W9-BYP-050

ALSO BY RICHARD WINSTON

Charlemagne: From the Hammer to the Cross

THOMAS BECKET

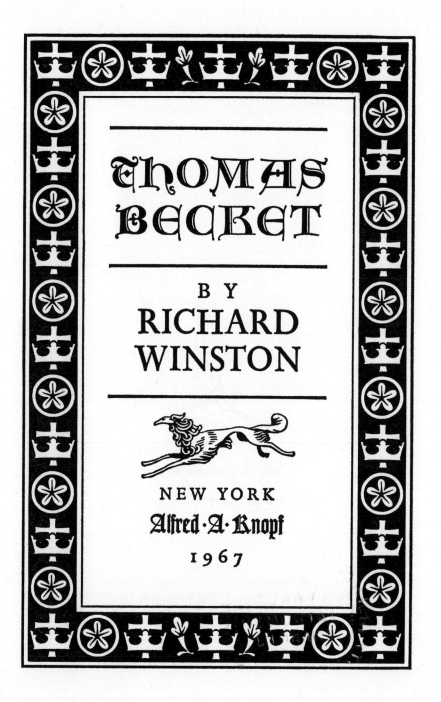

THOMAS BECKET

BY
RICHARD
WINSTON

NEW YORK

Alfred·A·Knopf

1967

THIS IS A BORZOI BOOK

PUBLISHED BY ALFRED A. KNOPF, INC.

Contents

A Prefatory Note on Sources

THE STANDARD BIOGRAPHIES of Thomas Becket date back more than a century; the last Life based on primary sources was published more than forty years ago. Not that the scholars have been idle; they have produced brilliant monographs on aspects of the Becket controversy, on the struggle between Church and State, and on the social and political setting of twelfth-century England. Playwrights and novelists have availed themselves, with varying success, of some of this material. But biographies have been few.

Perhaps the reason lies in the very abundance of the contemporary sources, and the vast literature that has grown up around the great English statesman, archbishop, and martyr. We have more information about Thomas Becket than about almost any other personality of the Middle Ages. We know what he ate and how he dressed, whom he spoke to and what he said. We can follow in minute detail the whole course of his life after he entered public office. Seven stout volumes of the Rolls Series, collectively entitled *Materials for the History of Thomas Becket, Archbishop of Canterbury,* contain no less than eight Lives of Becket by his contemporaries, as well as public papers, pamphlets of the time, records of councils, and letters. There are three volumes of correspondence alone, with more than eight hundred letters by, to, or concerning Thomas Becket. The Master of the Rolls has also published, in two volumes, an early fourteenth-century Icelandic biography, the *Thómas Saga Erkibyskups,* which derives from a lost Latin Life. There is a vigorous contemporary Life in French verse by Guernes de Pont-Sainte-Maxence, written within four years of Becket's death. Guernes studied the records at Canterbury, and talked with many of Thomas's intimates, including his sister. The chroniclers of the time, among them Gervase of Canterbury, William of Newburgh, Ralph de Diceto, Roger of Howden, and Gerald of Wales, treat at length of the relations between Thomas Becket and Henry II, and round out the picture of the times that is drawn by the biographers. Walter Map's *De nugis curialium* contains a witty and entertaining record of court life, and an analysis of the character of King Henry II. Voluminous writings on history and statecraft testify to twelfth-century England's passionate interest in legal and political theory. The *Polycraticus* of John of Salisbury (who also wrote a brief biographical essay on his friend Becket), the *Dialogue on the Exchequer* of Richard FitzNigel, the *Laws of Henry II* ascribed to Glanville—all throw light on the life and times of Thomas Becket.

The reader may be surprised by the frequency with which Thomas Becket, King Henry, and other characters in the drama are quoted directly in this book. This dialogue is not a fictional device; without exception it is taken from the original sources. It may be asked, of course, whether the early writers did not invent their direct discourse, in the tradition of Thucydides; and in many cases it is certain that they did so. Herbert of Bosham, Thomas Becket's confidant and at times almost his alter ego, is a particular offender; in his biography he puts long speeches into the mouth of his master—who was not nearly so verbose as the disciple. The problem of deciding what quoted material is authentic is not unlike the problem of extracting from the Gospels the *logia,* the actual sayings of Jesus, which were recorded and circulated in manuscripts among the early Christian communities before the Gospels themselves were written. If five or six biographers agree on the substance, and often very nearly on the language of a conversation, we may feel confident that the words were spoken as quoted. Above all, we must not assume that accurate reporting was impossible. Memories were better when literacy was not universal; men of the twelfth century could repeat long sermons, pleas, or diatribes almost verbatim, as Irish peasants can still do today.

In addition, as Eiríkr Magnússon has pointed out, it seems almost certain that there were minutes of conversations, taken down on the spot by shorthand secretaries or written up immediately afterwards. Thomas Becket and Henry II were great statesmen engaged in a fierce controversy. It was only natural that they would take precautions to preserve the exact phraseology of an agreement, or the precise language in dispute. The participants themselves often went to considerable trouble to report what was said at a particular confrontation. To take but one example: after the reconciliation at Fréteval, Thomas Becket wrote to Pope Alexander a long account of the interview, giving his version of the words that had passed between himself and the king.

No conscientious historian accepts contemporary witnesses uncritically. He knows that they must be checked against each other and against such "objective" records as are available—charters, surveys, financial accounts. In the case of a man like Becket, a judicious and wary attitude toward the contemporary chronicles and biographies is all the more essential because so many of them were written in a spirit of intense partisanship. On the other hand, the very transparency of their bias makes them easier to use than more subtly slanted works would be. Moreover, the twelfth century was an age of high intellectual attainments, and many of those who observed or participated in the struggle between king and archbishop strove, when they wrote of it, to be faithful to the truth. On essentials, the facts can be found in the contemporary records. Since almost anything that is said about Thomas Becket still tends to stir controversy, I have given fairly full references to my sources. These will be found at the back of the book, together with a note on their arrangement.

In writing this biography I have leaned most heavily on the twelfth-century documents; but I have of course profited greatly from the work of modern scholars. My major debts to them are acknowledged in the bibliography.

I wish to express my gratitude to Patrick Gregory of Alfred A. Knopf for constant encouragement and invaluable advice on points large and small; and to my daughter Justina for her willingness to discuss, and her ability to clarify, some of the more trying obscurities of Latin prose. Finally, I cannot even begin to thank adequately E. Porter Dickinson, Research Librarian extraordinary of Amherst College, who for five years has stretched

librarianship to the limit, unearthing what has been deeply buried, finding the unfindable, lending the unlendable, all the while
effortlessly contributing fruitful suggestions and making sure that
no stone would be left unturned.

RICHARD WINSTON

Halifax, Vermont
May 1967

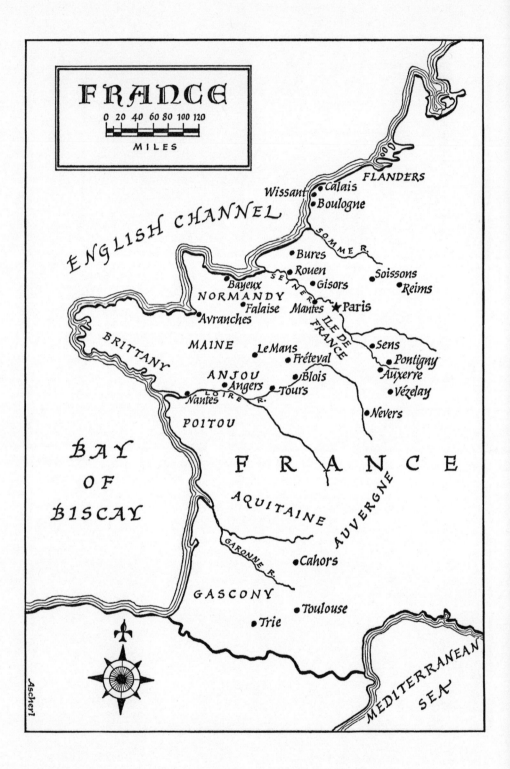

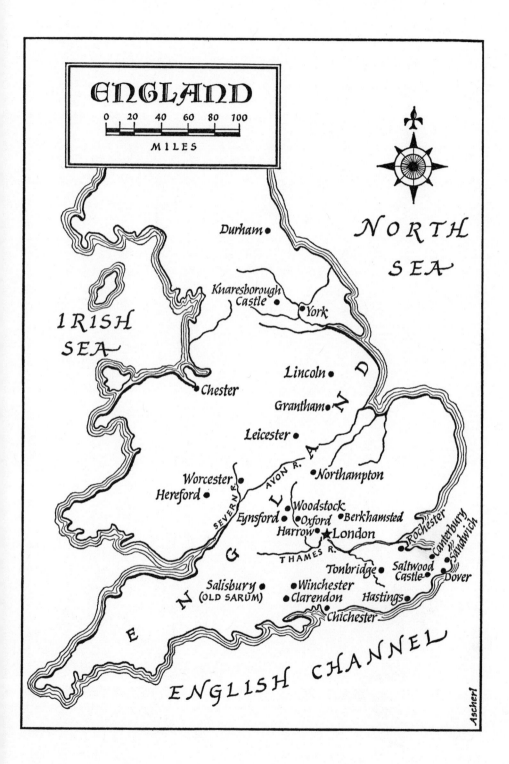

ENGLAND

0 20 40 60 80 100
MILES

NORTH SEA

IRISH SEA

Durham

Knaresborough Castle

York

ENGLAND

Lincoln

Chester

Grantham

Leicester

Worcester

Northampton

Hereford

AVON R.

SEVERN R.

Woodstock

Eynsford

Oxford

Berkhamsted

Harrow

London

Rochester

Canterbury

Sandwich

THAMES R.

Tonbridge

Saltwood Castle

Dover

Salisbury (OLD SARUM)

Winchester

Clarendon

Hastings

Chichester

ENGLISH CHANNEL

Ascher1

PART ONE

The King's Man

I

London

NEARLY eight hundred years have passed since Thomas Becket was done to death in Canterbury cathedral by four distinguished courtiers, barons whom tradition pictures as uncouth ruffians. Throughout that immense span of time—almost as long as the period from the assassination of Julius Caesar to the coronation of Charlemagne—the memory of Becket has remained green; the issues at stake in his great contest with his king have continued to be fought under different names; and the real or apparent contradictions of his character have given rise to controversy. He has been portrayed as a paragon, guileless and incorruptible, intolerant of immorality and dishonesty, an enemy of all evil. He has been pictured as violent, unscrupulous, self-willed, intolerant, foolish, and narrow-minded. Ultramontanists, royalists, Catholics, Protestants, Anglicans, political theorists, historians, and biographers have speculated on and wrangled over the riddle of Thomas Becket.

Opinions on Henry II have been equally divided. Yet fairness to Henry should not come hard. He is the more tragic figure of the pair. For a man of such fiery temperament, his patience with Becket was extraordinary. He believed as honestly as Thomas that he was fighting for principle. The clash was fated, precedented, inevitable; and had Henry not been essentially a foreign king, he would have known what to expect when he procured Thomas's election as archbishop. It has always been thought that Henry, despite Thomas's plain warnings, misjudged

3

the man; that he did not expect his worldly chancellor to put on the habit of religion spiritually as well as physically. But Henry also misjudged the office. Among other things, he was dazzled by the example of Emperor Frederick Barbarossa, who had made the Archbishop of Cologne his chancellor. Henry hoped to combine the two great offices of Church and State in a similar fashion. It was natural for him to think in Continental terms; and therefore he overlooked the historical relationship between the Crown and the primate of all England.

Thomas Becket, on the other hand, knew much more than his sovereign about English affairs, for he was a native of London. His merchant father, Gilbert Becket,[1] was a man of mark who at one time had held office as sheriff of London. Sheriffs were high-ranking officials; combining the functions of judge, tax collector, and chief of police, they were the executive arm of royal government. The rustics feared, the burgesses courted, and the barons respected the sheriffs. In 1130 the city of London offered King Henry I one hundred marks of silver for the privilege of electing its own sheriffs. The king condescended, although he probably made the Londoners match the Lincolners' bid of two hundred marks of silver and four marks of gold for the same privilege. Gilbert Becket, however, almost certainly held office before Thomas Becket was twelve years old. Gilbert, then, had been a royal rather than a municipal official.

London birth was not equivalent to Saxon descent, as Au-

---

[1] *Becket* means "little brook"—the word is related to the German *Bach* and is of Scandinavian origin. It was adopted into Norman French and has been preserved in such names as the abbey of Le Bec (which in the eleventh and twelfth centuries was the training ground for three archbishops of Canterbury). Hereditary surnames were just coming into use in the twelfth century; apparently they were brought into England by the Norman conquerors. But even long after secular Normans had adopted fixed *to-names,* as Old English had it, clerics were still known by their places of birth. In contemporary documents the name Thomas Becket is found only twice. Contemporaries referred to Gilbert Becket's son as Thomas of London, Thomas the Archdeacon, Chancellor, Archbishop—according to the office he held at any given time. After death he was known as Thomas the Martyr. During the fourteenth and fifteenth centuries the preposition *a* or *à* (from the Latin *a,* meaning *of*) crept into the name by analogy with such names as William atte Beck and Thomas à Kempis.

gustin Thierry, the nineteenth-century French historian, presumed. Having concluded that Thomas Becket must have been a Saxon, Thierry represented him as the spokesman for the Saxon underdog against the Norman overlord. This error has been perpetuated in belles lettres, although not in history; Conrad Ferdinand Meyer based his great novel, *Der Heilige,* and Jean Anouilh his play, *Becket,* upon Thierry's misconstruction of English conditions. In fact, both Gilbert Becket and his wife were Normans; Gilbert came from the same township in Normandy, Thierceville, as Archbishop Theobald of Canterbury (a circumstance which was to favor the admission of young Thomas Becket into the archbishop's household). There is no evidence at all for Thomas's Saxon ancestry, any more than there is for the legend that his mother was a Saracen.

The medieval mind, feeling that only some exotic parentage could explain Thomas's charisma in life and his miracles after death, fetched up this legend within a hundred years of Becket's death. In the earliest version, Gilbert Becket is captured on a pilgrimage to Jerusalem and made the slave of a Saracen emir whose daughter falls in love with the Christian prisoner. Gilbert escapes and returns home. The Saracen maiden, knowing only the two words "London" and "Gilbert," makes her way across the sea to him. She is baptized into the Christian faith, marries Gilbert, and in due time bears the child who is to be the future Archbishop of Canterbury, St. Thomas.

Even those of his biographers who were usually content with the more sober facts ascribed some element of the marvelous to Thomas Becket's birth. Thus several accounts include portentous dreams of Thomas's mother. While pregnant with the future archbishop, she dreamed that she carried the whole church of Canterbury in her womb. At another time:

> While Thomas was still a babe lying in his cradle, his mother dreamed that she rebuked the nurse for not putting a coverlet over him. The nurse replied, "Nay, my lady, he has the best of coverlets." "Show it to me," said her mistress. The nurse brought it and showed it to her, but when she tried to unfold it, she could not do so and said to the mother, "It is too large for

5

me to spread over the bed." Whereupon the mother answered, "Come into the hall and unfold it there." The nurse tried hard to do so but failed and said, "I simply cannot unfold the whole of it here." The astonished mother then said, "Go out into the market-place, which is now empty, and no doubt you will succeed in unfolding it there." But neither could the nurse do so there, whereupon she exclaimed, "The coverlet is so large that I cannot find the end of it; methinks all England would be too small for it to cover."

The Icelandic *Saga of Archbishop Thomas,* in its variant of this story, has these last words spoken by "a sweet voice out of the air." The *Saga* suggests an interpretation: that the cloth signifies "the holiness and goodness of this beloved friend of God." Guernes de Pont-Sainte-Maxence calls the cloth a *palie,* the word used for an archbishop's pallium, and sees it as symbolizing the saint's blood which was to spread over the whole world.

The infant for whom this supernatural coverlet was intended was born on December 21, 1118. By that time his father had been able to retire from trade and live on his income from rents. It is said that on the day of his son's birth Gilbert Becket suffered financial disaster from a great fire that swept London and burned down many of his properties. The coincidental date sounds improbable; but London did suffer from frequent fires, and at least one of them proved a severe blow to Gilbert Becket. Probably that was the great fire of 1135–6, which devastated most of the city from London Bridge to St. Clement's Dane.

Of Thomas Becket's mother we hear little beyond her gift for dreams and visions, her charity, and devoutness. Her name is generally given as Matilda, but one source calls her Roesa—that is, Rose—a native of Caen. The early biographers tell us that she took special pains to instill in her son the principles of religion, and, particularly, veneration for the Virgin Mary. Unfortunately this detail is such a commonplace in saints' lives that it can be regarded as no more than a standard hagiographical trope. Whatever the truth may have been, the biographers would inevitably have designated Thomas's mother as "pious and charitable." In this case we believe them only because we have the supporting

6

testimony of so scrupulous and close a friend of Thomas as John of Salisbury. "From an early age," says John, "he learned from his mother to fear the Lord, and sweetly to invoke the Blessed Virgin, taking her as his guide in all his ways, as his patroness in life, and placing all his trust in her, after Christ." The evidence is good, then, that Matilda Becket was unusually devout. Perhaps Matilda destined her son for the Church, as one biographer asserts. We may even, if we will, believe the charming tale of how she weighed out her gifts to charity: by placing her infant son in one pan of the balance, and the food, clothing, and money for the poor in the other pan.

Thomas Becket spent the first ten years of his life in the city of London, which in manhood he was to call "noble and famous beyond all other cities of this realm, the residence of our lord king and his notables, where the business of the whole kingdom is transacted." William FitzStephen prefaced his biography of Thomas with an elaborate and loving description of London, "the fruitful mother of noble men." He tells us that it was a city of churches—thirteen great ones, including the episcopal seat of St. Paul's, and no less than one hundred twenty-six parish churches. The Tower of London stood at that time outside the wall of the city, a great white mass of stone on deep foundations, which in fact were the remains of Roman fortifications. The Tower was fairly new at the time; it had been erected only forty years before Thomas Becket's birth. The Palace of Westminster, also a great tower with many breastworks and bastions, attached to the abbey church of St. Peter, lay some two miles from the city. Fine wide gardens surrounded the houses in the populous suburb that extended all the way from the palace to the city walls.

Estimates of the size of a medieval population are exercises in fancy guesswork. William asserts that during the wars of King Stephen's reign the city put into the field twenty thousand horsemen and sixty thousand foot soldiers. But medieval men were generally reckless with large numerals. Another contemporary, Peter of Blois, puts the total population of the city at the more reasonable figure of forty thousand. Whatever the precise number, London was a large and bustling city self-consciously proud of her metropolitan atmosphere. "The citizens of London are

7

regarded as conspicuous above all others for their polished manners, for their dress, and for the good tables which they keep." William was fond of good food, like his master Thomas, and he enlarges with delight upon a noted public cookshop:

> There daily you may find food according to the season, dishes of meat, roast, fried and boiled, large and small fish, coarser meals for the poor and more delicate for the rich, such as venison and big and small birds. . . . Those who would cater for themselves fastidiously need not search to find sturgeon or the bird of Africa or the Ionian godwit.

Smithfield, the market place of Matilda Becket's dream where the maid tried in vain to unfold the child's coverlet, was a broad "smooth field" just outside Aldersgate, near St. Martin's-le-Grand and the Augustinian priory of St. Bartholomew's. It was a short walk from the fine houses of Cheapside, where Thomas Becket was born; and we may imagine him as a small boy frequenting the great horse fair held on Smithfield every Friday. He would have slipped through the throng of earls, barons, and lesser knights who came to look over the latest offerings: the high-stepping palfreys with gleaming coats, the powerful sumpter-horses, and the costly and elegant chargers; he would have watched these noble *destriers* race, and would have wandered on to look into the pens of "swine with long flanks, cows with full udders, oxen of immense size, and woolly sheep."

A small boy could go about London safely, for it was a well-regulated city, divided into wards, governed by a senate and a lower magistracy, provided with courts that met on appointed days. Thanks to its sewers and aqueducts, and the old Roman paving of the main thoroughfares, it was also a fairly clean and wholesome place. Even as a boy Thomas Becket probably appreciated cleanliness, for in later life he was fastidious; it was noted as unusual that during his chancellorship he had his floors strewn with fresh rushes daily.

The city offered a variety of amusements for the young. "Instead of shows in the theater and stage-plays, London provides plays of a more sacred character, wherein are presented the miracles worked by saintly confessors or the sufferings which made illustrious the constancy of martyrs." (William FitzStephen makes his points gracefully.) On feast days the schoolboys matched wits in debates, oratory, recitation, and logic-chopping. "Sophists who speak paradoxes are praised for their torrent of words, while others seek to overthrow their opponents by using fallacious arguments." Less intellectual spectacles were the cock-fights held in the schools on holidays, the ball games after dinner, and the mimic tournaments on every Sunday in Lent. "At the Easter festival they play at a kind of naval warfare. A shield is firmly bound to a tree in midstream, and a small boat . . . carries on the stern a youth armed with a lance with which to strike the shield." Spectators stood on the bridge and quays, cheering and laughing as the youthful "knights" toppled into the water. In winter, boars, bulls, and bears were set loose to fight with each other or with hounds; and when the Mooresfield marsh was frozen over, the boys went skating by "tying on their feet the shinbones of animals."

William implies that young Thomas Becket took part in all these games, the rough as well as the fine. Thomas must have done well in the schoolboy disputations, for he was "quick of learning, keen of memory and clear of understanding in all things." Once he learned something, he could at any time recall it. His "sweet and merry" way of speaking is also noted—and these probably are not mere pious epithets, for they are proffered by a close but by no means uncritical friend.

There were a great many schoolboys, for London had three famous schools in her three principal churches (St. Paul's, Holy Trinity, and St. Martin's), as well as a number of lesser schools. It was said that England supported almost as many schoolmasters as tax collectors. Teaching was entirely in the hands of the Church; but for a boy to be sent to school did not necessarily mean that he was destined for a career in the Church. Education, as the twelfth-century writer and courtier Walter Map bears witness, was the path to a higher station in life. In the increasingly complex social and governmental structure of a country which the monarchy was steadily seeking to centralize, literacy was essential to thousands of persons. Charters had to be drawn, accounts rendered, the royal decrees read in the remotest corners of the realm. In England and Normandy many nobles and burgesses were thoroughly literate laymen. Nobles usually learned their letters from private tutors, either young scholars hired for the purpose or the priest in charge of the family's private chapel. The children of burgesses, however, went to the schools. Because schools and teachers were licensed by the bishop of the diocese, most scholars were officially considered clerics. They usually took "minor orders" and had the "simple tonsure"—a small shaved spot on the top of the head. Their status as clerics was a mere legal fiction, but a potentially troublesome one, as the Archbishop of Canterbury's dispute with the king over the question of "criminous clerks" was to demonstrate.

Thomas Becket's first schooling was not in London but at the priory of Merton in Surrey. He was sent there at the age of ten, and stayed for some years, learning to speak, read, and write Latin with a fluency which would later make that language his most natural mode of expression for complex ideas.

If Merton School followed—as it probably tried to do—the enlightened principles of Bernard of Chartres, "the most copious fountainhead of letters in Gaul in modern times," Thomas must have studied the trivium of grammar, rhetoric, and logic out of the classical authors, chiefly Cicero, Virgil, Ovid, and Seneca. Every student was required to repeat daily part of the lessons of the day before. Drill was reinforced by reprimands and, if necessary, by floggings. Classical texts were painstakingly analyzed for their rhetorical adornments and sophistical devices. Selected passages were related to other studies. Literature had to be read with close attention to the three levels of meaning: *historia,* the literal sense; *allegoria,* the recondite spiritual sense; and *sententia,* the implicit moral sense. Memorization was stressed; sizable sections of the texts had to be learned by heart every day. Yet the ideal was not omnivorousness. Bernard of Chartres recommended study of the best writers alone. "To study everything that everyone has ever said, no matter how insignificant, is either to be excessively humble and cautious, or overly vain and ostentatious," says John of Salisbury.

In the lower grades of a school such as Merton, grammar

was the main subject of instruction. According to the traditional definition given by Isidore in the early seventh century and still respected in the twelfth, grammar was the "science of writing and speaking in a correct manner." In a broad sense it prepared the mind to understand everything that could be taught in words. It was the mother and arbiter of all speech, the foundation of philosophy and virtue. John of Salisbury winds up his elaborate tribute to grammar with a quotation from Quintilian: "Necessary for the young, gratifying to the old, and an agreeable solace in solitude, it alone of all branches of learning has more utility than show."

A scholar needed persistence and devotion to survive the sheer physical hardships of his existence. At his lessons by six in the morning, often without breakfast, he continued studying until dusk, with breaks only for dinner at ten o'clock in the morning, a brief rest afterwards, and supper at five in the afternoon. Lecture halls were rarely heated in winter, and often had no furniture; the scholar sat on the straw which covered the floor. A stool or a bench was a rare luxury. If study did not continue after dark it was because candles were expensive.

After perhaps four or five years at Merton, Thomas transferred to one of the schools of London. As an adolescent, "bright and blithe of visage, and of a turn of countenance, as it seemed to wise men, that the sweetness of God's grace was clearly seen in him," he surely joined gladly in the urban pastimes described by William FitzStephen. He would also have had occasion to roam about the city, looking at the fine residences of bishops, abbots, and lay magnates; for most of the great men of England maintained town houses in London, and were even beginning to build in stone, although wooden houses were still the rule. Thus Thomas nourished that taste for luxury which came to the fore in later life. He would also have observed the economic life that made luxury possible. At the London waterfront he could watch the ships bringing wine from France and Gascony, the fish, timber, and furs from Norway and the Baltic countries, cloth from Flanders, olive oil, soap, leather, and "southern fruits" from Spain and Portugal. The ships carried away England's exports: wool and wheat, lead and tin, meat, hides, butter, bacon, and cheese. So profitable was the shipping trade that a single wharf in London yielded the enormous rent of ten pounds a year.[2]

Gilbert Becket was a hospitable man, with a spacious house and friends in high places who often were house guests on their visits to London. Among these guests was a nobleman named Richer de ·l'Aigle or Laigle, probably not much older than Thomas; we find him a member of the king's court and a signer of the Constitutions of Clarendon some thirty years after he first met Thomas, probably around 1132 or 1133. Although Richer may originally have been attracted to the house by Thomas's three sisters, Agnes, Mary, and Rose, he soon made a friend of his host's son, then a tall, spare, lively boy of fourteen or fifteen. Richer taught him the arts of venery and falconry—those aristocratic skills in which Thomas later excelled and which were to endear him to Henry II.

While hunting with Richer one day, Thomas had an accident which his biographers would subsequently represent as a miracle—proof that God wished to save him "to stand and fight for His tabernacles."

The man and the boy had come to a rapid millstream crossed by a narrow footbridge. The knight dismounted and led his horse swiftly across the bridge. Thomas followed, all muffled in his hood—it must have been a cold day and the bridge, a mere plank, possibly had a thin coating of ice on it. Halfway across, Thomas's horse stumbled; Thomas held fast to the reins, and boy and horse plunged into the stream. The violent current swept Thomas along toward the roaring mill, with Richer and the rest of the hunting party following on the banks "with great and piteous cries." It seemed certain that Thomas would either be drowned or crushed by the millwheel. At this moment the miller, knowing nothing of what was happening, suddenly shut off the water from his mill. In the ensuing silence he heard the shouts, came out of his mill, and "catching sight of Thomas in the water, quickly put in his hand and pulled him out, barely breathing and half dead."

---

[2] Thomas himself would one day enjoy that rent; for it was payable to Christ Church, Canterbury, of which he as Archbishop of Canterbury automatically became abbot.

In later life Thomas told this story often. The providential escape may have given him his sense of being singled out by destiny. At the time, however, his close brush with death seems not to have engendered any strong feeling that he was called to the religious life. His taste for hunting was not spoiled, and he continued to acquire the knightly attainments which were to stand him in good stead in his secular career. After all, there was no contradiction between the pursuits of a cavalier and the studies of a cleric. The minor clergy could marry; many of the higher clergy feasted, hunted, hawked, and fornicated as readily as any lay noble. At Coventry, according to a satirical poet, a bishop drove the monks out of the cloister and chapter house, and brought in harlots. Of course council after council of the Church cited the canons, deplored the moral decay, inveighed against simony, plural holding of churches, lay patronage, and priestly concubinage; but the conditions persisted. Although Duke William of Normandy had conquered England with the papacy's blessing, and presumably intended to reform the Church, he made only perfunctory efforts to do so.

II

Norman England

AFTER MAKING GOOD on the battlefield at Hastings his dubious claim to the Crown of England, William the Bastard consolidated his rule speedily and efficiently. He refused to acknowledge that the brief and turbulent reign of Harold Godwinsson had ever existed; and Norman lawyers devised ingenious circumlocutions when questions of land-tenure forced them to refer to "the usurper." For even during Harold's nine months as king, ordinary life had gone on, wills had been probated, lands had been bought and sold. The details of such transactions were carefully traced. The new Norman lords who stepped into the shoes of their English predecessors needed to know precisely what their holdings were.

There were many such new lords, for the land of England was won by the Normans in the most literal sense. The Anglo-Saxon Chronicle put the change succinctly and bitterly: "He [William] gave away every man's land." That is, William claimed the entire country for himself, and then parceled it out among his Normans. Most of the Anglo-Saxon nobles who escaped death in the great battles of 1066—Fulford, Stamford Bridge, and Hastings—and who also survived the subsequent revolts against William were forced into exile. Within twenty years after the Conquest, ninety per cent of the land of England had changed hands. The king retained for himself nearly one fifth of the country.

The English did not take expropriation tamely. "In this

year," the Chronicle records for 1068, "King William gave Earl Robert the earldom of Northumberland; but the people of the country surrounded him in the city of Durham and killed him and nine hundred men with him." That uprising, like so many afterwards, was crushed. "And King William came on them by surprise from the south with an overwhelming army and routed them and killed those who could not escape."

The English foot soldiers were unable to stand against the mounted and heavily armored Norman knights who had made a profession of warfare. That, at least, is one explanation that has been offered. Another might be that the English lost the flower of their fighting men in 1066, and did not soon recover. A Norman writer of the next generation, William of Malmesbury, suggests a further reason in his famous characterization of English and Normans. "They engaged William," he says, "more with rashness and fury than with military skill, and so they doomed themselves and their country to slavery by giving him an easy victory in a single battle."

William of Malmesbury describes the English as barbarians: "They wore short garments reaching to the mid-knee; they had their hair cropped, their beards shaven, their arms laden with gold bracelets, their skin adorned with punctured designs. They were wont to eat until they became surfeited and to drink until they were sick." More inclined to dissipation than to the accumulation of wealth, they "consumed their whole fortune in mean and despicable houses, unlike the Normans and the French who in noble and splendid mansions live with frugality."

Here William is in error. Far from squandering their resources, the English excelled in the accumulation of wealth. The Anglo-Saxon kingdom had had a sound currency, an efficient tax structure, and a highly developed judicial system to which the people often had recourse, for they were a litigious folk. England was rich, and far from primitive—as William unwittingly admits in other contexts, when he condemns the nobility for their luxury and wantonness, the monastic orders for the fineness of their vestments and the variety of their food. The land was fertile and not densely populated. Here and there one might find a peasant who owned a team of oxen, a cow, a mare, two pigs, or even nine sheep and eleven goats. Such prosperity was unusual, but the rustics by no means lived in grinding poverty. Moreover the villeins enjoyed a measure of freedom from arbitrary orders and assessments. Since the land was generally worked in common under the open-field system, all peasants, free and serf, regularly had a share in joint decisions.

William the Conqueror permitted a large part of that wealth to flow toward the Church, for he was a devout man who also recognized that the Church could aid him in consolidating his rule over a rebellious England. To serve as chief administrator of his ecclesiastical policy in England, William appointed as Archbishop of Canterbury Lanfranc, a Lombard monk who had become abbot of the monastery of Le Bec. Lanfranc reorganized and reformed the entire English Church. He created the structure that Thomas Becket would inherit when he in his turn came to assume the primacy of all England. Lanfranc established that primacy in fact by forcing all the bishops of England, including Canterbury's ancient rival, the Archbishop of York, to make profession of obedience to himself. In unifying and centralizing the English Church, Lanfranc strengthened William's hold over England. He also placed the Church almost totally under the monarch's control; so that we may say it was ultimately Lanfranc's work that Thomas Becket strove to undo.

As Archbishop of Canterbury, Lanfranc occupied virtually the same position in the English Church as did the pope in the Church as a whole. Lanfranc had the support of his king in asserting his own authority in England, while resisting the claims to suzerainty by the papacy, then controlled by the great Cardinal Hildebrand. In 1073 Hildebrand himself donned the tiara (not yet triple) and assumed the name of Gregory VII. As pope, he maintained that the divinely instituted Church was inherently superior to the secular State. He dramatized his thesis at Canossa, when he made Emperor Henry IV stand barefoot in the snow awaiting absolution. And although Henry afterwards grew strong enough to depose Gregory and set up an antipope, he could not drive the principles of Gregorian reform out of the Church. Gregory's successors continued to press their claims to universal authority; and a whole new generation of reformers set to work studying and codifying canon law in order to further justify these pretensions of the papacy.

In England, however, Gregorianism made little progress. William I rejected Gregory's demand that he pay fealty to him for the realm of England. Archbishop Lanfranc, although he avoided an open quarrel with Gregory, admitted no papal interference in English affairs. He issued a formal prohibition of simony and ordered priests to put away their wives; but in practice little changed. Parish priests in England lived openly with their wives, bishops with their concubines; and in spite of the stricture against simony, church preferments were often sold to the highest bidder. The bishops and abbots of England, accustomed to regard the king as God's Anointed, continued to accept the episcopal ring and staff from the king's hands and to apply for royal permission before attending a council abroad or going to Rome at the pope's summons.

In one fateful respect, however, Lanfranc complied with the papal demands for ecclesiastical reform. In Anglo-Saxon England bishops had sat with the sheriffs in the courts of the hundred, hearing "pleas" (*placita,* that is, "cases" or "suits") on ecclesiastical matters with the assistance of these secular officials. At the instance of Lanfranc, William the Conqueror commanded that henceforth "no bishop or archdeacon shall any longer hold pleas involving episcopal laws in the hundred [court]." Instead, the bishop was to maintain a separate court of his own in which to try such civil matters as marriage, wills, and debts (these because they involved oaths, hence "religion"), and criminal offenses committed by or upon all members of the Church.

The difficulty—which subsequently gave rise to the quarrel between Thomas Becket and Henry II—was that so many persons scarcely bound by ecclesiastical discipline could be classed as members of the Church. A clerk, that is a "cleric," was anyone who had received one of the minor orders, namely that of subdeacon, acolyte, exorcist, reader, or doorkeeper. In practice, anyone who could read and write a few scraps of Latin might claim ecclesiastical immunity and demand trial in the episcopal courts. The bishop's or archdeacon's court could fine or imprison a culprit, but could not order eyes to be put out or hands cut off, for canon law forbade the shedding of blood. In an age of savage penalties, that was a great mitigation. In the next century the episcopal courts, which in the meanwhile had expanded into a whole independent judicial organization, proved a refuge for dangerous criminal elements in English society. But it must be remembered that the system of two separate judicatures had functioned quite well for seventy or eighty years before Henry II determined to destroy it.

Many elements of feudalism were already present in England before the Norman Conquest. Fiefs and benefices existed, and the ceremony of homage was known. No doubt a full-fledged feudal society would ultimately have developed if Earl Harold had held the throne and passed it on to his sons. But the coming of the Normans accelerated the process. In granting out the land of England, the Conqueror provided for his military needs by assigning "knight service" to his barons, both lay and ecclesiastical. Each of the barons had to furnish a fixed number of knights—for convenience reckoned in units of five—to guard the royal castles and serve in the army. In order to supply these, the barons in their turn distributed their "honors" among vassals who either served in person or paid knights to take their place. Usually a reservoir of landless younger sons was available for this purpose. Since, as we have seen, ecclesiastics were not supposed to shed blood, the holders of church fiefs had to hire knights.

Although many aspects of the Norman system were imported into England, there was a vital difference between feudalism in Normandy and in post-Conquest England. As kings of England, William I and his successors were immeasurably stronger vis-à-vis their barons than the dukes of Normandy had ever been, because they exacted direct homage from the rear-vassals, that is, from the vassals of their vassals. Thus the ladder arrangement of feudal society in which each man owed fealty only to his immediate lord was shattered, in theory at least; practice would ultimately follow theory.

The most striking physical evidences of the new order that the Normans introduced into England were the ubiquitous castles. The Conqueror directed that every county seat be defended by a fortified place. In addition, he granted his barons the right to build castles to defend their own holdings. The earliest Norman castles were simple structures which could be erected very rapidly; the Anglo-Norman poet Wace describes one as having been put up in a single day. A space was cleared and a mound of earth, the motte, thrown up, preferably footed on native rock. Since earth was removed for the motte, a wide ditch naturally resulted, and this dry moat was further protected by a stockade of squared pales. The main keep was erected on the mound, and was eventually flanked by small towers. Except for the Tower of London and a few similar structures meant for the defense of major cities, the original Norman castles were built of wood. The next generation after the Conqueror, however, built in stone wherever possible, and added to their massive keeps such refinements as posterns, portcullises, and underground passages. And of course no castle was complete without "various dungeons or cells, in the depths of which prisoners are put away in hand shackles."

Such strongholds were occupied by a small contingent of Norman knights who commanded a swarm of Saxon retainers and domestics. The work of field and fold, stable and smithy, kitchen and bedchamber, was performed by "natives." But the Normans quickly won the confidence of their subjects. Although in the early days after the Conquest there had been considerable resistance, and Normans had been ambushed in woods and fens, no Sicilian Vespers ever took place in England.

The Conqueror's sons, William Rufus and Henry I, found that they could depend upon English soldiers to defend the Norman monarchy. And while French continued to be spoken at court, the lower ranks of the Norman nobility rapidly learned the speech of the conquered. It was, after all, very close to the language of their own grandfathers. Danish had been spoken in Normandy as late as 1028, and Danish, or a hybrid of Danish and Saxon, was still spoken in parts of the Danelaw after the Conquest.

Under the impact of the Conquest, however, the rich stream of Anglo-Saxon literature dried up. The Anglo-Saxon Chronicle was kept up (until 1154); but little else was written in English. English also disappeared from use in writs and records, to be replaced by Latin. By the time the writing of English recommenced in the thirteenth century, the language of King Alfred the Great had undergone profound changes. It had shed most of its complex inflections and had gathered into its vocabulary an enormous number of Norman-French or Latin words. Anglo-Saxon had become that idiosyncratic hybrid we call English—a lingua franca (to make the kind of pun medieval writers loved) of remarkable flexibility. The process was not to be completed until the fourteenth century, after another large infusion of French words; but the creation of English as we know it must be reckoned one of the consequences of the Norman Conquest.

✠　✠　✠

William the Conqueror, at war with his overlord, Philip I of France, was seized by his fatal illness just after he had sacked and burned the French town of Mantes. On his deathbed William reluctantly granted forgiveness to his eldest son, Robert Curthose, who had supported Philip, and bequeathed the duchy of Normandy to Robert. The middle son, William Rufus, received the greater prize: England. The Conqueror had nothing left for his youngest son, Henry, but five thousand pounds of silver. But as in the fairy tales, the youngest son proved the most fortunate in the end.

The throne of England was theoretically elective, and William's bequest might not have assured his son possession of it. William Rufus's prompt action did. He crossed the Channel at once, and arranged to be crowned by Lanfranc less than three weeks after his father's death. Within a year the barons, whose right of election had been ignored, rebelled against Rufus and attempted to place Duke Robert on the throne. But Robert never crossed to England to strike a blow for himself, and William Rufus won the English to his side by promising abolition of unjust taxes, freedom from the Conqueror's oppressive Forest Law, and respect for the laws and customs of the English. Saxon levies gave their blood to crush the revolt, and within a few months the Red King, as he was universally called, could proceed to the punishment of his enemies.

One of these happened to be a churchman: William of St. Calais, Bishop of Durham. The defection of this capable and popular prelate had been a serious blow to Rufus; the king, as soon as he had defeated the rebels, ordered the bishop brought to trial like any lay noble. Thus the issue of Church versus State, of lay versus ecclesiastical power, was joined. In fact, the contemporary[1] record of the proceedings often reads like an anticipation of the trial of Thomas Becket at Northampton seventy-five years later. The right of the king's court to try a churchman was stated with surpassing clarity. In this case, however, the Archbishop of Canterbury took the side of the State against the Church.

When the king ordered his land and property seized, the Bishop of Durham took refuge within the castle of Durham, and refused to appear at the king's court until he had been granted a safe-conduct. Firmly, he wrote to the king: "I beg you not to keep me unjustly out of my possessions. It is not for everyone to judge bishops, and I offer you such full justice *as is consistent with my order.*" (A phrase that Thomas Becket was to echo with his "saving my order.")

After much negotiation, the bishop appeared for trial at Salisbury on November 2, 1088. On orders from the king, the archbishops and his fellow bishops declined to talk with him or to give him the kiss of greeting. But although his brother churchmen had abandoned him, the Bishop of Durham insisted that a lay court had no right to try him.

He said to the archbishop: "I reject the judgment which has been pronounced against me, because I hold it to be against the

---

[1] H. S. Offler has argued (*English Historical Review*, Vol. LVI, 1951) that the account is not contemporary, but dates from the second quarter of the twelfth century. This contention flies in the face of the internal evidence, as Offler himself concedes. It requires us to admit the anonymous author to the pantheon of great dramatic writers. Norman Cantor (*Church, Kingship and Lay Investiture in England 1089–1135*) accepts Offler's thesis, and suggests that the Bishop of Durham could not logically take an extreme Gregorian position in 1088 and swing to the other side by 1095. But the character of William of Durham as revealed in the *De injusta vexatione Willelmi episcopi primi*—which is so favorable to him—is that of a wily, quick-thinking opportunist. I cannot help feeling that Cantor, though almost invariably right in his judgments, errs in this instance.

canons and against the law of our Church. . . . I have been deprived of my bishopric and now I am being constrained to plead my cause in a lay court outside my own province. . . . Moreover, my enemies . . . are in fact at the same time my accusers and my judges. I find that the law of our Church forbids me to accept a judgment of this nature. . . . Therefore, because I know that the king's hostility has made you all my enemies, I appeal to the Apostolic See, to the holy Roman Church, to the blessed Peter, and to his vicar."

Lanfranc answered: "We are not judging you about your bishopric, but about your fief. . . .

The bishop replied: "My lord archbishop, you have not today heard me mention my fief nor the fact that I possess one. It is about my bishopric that I have made my complaint."

"I may not have heard you speak of your fief," retorted the archbishop, "but I know you have a great fief, and it is in respect of that we now judge you."

The bishop obdurately refused to plead at all. At length the court declared that he had forfeited his fief. Between the lines of the narrative, written though it was by a partisan who wished to show Bishop William in the most favorable light, we can read the weakness of the bishop's actual case. Evidently he took his stand on ecclesiastical immunity because he was in fact guilty of rebellion and sedition. Had he been able to muster any proof that he had remained loyal to the king throughout the uprising, he would probably have contrived to offer it in evidence. In similar circumstances Thomas Becket would likewise deny the court's jurisdiction, but would also manage to mention the arguments in favor of his own case. William of St. Calais, however, offered only the lame promise that he would be able to expose the falsehood of the charges if he were allowed to plead in "the court of the Church of Rome."

Shabby though his motives may have been, Bishop William had set a mighty precedent. Alone, facing an episcopate united against him in support of a tyrannical and often choleric ruler, he had dared to assert the principle of ecclesiastical liberty. Unfortunately for the cause he briefly represented, he himself was hardly a man of principle. Later he quite readily sacrificed liberty to expediency. After three years in exile, he made his peace with the king, returned to England, received back his diocese and his temporal holdings, and thereafter displayed total subservience to the king. Seven years later we find him virtually assuming the role of Lanfranc.

Lanfranc had meanwhile died; and for five years William Rufus did not provide an archbishop for the vacant see of Canterbury. He had a number of reasons for procrastinating. During the earlier part of his reign Lanfranc, who had taken the prince into his household for "nourishing," and who had conferred knighthood upon him, exerted the frequently unwelcome restraint of an elder statesman upon the young king. In addition, the king could more easily control the bishops and abbots of England when they lacked their natural leader, the Archbishop of Canterbury. Money was also a factor. The revenues from Canterbury and other vacant sees helped finance Rufus's invasion of Normandy, his war with Scotland, his battles in the Welsh marches, and his preparations for conquest on the Continent. If he were going to lose such sources of income, he wanted compensation. He therefore treated ecclesiastical lordships as if they were ordinary secular fiefs: when he did permit election of a successor, he demanded a huge "relief," such as lay lords had to pay on entering into an inheritance. In 1091, for example, he collected £1000 for the see of Norwich and the abbey of Winchester. He taxed the monasteries heavily.[2]

William Rufus, when in good health, may have been indifferent to the Catholic faith; it has even been suggested that he was an apostate, a secret adherent of paganism, who was really swearing "by Loki" when he uttered his favorite oath: "By the Holy Face of Lucca." He saw schism in the Church as opportunity, not disaster. When after the death of Gregory VII two rival popes were elected, William Rufus sought his own advantage in postponing recognition of either Urban or Clement. But Wil-

---

[2] Such impositions, along with his notorious homosexuality and his skepticism toward religion, did not commend him to ecclesiastics. Since most of what we know of William comes from the pen of a monk (Eadmer), our view of his character and of the history of his reign may be seriously distorted.

liam's subjects were good Christians who found the schism pain-
ful and the prolonged "widowhood" of the Mother Church of all
England shocking. They pressed for a decision on both matters.
It was to force William's hand that the Earl of Chester in the
summer of 1092 invited Anselm, Abbot of Le Bec, to visit him.
Anselm came readily, since he had business in England; he
wanted to ask William Rufus to reduce taxes on his monastery's
English estates.

A native of northern Italy like Lanfranc, Anselm had originally been drawn to Le Bec by Lanfranc's reputation for learning. He soon surpassed his master in scholarship, rose like
Lanfranc before him to become prior and then abbot of the
monastery, and devoted his remarkable intelligence—his was the
finest mind in eleventh-century France or England—to providing
theology with a philosophical foundation.

This quiet metaphysician, who has been called the Father of
Scholasticism, preached ascetic rejection of the world; but he was
not unacquainted with secular affairs. An abbot necessarily carried a heavy load of administrative duties. Moreover, Anselm
knew England, having traveled there twice before on the affairs
of his monastery. If the magnates of England now wanted him to
be primate, he was probably prepared to bow to the will of God.
He was reluctant; but if he had been as violently opposed to
being Archbishop of Canterbury as his biographer Eadmer pre-
tends, he would never have come to England in 1092. For a
bishop-elect to protest his unworthiness for office was one of the
oldest traditions of the Church. How sincere these protestations
of *"nolo episcopari"* were in any given case is always difficult to
judge.

But if Anselm was reluctant to accept, William Rufus was
reluctant to consent. He kept Anselm in England by postponing
settlement of the abbot's affairs; but he refused to come to a
decision on Canterbury. Then he was struck down by an unspecified illness which everyone thought to be fatal. Faced with death,
the skeptic king agreed to everything his spiritual advisers recommended for the salvation of his soul: to release prisoners, pardon
debtors, and fill the vacancies of episcopal sees, especially of the
church of Canterbury. Anselm was called in and approved this

advice. Whereupon the king himself nominated Anselm for the archbishopric. Everyone acclaimed the step except Anselm, who had to be dragged struggling to the king's bedside and forcibly invested with ring and staff. Then he was "carried rather than led" to the nearby church.

As soon as the ceremonies were completed, Anselm reproached the bishops and the lay magnates. "Do you realize what you have done?" he said. "You have yoked together in the plow the untamed bull and the old and feeble sheep, and what good will come of it?"

His forebodings were proved correct as soon as the sick king recovered. William Rufus flew into rages when he was balked; and Anselm could be stubborn as an old ram. The new archbishop speedily developed into the leader of Gregorian reform in England. He clashed with Rufus over the return of certain temporal possessions of the see of Canterbury—as Becket was later to clash with Henry II. He refused to pay the "relief" William demanded, lest he incur the charge of having bought his office. He attacked the king for continuing to hold vacant abbacies. He bent every effort to enforce the authority of Canterbury. And he kept pressing for permission to go to Rome to obtain the pallium, the symbol of a metropolitan, from Urban II—whom Anselm had already recognized while still Abbot of Bec.

William, by now anxious to be rid of Anselm, decided to make an issue of this. "It is not in accordance with my custom or that of my father that any man should be recognized as pope in the realm of England without my leave or approval," he stated. "If anyone tries to infringe on my prerogative in this, it would be tantamount to depriving me of my crown." (This accusation that the Archbishop of Canterbury had designs upon the Crown was to be brought up repeatedly in Becket's struggle with his king.) Anselm maintained that allegiance to both powers at once was possible, and demanded that a council of notables be called to decide the question.

At the turbulent Council of Rockingham, held in February 1095, the king's chief spokesman was that same William of St. Calais, Bishop of Durham, who had refused to stand trial in 1088. Now Bishop William played Lanfranc's role of prosecutor and king's man. Anselm, after all a stranger in England, at first humbly asked the lay magnates and his fellow bishops to show him the way to resolve his conflict of loyalties. But, as in the trial of William of St. Calais, the bishops would only urge submission to the will of the king. The Bishop of Durham, who perhaps hoped to succeed to Canterbury himself, advised Anselm either to renounce obedience to Rome or to resign his archbishopric. Throughout the debate, Anselm remained gentle, forbearing, and friendly—a far cry from the conduct of Thomas Becket in a similar situation, as we shall see. But the mild Anselm was finally driven to an extreme Gregorian position. He invoked the argument that "the Archbishop of Canterbury can neither be judged nor condemned by any man, except the Pope, to answer any accusation against his will." Here was the doctrine of papal supremacy that dominated the thinking of Thomas Becket seventy years later.

A truce was patched up by the lay magnates, who were inclined to sympathize with any resistance to the royal power. Meanwhile William Rufus dickered with the pope, tempting him by offers of allegiance if he would sanction Anselm's expulsion from England. And as Alexander III was to do in the case of Becket, Pope Urban temporized; for Urban needed money, and he needed England's support for the First Crusade. William increased his exactions upon Canterbury and the other churches of England, and consolidated his hold over the other prelates of the realm. Only Anselm's extraordinary patience and sweet temper enabled him to maintain his precarious position for another two years, in spite of continual harassment by the king's men. He had the satisfaction, if satisfaction it was to him, that Bishop William of Durham died on the first day of the new year. But Anselm was finally forced into exile. And in exile he remained until William Rufus was felled by a mysterious arrow in the New Forest on August 2, 1100.

✠   ✠   ✠

It has been necessary to dwell on the affairs of William of Durham and Archbishop Anselm because their struggles with

William Rufus provided many precedents for Thomas Becket. To the royal power, the central issue had been the degree of State control over the Church. From the churchman's point of view, the issue was the right of the Church to freedom from secular restraints. This novel, not to say revolutionary, thesis of the Gregorian reformers had not won wide acceptance in England even among the clergy. But the prestige of the Church was on the rise after the dismal years of corruption in the earlier part of the eleventh century. And by his call for a crusade in the Holy Land, Urban had in a very real sense put himself at the head of all Christendom. With the accession of King Henry I to the throne of England, there began a period of remarkable growth in the powers and immunities of the Church in the island kingdom. There were setbacks, to be sure, and neither Henry nor his successor Stephen relinquished the royal prerogatives without a struggle. But we may fairly say that throughout the first half of the twelfth century a highly favorable climate existed for the Church in England.

Henry, the youngest son of William the Conqueror, was hunting in another part of the New Forest on the day his brother was killed. He immediately rode to Winchester Castle and seized the royal treasury. The leading barons of the realm accepted his claim to the throne, and three days later he was crowned at Westminster. At his coronation he issued the famous charter which was to exercise a direct influence upon the language and principles of Magna Carta. Its very first paragraph dealt with the affairs of the Church. After acknowledging the "unjust exactions" of the previous reign, Henry declared:

> I now, being moved by reverence towards God and by the love I bear you all, make the Holy Church of God free; so that I will neither sell nor farm out its property; nor on the death of an archbishop or a bishop or an abbot will I take anything from the demesne of the Church or from its vassals during the period which elapses before a successor is installed.

Henry's practice in the thirty-five years of his reign did not always conform to these noble principles. His financial needs at times forced him to revert to the methods of William Rufus, and his sense of the dignity of kingship made him resist what he regarded as the encroachments of the Church upon the rights of the Crown. But the piety he expressed in the coronation charter was genuine. He always preferred to compromise with the Church rather than push issues to extremes. Since Anselm, his friendly antagonist in the early years of his reign, was of a similar disposition, the potentially dangerous dispute over investiture never developed into a bitter confrontation of the two powers.

A real question of power underlay the efforts of the Gregorian reformers to abolish lay investiture of ecclesiastics. Their object, of course, was not merely to prevent a lay overlord from conferring upon bishops and abbots the spiritual insignia of office. The right to invest carried with it the right to accept or to reject a candidate; refusal of ring and staff could cancel an election. Hitherto, this issue had not been raised in England. Now Anselm, whom Henry had recalled from exile immediately after his accession, refused to do homage for his fiefs. He had attended the councils of Bari and Rome, where lay investiture had been roundly condemned; and he felt morally bound to uphold this stand. But he did not regard the king as his enemy, and helped to arrange the marriage between Henry and Eadgyth, daughter of the King of Scots, who came of the best English lineage—she was a direct descendant of Alfred and Cerdic. As queen, she took the name of Matilda and became the mother of that Matilda who married successively Henry V the Roman emperor and Geoffrey Plantagenet. The offspring of the second marriage was to be Henry II of England.

The negotiations over the investiture question were conducted principally between Henry and Pope Paschal, with Anselm often acting in the role of mediator rather than advocate of strict papal policy. Both Henry and Anselm preferred to gain their ends by diplomacy, and although some bitterness developed between them, it was mild compared to the acrimony which was to spring up sixty years later between Thomas Becket and Henry II. Nevertheless, at Easter in the year 1103 Anselm once more went into exile; he remained abroad, living at Lyons, until the question was finally settled by compromise four years later.

The terms of the agreement separated the issues of election, and of investiture and homage. The king would not grant free "canonical election," but he agreed to consult with the clergy before appointing bishops or abbots. He gave up the right of investiture by ring and staff. In return for this concession, candidates for church offices were to do homage to him for their feudal holdings. The settlement amounted to dividing the person of a bishop or abbot into two parts, one religious and one secular. This was virtually the position that Lanfranc had adopted in the trial of William of Durham: "We are not judging you about your bishopric, but about your fief."

After the death of Anselm in 1109, Henry's relationship to the papacy again became strained. Like his predecessor, he did not fill the vacancy at Canterbury for five years. But eventually piety and policy conjoined; the king made peace with Paschal once more, and throughout the rest of his reign on the whole favored the Church in England. Monastic foundations were encouraged—abbeys, and priories of Austin canons, were established by the dozen. New monastic orders entered the kingdom: in the last seven years of Henry's reign alone five Cistercian monasteries and three nunneries were founded. Henry freely permitted appeals to Rome and visits from papal legates, whom earlier in his reign he had barred from England. What was more, he supported the efforts of the Church reformers to enforce celibacy of the clergy. It was fine scrupulousness on his part to be concerned for the celibacy of others, in view of his own nineteen illegitimate children. But fines imposed on married priests filled his coffers. And the king needed money; while he kept England at peace, he financed his wars in Normandy and France out of the barrels of silver pennies stored at Winchester.

Those silver pennies, incidentally, were of good quality, worth four of the pennies of Rouen, and Henry was determined to keep them from being debased. In the year 1125—Thomas Becket was then just seven years old—he summoned all the mintmen of England to come to Winchester at Christmas. As the Anglo-Saxon Chronicle relates: "When they came thither, then were they taken one by one and deprived each of the right hand and the testicles beneath." The frightful mutilation was regarded as the men's just due—"for that they had ruined all the country with the great quantity of base coin."

The "Lion of Justice," as Geoffrey of Monmouth called

Henry, was feared as his father had been. But to the last he was more diplomat than soldier, preferring to gain his ends by negotiation and marital alliances rather than war. His dynastic schemes had failed when his only legitimate son, William Aetheling, drowned in the famous sinking of the *White Ship*. Lacking a male heir, Henry forced his barons to take oaths of fealty to his daughter Matilda, the former Roman empress. In 1133 Matilda bore to her second husband, Geoffrey of Anjou, a son who was baptized Henry. With that, the future of the legitimate line seemed secure.

On December 1, 1135, having dined too heartily on lampreys, Henry I expired.

Normans and Saxons alike had reason to regret his passing. His reign had done much to heal the wounds of the Conquest. Trade and industry had flourished, and thriving towns had bought important privileges. The prosperity of such a man as Gilbert Becket was probably due in part to the stable government that Henry I had provided. The times that followed were to be insecure.

III

Youth

THOMAS BECKET was "quick of learning, keen of memory and clear of understanding in all things"; he also had a mother who believed in the value of learning and a father wealthy enough to provide an only son with the best possible education. At the age of seventeen or eighteen, therefore—close to the time of King Henry's death—Thomas went to Paris to continue his studies. This meant that he was on the way to a career in the Church, although not necessarily in the priesthood; one could advance quite far in the ecclesiastical hierarchy without taking holy orders. There existed a whole shadowy realm of secular ecclesiastics and ecclesiastical seculars who performed much of the business of both State and Church. However, some evidence suggests that Thomas also felt a vocation; for around this time he began writing meditations on the Psalms. Intensified religious feeling seems to have been his reaction to the temptations of Paris.

Paris, as the Icelandic *Saga of Archbishop Thomas* puts it, "at all times has had the most renowned school in northern lands." London, too, had famous schools; but London was essentially a city of burgesses engaged in the earnest activities of an expanding commerce. Paris was more spirited, capital of that France which John of Salisbury called "of all nations the sweetest and most civilized." To Paris during Thomas Becket's stay came the sober young king and the gay young queen of France, Louis VII and Eleanor of Aquitaine, who was one day to be Becket's own queen

3 1

in England. The city attracted students of all nations, for then as now Paris was above all the city of the mind. The *Saga* reminds Icelandic readers that almost all the sons of wellborn fathers who attended the schools at Paris were of an age for "lust with fleshly desires and fleshly sweetness," and that most of them had at least one "woman-friend."

"Thomas the English" alone had no sweetheart of earth, says the *Saga;* his only beloved was the Queen of Maidens.

Now time passeth on and weareth towards Lent, the very time when in frail man lust is wont to pull at the rein after rather too forward a fashion. They now hold a great parliament, whereat in a brawly wise each praiseth his own beloved, saying that she is goodly of look, and wise of speech, and dealeth with all things with a deft hand. This is a meeting whereat Thomas the English sitteth and sayeth nought at all. They now cast glances at him with some rude jeering or mockery, saying that he is a lifeless mannikin, who findeth no game in things wherein there be the greatest joyance in this world.

A contest is to be held next day, at which each student is supposed to show the finest piece of needlework made by his mistress. Thomas, threatened with a beating unless he brings something, prays to our Lady to spare him some needlework fit to be shown among his companions.

Thus he prayeth and the night passeth away and the parliament taketh place. And he, as well as each and all of them, beareth forth unto the show-stand the glitter which each one hath got for himself. Now again they look askance to Thomas, asking what he might be about. He answered even thus: "I shall go forthwith and show you what mine own beloved brought to me last night," whereupon he went to his private study, where he found that a certain casket had come, snow-white, of shining ivory, locked and fashioned with images in a manner to surpass all polish that might be wrought by the hand of man. This little thing he now taketh with him and showeth to his companions. The casket being unlocked it appeareth what it containeth, which in short was this, that here was found, folded down, a full set of bishop's robes, so heedfully gathered together that even the staff was thereamong also. At this the noise of the clerks abateth somewhat, since by this wonder they understand that an election hath already fallen to the lot of this very Thomas, and that his path lieth somewhat higher than the ways of such folk, who sink into the sins and the filth of this miserable life.

The contemporary biographers and the chroniclers all agree that Thomas Becket took a vow of chastity in early youth. Some relate that King Henry II later tried in vain to tempt Thomas with "fleshly sweetness." We cannot penetrate into the motives for Thomas Becket's vow; we can only note that he seems to have kept it. In all the contemporary documents there is also no shred of evidence for (or for that matter against) his having had homosexual inclinations, such as Anouilh imputes to him. The sometimes excessive salutations of his letters—"to the better half of my soul," he addresses Conrad of Mainz—were typical of the age, not the person. The one letter of his addressed to a woman (see page 300) suggests that he had, within the bounds of propriety, a tender feeling for the sex.

Students made up a large part of the population of Paris, which has been estimated at 250,000. They swarmed by the thousands in the muddy, stinking streets of the Ile—for the paving of the city was not begun until the latter part of the twelfth century, in the reign of Philip Augustus. They crowded upon the Petit Pont to listen to the masters who held forth in their lodgings there, since there were houses on the bridge itself, and such famous teachers as Adam du Petit Pont were not averse to being overheard by the prelates, merchants, nobles, and scholars who crossed from Notre Dame to the Petit Chastelet. Notre Dame, incidentally, was not the cathedral we know today; that was begun in 1163. The cathedral Thomas Becket would have visited was a long, low basilica built in Merovingian times, with columns of black and white marble and gilded wooden ceiling beams.

Thomas Becket and his fellow students had come to Paris to "sit at the feet" of a corps of brilliant scholars whose fame had spread throughout Europe. Becket's friend, John of Salisbury, who arrived in Paris "in the year following the death of the illustrious King of the English" (1136), has left vivid sketches of some of them. Richard l'Evêque (who bore the name before ever he became a bishop) was "honest rather than vain, virtuous rather than ostentatious." Simon of Poissy was "a dependable lecturer but rather dull in disputes." Master Alberic was "full of subtle questions." Robert of Melun would never begin his discussion of a proposed point "without first taking up the contradictory side or showing . . . that there was more than one answer." This Robert of Melun, an Englishman, had been a pupil of Abelard and was the author of a *Book of Sentences* which formed a steppingstone to the more famous *Sentences* of Peter Lombard. He was also one of Becket's teachers, and Thomas later showed his gratitude by persuading Henry II to ask Robert to return to England—after forty years of teaching abroad—and accept appointment to the see of Hereford. Thomas himself, as archbishop, consecrated his aged teacher.

But the star of all that remarkable corps of masters who laid the foundation for what would be by the end of the century the University of Paris—the star of philosophy and the glory of the age, the thinker, singer, and sinner to whom all eyes turned when he walked in the streets—was Peter Abelard. The time of his greatness lay twenty years in the past, but in 1136 he returned briefly to Paris and once more taught on Mont Ste. Genevieve. John of Salisbury hastened "to sit at his feet drinking in every word that fell from his lips."

In all probability Thomas Becket, too, attended Abelard's lectures; few students of the time would have missed the opportunity. For Abelard's life had been as sensational as his ideas. His seduction of his pupil, Heloise, and the terrible revenge taken by her uncle—who had Abelard emasculated—was a story known to all the world. Abelard himself had told it in his *Historia calamitatum;* Heloise had written of it in the famous correspondence. Calamity followed Abelard wherever he went; his mind was too sharp and his tongue too quick to permit him to live in peace with his fellows. Twice, St. Bernard forced councils to condemn him for heresy; time and again he fled from monasteries where his presence had stirred contention. No teacher was adored more fervently by his students; no philosopher was hated more bitterly

34

by his fellow dialecticians. But he remains the truest representative of that great first half of the twelfth century when men's minds were shaken as they had not been for hundreds of years. Abelard and his contemporaries rediscovered the reach of the intellect, the potentialities of reason. "By doubting," Abelard proclaimed, "we come to inquiry; by inquiry we come to truth."

But in Abelard the mind and the heart were indissolubly joined. Of all the branches of philosophy, logic appealed to him most; but this logician had also written songs that, as Heloise testifies, were on everyone's lips. His passion for Heloise can still be felt across eight hundred years; and the love he was capable of awakening is equally apparent in every line of her letters, and in the testimonies of dozens of his contemporaries, even those of his enemies.

He was unfortunate in his enemies, or at least in one of them. For his great antagonist, Bernard of Clairvaux, was very close to being the spiritual dictator of Europe during the second quarter of the twelfth century. Fiercely orthodox, intensely mystical, conservative in thought and radical in action, St. Bernard dominated popes and princes by the force of his personality and the example of his ascetic life. By the age of twenty-four he had founded and become Abbot of Clairvaux. If Abelard stood for Reason, Bernard stood for Faith—although any such simplifications should be hedged around with a hundred reservations. Suspicious of philosophy, a preacher rather than a teacher, Bernard temperamentally carried everything to extremes. Thus with asceticism; thus with his appeals for the rescue of the Holy Land, which plunged all of Europe into the disastrous adventure of the Second Crusade. In retrospect he could say of his life: "All my works frighten me, and what I do is incomprehensible to me."

Thomas Becket in his youth must have felt the tug in two opposite directions exerted by Abelard and Bernard—how could he not, when all thinking men were taking sides? In later life he met Bernard several times and came under his spell. Walter Map recalls a time that he dined with Becket, by then Archbishop of Canterbury, and saw him grow quite angry when a malicious tale was told about the Abbot of Clairvaux. But this was the later Becket; in his youth Thomas probably admired Abelard as warmly as did his friend John of Salisbury, who speaks of "Master Peter" with unfailing respect, and specifically excepts him from those associates on Mont Ste. Genevieve whom he revisited after a long absence, to find that "they did not seem to have progressed so much as a hand's span; they had added not a single new proposition toward the solution of the old problems." Since John wrote so favorably of Abelard in a book dedicated to Thomas Becket, then Chancellor of England, he probably assumed that his admiration of the great dialectician was shared by Thomas.

Although Abelard at this time was only fifty-seven, he was virtually broken in body and spirit. Nevertheless, he still spoke with such brilliance and grace that his lectures resembled mass meetings. And even though his impingement on Thomas could only have been brief, "it is the privilege of such minds that they revivify everything they touch," as an eminent historian of philosophy has remarked. "Abelard imposed, so to speak, an intellectual *standard* which no one thenceforth cared to lower."

Thomas Becket has left no body of literary work. All that we have from his pen are the many letters he wrote during the controversy with Henry II. To judge by these, he must have devoted himself during his student years less to theology and philosophy than to obtaining a solid grounding in the classics and the scriptures. We find him quoting from Lucan, Juvenal, Ovid, Virgil, Horace, Terence, Suetonius, and Plutarch; but most frequently of all from the Old and New Testaments. Given the character of medieval education—so much of it was sheer memorization of tags from the classics—it is impossible to tell whether Thomas ever read deeply in all these authors. He certainly read the letters of Pope Gregory VII; he was also familiar with Eadmer's biography of Anselm, and with Anselm's letters.

One thing that Thomas undoubtedly learned in the schools of Paris was the intellectual swordsmanship of dialectic. In later life, at the pope's court in Sens, he would not be discountenanced by the debating techniques of Cardinal William of Pavia. Thomas then proved himself adept at explicating *"mot a mot"* the Constitutions of Clarendon, examining them with that minute logical and grammatical analysis which was the delight of the schools. On

36

this occasion he took a full half day to plead his cause. Excessive enthusiasm for argumentation was a general fault of the twelfth century, and one of the reasons for the interminable legal delays many unfortunate litigants complained of. That Thomas was by no means free of this fault is implied by several of his admiring biographers, and directly stated by John of Salisbury, who later admonished him to partake of more spiritual fare than the books of canon law.

John of Salisbury spent twelve years in study; Thomas Becket returned home after three or four. Possibly he was called home by the death of his mother and was so depressed by that event, as one biographer hints, that he could no longer apply himself to learning. As we have mentioned, Gilbert Becket's financial reverses also contributed to Thomas's decision. Our sources do not permit more than conjecture about his motives and the order of events. In any case, he was back in London by 1140, and for about a year devoted himself to solitary studies. At the end of his twenty-second year he departed from the home left "empty and desolate" by his mother's death, and found employment with a kinsman named Osbern Huitdeniers, or Eight-penny, a man "of many possessions and distinguished in the city." Since another biographer tells us that Thomas worked for a sheriff, it seems fair to assume that Osbern and the sheriff were one and the same; there is nowhere any suggestion that Thomas held two jobs after his return from Paris.

At this time the sheriffs of London were elected by their fellow citizens rather than appointed by the king. FitzStephen remarks that the sheriffs of London were comparable to the Roman consuls; they were elected for terms of one year, during which time they governed the city and were responsible only to the alderman. As the sheriff's scribe, Thomas Becket learned a good deal; he became both judicious and *curteis*—the second word meaning nearly everything from "genteel" to "practiced in the social graces." He also gathered wide experience in the administration of his native city. Since London was then the focal point of a governmental crisis, Thomas's work during those two or three years must have contributed enormously to his political education.

37

This crisis, in which so far as we know Thomas Becket played for a considerable time only the part of a passive spectator, centered upon the disputed succession to the Crown of England. Henry I had left only one legitimate heir, his daughter Matilda. But her husband, Geoffrey of Anjou, was unacceptable to the English and Norman barons, and their son, the future Henry II, was only an infant. At this perilous juncture, the one person who acted with boldness found the great prize his for the taking. He was Stephen of Blois, Count of Boulogne, grandson of the Conqueror and nephew of King Henry, a gallant knight noted for his generosity, forbearance, and intrepidity.

Stephen had the pride that went with his birth and bearing, and on at least one occasion in the past that pride had led him to impress on all men's minds a fact he might now wish forgotten. For at London on January 1, 1127, King Henry had presented his daughter Matilda to the assembled barons and asked them to swear that they would recognize her as their ruler if he should die without a male heir. The Archbishop of Canterbury, followed by the bishops, duly swore, and then Robert of Gloucester, one of the king's bastard sons, came forward. Stephen protested that he ought to take precedence over a bastard—and his point of protocol was allowed. But the consequence was that he had made it impossible for anyone ever to forget his oath of fidelity to Matilda.

It was as a perjurer and usurper, therefore, that Stephen had crossed the Channel with a small force "as soon as King Henry had breathed his last," and gone straight to London. London approved; the Londoners greeted Stephen with joy and hastily put forward the novel claim that they alone had the special privilege of electing the kings of England. With his brother Henry, Bishop of Winchester, manipulating the episcopate behind the scenes, Stephen was acclaimed king and crowned by William of Corbeil, the Archbishop of Canterbury. Personally well liked, with powerful kinsfolk in many parts of Europe and at least as legitimate a claim on the throne as a number of other possible claimants, Stephen seemed an excellent choice. For to have a woman on the throne or acting as regent for her young son seemed an invitation to anarchy.

But political event oftener deceives than fulfills expectations. Anarchy resulted from the accession of the strong and personable man in his late thirties, and anarchy continued until a boy of twenty-one—Matilda's son—came to the throne. Yet Stephen's reign began promisingly enough. He promptly paid his debt to the Church for its support by issuing a charter in which he granted virtually all the concessions demanded by the ecclesiastics. The customs and immunities of the churches were to remain inviolate; all ecclesiastical property was to be free of dues. Above all, Stephen conceded that "jurisdiction and authority over ecclesiastical persons and over all clerks and their property . . . shall lie in the hands of the bishops."

But after making these concessions, Stephen added a self-protective clause that was to echo again and again in Thomas Becket's controversy with Henry II: "All these things I grant and confirm *saving my royal and just dignity.*"

By placating the barons and the Church, by securing recognition of his kingship from Pope Innocent II, and by arranging a treaty with his dangerous rival to the north, King David I of Scotland, Stephen swiftly consolidated his position. But within a few years he found himself in difficulties at home and abroad. In 1138 he became embroiled in a war with Scotland, and simultaneously his Norman duchy was invaded by Geoffrey of Anjou. Whereupon Robert, Earl of Gloucester, that same bastard son of Henry whose precedence Stephen had disputed eleven years before, swung over to the cause of his half-sister, Matilda. Universally considered a gifted and honest man, he carried with him a large following. The subsequent struggle in England became largely a contest between Stephen and Robert.

A complicated series of marches and countermarches marked the campaigns of the civil war in England and Normandy. Castles were besieged, fell, were garrisoned or destroyed by the one side, only to be recaptured or rebuilt by the other side. The defense had the advantage almost always, for the Norman castles were highly resistant to direct assault. At any given time the number of men engaged in actual military operations was never very large, and most of them stayed safely in their strongholds, with the insurgents emerging to ravage the countryside when the king and his army were away trying to reduce some other focus of rebellion. The Anglo-Saxon Chronicle reflected the sufferings of the common people during this desultory warfare:

> When the wretched people had no more [protection money] to give, they [the rebels] robbed and burned all the villages, so that you could easily go a whole day's journey and never find anyone occupying a village, nor land tilled. Then corn was dear, and meat and butter and cheese, because there was none in the country. . . . If two or three men came riding to a village, all the villagers fled, because they expected they would be robbers.

Although Stephen enjoyed initial successes on the battlefield, he committed a crucial mistake in ecclesiastical policy which was to cost him dear—and which was also, incidentally, to advance the fortunes of a then unknown young man named Thomas Becket. William of Corbeil, Archbishop of Canterbury, had died in 1136, and Stephen's brother, Henry of Blois, Bishop of Winchester, hoped to succeed him. But Henry was already the most powerful man in England next to the king, and Stephen was unwilling to entrust him with the primacy. After a series of intrigues whose details are obscure, Henry of Winchester was outmaneuvered, and Theobald, Abbot of Bec, was elected fifth Archbishop of Canterbury since the Conquest. The Chronicle emphasized the influence of Stephen upon the election: "Te king makede Teodbald aercebisshop." Henry was deeply offended, and soon seized the opportunity to avenge himself upon his brother.

Thereafter, Stephen began having difficulties with the Church. The bishops, it will be recalled, were also great magnates of the realm. The family of Roger, Bishop of Salisbury, held so many of the seats of power within the political framework of feudal England that Stephen rightly feared the possibility of their changing sides. Roger was chief justiciar, his son was chancellor, his nephew, the Bishop of Ely, was treasurer, and another nephew was the Bishop of Lincoln. All held strategic castles in various parts of England. If they went over to the Angevins, Stephen's cause was as good as lost. As soon, therefore, as he felt in a position to do so, Stephen demanded that they surrender their castles. When they refused, he arrested Roger and Alexander.

Archbishop Theobald and Henry of Winchester promptly called a council to discuss this infringement upon the rights of the Church. The king spoke eloquently for himself, charging that everyone knew that as soon as the empress arrived in England the bishops would support her and let her use their castles. Roger and Alexander had been imprisoned not as bishops but as servants of the king, he declared. It was the old distinction which William Rufus had successfully upheld in the trial of William of Calais. The Archbishop of Rouen argued in support of Stephen that it was uncanonical for bishops to hold castles. Henry of Winchester spoke for the arrested bishops, but did not dare push matters too far for fear of Stephen's vengeance.

In the autumn of 1139 the long-expected invasion took place. Empress Matilda and Robert of Gloucester landed in England to renew the Angevin struggle against Stephen. Stephen chivalrously let slip an opportunity to capture Matilda, and paid dearly for his gallantry less than two years later when he himself was captured by the Angevins at the Battle of Lincoln. He had joined battle against great odds, for he "refused to sully his fame by the disgrace of flight." Although he fought like a lion, he was taken prisoner at last. The unknown author of the *Deeds of Stephen* tells us that

> when at length they disarmed him he kept crying out, in a humbled voice of complaint, that this mark of ignominy had come upon him because God was avenging His injuries, and yet they were not innocent of a monstrous crime in breaking their faith, disdaining their oath, caring nothing for the homage they had pledged him, and rebelling so wickedly and abominably against the man they had chosen of their own will as their king and lord. Then they were all so much softened by tender emotions of pity and compassion that they broke forth into tears and lamentation.

At the moment, however, the way seemed open for Matilda to become ruler of England. The greater part of the kingdom submitted to the empress and her followers. At a council held in Winchester on April 7, 1141, Henry of Blois took the position that God had punished Stephen for his infringing upon the liberties of the Church. "I must love my mortal brother," Henry declared, "but I have still greater regard for the cause of my immortal Father. . . . God has pronounced judgment on my brother by permitting him without my design to fall into the hands of the mighty." He then enunciated the novel doctrine that the clergy of England had the principal right to choose and crown the sovereign, and proposed that "invoking God's help, we elect as ruler of England and Normandy the daughter of that peaceful, glorious, rich, good and incomparable king [Henry I], and we promise her fidelity and support."

But London demurred; and although the Londoners were forced reluctantly to accept Matilda, they soon rose in revolt and drove her out of the city. The fortunes of the royal party revived; Henry of Blois changed sides once more; the war resumed, and with the capture of Earl Robert of Gloucester the way was open for the release of Stephen from captivity. An exchange of prisoners was effected, and at Christmas 1141 Stephen and his queen, Matilda, Countess of Boulogne, were crowned once more. The civil war continued, with varying fortunes, bringing its inevitable accompaniment of famine and disease.

✠   ✠   ✠

Soon after these stirring events, Thomas Becket reached a turning point in his career. An ambitious young man could not fail to recognize that the seat of stable power, in those troubled times, was the Church; a devout young man might also wish to be sheltered from the world's temptations within the bosom of the Church. And a partisan of the Angevins might not wish to go on working in a sheriff's office in London, for the city was now strongly committed to Stephen's cause. Ambition and prudence combined with opportunity, for friends of Archbishop Theobald frequented Gilbert's house. Two of these—their names are given as Master Eustace and Archdeacon Baldwin—were much taken with young Thomas. He was then slim and unusually tall, pale of complexion, with dark hair, a long nose, and straight features. His speech was marred by a slight tendency to stutter; on the other hand he was "so keen of discernment and understanding that he would always make difficult questions plain." Eustace and Baldwin gladly recommended this winning and intelligent young man to Archbishop Theobald. Gilbert Becket added a reminder that he had once been Theobald's neighbor in Thierceville in Normandy; and Thomas Becket was taken into the archbishop's "household"—that is, given a place on the staff.

There was something about Becket that provoked others to take a roughly chaffing tone toward him. For example, when he was residing at Pontigny during his exile, he asked the pope to send him a monastic habit. When it arrived, Alexander Llewelyn, his irrepressible Welsh cross-bearer, remarked that the hood was too small. Thomas smiled and said that it had been sewn thus on purpose so that Alexander would not again make fun of him, as he had done the other day. "The day before yesterday, when I was putting on the holy vestments for Mass, you asked why my posterior seemed to stick out. Now if a bigger hood dangled from my shoulders, you would ridicule me for being humpbacked."

Sometimes this chaffing assumed a hostile cast. That is what happened—with serious consequences for the future—at the very beginning of Thomas Becket's ecclesiastical career. The Archbishop of Canterbury owned a manor at Harrow-on-the-Hill, near London; a manor that comes into this story again at the very end. Instructed to join the archbishop's court at Harrow, Thomas went down from London accompanied by one Ralph, a menial official of the archbishop's household. Ralph's duties were those of a squire or arms-bearer; appropriately, he had the surname of Baillehache, or "axe-carrier." One member of Theobald's official family, Roger of Pont l'Evêque, saw something humorous in the combination and fastened upon Thomas the nickname of Baillehache, as if Thomas himself were the menial. Roger was the legal specialist in Theobald's court, and perhaps his jealousy had been aroused by the news that a young man learned in canon law was to join the household. In any case, the early biographers see in this raillery the seeds of the lifelong

enmity that Roger bore Thomas—an enmity nourished, after the
two men had become respectively archbishops of York and
Canterbury, by the traditional rivalry between the two
archiepiscopal sees of England.

Thomas quickly attached himself to Theobald's brother
Walter, then the archdeacon, and Walter protected the promising
canon lawyer against the intrigues of Roger. Twice, Roger
persuaded Theobald to dismiss Thomas; twice, Walter interceded
and procured Thomas's reinstatement. Thereafter there was no
checking Thomas's rise in the archbishop's favor. Ecclesiastical
preferments were heaped upon him: the church of St. Mary-
le-Strand, the church of Otford, a prebend in St. Paul's and at
Lincoln, are mentioned among others. What these gifts meant
was simply that his salary was steadily increased, for he had no
duties to perform in these churches. As in all cases of "pluralism," some poor priest read the Masses and visited the sick of the
parish, for which services Thomas paid him a meager portion of
the revenues. The Church had repeatedly fulminated against this
practice; as recently as 1128 the bishops and abbots of Normandy,
meeting in Rouen, had heard the legate of Pope Honorius
pronounce that "one priest shall not serve two churches, nor any
clerk hold prebends in more than one church; let him serve God
in the church where he is beneficed." But pluralism could not be
stamped out; it was too firmly rooted in the whole economic
order of feudal society. Only the most minor officials were paid in
wages; all others were compensated by benefices, ecclesiastical or
secular. Nor did any stigma attach to such holdings. Becket's
biographers note them as proof that he early found favor in the
eyes of his superiors, and Thomas himself would later cite them
as evidence that he had not been "poorly provided with worldly
goods" at the time that King Henry made him chancellor.

At the court of Theobald Thomas encountered a group of
brilliant men, the nearest equivalent to a university that England
then boasted. Four of these men were later to become archbishops, six bishops, and many of them afterwards held important
posts in the secular government. Theobald himself, in fact, was a
lesser luminary among these distinguished scholars. Thomas, like
any young man arriving at a university, discovered that he was

44

not so learned as his companions; but instead of despairing, he set out to fill the gaps in his education. Later, FitzStephen tells us, he became an accomplished scholar—*literatissimus*. Yet he was never a man of letters in the formal sense (although an indefatigable correspondent). No studies of *The Degrees of Humility and Pride* or *On Grace and Free Will* (St. Bernard), no examination into *The Nature of the Body and the Soul* (William of St. Thierry), no *Proslogion* or *Monologion* (Anselm) from his hand have come down to us. He devoted himself to action, to administration and law rather than theology or philosophy.

In pursuit of a superior grounding in civil and canon law Thomas went, at Theobald's expense, to study in Bologna for a year, and then for some time in Auxerre, where there was also a famous school of law. Unfortunately, nothing whatsoever is known of these two periods of what might be called postgraduate education in Thomas Becket's life. Nor has their date been established, although it probably fell about the middle of the decade, perhaps around 1145, after Thomas had proved his merit in Theobald's service for a number of years.

The middle of the twelfth century saw a great revival of Roman civil law, and the codification of canon law. The heart of this movement was the school of Bologna, where the Benedictine monk Gratian published his *Concordia discordantium canonum* at this time. At Bologna Thomas Becket probably met the Lombard canonist, Master Vacarius, and persuaded him to act as legal adviser to Theobald; the archbishop, as we shall see in a moment, was engaged in a legal suit at the Curia against Bishop Henry of Winchester. Theobald subsequently invited Vacarius to England, where for a time he lectured on Roman civil law (as an adjunct to canon law) at Oxford. The English barons objected. They saw Roman law as a threat to feudal customs and a potential invasion of their judicial rights, for the tendency would be for clerks to monopolize a system of law based on learning. King Stephen agreed with his barons, silenced Vacarius, and forbade the teaching of civil law altogether.

Thomas was sent to study law because Theobald was grooming him for the post of archdeacon, the key legal and administrative office of a diocese. Archdeacons were primarily lawyers, and had the reputation of being bloodsuckers. Like the sheriffs, who practiced extortion for the king's exchequer and their own, they were hated for their rapacity. They blackmailed, boasted of their mistresses, and were alleged to have learned in their studies at Bologna the Italian arts of poisoning. Henry II complained that the archdeacons extracted more money from the people by fines than the king himself received in revenue; and John of Salisbury raised the question whether eternal salvation was possible for them. Thomas himself, after he became archbishop, would regularly refer to his own archdeacon, Geoffrey Ridel, as the archdevil—*archidiabolus* instead of *archidiaconus*.

But ten years were to pass before Thomas rose to that soul-endangering eminence; and indeed he did not remain archdeacon for long, since he soon passed into the secular service of Henry II. Very few details of those ten vital years under Theobald have been preserved by the early biographers. We catch only glimpses of Thomas during that period, as he gradually became Theobald's most trusted adviser, formed friendships among the great men of his time, was dispatched on missions that called for consummate diplomatic skill. We know also that he ghostwrote speeches for Theobald, who was not so ready of tongue as others of his contemporaries in high places.

He was sent on a number of missions to Rome, where he won the favor of the several popes who reigned between 1143 and 1154 (Celestine II, Lucius II, Eugenius III, Anastasius IV, and the only English pope, Nicholas Breakspear, who took the name of Adrian IV). On one occasion Thomas successfully negotiated with the pope to procure the office of apostolic legate for Archbishop Theobald. The legateship had been held by Henry of Blois, who had attempted to use it to dominate the Church in England. Disappointed in his hopes of becoming Archbishop of Canterbury, Henry sought the power if not the title. He also tried to persuade the pope to raise his see of Winchester to the dignity of an archiepiscopate. "The legate," says a contemporary, "wished to seem greater than the archbishop."

In thwarting Henry of Blois's plans, Thomas acted in the

interests of his own master; but he also asserted the hierarchical principle in ecclesiastical affairs for which he was to stand during his own tenure of the archbishop's office. Evidently, he came early to regard the rights and dignities of the primate of all England as sacrosanct. Fortunately, Henry of Blois seems to have borne Thomas no grudge. Fifteen years later, during the conflict between King Henry and Thomas, Henry of Blois—then one of Thomas's suffragan bishops—met his obligations loyally and gave his superior temperate advice.

Another glimpse of Thomas during his service under Theobald reveals him in a situation that without doubt made a profound impression upon his mind and influenced the whole course of his career. Pope Eugenius III had called a council of the Church at Reims to deal with a number of political and ecclesiastical problems. Among the latter was the trial of Gilbert de la Porrée, whom St. Bernard had charged with heresy; among the former was the validity of the election of William, King Stephen's nephew, whom Stephen had virtually appointed Archbishop of York. When the call to the council was issued, Stephen promptly retaliated by forbidding the English bishops to attend. This was the traditional policy of his predecessors since the Conquest, who had limited contacts between the English episcopate and Rome. Stephen's ban was a measure of the increasing strength of his position against his enemies at home. It was also the beginning of an open break between Stephen and his brother Henry on one side, and Archbishop Theobald on the other.

Stephen suspected that Theobald would attempt to disobey, and ordered the ports watched. Meanwhile, he himself remained at Canterbury to keep an eye on his archbishop. But one night in March Theobald slipped out of Canterbury accompanied by a single clerk, Thomas Becket. They crossed the Channel in a vessel so leaky and in such stormy weather that Pope Eugenius afterwards commented that they had come swimming rather than sailing—a play on words in Latin (*natando potius quam navigando*). The sentence comes from a letter by Thomas himself, who thus learned from Theobald an Archbishop of Canterbury's obligation to defy his king.

This witty Pope Eugenius had proved to be one of the surprises of the mid-century. Originally a Cistercian abbot, he had a reputation for being devout, but simple and ineffectual. He had been elected because of his friendship for St. Bernard, who with somewhat unsaintly immodesty, if half jokingly, had told him: "They say you are not the pope, but me." The times were troublous for the papacy. Eugenius's predecessor had died in battle at the head of troops, trying to recapture Rome from democratic republicans led by that idealistic revolutionary and proto-Protestant, Arnold of Brescia, who for a short time had succeeded in setting up in Rome a shadowy restoration of the *res publica Romana*. Eugenius himself was driven out of Rome three days after his election, but succeeded by his own energy, and by adroit intrigues with the neighboring cities around Rome, in regaining his position there. Expelled once more in 1146, in one of those March uprisings that were a commonplace in the volatile city of Rome, he eventually crossed the Alps to France, the heart of orthodoxy. It was, then, as an exile and fugitive that he greeted the fugitives Theobald and Thomas Becket at the Council of Reims. No wonder he was moved by their testimonial of unquestioning obedience to him as pope.

Although the full import of the terrible failures of the Second Crusade was not yet known in Europe, some inkling of disasters had already reached France in King Louis VII's reports to Abbot Suger. The blame for defeats on the battlefield and for thousands of deaths by pestilence, as well as for quarrels among the leaders of the Crusade, could not logically be laid at the door of Bernard of Clairvaux. But he had persuaded men to take the cross, and his prestige suffered as the rumors reached home telling of betrayals by the "Greeks," of ambushes by the Turks, of lives and treasure squandered to no useful end.

At the Council of Reims Bernard of Clairvaux failed for the first time to secure a condemnation for heresy. Thomas Becket must have thought himself once more back in the schools of Paris as he listened to the debates on "substance," "accidents," and "subsistence." But Gilbert de la Porrée was not to be overwhelmed by such tactics as had secured the condemnation of Abelard. He came to trial with his clerks staggering under a load of heavy volumes, the collected Fathers of the Church, and

48

stalwartly met the assaults of Robert of Melun and Peter Lombard, who spoke for the prosecution.

The heart of the argument against Gilbert focused upon his commentary on Boethius' *De Trinitate*. Boethius, and Gilbert following him, distinguished between what a thing is and the essence which makes it what it is: the *id quod est* and the *quo est*. In God, both coincide: the *quo est* of God is divinity. To Bernard and his followers, Gilbert seemed to be saying that God and divinity were separate essences, and this appeared to them as rankest heresy. The rapid spread of Manichaean doctrines in Languedoc around this time was prompting orthodox theologians to scent heresy in anything that resembled a dualistic view of the universe. Hence the barbed questions directed to Gilbert at the Council of Reims: "Do you teach that Divine Essence is not God, but the form by which God is?" To which Gilbert stoutly replied: "No. The form of God, the divinity by which God is, is not itself God." He haughtily recommended that Bernard go to school for a while if he wished to discuss philosophical questions.

Most of the church dignitaries could not follow the subtleties of the argument. Pope Eugenius may or may not have understood it; the degree of his comprehension can scarcely be made out from his decision that "the essence of God should be predicated not in the sense of the ablative case only, but also of the nominative." But presumably he meant by this that God is both the *quo est* and the *id quod est*. At any rate, he availed himself of the opportunity to declare his independence of Bernard, and refused to consent to a condemnation of Gilbert.

However, on the political matter discussed at the council, Eugenius went along with Bernard. He insisted on the resolution deposing King Stephen's nephew, William, from the see of York, and prepared to excommunicate Stephen for his highhanded conduct toward both his archbishops. The candles had already been lit for the solemn ceremony of excommunication, but before they could be dashed to the ground and thus extinguished, Theobald surprised the pope by pleading with him to spare Stephen. Eugenius praised Theobald for loving his enemies and praying for his persecutors, and suspended the sentence. Theobald's lesson in policy and moderation was not to be lost on his clerk, Thomas Becket.

Stephen's anger was not placated. He had the property of the see of Canterbury confiscated, and when Theobald returned armed with papal suspensions of the bishops who had not obeyed the summons to the council, Stephen ordered him to leave the country. Thus, like Anselm before him and Thomas Becket after him, Theobald went into exile. And as was to happen in Becket's case, most of his suffragan bishops took the king's side in the quarrel. They disobeyed the interdict which the pope had laid upon the country, and in effect declared, with the king, the independence of the English Church.

The exile did not last long. The contention between the houses of Anjou and Blois continued to rack England. Stephen could not long affront the Church, for he needed Theobald's help in securing the succession of his son Eustace, whom he wished to crown during his lifetime to assure the continuity of the line of Blois. Before the end of the year, therefore, he patched up the quarrel; mutual concessions were made, and Theobald returned to England. Nevertheless, he went on opposing Stephen's plans for the succession. Thomas Becket, ever an Angevin sympathizer, loyally supported his archbishop throughout this period of tense relations with the Crown. We are told that Thomas "by his most subtle foresightedness" frustrated Stephen's efforts to secure papal assent to his son's coronation. Thomas also traveled back and forth between England and Rome, and although we do not know the details of his negotiations the mere fact of these journeys was something of an innovation. Weak though the papacy was at home, threatened by rebellion in Rome herself and schism in the Holy Roman Empire, it remained strong in its relationships with England. The English clergy themselves grumbled at the unprecedented frequency of appeals to Rome, which prolonged disputes, cost a great deal of money, and permitted the intervention of a foreign power in the affairs of England.

✠   ✠   ✠

While Stephen was engaged in futile negotiations with his recalcitrant churchmen, the Angevin power on the Continent was

50

growing by leaps and bounds. In September 1151 Geoffrey of Anjou died at the age of thirty-nine. His eldest son, Henry FitzEmpress, already Duke of Normandy, inherited Anjou and Maine. The following March, Louis VII of France divorced Eleanor of Aquitaine; two months later, Henry triumphantly led her to the altar, carrying away a prize that both his brother Geoffrey and Theobald of Blois had eagerly sought. Eleanor was not only beautiful and accomplished; she was also mistress of vast domains. With her land joined to his, Henry held almost the entire western part of France and was in a much stronger position to assert his mother's claim to England. In January 1153 the twenty-year-old duke invaded England. He brought with him only 140 knights and 3,000 infantrymen, for he was relying mainly on gold and the Angevin supporters already in the country to win him his heritage. His infantrymen, mercenaries schooled to cruelty in the incessant wars of the Continent, stormed the town of Malmesbury with a military efficiency such as England had not witnessed for years. They then proceeded to murder and pillage in town, monastery, and church with such ruthlessness that the English barons in Henry's own camp insisted they be sent home.

Within a few months, Henry FitzEmpress, aided by defecting nobles, had brought almost half of England under his nominal control. With an army that had grown enormously since his landing, he laid siege to Crowmarsh, a castle on a high mound near Wallingford. Stephen made one last effort. He gathered, says the author of the *Deeds of Stephen,* "an unspeakably large army of knights as well as infantry, accompanied also by his son Eustace, by many earls and innumerable barons, and came to Wallingford." The two armies drew up in battle array with the Thames between them. There were kinsmen in both, and the barons were not eager for either side to win a clear-cut victory since the existing anarchy favored their own relative independence. A temporary truce was arranged, the armies went home, and negotiations between the parties continued. Eustace departed in anger, feeling that his father had betrayed him. Shortly afterwards, Eustace's untimely death broke Stephen's spirit and removed the last obstacle to a permanent settlement.

Archbishop Theobald, probably aided by Thomas Becket, labored mightily to work out a compromise; and in November 1153 a treaty was signed between Stephen and Henry. Stephen adopted Henry as his heir, on condition that he, Stephen, be permitted to hold the kingdom for the remainder of his life.

He had not long to live. On October 25, 1154, he died at Dover. Six weeks later, having been delayed by bad weather, Henry FitzEmpress crossed the Channel, to be greeted joyously as the pledge of a new era of peace and prosperity. Archbishop Theobald had kept the realm tranquil during the interregnum. Henry was crowned without opposition at Westminster on December 19, 1154. As Duke of Normandy, Count of Anjou, Duke of Aquitaine, and now King of England, this young man of twenty-one had suddenly become one of the most powerful monarchs in Europe.

IV

The King and His Chancellor

LEGEND HAD IT that King Henry II was descended from a demon. His ancestor, Fulk the Black of Anjou, had a wife who entered church with great reluctance and always left before the consecration of the Host. One day Fulk ordered that she be restrained by force. Thereupon she slipped out of the cloak by which his men were holding her, caught up two of her children, flew out through the window with them, and vanished forever, a medieval Medea.

The Angevins were fond of this story and told it with relish. It served to explain to themselves as well as to the rest of the world the paradoxes of their characters: their vehemence combined with coldness and shrewdness; their fits of epileptic rage coupled with sagacity, prudence, and administrative genius; their genuine devoutness and temperamental anti-clericalism; their sense of honor and their inclination toward the dishonorable. Henry II, the greatest of the Angevins, contained within himself all the contradictions of his line. He had a unique capacity for friendship, by all accounts; yet we are also told that he "mourned the dead with a grief far greater than he loved the living." He was a great organizer who laid the foundations of many institutions by which England is still governed today; yet in his personal life no one could have been more disorganized. Incessantly active, on his feet from dawn to dusk, changing his plans from moment to moment, he made life a hell for his courtiers, who tried in vain to bring order into the chaos the king half deliberately created

53

around him. For although he revered the memory and frequently adverted to the customs of his grandfather, Henry I, he managed his household with none of the efficiency of that disciplined king. Under Henry I, every courtier had known exactly how many loaves of bread and candle ends he was entitled to receive for himself and his men. All was set forth in detail in the *Constitutio Domus Regis*, the Establishment of the King's Household. ("The chancellor shall receive 5 shillings a day and 1 lord's simnel loaf, and 2 salted simnel loaves, and 1 sextary of clear wine . . . and 1 fat candle and 40 pieces of candle. . . . The fruiterer shall live in the king's household and shall receive 3 pence a day for his men. The carter shall have the customary food and an allowance for his horses.") When Henry I went on a royal progress, the stages of his journey were set in advance, the supplies that must be taken along predetermined, and the king's itinerary widely published so that those who had business with him could assemble to meet him. Each day was carefully ordered; public affairs were conducted at set times, amusements and conversation reserved for the after-dinner hours.

The disorder, the seeming carelessness, the breathlessness and excitement in household and court of Henry II, seemed all the more disconcerting by contrast. A contemporary, Peter of Blois, complained bitterly about it:

> If the king has promised to spend the day in a place—more especially, if his intention so to do has been publicly proclaimed by a herald—you may be quite sure he will upset everybody's arrangements by starting off early in the morning. Then you may see men rushing about as if they were mad, beating their packhorses, driving their carts one into another—in short, such a turmoil as to present you with a lively image of the infernal regions. If, on the other hand, the king announces that he will set out early in the morning for a certain place, he is sure to change his mind; you may take it for granted that he will sleep till noon. Then you shall see the packhorses waiting with their burdens, the carts standing ready, the courtiers dozing, the purveyors worrying, and all grumbling.

And after all had finally set out for a destination, "the king would turn aside to some other place where he had perhaps one single house, and just enough provisions for himself and no one else.

54

. . . I truly believe he took delight in seeing the straits to which he put us! After wandering a distance of three or four miles in an unknown wood, and often in the dark, we thought ourselves lucky if we stumbled upon some dirty little hovel."

There was method in this madness, of course. The possibility of the king's unexpected appearances struck terror to the hearts of dishonest or disloyal officials. But there were grave disadvantages also, especially in the delays of justice, for which the royal court became notorious. To obtain judgment of a case from Henry, suitors were compelled to go to enormous expense in chasing the king about the country, bringing documents and witnesses with them. When they succeeded in catching up with him, they could never know whether he might decide to go hawking or hunting rather than hold court. Even if he did hear the case, he might reserve decision to some future session. Walter Map relates that he was so slow in settling the business of his subjects that many died unheard or departed empty-handed. Map attributes Henry's dilatoriness to deliberate policy, the consequence of his mother's teaching. But the slowness of justice in the realm of a ruler so concerned with reform of the courts is more likely to have resulted from administrative slackness and the king's restiveness of mind and body.

He kept his mind as active as his body. Henry Curtmantel, as his contemporaries called him because he introduced into England the short Norman cape, was well-read and well-spoken. He knew "all the languages which are spoken from the Bay of Biscay to the Jordan, but made use only of Latin and French." When he was not otherwise engaged, he would be found with a book in his hand; and he remembered what he had read, just as he never forgot a face. Although he liked to shut himself off with a few chosen friends, so that jealous courtiers grumbled, he was affable and accessible when he reappeared. Men loved him and were fiercely loyal to him, but many wished that he would be more conscious of his royal dignity. Anyone could address him freely in the streets or on public highways; he put up with being jostled and buffeted when hordes of suitors crowded round him.

His physical appearance has been carefully described by many contemporaries. Evidently he worried about it, for he kept his reddish hair close-cropped to avoid baldness, and he fought his tendency to corpulence by constant exercise and frugal meals. Slightly above medium height, he was stocky, freckled in complexion, with a large round head, "gray eyes which glowed fierce and grew bloodshot in anger, a fiery countenance, and a harsh and cracked voice. His neck was somewhat thrust forward from his shoulders, his chest was broad and square, his arms strong and powerful." Yet, although he was concerned about keeping fit, he dressed so carelessly that he could hardly be distinguished from his servants. Moreover, his clothes were frequently caked with mud and dust; indeed, he seemed to take pleasure in subjecting his powerful frame to constant hardship.

This description, of course, applies to Henry in middle life. We would have to retouch some elements in the portrait to see the young man who, in the beginning of 1155, set out on a prolonged royal progress to show himself to his new subjects. Born in Le Mans in 1133, Henry had spent the first nine years of his life in Angers, under the tutelage of an Aquitanian, Master Peter of Saintes. At the end of 1142 he was sent to England for "fostering" in the household of his uncle, Robert of Gloucester. There he stayed for four years, and at his age would undoubtedly have picked up Anglo-Saxon from the servants, although there is no evidence that he ever spoke the language. He received a sound education at Bristol. More important, he had an opportunity to witness the effects of bad government during his uncle Robert's prolonged struggle with Stephen: the raids, the ravaging of the countryside, the intrigues. From the age of sixteen, when his father, Geoffrey of Anjou, appointed him Duke of Normandy, he personally participated in the Angevin attempt to wrest England from the House of Blois. But young as he was, he even then showed none of the impetuosity of youth in warfare. He avoided pitched battles whenever possible, as he was to do throughout his life, preferring the threat of force to its application, and the byways of diplomacy to the bloodstained highway of battle.

✠ ✠ ✠

Such was the man Thomas Becket must have confronted—or rather, looked down upon from his own towering

56

height—at Westminster in the last days of December 1154. Archbishop Theobald brought his recently appointed archdeacon with him to the coronation, and kept Thomas by his side as the court followed the king from Westminster to Bermondsey to Oxford to Silverston to Northampton. For Theobald remained in attendance upon the king during this journey, which must have been exhausting for a man of his age. (Theobald's presence is attested by his signature attached to charters that Henry issued all along the route.) He stayed with the king not only as a matter of duty, but also in order to place his trusted assistant in a position of power at the king's court.

Theobald himself had been virtually governing England since the death of Stephen. During that interval before Henry's arrival he would have had ample opportunity to observe Thomas's aptitude for the tasks of secular government. He himself must return to his ecclesiastical duties; but he wished to have his own man in the counsel of the king. He feared for the future of the Church and of the people of England under a foreign king, a young man surrounded by advisers whom he believed to be hostile to the Church, and a new ruler who might be tempted to punish severely those who had formerly opposed his accession. To install in the king's court a capable administrator old enough to gain a certain ascendancy over the young king's mind (Thomas was then thirty-seven) would provide some assurance that Henry could be guided in the right direction—that is to say, prevented from making inroads upon the property and prerogatives of the Church.

Theobald therefore recommended Thomas Becket for the post of chancellor in the new administration. During the long struggle between the Angevins and the House of Blois, Henry's mother had pledged the chancellorship to William de Vere, who at this time was Archbishop Theobald's chaplain. But Henry owed a good deal to Theobald, he had had proof of his loyalty, and he could assume that Theobald would know the members of his own household. If the archbishop believed that Thomas Becket was the better man for the office, Henry as a foreigner would do well to be guided by him. Then, too, Henry had an instinct for quality in men; his choices of his "cabinet" demonstrate that. And in view of the later relations between Henry and Thomas we are safe in assuming that the king felt an immediate sympathy when the tall, merry-faced cleric was presented to him.

In any case, Theobald's suggestion was accepted. Whether Bishop Nigel of Ely, the treasurer, briefly preceded Thomas as chancellor depends upon the interpretation of a single manuscript. For all practical purposes Thomas Becket served as Henry's first chancellor. By January 1155 his name appears as a witness to charters. FitzStephen states distinctly that Thomas was chancellor within the first three months after the king's coronation.

The office was not originally so important as Thomas made it. "The Chancellor of England," William FitzStephen tells us, "holds the custody of the royal seal and seals his own orders with the obverse of it; he takes charge of the arrangements in the king's chapel; he receives and carefully guards the vacant archbishoprics, bishoprics, abbeys and baronies which fall into the king's hand; he sits in on all the king's councils and may enter even when not summoned. Everything is signed by his clerk, who carries the royal seal, and everything is done by the chancellor's advice."

FitzStephen was magnifying the chancellor's importance to glorify the martyr; but he and his contemporaries agreed that Chancellor Thomas, at any rate, was second only to the king in the realm. Richard FitzNigel remarks that the chancellor "is as great at the Exchequer as at court, so that nothing of great moment is done, or ought to be done, without his consent and advice." Thomas, at any rate, managed all the secretarial work of the royal household; it is scarcely surprising that he employed fifty-two clerks. And within a short time he was more powerful than the justiciar (at this time Richard de Lucy) or the treasurer (Bishop Nigel), although he ranked below them in the official hierarchy. As chief of the royal chapel, which was the collective name for the household clerks, his functions were mainly secular. And he quickly made it plain to all that he regarded himself as a man of this world rather than the next. As his contemporaries phrased it, he "put off the deacon and put on the chancellor."

58

The revenues of a whole kingdom now flowed through Thomas's hands: receipts from vacant abbeys and bishoprics, dues, payments for royal charters, and the rapidly multiplying royal pleas. In addition, his own private revenues were vastly increased by the "honors" (such as the stewardship of the Tower of London) that the king heaped upon him. Thomas seems to have made little distinction between the public and his private purse. This is no comment on his ethics but on his conception of his position; he viewed himself as representative of the king, and was more solicitous about his master's public "image," to use the ugly modern word, than Henry himself. The concept of "conflict of interest" did not exist. Thomas deliberately used his new wealth to set up a household whose magnificence was the wonder of England. He dined in more than regal splendor, and served his guests the most delicate dishes, although he himself continued to eat frugally. We have mentioned the fresh rushes that were strewn daily on his floor—an example of fanatical hygiene for the times. His contemporaries, however, regarded this as testimony to his considerateness; for there was often not room enough at the trestle tables, and those guests who dined on the floor had the comfort of not sitting on fouled rushes. Gold and silver plate sparkled on his tables; pages who were the sons of the greatest nobles of England handed round rare and precious wines.

These pages, sent to him for "nurture" after the custom of the day, ultimately included young Henry, the king's son, who was born to Henry and Eleanor on February 28, 1155, shortly after Thomas was appointed chancellor. It would have been surprising indeed if many of these boys, raised in his household, enjoying daily the example of his munificence and the lessons of his intelligence, had not grown up to be ardent partisans of their foster father. This must be remembered when we consider Henry's alarm and anxiety after he had, as he believed, made an enemy of Thomas Becket. By the time the struggle between the two began, most of those pages had reached manhood and were heirs to or holders of some of the most important fiefs of England and of Henry's Continental lands.

But struggle was far in the future, and in the early days of

Thomas Becket's chancellorship there sprang up between him and the king an intimacy so close that the disparity in their positions and years seemed to vanish. They played and sported together "like boys of the same age." They laughed, talked, sat over the chessboard together, went hawking and hunting and riding. The king might, at the spur of the moment, come riding on horseback into Becket's hall "to see whether the talk about his house and his table were true." Never in Christian times, says FitzStephen, were two men more of one mind or better friends.

The king, who went about drably dressed, often in mud-spattered clothing, was fond of chaffing his chancellor for wearing a fortune on his back. The famous story of the beggar must stand for many a similar occasion. One cold winter day the king and his chancellor were riding in the streets of London. The king saw an old man, raggedly dressed, and said to the chancellor: "Do you see that poor, feeble and scantily clad old man? Would it not be great charity to give him a thick, warm cloak?" Thomas agreed: "It certainly would be, and you ought to see to it." Henry replied: "You shall do this great charity." He reached over and tried to pull off Thomas's elegant new scarlet and gray cape. Thomas resisted, and the two grown men struggled, shouting and laughing, several times on the point of tumbling from their horses. The knights in their train hurried up, not knowing what to think, and Thomas at last let the king win. The cloak was taken and given to the startled man, who hurried away happily, "rich beyond expectation and giving thanks to God." Laughing heartily, half a dozen of the king's attendants offered their cloaks and capes to the shivering chancellor.

The anecdote, one of the best-known stories about Thomas Becket, has traditionally been cited as an instance of the easy familiarity between Henry and Thomas. But it is more than that. If we apply to it the exegetic techniques that the Schoolmen loved, we may come up with a rather surprising conclusion. As the story is told, we hear part of an interrupted conversation. Thomas and Henry, riding together through the streets of London, were chatting as was their wont. And evidently they were talking about charity. The chancellor had not altogether put off the deacon; apparently he still considered it his duty to exhort the king on Christian virtues. In the twelfth century men fell readily into the hortatory tone, especially if they had had training in the Church. Thomas himself was the recipient of many a lecture from such intimates as John of Salisbury, as their correspondence amply testifies; and even so timeserving a "friend" as Arnulf, Bishop of Lisieux, took it upon himself to tell Thomas how to behave. As the elder of the two, and as a churchman, Thomas could sincerely feel called upon to instruct the king; their friendship and Henry's youth seemed to permit what otherwise would be impertinence in a subject. Evidently Henry usually took such impromptu sermons in good part. But in the present case he replied to a speech that may have been too pious for his taste by putting the preacher to the test in rough-and-ready fashion.

Such intimacy with a sovereign is bought at a price. The king's favor aroused the jealousy of the courtiers, the king's policies their hatred; and as the king's alter ego the chancellor became the target of endless intrigues. Henry was king, but England was not yet wholeheartedly Angevin; the House of Blois still had many adherents. In the first year of his reign, for example, Henry found it necessary to send Henry of Winchester, Stephen's brother, into temporary exile. This meant, of course, that Thomas Becket administered the vacant see, since that was one of the chancellor's duties. Bishop Henry's castles were demolished, along with nearly all those that had been built under Stephen; and the chancellor was charged with supervision of the demolition work. That, too, did not endear him to the barons. His difficulties were so many, at least in the early days of his chancellorship, that he often complained bitterly to his friends and to Archbishop Theobald. There were days when he was weary of life, he told them (*tearfully*, says John of Salisbury) and he would have resigned if he could have done so without disgrace. Theobald had repeatedly to urge him to stay on. This weariness, this sudden relaxation of the tension of the will, was to remain characteristic of Thomas in the later crises of his career. He loved the exercise of power and its accompanying glory, but he disliked the complications that were attendant upon both. More than anything, however, he feared disgrace; and this fear motivated much of his intransigence in later life.

The policies that aroused so much antagonism sprang naturally from Henry's situation and intentions on coming to power. As Duke of Normandy, engaged in a struggle with Stephen for the Crown of England, Henry had made promises which after his coronation he preferred not to keep. He had, for example, given a solemn undertaking to restore to the Bishop of Salisbury the formidable castle of Devizes, which had figured prominently in the Civil War. After he secured the throne, he refused to honor this pledge, although he offered the bishop compensation. He also, as we have seen, broke his mother's promise to grant the chancellorship to William de Vere. Likewise he disregarded his assurances to many of Stephen's former supporters that they would be left in full possession of their estates.

Such perfidies, if the strong word is justified, inhered in kingship, and Henry did not hesitate to commit them. With no more hesitation he expelled from the country the remaining Flemings who had come to serve either as Stephen's mercenaries or as his own. According to a contemporary, they vanished from one day to the next; but in fact many must have lingered or afterwards returned to England, for they later appear as prominent merchants in the wool trade.

There was much work for the new chancellor when Henry ordered reclamation of the Crown lands which had been alienated under Stephen. The records of such matters would ordinarily have been kept in the chancery or the Exchequer; but during the long Civil War many document rolls had been burned, stolen, lost, or simply not kept. The king did not know what he owned; Thomas Becket, out of his knowledge of England, his experience at Canterbury, and what written evidence he could track down, had to find out. He showed great zeal in behalf of the king, reclaiming even parts of the royal demesne that Henry or his mother had given away in order to win supporters. Some Angevin partisans of long standing were ousted from royal castles and the revenue-producing lands that went with those castles. To administer such a program of restoring the demesne was a good way to make enemies; the dispossessed barons did not thank the chancellor. But Thomas ignored their resentment. He was the king's man.

In some few cases, a military demonstration was needed before the demands upon some of the greater nobles could be enforced. During most of Henry's first year, the king traveled incessantly about his new realm, with Thomas Becket in constant attendance and Archbishop Theobald often accompanying. By the end of the year Henry had shown himself to most of his people and made it clear that England would once more be firmly ruled by a strong central government. The "Anarchy" was over. Except for the few barons who felt cheated, the whole country breathed easier as economic life revived, crops were reaped as well as sown, and the livestock of villeins and gentry alike multiplied instead of being slaughtered by marauding bands of soldiers. Rents began to be collected regularly; fees and fines filled the coffers of the Exchequer. By the end of 1155, it became possible for Henry to turn his attention to his vast overseas dominions.

It was high time, for his younger brother, Geoffrey, had raised the standard of rebellion. Geoffrey claimed that their father had intended him to receive Anjou and Maine once Henry obtained the throne of England. At present Geoffrey held only three formidable castles in Touraine: Chinon, Loudun, and Mirabeau. After fortifying these until he had reason to think them impregnable, Geoffrey invaded his brother's neighboring lands.

In January 1156 Henry crossed the Channel and raised a mercenary army. Thomas Becket stayed at his side, no doubt to oversee payment of the soldiers. Gervase of Canterbury tells us that Henry relied on the considerable assistance of his chancellor; but we do not know definitely what form that assistance took. It seems likely that Thomas also had a taste of fighting; the desultory campaigning would have provided good training; and without previous experience Thomas could hardly have commanded an army in 1159, only three years later.

Within six months Henry had forced the surrender of all three of his brother's castles. The last to fall was redoubtable Chinon, destined to be the site of Henry's death and, some centuries later, of the famous meeting between Charles VII and Joan of Arc. Henry stripped his brother of all his possessions except one small estate, just enough to provide a bare livelihood. Fortunately for Geoffrey, the citizens of Nantes chose him for their lord, presumably hoping that a landless liege would be less rapacious than the Count of Brittany.

Thomas did not stay on the Continent for the full fifteen months of Henry's absence from England. He returned to England before the leaves fell, possibly because two of the chief personages in the government were temporarily out of action. Theobald fell severely ill during the summer of 1156; and Queen Eleanor, having been delivered of a daughter, the Princess Matilda, in June, crossed to Normandy in July. In any case, the chancellor's services would be required at the Michaelmas session of the Exchequer at the end of September, when full accounts for the year were rendered. The chancellor's clerk rather than the chancellor in person carried the major burden of the work in the Exchequer. Nevertheless at important sessions, when the accounts of tenants-in-chief of the king were received, Becket himself took his seat on the left of Richard de Lucy, the justiciar, before the ten-by-five-foot board covered with striped cloth from which the institution of the Exchequer took its name. The entire system of financial administration was at this time being reformed by Bishop Nigel of Ely, for it had been "almost abolished by the continuous storm of war lasting for many years." The treasury was in process of becoming the Lower Exchequer, or Receipt, as it was also called, where the money was actually taken in. What precise part Thomas played in the reorganization our sources do not reveal; but there can be no question that many problems must have come to him for decision. For the biographers make it quite plain that Thomas swiftly became the second man in the kingdom; and when the king himself was absent from England, his chancellor was first. The Icelandic *Saga* compares Thomas with Joseph in Egypt, and adds:

Nearly all the affairs of the king and of the government have fallen under his power and will, as have also cities and townships, trade ports and castles, gold and treasures, and all royal armories. Herewith also goeth the freedom, wheresoever the king hath outstanding moneys, to give thereof to rich and poor, as if they were his own patrimony. But with wisdom and wari-

6 4

ness he dealeth therewith, and in such a heedful manner that the king is well content, and findeth things best done even as Thomas chooseth to ordain.

In addition to his fiscal and administrative duties and his work of restoring the Tower of London and the Palace of Westminster, Thomas acted upon occasion as an itinerant justice. By virtue of his membership in the Exchequer, he also functioned in the king's court. The biographers insist that he heard many cases, but the surviving records contain only scattered notices of his judicial activities. He has been credited with a major share in Henry's great reforms of the legal system of England, but not a shred of documentary proof remains. For one very prominent case, however, we do have ample evidence of the chancellor's active participation. This case throws some light on Becket's attitude toward the "freedoms" of the Church while he served as the king's chief minister, although that light is much obscured by conflicting interpretations.

The case came before King Henry's presence—*coram rege,* as the contemporary phrase had it—in May 1157, shortly after the king's return from Normandy. It concerned the right of Hilary, Bishop of Chichester, to exercise his authority over Battle Abbey, whose abbot was Walter de Lucy, the justiciar's brother. The litigation had already arisen in the reign of King Stephen, but Stephen died before he could pass judgment. Battle Abbey had been founded by William the Conqueror on or near the site of the Battle of Hastings, to commemorate the great victory. It therefore enjoyed the status of a royal chapel, and any infringement upon its privileges might be considered a diminution of the king's rights. Always, but especially at the beginning of his reign, Henry was jealous of his prerogatives and determined to restore to the royal power the ground it had lost during the Civil War.

As soon as Henry acceded to the throne, Abbot Walter applied to him for confirmation of Battle Abbey's traditional status. Bishop Hilary protested, and obtained the support of Archbishop Theobald, who regarded the abbot's exemption from episcopal jurisdiction as a poor precedent, endangering hierarchical obedience. Henry thereupon ordered his chancellor to affix the royal seal to the charter, but to hold it in his chancery until the parties could agree on revision of the objectionable clauses. If no agreement could be reached, the king would hear the case in person. Thomas, Archbishop Theobald, Bishop Hilary, and Abbot Walter then met at Lambeth to discuss the dispute.

The whole question of proprietary churches and the delicate relations between monastic foundations and the episcopate was involved in this suit. But we are concerned here with Thomas, for whom Henry's order amounted to a test of his chancellor's loyalties. Theobald had recommended Thomas to Henry in the expectation of having a faithful defender of the hierarchy at the king's side. Here was a clear-cut case of conflict between royal grant and episcopal privilege, as Theobald and Henry pointed out. The discussion at Lambeth became loud and heated; the bishops held that Battle Abbey's exemption was a violation of canon law and of the rights of the see of Canterbury itself.

Thomas made his choice—a fateful one which marked the beginning of a breach between himself and his old patron. He was the king's chancellor now, and he acted for the king and the court party, as represented by the de Lucys. Since the disputants could not agree, for the time being Thomas obeyed the king's order to the letter and held the charter in his chancery. The act was a deliberate defiance of Archbishop Theobald, who had demanded removal of the offensive clause exempting the abbey from episcopal jurisdiction. And shortly afterwards Thomas compounded his defiance: upon a renewed application from Abbot Walter, he released the charter, sealed, to the abbot. He could have given no plainer declaration of his conception of his new position: as chancellor, he represented the Crown against the Church.

Bishop Hilary did not let the matter rest. He appealed to the papal court, and obtained from Pope Adrian IV (the close friend of Theobald's secretary, John of Salisbury) a letter ordering the abbot to submit. The abbot refused, and the case then came before Henry.

The trial was a full-dress affair, for it took place at Whitsuntide, when the king wore his crown—a solemn occasion at which most of the nobles and high clergy of the realm were in attendance on the king. Justiciar Richard de Lucy presented the case for his brother. The king then asked the abbot to read out his charters. Abbot Walter had a goodly collection: successive grants by William the Conqueror, William Rufus, Henry I, and now Henry himself. If he had also obtained a charter from Stephen he wisely did not present it, for Henry made a point of ignoring Stephen's reign as his great-grandfather had ignored the reign of Harold.

There was no question about the content of William the Conqueror's original charter; it distinctly granted the abbot exemption from the bishop's jurisdiction. Whether the charter was a forgery, as has been suggested, was a question apparently not raised at the time. The king examined each of the documents carefully and found them formally correct. Thomas Becket then addressed the abbot. The bishop claimed that he had made a profession of obedience, Thomas said. Was this true? The abbot denied it. Richard de Lucy then paid tribute to the abbey as a memorial to the great days of the Norman Conquest. Norman feelings would be offended, he said, if the abbey were deprived of rights that the Conqueror had conferred upon it.

The session had been held on a Friday. At this point in the proceedings, the court adjourned for the weekend; but only after the king had declared publicly that from what he had heard so far, he was inclined to favor the abbey. At the second session both of England's archbishops, Theobald of Canterbury and Roger of York, attended. In addition, Bishop Richard de Beaumais II of London, Bishop Robert de Chesney of Lincoln, and Bishop Robert Warelwast of Exeter were present, as well as the abbots of Holme and St. Augustine's. Encouraged by the heavier ecclesiastical representation, Bishop Hilary now stated his own case. He emphasized the immunity of the Church from secular interference. The spiritual power had been confided by St. Peter to the bishops, he said. No layman, not even the king, could grant any ecclesiastical exemption without the consent of the pope.

At this point the king angrily interrupted him. "This is a strange thing I hear, that the charters of the kings my predecessors, confirmed by the full authority of the Crown of England, and by the testimony of our great men, should be pronounced arbitrary by you, my lord bishop." Chancellor Thomas added his own remonstrance: "You are disloyal to my lord the king, to whom you have taken the oath of allegiance, as all men know." Whereupon Bishop Hilary beat a hasty retreat. The other ecclesiastics had not supported him, as he had hoped. Hilary now insisted on his own loyalty, argued that the abbot had already submitted to him on various occasions, and complained of the abbot's obstinacy at the conference two years before, when the king had commanded revision of the abbey charter.

The abbot's supporters withdrew to discuss the matter. They chose Thomas Becket to deliver the speech setting forth their position. The chronicler of Battle Abbey testifies that he spoke "eloquently." His oration concluded with a charge which, a few years thereafter, would be seen as a crowning irony: he berated the bishop for having appealed to Rome against the abbot. Bishop Hilary realized that he had been thrust into the role of directly defying the king, and sought to escape by denying any such appeal. But letters from the pope were in Abbot Walter's possession, and Hilary's perjury succeeded only in alienating Archbishop Theobald as well as the king. Theobald tried to save the situation and keep the whole matter within the fold of the Church by indicating to the king that he had changed sides and would prefer to settle the issue to the abbot's satisfaction. But Henry, by now thoroughly angered, refused this offer. "No," he said bluntly, "I will not order these matters to be decided by you."

Henry's decision was a foregone conclusion, although he went through the form of withdrawing to consult the entire council. The bishop was ordered to renounce publicly all his claims upon Battle Abbey, and to exchange the kiss of peace with Abbot Walter and his brother, Justiciar Richard. To assuage the feelings of Theobald, who saw the vital principle of ecclesiastical liberty at stake, Bishop Hilary was also required to state that he was making peace voluntarily, not under coercion.

Thomas the Chancellor helped to bring about a verdict that accorded with the royal dignity, and he evidently took satisfaction in stressing a bishop's loyalty to his king. Thomas the Archbishop saw the issue in an entirely different light. In a letter to

68

Pope Alexander written many years later, he alluded to the trial. "What success did the Bishop of Chichester have against the Abbot of Battle?" he wrote. "Relying on his papal privileges, he mentioned them in court and pronounced the abbot excommunicate. Whereupon he was at once compelled to communicate with him in the presence of everybody, and to receive him in the kiss of peace, although the abbot had been given no absolution. For so the king wished, and the court, which did not dare to contradict him in any matters."

This letter has been taken as evidence that the writer of the Battle Abbey Chronicle misrepresented, perhaps unwittingly, Becket's part in the trial. It seems rather to confirm the story. In the passage cited, as in the whole letter of which it forms a part, Thomas is bent on exculpating himself. Elsewhere in the same letter he mentions other attacks upon the liberties of the Church, in Henry's time and in the times of his predecessors, and asks: "Was I archbishop then?" He charges that from the time he came to power Henry persecuted the Church "as if by hereditary right"—*quasi jure hereditario*. But all this was written after years of conflict and exile, when Thomas was prepared to interpret past acts on Henry's part as autocratic invasions of ecclesiastical privilege. And he now reinterpreted his own support of such acts during his chancellorship as crawling subservience shared with the rest of the court. Perhaps by this time he recognized that in the affair of Battle Abbey he had, as a biographer of Theobald puts it, "knocked another nail in his coffin." Certainly it can be said that Thomas involuntarily misled Henry by the position he took; the future high Gregorian was not in evidence in 1157. But in asserting that no one dared contradict the king, Thomas was being unfair to Henry as well as to himself. Actually, the Battle Abbey Chronicle reveals the freedom with which matters touching the royal "dignities" could be discussed in the king's presence. Hilary went so far as to assert that a royal charter could not, without papal assent, confer immunity upon an abbey. This angered Henry, and Hilary lost his case, but he was not otherwise punished. Although Henry insisted on his rights he was not tyrannical. There is no reason to assume that Thomas and the other members of the royal court agreed with the king's view out of fear. Rather, at the time of the Battle Abbey trial, Thomas acted in accordance with his conscience and his view of the facts. As archbishop, he repudiated this conduct. When he wrote the letter quoted above, he was succumbing to the very human inclination to revise the past in the light of the present.

No doubt Thomas regretted distressing the aged Archbishop of Canterbury to whom he owed so much. But dissension between the two men had become inevitable as soon as Thomas changed masters. Theobald's interests were necessarily restricted to the country and the Church of England at the widest, to the see of Canterbury at the narrowest. Thomas Becket was now the friend and chief adviser of a king whose possessions extended to the Pyrenees, who even while he was securing the north of England and invading Wales during the year following the Battle Abbey trial had to be thinking about his dynasty (Queen Eleanor was pregnant again; her son Richard was born on September 8, 1157), about the Vexin (the border county between Normandy and France), about the county of Nantes, which he could claim as an inheritance from his recently deceased brother Geoffrey, and about the whole complex of his relations with Louis of France, his overlord for his Continental dominions. Chancellor Thomas—perpetually busy, holding in his hand a thousand threads, receiving ambassadors, raising money, maintaining a brilliant household, virtually ruling England while keeping a watchful eye on events overseas—was often forced from sheer lack of time to ignore the requests Theobald made to him to take care of some Church affair, or the remonstrances that Theobald addressed to him as his ecclesiastical superior; for in addition to his other employments, Thomas continued to hold the archdeaconry of Canterbury. At one point in their troubled relationship Theobald asked him to renounce voluntarily some of the income which accrued to him as archdeacon. Thomas refused. He needed every silver penny he could lay hands on in order to carry out such extravagant projects as his famous embassy to Paris in 1158.

The purpose of this embassy was to arrange a marriage between young Henry, the three-year-old son of Henry and Eleanor, and Marguerite, infant daughter of Louis VII by his second wife, Constance of Castile. The project quite possibly originated with Thomas Becket. In any case it is a telling indication of the position he had won in Henry's confidence that he, rather than Richard de Lucy or Archbishop Theobald, was chosen to make the arrangements.

The thought of such an alliance was natural enough. Henry and Louis were, after all, the two most powerful monarchs in western Europe. They had long contiguous frontiers, and their two countries were linked by interlocking feudal ties, economic relations, and a common language. Moreover, if Louis failed to have male heirs—and so far he had none—young Henry Plantagenet might possibly unite the two thrones. It was worth staking a good deal on such a prospect.

Thomas resolved to spare no expense. His embassy would be such a display of the wealth and magnificence of England that the French would be prompted to say: "If this is the king's chancellor, what must the king himself be?" Possibly the idea had come to Thomas from reading the Monk of St. Gall's tale of Charlemagne's reception of envoys from the eastern emperor: the bewildered Greeks passed on from one underling to the next, each more splendid than the last, each seated on a high throne, so that they repeatedly abased themselves in the mistaken notion that they were in the presence of Charlemagne himself. When at last they were brought before the emperor, he was so decked out in gold and jewels that he glittered like the rising sun, and the overwhelmed envoys fell to the ground in a faint.

William FitzStephen dwells with fond delight on the splendors of Thomas's person and train. He had with him twenty-four changes of clothing, much of it pure silk, as well as rare furs, tapestries, and carpets "such as adorn the bedchamber of a bishop." In his train were some two hundred members of his household: knights, clerks, stewards, servants, squires, and pages. (Since he undoubtedly left many of his men behind, the figure suggests the vast size of his *mesnie*.) Hounds and hawks accompanied him, that the pleasures of the chase might not be neglected during the journey. Eight baggage wagons, so huge that five horses were required to draw them, carried supplies and appurtenances: the furnishings for the chancellor's chapel, for his

7 1

chamber, his wardrobe, his kitchen, and so on. Two of the wagons were laden with iron-hooped casks containing "a clear, wholesome beverage, the color of wine but superior in taste" to be given to the marveling Franks. Gilbert Becket's son was not without commercial instincts; he evidently hoped to foster a taste for beer among the French.

The wagons did not nearly suffice. A dozen packhorses were also required, to carry the chancellor's gold and silver plate, his money, clothes, and even books. One horse, leading all the rest, bore the sacred vessels for the chapel, and the altar ornaments and books. A huge mastiff was chained to each wagon to protect all these valuables; and since the intent of the display was to amuse as well as to impress the French populace, a monkey rode on each of the packhorses. The procession kept to a strict order as it passed through the French villages. First came footmen walking in groups of six and ten and singing songs in English. They were followed at an interval by leashed hounds and their keepers. Then came the wagons, with contents covered with hides. These were followed by the packhorses with their grooms and monkeys; then the squires bearing the knights' shields and leading their chargers; after these the servants; then the knights and clerks. Last of all came the chancellor, riding with a few of his close friends.

A game of mutual courtesies was played out when Thomas arrived in Paris with this enormous following. It was customary, so FitzStephen tells us, for the French king to provide for all the needs of the foreigners who came to his court. Louis therefore issued a proclamation ordering his subjects not to sell anything to the chancellor or his agents. Thomas circumvented this generous precaution by sending his men in disguise to the suburban markets and fairs around Paris. They bought lavishly enough to feed a thousand men for three days; and the story went—magnified in the telling, no doubt—that they paid a hundred shillings for a single dish of eels. Incidentally, the fact that some of the purchasing was done at St. Denis may establish the month of the visit, for the fair of St. Denis was held in June. This would agree well with the dates of subsequent events.

Thomas lodged at the Temple, a large group of sturdy

houses built by the Knights Templar just outside the stockade which enclosed the right-bank suburb of Paris. Probably a large part of his retinue camped in the nearby open space known as the Grève, on which the houses of the wealthy fronted. For even the huge Temple would not hold them all.

Reasons other than mere comfort had dictated the chancellor's choice of lodgings. The Temple was the European headquarters of the "Poor Knights of Christ and of the Temple of Solomon." Founded the year after Thomas Becket's birth, the order had long since ceased to be poor. It had been particularly favored and well endowed by the kings of England, and was by now one of the wealthiest monastic orders in Europe. Independent of episcopal jurisdiction, acknowledging the commands of the papacy alone, it had devised ways to evade the general prohibition against the taking of interest. As a result, the Templars were the nearest thing Europe possessed to international bankers, and the Paris Temple was the center of the world's money market. This was particularly convenient to Thomas, since he could not possibly have carried with him all the money he intended to spend in Paris. In addition, while staying at the Temple he had an opportunity to discuss the diplomatic role he expected the Templars to play in the forthcoming negotiations.

A banker was certainly needed, for the chancellor's visit to Paris was conducted in the atmosphere of what a modern anthropologist would call a potlatch. Thomas gave away everything he had brought with him: his gold and silver plate, his precious robes and cloaks, the furs and even the destriers. Everyone high and low at the French king's court received a gift. And like any old grad returning to the city of his student years, Thomas did not forget his alma mater. The masters and students of the English Nation at the university came to see and cheer their king's chancellor, and were richly rewarded for their courtesy. Not content with gifts alone, Thomas even paid off the students' debts.

Louis VII of France, who had lost his wife and the duchy of Aquitaine to Henry II, and was now about to lose his six-month-old daughter, took the display of wealth in a philosophical spirit if we may judge by a conversation Walter Map reports:

It was my good fortune to spend some time in Paris with Louis, and he discussed with me among other matters the riches of kings. He said: "Just as the resources of kings are diverse, so they differ distinctly in kind. Precious stones, lions, leopards and elephants constitute the riches of the King of the Indies; gold and silken garments do the Emperor at Byzantium and the King of Sicily boast; but men they have not who know anything else than talk, for in things pertaining to war they are fools. The Roman emperor, who is called emperor of the Germans, has men fit for arms and war horses, not gold, not silk, nor any other luxury. . . . Your master, however, the King of England, lacks nothing; he possesses men, horses, gold and silk, gems, fruits, wild beasts, and all things else. We in France have nothing except bread and wine and joy."

Medieval chroniclers often, as in this case, tell us more about the outward show of a political event than the substance. We have no idea how the negotiations between Thomas Becket and Louis VII went, aside from the brief statement that Thomas obtained all he asked. This is a gross exaggeration. In fact, he made a great concession, or so it must have seemed to the French; whatever mental reservations the king and his chancellor had were not apparent at the time the treaty was signed. For it was settled that Princess Margaret's dowry would be five castles in the Vexin (formerly ceded by Henry's father Geoffrey to Louis) and the lands they controlled. Possession of these castles would extend the boundary of Normandy to the river Epte, dangerously close to Paris. But the agreement as it stood appeared highly favorable to Louis, since surrender of the castles would be postponed until the children were of an age to marry. Meanwhile neutrality of the disputed territory was guaranteed by a clause placing possession of the castles in the hands of the Knights Templar. That Thomas came to a private arrangement with the Templars during his stay in Paris cannot be proved; but the possibility is strongly suggested by the sequel.

Terms of the treaty settled, Thomas turned homeward. If our ordering of events is correct—some guesswork is involved— Henry then crossed to Normandy in order to confirm at a "summit conference" the agreement that his chancellor had nego-

74

tiated. The two kings met at the Epte River in August. Queen Eleanor remained at Westminster where in September she, who had borne only girl-children to Louis, gave birth to yet another son, Geoffrey. That the event stirred the jealousy of Louis, a monarch oversupplied with daughters, can scarcely be doubted. But for the present, relations between the two kings could not have been more amicable. The agreement on the marriage of the two children was ratified. Louis granted Henry a free hand in Brittany. Henry accepted an invitation to Paris, where he was royally entertained. Princess Margaret was given into his custody, and Henry turned her over to a Norman baron to be "fostered."

After suppressing a minor rebellion in Brittany, Henry met Louis once more. Together the two kings visited the Abbey of Mont-St.-Michel on its rocky islet above the sea, heard Mass, and dined in the hall now called the Promenoir. Then Henry conducted the king on a progress through Normandy. The year ended with Louis VII and his excessively powerful vassal in the best of harmony, thanks largely to the skillful diplomacy of Chancellor Thomas Becket. The two kings even discussed joining forces for a crusade against the Spanish Moors, and wrote a letter to Pope Adrian to ask his blessing.

V

Thomas the Soldier

THE GOOD FEELING between the two great Continental powers did not last long. Within three months, the two kings were at odds over lands which neither owned. The county of Toulouse, now ruled by Raymond V, had anciently formed part of Aquitaine. In 1141 Louis VII unsuccessfully claimed overlordship of Toulouse by virtue of his marriage to Eleanor. After their divorce, Aquitaine and the claim to Toulouse passed, with Eleanor, to Henry II. In these circumstances, an alliance between Toulouse and France was only natural, and in 1154—the year that Henry succeeded to the throne of England—it was strengthened by marriage: Louis VII gave his widowed sister, Constance, to Raymond.

Henry's decision to enforce his claim upon Toulouse seems to have come as a direct result of his recent agreement with Louis and the neutralization of the Vexin. Thomas Becket had had the opportunity, during his recent negotiations in Paris, to form a close and surely contemptuous judgment of French power and the personality of Louis. There is no doubt that Becket advised the expedition against Toulouse—John of Salisbury calls him the "author and leader" of it—and that he, among all of Henry's counselors, pursued the undertaking with the greatest ardor. He devised the means for financing it, and he himself led an army into the field.

Henry and Louis met at Tours to confer on the question of Toulouse. Louis temporized, and Henry seems to have come away with the impression that he would not or could not offer serious opposition to a conquest of Toulouse. In the spring of 1159, therefore, Henry issued the formal summons to his host to assemble at Poitiers on Midsummer Day.

The great barons of the south, Raymond Trencavel, Viscount of Béziers and Carcassonne, and Raymond-Berengar, Count of Barcelona and husband of the Queen of Aragon, welcomed the opportunity to discomfort a neighbor with whom they were perpetually skirmishing. As their sons and grandsons of the same names would be fifty years later, during the Albigensian Crusade, they were woefully disunited against the threat of invasion from the north. They agreed to an alliance with Henry. And Henry, with that faculty for conjoining military, diplomatic, and dynastic advantages which was certainly due in part to his chancellor's foresight, purchased the cooperation of Raymond-Berengar at a mutually advantageous price. He arranged another infant betrothal, this time of his son Richard with the daughter of Raymond-Berengar and Queen Petronilla of Aragon. It was stipulated that at the time of the marriage Richard would be given the duchy of Aquitaine and could hope, of course, that if there were no male heirs to Barcelona and Aragon he would inherit those lands also *jure uxoris*.

It was a vast and brilliant host that assembled in Poitiers for the first major war of Henry's reign. Thomas Becket arrived at the head of no less than seven hundred knights of his own household—a stupendous force for the times, and an indication of the wealth that Henry had heaped upon him during the four years of his chancellorship. Malcolm, King of Scots, also answered his overlord's summons, hoping to win the belt of knighthood which Henry had refused to grant him the previous year. The barons of Aquitaine, Anjou, and Maine contributed their quota of men. Many of the greater nobles of Normandy and England were likewise present in the host, for fighting was the major entertainment of the medieval knight. Moreover, Languedoc was a wealthy land, as the Crusaders were to discover fifty years later, and any war offered the promise of spoils.

The Norman and English barons, however, came without the fighting men who owed them service. Given the state of the king's navy, it would have been a logistical impossibility to transport the bulk of the English knights and their attendants across the Channel. Thomas Becket had been striving, among his multitudinous other activities, to build up England's sea power. Henry had had only one ship at his disposal until his chancellor presented him with three more. Thomas himself had the use of six and even more vessels when he wished to cross the Channel, and was in the habit of giving free passage to all who needed it. But his seven hundred knights, with the numerous footmen, squires, and pages who attended them, must have strained the shipping resources of England. If all the men of England who owed knight's service had swarmed to the ports, they would have waited months for transportation to Normandy. Once there, moreover, the long march to the south of France would still remain.

Henry had confronted this problem three years earlier, on a smaller scale, when he crossed from England to fight his rebellious brother. At that time he had spared his English tenants the necessity of fighting on alien ground, and himself the difficulty of finding shipping for them, by hiring mercenaries with money paid in lieu of personal service. The scheme had worked well, and either Henry or Thomas Becket decided to apply it once more, but more comprehensively. Accordingly, a proclamation was issued stating that "King Henry, considering the length and difficulty of the way and not wishing to trouble the country knights, the burghers and the multitude of yeomen" had decided to levy the sum of sixty Angevin shillings on his Norman *feuda loricae*, "fiefs of the hauberk" or knights' fees, and similar sums on his other lands. In England the amount seems to have been two marks per knight's fee. A rough idea of the value of this can be gathered when we learn that five or six marks were sufficient to pay a student's expenses in Paris for a year. The mark was not a coin but a unit of account equivalent to eight ounces of silver or 120 silver pennies.

The Great Scutage, as this impost came to be called, aroused considerable bitterness among churchmen. Years later Gilbert Foliot, Bishop of London, charged that Thomas had plunged the sword of state "into the vitals of Holy Mother

78

Church with your own hand when you despoiled her of so many thousand marks for the expedition against Toulouse." The burden apparently fell more heavily upon the Church than upon the lay barons. And the Church, which had looked to the chancellor to champion its causes, felt betrayed. It was generally held that Thomas Becket himself had conceived the plan; and certainly he was responsible for its execution, as we learn from John of Salisbury's attempt to defend him. "Some will say," John wrote to Bartholomew, Bishop of Exeter, "that this taxation and vexation of the churches ought to be charged against his chancellor, who now either is the archbishop, as I believe, or is seeking to be the archbishop, as his rivals mendaciously assert. They say that he urged this and many other evils upon the king. That is false, and I know it. I know that he did not lend his authority to license, but his consent to necessity. Still, I do not doubt that he was indeed the agent of wickedness."

This letter was written at the height of Becket's struggle with the king, and is surely colored somewhat by John's partisanship even though John of Salisbury had a gift for remaining remarkably free from prejudice under the most trying circumstances. Given Becket's enthusiasm for the Toulouse campaign, his conviction that if a thing was done at all it should be done wholeheartedly, and the obvious need for additional sources of revenue, it is probable that he did not dissemble assent to a measure that was repugnant to him, but on the contrary either recommended taxation of the churches or willingly agreed, if the suggestion came from other quarters. John actually suggests this possibility when he adds, a few lines later: "If, with Saul, he once assailed the Church, with Paul he is now ready to give up his life for it."

It was formerly thought that the scutage of 1159 was "as regards England, the most important matter connected with the war of Toulouse" and that it marked "a turning-point in the history of military tenure." Bishop Stubbs in his famous *Constitutional History* asserted that the war of Toulouse was the time "at which the institution of scutage, as a pecuniary commutation for personal service in the host, is fixed by the common consent of lawyers and historians." Recent research has diminished the importance of this scutage as an innovation; the "feudal army" was not so definite a concept as nineteenth-century historians imagined, and knight's service was as much a method of accounting as an actual obligation to military service. Nevertheless, the use of scutage to raise money, and the actual revenue it afforded, did essentially stamp the character of Henry's reign as a long period of peace for England in spite of his many wars. Englishmen stayed at home, tended their fields and flocks, engaged in trade, built fulling mills where water power was available, and laid the foundations for a great commercial prosperity. Mercenaries did the fighting for the king, while at home arms rusted and men grew pacific to such an extent that in the latter part of his reign Henry became alarmed. (The Assize of Arms of 1181 attempted vainly to reverse the trend by decreeing the equipment each man was required to maintain according to his wealth.)

Some portion of the scutage must have been used to defray Thomas Becket's own enormous expenses for the Toulouse campaign. We do not have his accounts; but we know that he asked the king for five hundred marks and borrowed another five hundred from a Jew, with Henry guaranteeing the loan. Although these sums were obviously expended in the king's interest, Henry five years later demanded repayment.

Considering Thomas's services to him in the county of Toulouse, the demand was more than unfair; it was an act of churlish ingratitude. For by general agreement, Thomas commanded the flower of the king's army; and if the campaign was ultimately a failure, that was certainly not his fault.

The war began auspiciously enough. Two conferences between Louis and Henry had failed to dissuade Henry from his purpose. Immediately after Midsummer's Day, the host marched south from Poitiers. The Toulousain countryside was rapidly overrun, the fortress of Cahors taken, and the army advanced on Toulouse. At this point a hesitant Louis at last responded to the appeals of his brother-in-law and the anguished citizenry. Louis had only a few troops with him in the south; he sent for reinforcements and meanwhile entered Toulouse, hoping evidently that his presence alone would encourage the defenders. His act was a gamble based on his estimate of Henry's character.

8o

At this point, Thomas Becket and Henry Plantagenet had their first recorded disagreement. Thomas, ever ready to play for high stakes, saw a golden opportunity. If the city were assaulted before the reinforcements arrived, it could probably be taken and Louis himself made prisoner. Thomas's military judgment was good; that was demonstrated later in the campaign by his success in storming three strongholds. And if the swift, bold stroke succeeded, the capture of Louis could undoubtedly be turned to profit.

But Thomas was after all a commoner. He did not understand the noble's mentality. Henry had done homage to Louis as his feudal lord; to attack him personally would set a bad example to his own vassals. Moreover, he had only recently signed a peace treaty. In vain Thomas argued that Louis himself had violated the treaty by siding with Henry's enemies. Henry's other barons supported the king's decision; and the army withdrew without having accomplished its purpose. The sources hint, without stating so explicitly, that the disagreement between Thomas on the one side and the king on the other grew heated and left a heritage of ill will. If FitzStephen's words are an echo of Thomas's opinion, the chancellor accused the king of giving way to "foolish superstition." In any case, when the king retreated, the other barons insisted on accompanying him. They refused to garrison the town of Cahors and a number of other castles in the vicinity of Toulouse. Thomas was left behind to hold these, and for a while he continued the war on his own. It was at this time that he personally donned helmet and cuirass and led his men in successful assault upon three reputedly impregnable castles. He then pursued the enemy across the Garonne and forced "the whole province" to swear allegiance to Henry. The king, by the time Thomas rejoined him in Normandy, had forgotten his pique; he welcomed the chancellor warmly and praised him for his redoubtable performance as a warrior.

The taste of military victories was sweet to Thomas. War suited his temperament; throughout his career he was a warrior, whether for the king or for the Church. And as a soldier he fought *à l'outrance,* just as he was later to do as archbishop. There is a reminder, in the words of the devoted biographer

Edward Grim—who nearly lost his arm defending the archbishop against the murderous knights— that the future saint had
scarcely been a man of mildness and compassion in his secular
career. "Who can enumerate the number of persons he did to
death, the number whom he deprived of all their possessions?
Surrounded by a strong force of knights, he attacked whole
regions. He destroyed cities and towns, put manors and farms
to the torch without a thought of pity, and showed no mercy to
any of the king's enemies."

Grim's tone is scarcely regretful; that sturdy Englishman
saw nothing odd in the fact that a man in deacon's orders should
wage war. Ecclesiastics far higher in rank did not hesitate to
fight, as was shown in the immediate sequel to the Toulouse
campaign. For Henry's scruples against attacking his overlord
did not extend to the overlord's vassals. The war, which had
subsided in the south, broke out anew on the borders of Normandy where Henry's ally, Theobald of Blois, harried French
territory to create a diversion. Henry, Bishop of Beauvais, who
was the brother of Louis VII, then raided the Norman marches in
retaliation.

Thomas Becket hastened to the scene of the new fighting. In
addition to his seven hundred household knights, he now provided at his own expense twelve hundred mercenary knights, as
well as four thousand foot soldiers. At three shillings a day per
knight for forty days, the cost was enormous. In addition, Thomas
had all his knights dine at his table. No wonder that he was
forced to borrow and that he was unwilling to give up any of his
sources of revenue.

On the frontier between Gisors, Trie, and Courcelles, the
chancellor led his troops in person, marshaling them with a
long, thin bugle that was peculiar to his personal following.
"Clerk though he was," as FitzStephen says—and the remark is
intended to stress his lack of practice in jousting rather than any
impropriety—he even met a valiant French knight, Engelram de
Trie, in single combat. Lance at rest, he charged in the approved
fashion and succeeded in unhorsing his opponent. That sufficed
for honor; a cleric was forbidden to shed blood, and in any case
knights did not like to kill each other. For them, "death was an

accident of battle." Thomas rode back to his own lines with Engelram's destrier as his prize. "And in the whole of the English king's army, the chancellor's knights were always in the van, always risking more than others, always performing gloriously. He himself taught them, led them, exhorted them." Although the combat with Engelram is the single specified instance of his personal military conduct, we have the testimony of the French poet Guernes that he was in the forefront of his troops more than once. "I myself saw him riding against the French several times," says Guernes (*E jeol vi sur Franceis plusurs feiz chevalchier*).

But diplomacy rather than fighting settled the issue, at least temporarily. Simon, Count of Evreux, was persuaded to do homage to Henry for the lands he held of the King of France, and to surrender to him the castles of Montfort, Rochefort, and Epernon. This was a severe blow to Louis, for Henry thus obtained command of the lines of communication between Paris, Orleans, and Etampes. Paris itself seemed threatened, and although Henry probably would not have attacked his overlord's capital, an anxious Louis resolved to ask for a truce. Once again the negotiations were entrusted to Thomas Becket. In keeping with the spirit of the age, Louis bore Thomas no grudge for his military exploits against the French. The discussions proceeded in an atmosphere of good will, and in December a truce was arranged, to last until the Octave of Pentecost, that is, May 22, 1160. Neither side could have fought in any case, for the winter proved to be unusually severe. Despite the weather, Queen Eleanor sailed for England after Christmas. For the next nine months she acted as regent of England; the Pipe Rolls contain many references to her writs during this period. The great lady of the century was coming into her own as Queen of England. She knew how to rule as well as any man, and at present her relations with Henry were good—how could they not be, when she was so successful at presenting him with male heirs! The explanation for her independent activity is, of course, that Thomas Becket had remained on the Continent with Henry. Once more negotiations with Louis were placed in the hands of Thomas, who carried them through to a successful conclusion. Before the truce ran out, a treaty of peace was signed. Its terms amounted to a restoration of the *status quo ante bellum,* except that Henry kept his conquests in the county of Toulouse.

The harmony that had hitherto prevailed between Henry and his chancellor had been disturbed, for the first time so far as we know, by the disagreement over policy at Toulouse. Henry had been reigning for five years; his position was secure, his knowledge of public affairs enriched by experience, and it is possible that he was beginning to chafe somewhat under the tutelage of his older friend. Now a further disagreement troubled their relations.

William of Warenne, Count of Boulogne and the last surviving son of King Stephen, had died in October 1159, during the withdrawal from Toulouse. His sister Mary, Abbess of Romsey, thus became sole heiress to the county of Boulogne, and Henry, exercising his feudal right as overlord, resolved to marry her to his cousin Matthew, brother of Philip, Count of Flanders. As he conceived it, the alliance would attach Flanders more closely to England and weaken the influence of Louis VII in that strategic area.

Thomas Becket protested vigorously against this project. But after his recent experience at Toulouse he knew better than to oppose Henry on political grounds. The royal court had been in existence long enough to engender that typical byproduct of court life, sycophancy. The king, his self-confidence nourished by flatterers, would no longer brook an outright challenge to his political acumen. Thomas therefore raised religious objections. As the king's chaplain, such questions of conscience fell within his province. He spoke of the "enormity" of causing a nun to break her vows, and used his influence in Rome to prevent the granting of a dispensation. It is likely that his religious concern was a genuine one. But his insight into the personal character of Matthew and his awareness of the strategic potentialities of a Flanders allied to the county of Boulogne were likewise factors in his opposition. The event was to prove his judgment superior to Henry's; for Matthew, after he had become Count of Boulogne, acquired along with his wife some of the traditional hostility of the House of Blois to the House of Anjou. In the course of the tensions that repeatedly flared between Louis VII and Henry II,

Matthew was to change sides several times; and in 1167 he would actually contemplate an invasion of England from Boulogne.

✠   ✠   ✠

Possibly Becket's intervention at the Curia would have been more successful if Pope Adrian IV had still been living. The only pope of English birth, Nicholas Breakspear, had died on September 1, 1159. In the five years of his reign as Adrian IV he had proved to be an active and courageous leader of the Church. Despite his lowly birth—William of Newburgh tells us that he was "raised from the dust to sit in the midst of princes and to occupy the throne of apostolic glory"—he had not hesitated to challenge the emperor himself. Many high churchmen of the age were men of the best families (Henry, Bishop of Winchester, is an example) who made much of their ancestry. But the Church was also an avenue of social mobility: Thomas Becket and Nicholas Breakspear may serve as types of the commoner who proved that a good measure of equal opportunity existed in the twelfth century. Adrian, indeed, began life under greater disadvantages than Becket. The son of a minor English cleric, he had started life in direst poverty and risen through the ranks of the ecclesiastical hierarchy, becoming first abbot, then bishop, then a missionary legate among the "wild and savage peoples of Denmark and Norway." Upon his return to Rome from his sojourn among "these barbarians," he was received with honor and in triumph by the pope and the cardinals. After the death of Anastasius IV, Adrian was elected to the Chair of St. Peter by unanimous vote.

His elevation naturally increased the influence of the English clergy upon the affairs of the Church. The coterie of English intellectuals whom Archbishop Theobald had gathered around himself at Canterbury suddenly found one whom they could regard as their own representative at the highest seat of ecclesiastical power. Among those intellectuals, John of Salisbury takes first place. And he could speak without boasting of his intimate friendship with the pope. In his *Policraticus,* John relates that he spent three months with Adrian in Benevento (this must have been between November 1155 and July 1156).

They conversed with the utmost frankness, John relates. At one time Adrian asked John to tell him in confidence what men were saying about him and the Roman Church. John replied with a long list of shocking charges against Rome. The Roman prelates lorded it over the clergy instead of serving "as a pattern to a flock treading the straight and narrow path which leads to eternal life." The princes of the Church loaded their tables with gold and silver, but seldom invited a poor man to feast with them. They dispensed justice for money rather than in accordance with truth. "The palaces of the priests shine in splendor, while the Church of Christ is defiled at their hands. They pillage and despoil the provinces as if they were intent on restoring the treasury of Croesus."

After hearing a recital of the people's grievances against the Church, the pope placed John in the uncomfortable position of having to give his own opinion. "And what do you yourself think?" Adrian asked. John rose to the occasion. "Troubles beset me on every side," he replied. "I fear to incur the charges of falsehood and flattery if I were the only one to contradict the people. On the other hand, if I do not do so, I dread being found guilty of treason." He went on to say that the sins of a few popes had disgraced the universal Church, and that in his opinion popes died so often lest they should corrupt the whole Church. But, he added, "the good popes are sometimes also carried off, lest they be turned to evil, and because corrupt Rome is found unworthy of them in God's sight. Do you, therefore"—and here John of Salisbury began to lecture the pope as he was wont to do to his good friend Thomas Becket—"who now occupy the papal chair, speak out and cultivate the meek and them that despise vainglory and wealth. But I fear that so long as you persist in following your own will, you will continue to hear unpalatable truths from your indiscreet friend."

John's candor appears in no way to have affected their friendship. In his *Metalogicon,* John has recorded: "Alike in public and in private he made no secret of the fact that no one was so dear to him as I. . . . While he was pope, he took pleasure in inviting me to his table and in making me, against my will, eat from his plate and drink from his cup." It was John who obtained from Pope Adrian the hereditary possession of Ireland for Henry II. John records that Adrian sent Henry a gold ring set with a handsome emerald in token of his investiture with the government of the Emerald Isle.[1]

Adrian had scarcely enjoyed a peaceful pontificate. At the time of his election, the city of Rome was controlled by that tragic, idealistic revolutionary, Arnold of Brescia, the one-time pupil of Abelard. Unfrocked monk and charismatic leader, Arnold had initiated a ghostly restoration of the institutions of republican Rome. A powerful orator, he denounced the corruption of the priests and preached return to the supposed purity and austerity of ancient Rome. His strictures against the Church differed little from those that John reported to Pope Adrian. But John had the good sense to utter them in private. Arnold inflamed the populace by attacking the cardinals and other high clergy for their pride, avarice, and hypocrisy. Was not the Church of God a house of business and a den of thieves? The volatile Roman populace responded warmly to these denunciations, which were on the whole justified; and Adrian was able to procure Arnold's banishment only by laying an interdict upon the whole city. For the first time since the triumph of Christianity, the confessionals were closed and the bells ceased to ring in the churches of Rome. The people were quite capable of attacking a cardinal and fatally wounding him, but they could not long bear to be deprived of their religious rites. Interdict, not yet

---

[1] The papal claim to dominion over Ireland rested, of course, upon the spurious Donation of Constantine, which purported to grant to the papacy sovereignty over all islands "which have received the doctrines of the Christian faith." The terms of the grant of Ireland are set forth in the bull *Laudabiliter*. The authenticity of this bull is still a matter of controversy, but whether or not it is genuine, there can be no question that Adrian did sanction Henry's conquest of Ireland. John's account is confirmation of Robert de Monte's statement (Stevenson, Vol. IV, Pt. 2, p. 739) that Henry planned this conquest in the early days of his reign, very likely with the enthusiastic cooperation of Thomas Becket, although he was not able to launch his project until after Thomas's death.

weakened by overuse or by defiance of the lower clergy, was still a strong weapon. Arnold was driven from the city. The short-lived new Roman republic came to an end, and Adrian was once again ruler of Rome. He enlisted the aid of Emperor Frederick Barbarossa, soon to be his bitter enemy, to free himself of the menace that Arnold still represented. Barbarossa's men captured Arnold and handed him over to the Prefect of Rome, who held the castle of St. Angelo for the pope. Adrian ordered Arnold's execution. The revolutionary's body was burned and the ashes scattered in the Tiber "lest perchance something might be left to be honored."

In his dealing with Arnold of Brescia, whom even the executioners pitied, Pope Adrian acted with the harshness of a secular ruler. In his dealings with Barbarossa, he displayed all the imperiousness of a high-Gregorian ecclesiastic. He refused to crown Frederick until the emperor had held his stirrup, as Charlemagne had done for the first Pope Adrian. But Frederick had the temper of a Charlemagne. Like his great predecessor, he regarded himself as *rector* as well as *defensor* of the Church. Papal interference with his control of Italy did not fit into his conception of imperial grandeur. He insisted upon extending his authority to the city of Rome itself, and haughtily rebuked the claims of the Roman republicans, in whose minds the spirit of Arnold still lingered. Adrian, for his part, encouraged the cities of Lombardy in their opposition to the emperor, and summoned the prelates of Germany to treason. At the time of his death he was preparing for a virtual declaration of war: excommunication of the emperor. The struggle against the imperial claims, which he had waged to his dying hour, led directly to the schism that was to have so momentous an influence upon the history of Europe and the affairs of Thomas Becket.

VI

Schism

WITH THE DEATH of Adrian, the papacy became the prize for three contending parties: the Roman republicans, still clinging to the ideals of Arnold of Brescia; the papal supremacists, the heirs of Adrian's policies; and the emperor's adherents, who were prepared to place their man on the papal throne by armed force. The papal supremacists were naturally in the majority at the conclave, and they elected Cardinal Roland of St. Mark, chancellor of the Roman Church and a former professor of canon law at Bologna, where Thomas Becket may have heard him lecture. Their choice was a direct affront to Emperor Frederick Barbarossa, for Cardinal Roland had been involved in one of the most dramatic confrontations between Church and State since the days of Henry IV and Gregory VII. At the Diet of Besançon a letter of greeting from Adrian to Frederick had been read aloud before a glittering assemblage of nobles and ecclesiastics from all parts of the Empire and the world. The reproving tone of the letter aroused indignation among the German nobles; one of its phrases stirred them to fury. The pope spoke of the *beneficia* he had conferred upon the emperor. The word could, by a stretch of the imagination, be interpreted in the ordinary sense as favors, "benefits"; but everyone present took it in the technical sense of the age, to mean fiefs or "benefices." Although the pope himself later alleged that he had meant the word in the first sense, Cardinal Roland himself, who was present at the Diet, initially accepted the technical use of *beneficia.* In answer to the outraged cries of the German nobles, he intrepidly called out: "From whom does he hold the Empire, if not from the pope?" His daring nearly cost him his life; Frederick had to intervene personally to save him from Otto von Wittelsbach, the Count Palatine, who drew his sword threateningly.

Now this same Count Otto was in Rome during the conclave of cardinals, and had already laid his plans. As the great white semicircle of silk called the cope was being placed on Roland's shoulders, the cardinal struggled and protested in keeping with the time-honored tradition of *nolo episcopari*. Whereupon Cardinal Octavian, one of the minority who had voted against Roland, cried out that he must not be compelled, and snatched the cope. The partisans of Roland refused to let go of it. A hand-to-hand brawl ensued among these highest dignitaries of the Church of the Prince of Peace. Octavian lost his hold on the cope; but another was being held ready by his chaplain, and was placed on him. In the confusion, it was put on backwards—"by divine judgment," the contemporary chronicler adds.

The Church was divided once more, after a twenty-year interval of unity. Roland assumed the name of Alexander III, Octavian that of Victor IV. Which was to be called pope and which antipope became the central question for an anguished Christian world.

The scandalous scene at the conclave, and the ensuing schism, deeply affected the contemporaries of Thomas Becket. John of Salisbury could be certain that his friend shared his feelings when he wrote (in the last chapter of the *Metalogicon*, which he sent to Becket at this time):

> Yet Adrian's death is not all. The worst catastrophe which perturbs all our minds is the schism in the Church, which broke out, in punishment for our sins, as soon as our great father was withdrawn. Satan, who has lusted to lay hold of the Church that he might sift her like grain, is now sowing bitterness and scandal on every side, by means of his tool, that perfidious second Judas [Octavian]. Wars have broken out that are worse than civil, for they are wars between brother priests.

Becket shared John's anxiety and, after a while, his commitment to Alexander III. But not everyone could be so certain at

the outset which pope should be recognized as legitimate. Each
pontiff sought by reciprocal excommunications and incessant
attempts at persuasion to win the allegiance of Christendom. (On
the whole, northern and eastern Europe followed Victor, western
Europe Alexander. But everywhere there were individual prelates who adhered to the minority party in their country.) Among
the most effective of the apocryphal tales spread by the advocates
of Alexander III was the allegation that Victor IV had surrendered his Fisherman's Ring to the emperor, receiving it back
from Frederick as a sign of his investiture with the Holy See.

The story was repeated by Bishop Arnulf of Lisieux, the
ambitious, ambiguous, and agile prelate who before the advent of
Thomas Becket had been a principal adviser to Henry of Anjou.
Immediately after the disputed election, Arnulf took it upon
himself to urge Alexander's cause on Henry II. Archbishop
Theobald, through the pen of John of Salisbury, did likewise. He
wrote to Henry:

> I know that if you gave your consent, we would all favor
> Alexander. I have heard that the emperor is trying to bring you
> over to the faction of Octavian, but may it never be that you
> would do anything for the love or honor of man, when the
> Church is in such great peril, unless you thought it would be
> pleasing to God. Nor does it befit your majesty to place at the
> head of the Church of your kingdom, without consulting it, a
> man who was not elected and is commonly said not to have the
> grace of God. He dared to seize this position only because of the
> favor and decrees of the emperor, for the Roman Church is
> almost entirely in favor of Alexander.

Becket, although he leaned toward Alexander, evidently
urged Henry to temporize, partly to preserve his good relations
with Frederick Barbarossa, partly in order to reap political advantages from the schism. Henry readily assented to delay, for he
wished his ecclesiastics to understand that the decision on so
important a question rested with him alone, although he would
take counsel with his clergy. He pointedly made this claim in a
letter to Archbishop Theobald and the rest of the English Church
forbidding recognition of either faction until he had made his
choice, as his grandfather Henry I had done thirty years before.

Since at this time Theobald was gravely ill, suffering from a stomach ulcer, the letter was received by John of Salisbury, then virtually in charge of the diocese as he had been for the past several years. King Henry had long directed toward John the hostility he did not quite dare display toward the venerable Archbishop of Canterbury who had helped him to ascend the throne. Three years before, Henry had been so angry with John, for reasons unspecified, that John had considered going into exile. It had required the intervention of the pope, the archbishop himself, and his friend Thomas Becket to placate the king.[1] The incident is a significant suggestion of the normally tense relationship between an English king and his Archbishop of Canterbury, and as such throws light upon the subsequent conflict between Becket and Henry. John was as sweet-tempered and mild as Becket was belligerent; yet both incurred the king's wrath. Although Henry's anger cooled at the time, he remained suspicious of John—in 1160 John could still write that he lived "in fear of banishment," and he composed or extracted another testimonial from Theobald commending himself to the king. For John's premature adherence to Alexander had again incensed Henry. Ever jealous of the royal prerogatives, Henry felt that John, using the powers of Theobald's office, was attempting to usurp the royal privilege of deciding the issue.

Powerful English ecclesiastics sympathized with the antipope. Among these were said to be Henry of Blois, the Bishop of Winchester, and his nephew Hugh of Durham, who were distantly related to Octavian—or at least so the antipope claimed (relationship to the House of Blois would not endear Octavian to

---

[1] John had complained at the time that the king held him responsible for everything that happened at Canterbury. In a letter to his friend Peter, Abbot of Celle, he wrote: "I alone in the kingdom am said to belittle the royal majesty. . . . If any one among us invokes the name of Rome, they blame me. *If the English Church dares to claim even the shadow of liberty in holding elections or in trying ecclesiastical cases*, it is imputed to me, as if I alone teach my lord of Canterbury and the other bishops what they ought to do." To Thomas, in a letter pleading that the chancellor "assuage the indignation which our most serene lord the king has conceived against me without cause," he said: "If anything is done rightly, others get the credit; if anything is done badly, it is ascribed to me."

92

King Henry). They had rallied around them a considerable party
by the time the English clergy met in council at London, probably in June 1160. However, the eloquent arguments of Arnulf
of Lisieux, whose letters were read out to the council, and the
intimation that Henry favored Alexander, swayed the decision.
Some uncertainty remained, for Theobald sent a number of urgent and anxious letters to the king, and his report on the council's decision was couched in extremely circumspect language:

> On the issue before us, we gave no definite judgment, since
> that was not permitted. We decided nothing to the prejudice of
> the royal majesty, for that would not have been right. But . . .
> as your majesty commanded, with God our witness and judge,
> we shaped our advice. Indeed, as loyal and prudent subjects we
> would have been obliged to offer it unasked to our prince.

It is well to stress again, in view of the subsequent struggle
with Becket, that the relationship between king and Church was
not always one of amity and concord during the early part of
Henry's reign, as the above letter plainly indicates. Around the
same time we find John writing to Henry in Theobald's name:
"The sons of the world counsel you to lessen the authority of the
Church that your royal power may be increased."

The tense situation was at last alleviated in July of 1160,
when Henry held counsel with his Norman bishops at
Neufmarché, a small market town on the border between Normandy and France. Choice of this obscure and seemingly incon-
venient place was dictated by its nearness to Beauvais, where the
French king was likewise conferring with his clergy on the same
problem. Alexander's legates, Cardinals William of Pavia and
Henry of Pisa, attended and presented their case. From Theobald's letters it is apparent that the French Church had already
made its decision in favor of Alexander, perhaps informally.
Nevertheless Queen Eleanor, writing decades later, asserted that
Henry had led the way in giving allegiance to Alexander, and
that he had persuaded King Louis of France to follow his example.[2] In fact, joint sessions were held at which the legates of both

---

[2] Eleanor's memory of the events may have been confused after
the passage of more than thirty years. She was not present at the

popes pressed their cause. Louis and his prelates came to the same decision as Henry, but without obtaining the same benefits.

The presence of the papal legates in Normandy gave Thomas Becket the chance for a diplomatic coup, which again clouded the good relations between Louis and Henry. Thomas must have prepared the ground for his present stroke during his memorable visit in Paris, when he had arranged the marriage between young Henry and the infant Marguerite. The responsibility is clear; Herbert of Bosham states distinctly, with no trace of embarassment over his master's trickery, that the chancellor procured for his king the border fortresses of the Vexin "by matrimony, without iron, without sword or lance or fighting." (The fighting came later, to be sure.) The smoothness of the whole maneuver, and above all the involvement of the Templars, suggests that Becket had prepared it long before, perhaps from the moment that he lodged in the Temple at Paris. Execution of the plan had been delayed by the death of Adrian, on whose amiable consent as an Englishman Thomas had no doubt reckoned. The precarious situation of Pope Alexander III now enabled Thomas to extract a *quid pro quo* from the legates.

The immediate pretext for action was a series of events in France. Queen Constance of France gave birth to another daughter—Louis's fourth—and died in childbed on October 4. France still had no male heir; the anxious king hurriedly remarried before Constance was cold in her grave. His third wife was Adela of Blois, the sister of his own prospective sons-in-law, for the two counts of Blois were already betrothed to Louis's daughters by Eleanor of Aquitaine.

This triple alliance with the House of Blois spurred Henry

---

council session herself, for she remained in England until September. Moreover, she was writing with polemical intent, for she was trying to persuade Pope Celestine III to procure the freedom of her imprisoned son, Richard. Hence she stressed England's services to the Church. Logically, Louis should have been more eager than Henry to acknowledge Alexander; he had more to fear from his neighbor, Frederick Barbarossa, with whom Henry was on good terms. On the other hand, Pope Celestine would himself have remembered the circumstances; as Cardinal Hyacinth, he had been a good friend of Thomas Becket's, recipient of many of Becket's letters, and a member of the Curia throughout this period.

to immediate counterattack. Just before the death of Constance, Henry and Louis had met once more, and five-year-old Prince Henry had formally done homage to Louis for the duchy of Normandy. Now, while Louis was preoccupied with preparations for Adela's and his own coronation in Paris on November 13, another wedding was hastily celebrated, though it could not very well be consummated. With the consent of the legates, the two children, Henry and Marguerite, were married on November 2, 1160. The Templars with whom Thomas Becket had been so friendly promptly handed over Marguerite's dowry: the castles of the Vexin. King Henry's troops immediately occupied these castles; his frontier thus advanced to the river Epte. Baffled and furious, Louis could do no more than banish from France the three Templar knights, Robert of Prion, Tostes of Saint Omer, and Richard of Hastings; they were warmly received in Henry's lands. The following spring, Louis made a halfhearted attempt to regain by military means what he had lost by diplomacy. He accomplished nothing.

Thomas Becket had played a devious game to secure this great advantage for Henry. In another respect also he was playing a devious game at the time, and his motives are not easy to penetrate. Indeed, the game was so subtle that his best friends could not readily understand it. He was eager to return home to England, and wrote privately to John of Salisbury, or communicated with him by messenger, requesting that Theobald beg the king to come to England to receive his last blessings, or, if that were impossible, at least to send the chancellor to him. We possess only one side of the correspondence. There is a strong letter from Theobald in which he reproves Thomas for not obeying his repeated summons. This letter has been interpreted as indicating a breach between Thomas and Theobald; but it seems to have been written at Thomas's instigation. Clearly, Thomas wanted to escape from the atmosphere of the court for a while; but whether this was due to a desire to be in England because Theobald was dying, or to recent strains between Henry and himself, is difficult to say. The private letter in which John reported to Thomas on his efforts tantalizingly reveals and conceals the intrigue that was going forward. John wrote:

As you commanded me, my dear friend, I originally framed
my lord's letters to the king and to yourself in terms of extreme severity. In my draft they were meant to impress on you
the wisdom of your returning quickly. Otherwise you might be
taxed with disobedience and suffer my lord's condemnation and
loss of all the possessions the church of Canterbury has given
you. . . . But my lord has insisted that I temper my rigorous
language and make concessions to political necessities. Those
returning from overseas say—and I hope it is true—that the
king and all his court are utterly dependent on your advice, so
that there is no hope of peace in the near future unless you pave
the way for it. This is why my lord is puzzled at times by the
contradictory requests that you or the king make, and by the
different reasons you both give in your letters for hastening or
postponing your return. For common report and rumor suggest
that you are of one heart and mind. In view of such intimate
friendship, your desires and dislikes ought to coincide. He [i.e.
Theobald] has also sometimes asked whether there may not be
some collusion between you in this matter. But I think I have an
inkling of the truth, and realize your situation almost as vividly
as if I were on the spot. . . . All the same, you ought to realize
that it is in all sorts of ways expedient for you to return before
our lord dies, even if you have to cross the sea at once.

There are a number of reasons, personal and public, for
Becket's venturing to intrigue behind the king's back. In all
loyalty to Henry, he may have felt it unwise for both the king and
his chief minister to remain so long away from England, particularly when the control of affairs was slipping from the hands of
Theobald. At Toulouse he had taken an unpopular stand and
urged assault upon the city against the convictions of Henry and
the advice of the barons. Now he had apparently been recom-
mending, urgently but vainly, that Henry return to the kingdom
he had seen so little of since his accession. And since Henry was
disinclined to follow his advice, he wished at least to return
himself. This explanation would accord well with the characters
of the two men. Throughout his life, Henry was always impatient
to go back to his Continental dominions whenever he had so-
journed for a while in England; while Thomas, London born,
regarded the Continent as a place of exile.

Another possible explanation is less charitable to Thomas. Gilbert Foliot would later charge him with having long schemed to obtain election as Archbishop of Canterbury. John's remark that it would be expedient for him to return before Theobald died is fully consonant with such ambitions, and might be interpreted to mean that John knew and approved of them. But John's words can also be explained as entirely consistent with Thomas Becket's distaste for that high and extremely burdensome station, despite Theobald's known desire to have him for his successor.

The likeliest explanation is that Thomas was doing what he considered to be best for the king, even at the risk of crossing his will and engaging in a mild conspiracy against him. This ungrateful part fell rather frequently to Thomas. Remaining Henry's friend and wise counsellor had required learning how to deal with the king's temper. Two anecdotes will serve as examples. While the question of Alexander's recognition was still pending—during the council at Neufmarché, in fact—Henry heard that the Archbishop of Rouen had already approved Alexander, and through Giles, his archdeacon and nephew, had sent orders to his suffragan bishops to do the same. Typically, Henry's anger flared against the immediate object, and he ordered the archdeacon's house to be demolished. Becket forestalled this drastic punishment by pleading: "My lord king, it is true that the house you have ordered demolished belongs to Archdeacon Giles; but it also happens to be my lodging."

Thomas saved the house, but the king's determination to show his authority was not sated. The following day Henry heard that the Bishop of Le Mans had obeyed his archbishop's summons and promised obedience to Alexander's legates. Henry promptly signed orders for all the bishop's houses to be destroyed. The clergy of the two kingdoms pleaded with him, the chancellor above all; but Henry refused to give way. Knowing Henry's character, Thomas ordered the king's messengers to travel as slowly as possible toward Le Mans, taking four days instead of the usual two. Meanwhile he kept up his pleas. At last Henry yielded—when he thought the messengers would already have reached Le Mans and seen to the work of destruction. He issued the countermanding order, whereupon Thomas instructed

97

the messenger not to rest day or night until he arrived at Le Mans, which he easily did in good time, so that the bishop's houses remained intact. Afterwards the king was pleased with the outcome of the chancellor's well-meaning deception.

Throughout those last years of his chancellorship Thomas more and more often had to exert all his diplomacy to direct the king's wrathful impulses into useful and constructive channels. "There is no hope of peace in the near future unless you pave the way for it," John of Salisbury had written to him in the letter quoted above. He was referring to internal as well as external peace, and Thomas did his best. He persuaded Henry to forgive the Bishop of Le Mans, and it was probably for that reason that Henry and Queen Eleanor spent their Christmas at Le Mans. At the same time, Thomas turned Henry's thoughts from the razing of houses to the nobler art of building. He and Henry were able to use the income from the reviving economic life of England to engage in construction on a princely scale. The border was fortified by new castles at Gisors, Néauphle, and Châteauneuf-sur-Epte. A palace and park were built near Rouen. A leperhouse was founded at Caen and another castle built at Osmanville on the Vire.

During this winter of 1160-1, it may be that Thomas Becket found time to read and perhaps to discuss with his friend and king a voluminous work that had been sent to him during the siege of Toulouse. The book was John of Salisbury's "Statesman's Book," the *Policraticus,* a lengthy and often highly digressive discourse on political theory and many other matters, which must be reckoned among the great books of medieval times. That John found leisure for such ambitious literary work while conducting the affairs of Canterbury, handling most of Theobald's correspondence, and going on frequent missions to Rome, is testimony to his enormous energy and competence.

These qualities had long been recognized by all who had dealings with him. As we have seen, he was about the same age as Thomas. Beyond the fact that he was born in Salisbury (the twelfth-century Salisbury now called Old Sarum), nothing is known of his childhood except the story he tells in the *Policraticus* of the priest who tried to use him for crystal-gazing. John refused to see anything in the polished basin, and was therefore barred from the "sacrilegious proceedings," as he calls them. The anecdote tells us as much about the superstition of the clergy as it does about John's good sense.

His early career in Paris and his meeting with Thomas Becket there have already been mentioned. One of his teachers at Paris, Robert Pullen, probably introduced him to the papal court, where he served as a clerk under several popes until 1154, the year Henry II succeeded to the throne. Then he became a member of Theobald's household.

In his letters, John complains frequently of the burdens of his official duties. It may be, therefore, that much of the *Policraticus,* and possibly its sequel, the *Metalogicon,* had been drafted during his period of disgrace in 1156, when he had withdrawn somewhat from public business, and that the books were only completed in 1159. That he dedicated them to Thomas Becket at a critical juncture in the affairs of England and Canterbury, when it seemed likely that Theobald might die at any moment, suggests that John expected Thomas to succeed Theobald, and hoped to influence him toward those conceptions of Church and State which he set forth in the *Policraticus.*

An extensive literature has grown up around the book and John of Salisbury's notions of the Christian polity. John had one of the most fertile, well-stocked, and reflective minds of his age; it would be unfair to the complexity of his thought to attempt to summarize his ideas in a few pages. But it will be well for us to note some of the more striking remarks, implicit attitudes, and explicit theories that were later to be reflected in the actions or opinions of Thomas Becket during his years of struggle with his king.

The underlying argument of the *Policraticus* is the ancient organic theory of the "body politic" as analogous to the human body: the prince is its head, the priests its soul, the judges its eyes and ears, the officials and soldiers its hands, the peasants its feet. The theory fitted well into the medieval churchman's feeling for hierarchy and love of metaphor, and John elaborates it with a wealth of lively anecdote and quotation drawn from his reading in the ancient authors and the Fathers of the Church. For the book was intended to amuse as well as instruct; and since John expected, hoped, and feared that it would be read by the great men of his day, he was careful to give plenty of easily digested milk along with the solid food of his wisdom (to use a favorite medieval metaphor).

It took courage for a cleric who had suffered King Henry's disfavor to write that a prince ought to be chaste (when Henry was already as notorious as his grandfather had been for disregard of marital bonds) and moderate. "All excess is a fault; nothing is worse than the immoderate practice of good works." It took courage to stress that a prince ought to obey his own laws, serve his subjects, and fear God. It took even more courage to dedicate such a book to the king's chief minister who, friend though he was, by his position must necessarily represent the spirit of the king's court. John was courageous but not foolhardy, and he did not send his book directly to Thomas Becket. He took the precaution of submitting it first to his best friend, Peter, Abbot of Celle, with instructions "to keep it back unless you approve of its proceeding on its journey to the illustrious chancellor of the English king." For, John added, it would "scarcely find a single friend at court."

His fears are evidence that he understood the temper of Henry's court. For in addition to those comments on the necessary qualities of a prince which could easily be read as criticisms of King Henry, the book contained a lengthy and insistent statement of the high-Gregorian position that the secular power was by its nature inferior to the spiritual power. The prince, John said, "receives his sword from the hand of the Church." To illustrate his point, John recalled the supposed "fact" that at the Council of Nicaea the Emperor Constantine took the lowliest seat, not daring to sit among the priests. Moreover, when petitions bearing accusations against priests were brought to him, he burned them without examination, saying "that it was not permissible for him, as a man, and one who was subject to the judgment of priests, to examine cases touching gods, who cannot be judged save by God alone."

When John wrote these words he must have been well aware that Henry II had no inclination to imitate the example of Constantine; that, in fact, he was deeply disturbed by the conduct of priests in England and was already seeking ways to bring erring members of the clergy to justice in his own courts. John's insistence is a clue to the historical situation, and corroborates the evidence from other sources that the question of clerical immunities was being agitated before Thomas Becket became primate. For John returned to this argument repeatedly. "The prefects of religion preside over the entire body [politic]." "God's ministers are they that have been called by the divine governance to procure the salvation of themselves and others by rooting out and correcting vices or by implanting and increasing the virtues. But those who minister to Him in the sphere of human law are as much inferior to those who minister in divine law as things human are below things divine." It followed directly that "to outrage the immunities of sacred things is to rebel against God Himself," and that "the clergy shall have nought to do with proceedings at law or those which pertain to the royal court. . . . The nature of these privileges of churches and holy places and ministers is made clearly known by the law both divine and human, although it is now obvious from usage that they can only be determined before ecclesiastical judges."

Such sentiments, widespread though they were among the clergy, could not have been stated to the face of any English king, let alone Henry, without enraging him. And the chances were good that Henry would read at least parts of the book, for Henry was more than literate; he was lettered. In fact, one of his tutors, William of Conches, had also been a favorite teacher of John. John therefore saw to it that his bulky volume contained generous praise of Henry. The young king, he wrote, "was destined to be the greatest king of the whole age among the British lands, as well as the most fortunate duke of the Normans and Aquitanians, surpassing all others, not only in power and wealth, but also in the splendor of his virtues." John combined such tributes to Henry with eulogy of his grandfather, Henry I, on whom Henry liked to model himself, and with a sweeping condemnation of Stephen. Yet he linked even that condemnation with the obsessive theme of ecclesiastical immunities. While Stephen "did many things ill, and few things well," John wrote, "his worst act was that in contempt of God he laid hands on His anointed. . . . The seizure of the bishops was but the beginning of his ill deeds, and from that day the sword was never absent from his side, and each new act of the man was worse than those which had gone before."

With the best will in the world, John could not be a discreet courtier. He had spoken his mind freely to Pope Adrian; in the future he would reprove Thomas Becket with equal freedom. And even now, when his aim was flattery, his honesty and bluntness got the better of him. He could not resist interlarding his panegyric of Henry with admonitory phrases: "If the merit of his virtues cleaves until the end to the grace which has already been bestowed on him," or: "However, the period which marks the end of a man's youth is looked upon by some with suspicion, and may it prove that the fears of the good are groundless." Again and again John struck the note of mingled submissiveness and resistance to the secular power:

I am satisfied and persuaded that loyal shoulders should uphold the power of the ruler; and not only do I submit to his power patiently, but with pleasure, so long as it is exercised in subjection to God and follows His ordinances. But on the other hand, if it resists and opposes the divine commandments, and wishes to make me share in its war against God, then with unrestrained voice I answer back that God must be preferred before any man on earth.

Thomas Becket was to echo that note frequently.

PART TWO

Lord of Canterbury

VII

Toward Canterbury

IN HIS LAST LETTER to the king, the dying Theobald had written pathetically:

> My flesh is worn, my limbs wearied by age and toil, and long and grave illness warns me that the end of my days will soon be upon me. I was hoping that I might once more look upon your face, so long desired, before I die. . . . But since I am being summoned more quickly to His weighing before Whose judgment seat we shall all stand, I speak to your Serene Highness in these letters. . . . I commend to you the holy church of Canterbury, from which you received the governance of the realm by my ministry. Guard it, I beg you, against the attacks of wicked men.

The long-expected end came on April 18, 1161. After spending his last hours with John of Salisbury, whom he appointed an executor of his will, Theobald died.[1] He had been an effective, if not brilliant prelate, brave when he had to be, forbearing and conciliatory whenever possible. Although a Canterbury monk, who was only a young man at the time of Theobald's death, declared later that he had conferred few advantages and inflicted many evils upon the church of Canterbury, it cannot be denied that during his episcopate the prestige and the immuni-

---

[1] Twenty years later, during repairs on the cathedral, his body was found incorrupt—"perfect as to the bones and the nerves, the skin and the flesh." A movement for his canonization was thereupon set afoot, but nothing came of it.

ties of the Church had risen to a great height in England. He had had his difficulties with the secular power, but had on the whole avoided prolonged clashes with it. He had steered the Church of England through a schism and, with the very considerable assistance of his "clerk of London," Thomas Becket, had been largely instrumental in preparing the way for the change of dynasties. He had been least successful, in those troubled times under Stephen, in protecting the property of his see against the inroads of greedy neighbors. To the last, the possessions of Canterbury remained a deep anxiety to him,[2] and in his testament he declared, under pain of anathema:

We forbid the alienation of any of the lands belonging to the archbishop, and prohibit all cutting down and damage to the woods until our successor be appointed, save only for some essential purpose of the church, or if the king command it with his own lips, or discreet pity should make some slight indulgence to the claims of the poor.

---

[2] Perhaps a word should be said about this anxiety, so common in the documents of churchmen, over the possible alienation of church lands. It is one of the venerable clichés of historians that "one third of the land was owned by the Church" at almost any given period under discussion. And it is true that there was a steady flow of land, through wills and grants, into the "dead hand" of the Church. But there was also a steady flow out of that hand. Heirs often refused to recognize the bequests of parents or kinsfolk, which would deprive them of parts of their inheritance. Hence, there were constant encroachments on ecclesiastical property. In addition, ecclesiastical lords had to enfeoff secular knights to pay the service they owed to the king. After a generation or two, the terms of an original contract would be forgotten, and the tenants would no longer recognize their obligation to the ecclesiastical lord. The *Cartae baronum*, the returns of an inquiry conducted by Henry II in 1166 into the number of knights' fees in England, are full of complaints by bishops over refusals of service. Thus the Bishop of Exeter: "Henry of La Pommeraye holds . . . half a knight's fee in Devon. He denies the duty of service in respect of this half knight's fee. But it is owing from him. . . . Joel of St. Winnow holds half a knight's fee but claims that it should belong to his demesne. Roger . . . holds half a knight's fee but claims that it ought to belong to his demesne." Much of the business of the courts dealt with the question of whether or not services were due. Since such services were usually commuted for a money payment, these cases were suits at civil law in the modern sense. And then, as now, the costs of going to court might exceed the value of the property or the sum involved.

VII · TOWARD CANTERBURY

After Theobald's death the administration of Canterbury passed, like that of all vacant sees, into the hands of Chancellor Thomas Becket. The large revenues of the archiepiscopate were more than welcome to the chancellor and his king. For Louis VII had taken the field in the Vexin, and there was no telling how seriously he intended to prosecute his campaign to recover the lands that, he felt, he had lost by trickery the previous winter. Henry preferred to use mercenaries rather than raise his host in Anjou and Normandy, and mercenaries, of course, meant a heavy outlay of money. As it turned out, Louis did not regard serious fighting as worth his while—especially since the initial successes went to Henry—and by the end of June he agreed to a truce. The cessation of the fighting on the border of Normandy gave Henry the opportunity to make a show of force in Aquitaine, and during the summer he put down a minor rebellion there. For once he was not accompanied by his chancellor, who remained behind in Normandy. Around this time, Thomas fell ill at Rouen,[3] and there took place the famous conversation recorded by William FitzStephen.

At length, FitzStephen relates, Thomas began to improve. One day he was sitting playing chess, dressed in a cape with long sleeves (distinctly secular garb) when Aschetinus, the Prior of Leicester, came to see him straight from the king's court in Gascony. He addressed the chancellor in that familiar, chaffing tone that Thomas seemed to evoke in those who knew him well: "What is this long-sleeved cape you have? It is more suitable to the sort of men who carry falcons; but you are an ecclesiastic,

---

[3] The nature of the illness is not specified, but the time can be determined fairly closely. During Becket's illness, FitzStephen tells us, two kings came to see him at the same time, the King of France and his own lord (*Materials* III, 25). This would place the illness around June 30, when Henry and Louis arranged their truce (Eyton 54). In fact, it seems likely that the kings would have come not only to pay a sick-call, but also to consult with the chancellor on the terms of the truce. The conversation with the Prior of Leicester took place while Henry was in Gascony, FitzStephen records (*Materials* III, 26). On August 10 Henry captured the castle of Castillon on the Dordogne in Gascony. This would suggest that Becket's prolonged illness lasted over a month. Dom L'Huillier (I, 160) states that Thomas fell ill at the time of Theobald's death, but gives no evidence.

singular in person but plural in dignity: Archdeacon of Canterbury, Dean of Hastings, Provost of Beverley, canon here and canon there, even administrator of Canterbury, and it is common rumor at court that you will be archbishop."

The chancellor replied: "I assure you, I know of three poor priests in England any one of whom I should rather wish to see advanced to the archiepiscopate than myself. For if I should by chance be promoted, I would either lose the favor of my lord the king, whom I know 'from his skin to his soul,' or neglect the service of the Lord God."

It is a wonderfully vivid anecdote that catches the living Thomas: his fondness for gay and expensive clothing; his delight in chess, that subtlest of games, pure battle of intellect, will, and above all foresight; his ability to be relaxed and on his guard at the same time; his genuine religious feeling and his authentic compound of humility, pride, and ambition. The story might be dismissed as a typical piece of medieval hagiography; but it is validated by all the circumstances, by the details, the naming of the person involved, the fact that we are able to date it so closely, the information that the Prior of Leicester had come directly from the king's court. The wryness of Thomas's reply to the prior suggests, furthermore, the ambiguities of his present relations with a Henry no longer willing to accept his friend's guidance in all things. Thomas had not failed to draw conclusions from their recent clashes: over Toulouse, over the marriage of Matthew of Boulogne, over the Archdeacon of Rouen and the Bishop of Le Mans, and over his desire to return home to see the dying Theobald. He truly knew the king inside and out (as we would nowadays phrase the tag from the Roman satirist Persius that Thomas used). He knew the king's courage, sense of justice, and capacity for friendship; he knew also his cunning, lack of principle, skepticism about religion, and ungovernable temper. From his knowledge of the whole man he could easily predict the result if he were to succeed Theobald and attempt to meet his own responsibilities to the Church perhaps somewhat better than Theobald had done. As John of Salisbury tells us: "By long familiarity he had learned what the burden and the honor of that office really were. For he had grown to know the character of the king and the wickedness and obstinacy of his officials, and how effective was the malice of informers at court. From these considerations he rightly drew the conclusion that if he accepted the post, he would lose either God's favor or the king's. For he could not cleave to God and obey the royal will, or give precedence to the laws of the saints without making an enemy of the king."

Thomas's disagreements with Henry hitherto had concerned different opinions on how best to prosecute the king's aims. They were conflicts of method but not of principle. If the time ever came that their aims should differ—and John of Salisbury's own troubles with Henry were indication enough that they would—irreconcilable antagonism was in prospect. It required no supernatural prophetic spirit, such as the hagiographers later attributed to Thomas the Martyr, for him to realize that.

Until a direct offer was forthcoming, Thomas could not in modesty advise the king against his own promotion. Yet if he let matters drift he might well find himself Theobald's successor. Was propriety the sole reason for his silence? Was he in fact swayed by ambition, willing to accept the foreseen difficulties for the sake of power? Or did he passively accept whatever might come in a religious spirit: let God's will be done? Or again, did he believe that ultimately he of all men in Henry's realm was best fitted to head the English Church, to save her from Henry's potential tyranny, and to guard Henry himself from the perils of conflict with the Church? This seems likelier than the alternative that from the first he desired the primacy in order to thwart Henry's designs on the liberties and properties of the Church. For Thomas loved Henry, despite his reservations. Henry, like Thomas himself, was a man who with all his faults inspired the deepest loyalties.

We cannot hope for an unequivocal assessment of Thomas's motives. Yet we must recognize that Thomas could have escaped the onus of advancement if he had wished. Not every man wanted to be a bishop, as King Henry's own illegitimate son Geoffrey was to demonstrate in after years.[4] Thomas could simply have refused. Since he did not do so, he must have desired the

---

[4] Geoffrey was nominated bishop-elect of Lincoln in 1173, but could never bring himself to accept consecration.

office as much as he feared it. His reasons for wanting it would not have been entirely personal; he was a dedicated public official with a high sense of duty. But he may also have sensed that his years as second in command under the king were approaching a natural term; that Henry would not tolerate an equal at his side much longer. A man who had grown used to power would naturally look for a sphere of his own in which to exercise it. That applied to both Henry and Thomas.

✠   ✠   ✠

The offer, when it came, was linked with Henry's dynastic ambitions. Henry returned from the campaign in Aquitaine by autumn, in time to see his new daughter, the Princess Eleanor. With Thomas now well again, a definitive peace with Louis was arranged. Life expectancy was short in the twelfth century. Henry, who was approaching the age of thirty, had to take steps to establish the succession.

Young Henry, his firstborn son, was seven years old. Henry had already sent the boy for "fostering" under the tutelage of the man he trusted most, in whose household the sons of so many great nobles already served as pages: Thomas Becket. Who could better teach the boy the duties of a prince than the older friend who had already guided Henry himself in the art of kingship? Henry was luckier than his grandfather had been, than Louis of France now was: he had heirs. His newly wedded son might some day add the throne of France to that of England, if Louis's ill-luck held and his new wife gave him only daughters. But that was speculation; the more immediate problem was to make certain that the boy would not find his natural heritage as difficult to win as Henry had found his. For no regular principle of succession to the throne of England yet existed.

Henry resolved to adopt the solution that had been initiated by Charlemagne, who had crowned his sons kings and his surviving son emperor during his own lifetime, a practice that had since become accepted in France and Germany. Henry therefore decided to send his son to England to receive the homage of the barons, as a step toward his subsequent coronation. Stephen had attempted similarly to have his son Eustace crowned in his lifetime, but the project had foundered on the opposition of Theobald and the pope. With Thomas Becket to manage the ticklish affair, Henry believed that it would succeed.

He ordered Thomas to prepare to return to England. There was in any case much business to attend to there, since he himself had not set foot in his kingdom for more than three years. With the stabilizing personality of Theobald gone, it became important for Henry to have his most capable administrator in England. Beside secular matters, ecclesiastical affairs were pending. The see of Canterbury had been vacant for a year, which meant that bishops could not be consecrated, appeals went unheard, and the whole Church of England—an organization much more tightly integrated than the state—lacked a head.

Above all, only the Archbishop of Canterbury could crown an English king. If young Henry were to be crowned, the church of Canterbury must be given a shepherd. The two projects were one.

Henry had already made his decision, and Thomas had some inkling of it. But the king, "following the bent of his mind," dissembled his intention; and Thomas also kept silent. Yet the matter was certainly no secret; courtiers talked openly about it, and the *vox populi* already heralded it.

In May 1162 Henry was staying at the castle of Falaise, where his great-grandfather William the Conqueror had been born. To this square Norman structure, set on a high crag dominating the town, came Thomas Becket to pay his respects to the king before departing on his mission to England. Calling him aside, the king said to him privately: "You do not yet know fully the reason for your mission." And he added: "It is my will that you shall be Archbishop of Canterbury."

With a smile, the chancellor looked down at his gay robe. "How religious, how holy a man you wish to appoint to that holy see and over so famous and saintly a congregation of monks. I know for sure that if God should permit it, you would swiftly turn against me, and the affection which is now so great between the two of us would soon be changed to violent hatred. I know that you would demand many things that I would not be able to bear with equanimity—for already you presume too much in ecclesiastical affairs. And so the envious would find opportunities to stir up constant animosity between us."

Herbert of Bosham and the *Saga of Archbishop Thomas* agree fairly closely on the content of this dialogue. It may be suspected that Thomas did not actually tell the king he already presumed too much in ecclesiastical affairs; that sounds like an invention typical of Herbert's mind. The *Saga* has Thomas warn the king further that if he took office he might become "unlike him who now stands before you." Almost all accounts stress the potential malice of envious courtiers, but that was so much a standard *topos* of literary composition that perhaps not much importance should be attributed to it.

Whatever the exact words, the contemporary accounts agree that Thomas warned Henry against nominating him. He may not have insisted long: the *Saga* says that after making his protest he bowed to the king and walked out of the chamber. But he satisfied his conscience; he gave the king the benefit of his foresight, as was his duty while he remained chancellor. It was later alleged that when Henry consulted his mother, the Empress Matilda, she likewise advised against the appointment. But Henry would not be gainsaid; he enlisted the aid of the cardinal legate, Henry of Pisa, who happened to be in Falaise at the time, to persuade Thomas to accept. And Thomas, against his better judgment surely, bowed to the authority of his ecclesiastical superior and to his notion of the divine will.

With Thomas's reluctant acceptance in hand, Henry promptly called Richard de Lucy, his justiciar, to his side. Richard bore the epithet "the Loyal," and merited it. He had been justiciar under Stephen, and he was to serve Henry for a quarter of a century. Although he firmly opposed Thomas during the quarrel with the king, he subsequently founded Lesnes Abbey in honor of the martyred saint, and himself retired there to end his days in the garb of religion. Next to Thomas, Richard must be reckoned among the most gifted of Henry's secular officials; and it was to him that Henry now entrusted the task of enforcing his will upon the English episcopate and the frequently stiff-necked

monks of Christ Church, Canterbury, who must elect the archbishop. The obstacles to which Thomas himself had alluded—his
secular mode of life, his luxury and ostentation, his part in
exacting money from the Church for the king's purposes—would
loom large in the minds of ecclesiastics.

The king's words to his justiciar have been preserved. The
opening phrase suggests the gloomy forebodings that were in his
mind at the time—for what specific reasons we do not know.
"Richard," he said somberly, "if I lay dead in my shroud, would
you see to it that my firstborn son Henry were raised to the
kingship?" Richard replied: "I would, my lord, by my life and
limbs." Then the king said, suddenly reverting to the formal
plural of royalty: "Very well. It is our will and bidding that you
help Thomas, our chancellor, to become archbishop of Canterbury."

Richard obeyed. He crossed to England, as did Thomas
Becket, and the two presided at the council held in London at
which the magnates of the kingdom swore fidelity to young
Henry. Thomas knelt before the boy to take the oath, and the rest
of the assemblage then followed his example to everyone's surprise without a murmur, for it had been thought that such an
innovation could scarcely be introduced without trouble even
had the king himself been present. No formal coronation was
undertaken at this time; but the little king evidently wore a crown
and carried the regalia, the symbols of royalty, for the Pipe Roll
records that the great financier William Cade was paid £38 6s.
for supplying gold for the king's son's crown and for preparing
the regalia.

The council over, Richard set out for Canterbury with his
brother Walter, the Abbot of Battle, and three of the bishops,
Walter of Rochester, Bartholomew of Exeter, and Hilary of
Chichester. Bishop Walter was that brother of Theobald and
one-time patron of Thomas who, twenty years before, had saved
young Thomas from the intrigues of the then Archdeacon Roger,
now Archbishop of York. Bartholomew of Exeter had held office
only a year. He was one of John of Salisbury's closest friends, and
during Theobald's last days John had labored long and hard to
procure his appointment, for King Henry had proposed another

candidate. Bishop Hilary, a one-time clerk in Henry of Winchester's household, had a considerable reputation as a canon lawyer. We will recall how he had tried to defend himself before the king in his conflict with Abbot Walter, with whom he was now traveling harmoniously to Canterbury, and how he had capitulated before the arguments of Chancellor Thomas and the royal wrath. Evidently he bore Thomas no grudge at this time, for he used his quick wit and ready tongue to subdue the recalcitrant Canterbury monks. Or if he bore a grudge, he repressed it. Hilary was an opportunist above all else.

The bishops brought with them letters from the king ordering the monks to convene the Canterbury chapter for the election of an archbishop. The bishops themselves spoke first, and at great length, to the assembled monks, alluding frequently to the king's generosity in allowing them the free election required by canon law. They dilated upon the king's devotion to the Church, and especially to the church of Canterbury. Richard de Lucy then took up the theme, treading nicely the narrow path between a free and coerced election. "The king grants you full freedom of election," he told the monks, "provided you elect a man worthy of the office and equal to the burdens. . . .[5] It behooves you to elect one under whose protection you may rejoice before God and men. For if king and archbishop are linked by affection and cherish one another in friendship, there is no doubt that the times will be happy and the existing gladness and tranquility of the Church will continue. But if, God forbid, things should turn out otherwise, crises and confusions, troubles and tumults, damage to property and peril to souls will follow."

The speech adroitly mingled cajolery, threat, and information. Without technically infringing the canonical provisions for free election by naming Henry's candidate, Richard made plain whom the king had in mind. The monks could not help being intimidated by the weight of authority; but they were determined not to be put upon. The very presence of Bartholomew of Exeter

---

[5] . . . *ut personam tanto oneri et honori eligatis*—apparently the standard pun, for it was used by John of Salisbury and other contemporary writers.

among the envoys was proof that Henry's will did not always prevail in episcopal elections—although it might serve as evidence that Becket's did. And what most troubled the Canterbury monks, aside from their suspicions of the chancellor's attitude toward the Church and their natural inclination to assert themselves, was the fact that the Archbishop of Canterbury had usually been chosen from the regular clergy whereas Thomas was not even a secular priest.

After Richard de Lucy had spoken, the prior and some of the older monks withdrew to consult among themselves. But they came to no decision. Blandly pretending that they did not understand Richard's broad hints about a person with whom the king was linked in friendship, they called in the royal commissioners and once more asked advice on the king's wishes since, they declared, the whole question of the election must depend on that. Richard and the bishops were compelled to identify the king's candidate by name. Only then did the monks declare their unanimous agreement. Their hesitation arose, says the contemporary biographer, not because they did not know Thomas to be a man of virtue, but only because "he did not wear the habit of religion."[6] But "his other virtues and graces shone so brightly" that they considered this sufficient compensation, and elected Thomas at last "with one heart and will."

Such is the account of the biographer who lived in close intimacy with Thomas during his exile, heard the story from his own lips, and may be taken as representing Thomas's own view. Like Anselm before him, Thomas "regarded the appointment of a bishop or abbot as a royal appointment." The king's influence did not mean, to his mind, that he had not been canonically elected; in fact it was part of the process of canonical election, as was the consent of the electors. "You insinuate," he wrote years later to the bishops of England, "or say openly, that I was promoted amid the sighs and groans of the Church. Consult your consciences, look at the form of the election, the consent of all the electors, the assent of the king through his son and his envoys,

---

[6] Subsequently, after the election, they continued to make a point of this until Thomas adopted monastic habit.

the assent of the son himself as well as all the magnates of the kingdom." Afterwards, too, Thomas declared that if the queen mother had indeed opposed his election, she had not revealed that fact to the public. It should be remembered, however, that the letters just quoted were written as polemics in answer to a polemic.

There is another account of the proceedings that presents the discussions in a very different light. According to the Icelandic *Saga,* the monks promptly divided into two factions after hearing the king's emissaries. Some said that the election of Thomas would necessarily be a great good; others vehemently disagreed. The latter party argued that the "king's court would open its mouth and gulp down the Church's wealth and freedom." They likewise protested that such a worldly man should not be permitted to lord it over monks living under the rule. "Now that the king's messengers come to understand that they have to deal with contentions instead of an election, and with tardiness instead of good will, they name a certain number out of the Canterbury chapter to meet for the election on a settled day in the king's court in London, together with the bishops thither summoned and other great folk; and in this way they depart therefrom and ride to London."

The two narratives stand in direct contradiction. According to the *Saga,* the bishops and Richard de Lucy left Canterbury without having accomplished their purpose of procuring the election, and the matter had to be debated all over again at the meeting in London. According to the other biographers, and to the testimony of Ralph de Diceto, Thomas was elected at Canterbury. The *Saga* confirms the charges later made by the suffragan bishops and Gilbert Foliot in the course of the polemics. All the other testimony supports the position of Thomas.

There is a possibility of reconciling these two narratives. It may well be that the writer of the *Saga* either misunderstood his Latin source or overdramatized the opposition of the monks of Christ Church. That there was some resistance to the king's choice is admitted by all. Probably the monks were in fact overawed by the royal commissioners and agreed to the election despite their misgivings. But there was more opposition in London, as we shall see; and possibly the author of the *Saga* con-

cluded from this fact that the election by prior and monks had
not yet been accomplished at the time of the assembly in London.
Remote from the scene, he would be trying to make sense out of
his documents, and would ask himself how further opposition
was possible if the election were already completed. In fact, he
may have been right in the formal sense, for Roger of Pontigny's
account mentions that after the monks had unanimously elected
Thomas, the bishops appointed a day for the prior and monks to
meet in London "in order that whatever remained necessary to
complete the formalities of the election might be publicly performed before all the bishops and abbots of the realm and in the
presence of the young king."

The principal opposition to the election of Thomas came
from the man who next to the now venerable Henry of Winchester was personally the most formidable of the English bishops:
Gilbert Foliot, Bishop of Hereford, who was subsequently to
become the leader of the anti-Becket party in England. Although
his own actions and the verdict of posterity cast him as the villain
of the drama, Foliot was a man to whom many of his contemporaries paid tribute in terms approaching adulation. Hugh, Abbot
of Cluny, called him the foremost of teachers, the mirror of
religion, and the glory of the present age, and declared Cluny
happy to have merited such a man. Gilbert was related to several
of the noblest families of England, and must even as a young
man have been extremely promising, for he was a prior by the age
of twenty-five. He acquired a reputation for both learning and
asceticism, and in 1139 was called by Stephen to be Abbot of
Gloucester. Since that city was the capital of Earl Robert's territory, it naturally served as headquarters for the Angevin party
during the Civil War; and Gilbert had a difficult time steering his
abbey between the contending factions. As far as possible he
kept out of politics, and seems to have preserved neutrality without forfeiting the good will of either side. In 1148, Theobald
ordered him to attend the Council at Reims, in spite of Stephen's
prohibition. Gilbert obeyed, with some hesitation. This opposition, although reluctant, proved fortunate for him. During the
council the Bishop of Hereford died, and he was rewarded with
that see.

This was the occasion for an act of perjury that stained

Gilbert's impeccable record. The see of Hereford was controlled by Henry, then Duke of Normandy. Henry refused to confirm the election until Gilbert swore on the Gospels to do homage to him within a month after his consecration, and not to swear fealty to Stephen, whom the whole Church of England, by papal decree, was bound to obey. Gilbert took the oath and was consecrated in St. Omer by Archbishop Theobald, the other English bishops refusing to attend on the ground that it was a violation of custom for a bishop to be consecrated outside the kingdom and without the consent of the king.[7] As soon as Gilbert returned to England, however, he violated his oath and swore fealty to King Stephen for the temporalities of his see. Henry angrily denounced the act to Theobald, "protesting that a man was not worthy to be a bishop if without fear or shame he could break an oath publicly sworn on the gospels." But the archbishop succeeded in placating him, arguing that "a bishop had no right to divide the Church by refusing fealty to the prince whom the Roman Church has accepted."

From Gilbert's voluminous correspondence the picture of an extremely competent administrator emerges, a clear, forceful, sometimes sarcastic writer, a man of tact, learning, considerable shrewdness, and literary as well as ecclesiastic ambition. There are few personal notes in these letters, and his colleagues seem to have respected him more than they loved him. But beneath the cold exterior was a man who could give way to passion. The clue to his personality is perhaps best given by that contemporary who knew him well and saw so clearly into the minds of all around him: John of Salisbury. In his *Policraticus* John relates that Gilbert once said to him that "when he was a simple monk, he would blame his superiors' lack of zeal; when he was somewhat advanced in the Order, he pitied the faults of his equals, but did not spare the shortcomings of those of yet higher rank; when a prior he had sympathy with priors, but still carped at abbots; when an abbot he felt kindly toward his fellow-abbots and turned

[7] The conduct of the bishops on this occasion is an interesting example of the English episcopate's tendency to side with the secular power in a disagreement between their archbishop and the king.

his attention to the defects of the bishops; now at last, a bishop himself, he dealt gently with his colleagues in the episcopate." John did not add that the only superiors to a bishop were the archbishop and the king! This remarkable glimpse into Gilbert Foliot's character was written while Theobald was still living, at which time John speaks of Gilbert with the utmost respect.

Such was the man who alone among the bishops of the realm had the courage to raise his voice against the chancellor's election as archbishop. If it were not for the suspicion of envy, the protest would redound to his credit. As David Knowles points out: "No one could have foreseen the change that took place in the new archbishop, and for a worldly chancellor to be forced upon a recalcitrant electing body was a thing deplorable in itself and (so far as man could see) in its consequences." But envy there certainly was, for Gilbert Foliot had every reason to believe that he was better fitted for the office than Thomas Becket. Both Thomas and John of Salisbury believed that he aspired to be archbishop, although Gilbert himself always denied any such ambition.

A vast concourse of "both learned and unlearned," all the bishops, abbots, priors, earls, magnates, and royal officers, assembled at Westminster on May 23, 1162. The three bishops set forth their mission to Canterbury, and declared that "by the inspiration of the Holy Spirit" Thomas had been elected canonically and "harmoniously" (*concorditer*)—whether pointedly or not, they did not say "unanimously." An abbot once again raised the question of Thomas's secular status, saying that it had been customary for members of the regular clergy to be chosen for the see of Canterbury ever since the time of St. Augustine, the first archbishop. Bishop Hilary of Chichester promptly silenced this protest with the tart retort: "Do you think that none are acceptable to God unless they are like yourself? Far from it!" If we may believe the Icelandic biography, which alone among the accounts stresses the extent of the opposition, the arguments raged back and forth all day. At one point Bishop Foliot "grumbled that Thomas had been a persecutor of the Church" and proposed that the matter be postponed until the king himself could come to England and participate in the deliberations. Again Hilary took up the challenge, insisting that the king had already made his stand perfectly clear and had not changed his mind. Gilbert's opposition was finally broken by the authority of the two men who might be regarded as his ecclesiastical superiors, Bishop Henry of Winchester, King Stephen's brother, and Cardinal Henry of Pisa. After both had emphatically urged the election of Thomas, Foliot withdrew his objections.

All this time, Thomas had been waiting outside the hall in which the discussions were being held, no doubt, sure of the outcome of the deliberations, but perhaps wondering at their prolongation. At last he was called into the august gathering, and Bishop Henry addressed him:

"By Almighty God's providence and our common consent, you are chosen archbishop of the highest episcopal see in all England, for the glory of the Holy Trinity, for the governance of the Church and for the good of the people; and in God's name we now ask you to assent to our will."

Thomas replied, as custom required, that he was unworthy in the eyes of the Heavenly Judge. He pointed out that the weight of his new burdens would be unbearable, for he had not been relieved of the old. This was a matter that, with characteristic foresight, he had evidently discussed beforehand with the men who would be his suffragan bishops. For Henry of Winchester then addressed the seven-year-old Henry as if he were in fact the king:

"The lord chancellor, our archbishop-elect," he said, "has now for a long time held the highest place in the household of the king, your father, and in the whole realm, and has had the kingdom in his charge, nor has anything been done in it during his time except by his authority. We ask, therefore, that he be handed over to the Church of God and to us free and absolved of all service and connections to the court, and from all suits, accusations or any other charges, and that from this hour and henceforth he may be emancipated and unencumbered, freely able to perform the duties of God. For we know that the king, your father, has delegated his authority to you in this business, and that he will gladly ratify your decision."

The young king (Thomas's page!) gave his formal consent

120

to a request that he could not possibly understand. It was an important point, this release from secular obligations, and was to become a matter of great moment two years later. But still Thomas hesitated to pronounce the decisive words of acceptance before the whole council; and it is difficult to believe that his hesitancy was only feigned. He alone, of all those present, knew what he was about to do; and renunciation of the pleasures and privileges of secular power was not the least of his sacrifices. Henry of Winchester, who was then over sixty, used all the authority of his years to overcome Thomas's last scruples. He spoke paternally: "Sweet son of mine, do not grieve, for hereafter you will mend whatever you have broken. Remember how Paul opposed the Church of God and later upheld her most of all, and glorified her at last with his blood."

And Thomas answered: "God's hidden will and yours seem to be alike in this matter. I assent, although in great fear."

Whereupon everyone rose, to the ringing of bells, and sang the *Te Deum*.

☩ ☩ ☩

Now that the matter was settled, a contention arose among the bishops as to who should consecrate the new archbishop since there was no Bishop of London, to whom the privilege would ordinarily have fallen. Roger of York, Becket's old enemy and the highest ranking ecclesiastic in England, claimed the right, but abandoned his claim when Thomas declared that in that case he would have to make a profession of obedience to Canterbury. The matter seems trivial, but it serves to remind us of the twelve years that Thomas had spent in Canterbury as Theobald's secretary. He was by no means ignorant of the requirements and ancient rivalries of his new office, and immediately took opportunity to assert Canterbury's primacy, in the fullest sense of the word.

It was finally agreed that Henry of Winchester, brother of a king and dean of the bishops, was the obvious choice. As a kind of consolation prize, Walter of Rochester, who had briefly put in a claim, was allowed to confer the priesthood on Thomas. The ordination took place on Saturday June 2.

The consecration was set for the octave of Pentecost, that is, the Sunday after Whitsunday, which that year (1162) fell on June 3. An "infinite multitude" of dignitaries of Church and State left London to accompany the archbishop-elect to Canterbury: no less than fourteen bishops, innumerable priors, abbots, earls, sheriffs, and officers of the court, as well as seven-year-old Henry, the young king. In their wake came crowds of the common people, to watch the spectacle and to cheer the new archbishop. They rejoiced that the vacancy was ended; they rejoiced the more because Thomas the Chancellor had been popular as much for his luxury and ostentation as for his generosity. And they rejoiced also because he was both an Englishman and a Londoner.

Christ Church, where the consecration was held, burned down four years after the death of Thomas (the present more imposing cathedral was founded upon the ruins). Gervase of Canterbury has left a description of the building as it had been when it was dedicated in 1130.

I will first describe the work of Lanfranc, beginning from the great Tower, for not the whole of that church has been destroyed, although a part of it has been altered. The tower is raised on great pillars and . . . had on its summit a gilded cherub. On the West of this tower is the nave, supported on each side by eight piers. Two lofty towers with gilded pinnacles end this nave. In the middle of the church hangs a gilded cross. This tower was separated from the nave by a screen with a loft, and in the middle of this, on the side toward the nave, was the altar of the Holy Cross. Above this loft-screen, and placed across the church, was a beam bearing the great cross, with two cherubim and the images of St. Mary and St. John the Apostle. . . . The great tower had on each side a transept, one on the south and another on the north, and in the middle of each transept was a strong pillar which sustained a vault. . . . The two transepts are almost exactly the same in design. The south transept was used to carry the organ above its vault, and an apse extended from the east side of the transept, above and below the vault. . . .

The east piers of the great tower stood out from the solid mass in semicircular relief. From here, down the choir, stretched a line of eight pillars on each side of it, almost equidistant from each other; and then came six in a semicircle, arranged from the ninth pillar on the south side to the ninth on the north side. . . . Arches were turned from pillar to pillar; and above these the solid wall was set with small blank windows. Above the wall was the passage which is called the triforium, and then the upper windows; this was the continuation of the interior wall. On this rested the roof and ceiling, ornamented with excellent paintings. At the bases of the pillars was a wall of marble slabs which surrounded the choir and presbytery, this dividing the body of the church from its sides, which are called aisles. . . .

Above the wall, in the apse behind and opposite to the altar, was the patriarchal chair formed out of a single stone, in which, following the custom of the Church, on high festivals the archbishops used to sit during the solemn Mass until the time of the consecration of the holy elements, whereupon they descended to the altar of Christ by eight steps. . . . At the eastern horns of the altar were two wooden columns gracefully ornamented with gold and silver, which carried a great beam, of which the ends rested on the capitals of the two pillars. This beam, decorated with gold, was carried across the church, above the altar; and bore on it the image of the Lord and the images of St. Dunstan and St. Alphege; also seven chests worked over with gold and silver and filled with the relics of many saints. Between the two wooden columns there was a gilded cross surrounded by a row of sixty transparent crystals. . . . From the middle of the choir there hung a gilded crown carrying twenty-four candles.

When Thomas arrived at Canterbury he was greeted by the bishops and nobles who had preceded him, by the monks and clergy of Canterbury, and by an "innumerable multitude of people." Words cannot express, Roger of Pontigny tells us, "the devotion and exultation of those who came running up to meet him." But far from exulting himself, Thomas moved forward slowly with "tears flowing from his eyes, in a mood of humility and contrition, thinking less of the honor than of the burden." The long, solemn rite of consecration over, he mounted the eight steps to the great stone seat to say his first Mass and to declare that a new festival would henceforth be kept in England on this day. The festival—Trinity Sunday—was ultimately adopted by the whole of western Christendom at the command of Pope John XXII.

That act should have served as a warning to those who thought that the worldly minded chancellor would continue as before in his new office. The institution of a feast day is no small matter; it is a manifestation of religious authority and bespeaks an intimate bond with the ritual life of the Church. Thomas could not have said more clearly that he was determined to become a new man; that as Archbishop of Canterbury he meant to be the ruler of the Church of England, the subject only of the Holy Trinity to whom he dedicated the day of his consecration, and something perhaps more dangerous to the secular power than either of these: an innovator.

Amid the general rejoicing, however, there was one man who was not content and who did not see the implications. Gilbert Foliot, Bishop of Hereford, vegetarian and teetotaler, sneered: "The king has worked a miracle. Out of a secular man and a soldier he has made an archbishop!"

VIII

The New Archbishop

DURING THE JOURNEY to the consecration in Canterbury Thomas rode a little apart from his large following, lost in meditation. He "mused with his own heart," Herbert of Bosham tells us. Suddenly Thomas called Herbert to him and said: "I had a vision last night."

"What kind of vision?" Herbert asked.

"I saw a venerable man who stood by me and handed me ten talents."

Herbert, ordinarily ready enough to offer his opinions, did not venture an interpretation of the dream. But the reference to the parable of the talents (Matt. 25:14) must have been perfectly clear to both of them. In confiding the dream, Thomas was virtually promising that he did not intend to be a fearful servant who would bury his talents in the ground. Significantly, he referred to the dream as a vision; it must have seemed to him, coming at this moment, a direct revelation, a divine injunction. Humility and self-doubt followed naturally. For seven years at King Henry's side Thomas had observed the dangers of power. He himself had been able to warn Henry against mistakes, and had been saved from mistakes of his own by his subordinate position. But now?

As they drew near to Canterbury, their horses stepping gingerly on the ancient Roman pavement of Watling Street, Thomas said as if continuing the conversation about the dream: "Hereafter, Herbert, I want you to tell me, candidly and in secret,

1 2 5

what people are saying about me. And if you see anything in me that you regard as a fault, feel free to tell me in private. For from now on people will talk about me, but not to me. It is dangerous for men in power if no one dares to tell them when they go wrong. And four eyes see more than two."

It is characteristic of that humorless and exasperating writer, Herbert of Bosham, that he gives us no more of this important conversation, but instead launches into one of his interminable invocatory digressions: *"O prudentia viri!"* and so on. Herbert could not keep his mind on his subject, but he loved to write. In an age of verbosity, when a simple business letter could easily turn into an elaborate essay, Herbert was notorious for his prolixity. As we have mentioned, he was also given to inventing speeches, and it is as much the brevity of the above conversation as its psychological verisimilitude that marks it as probably authentic.

From other sources as well as from his own biography of Thomas we can see Herbert as a proud, quick-tempered, and courageous man, but also at times vain, obstinate, and foolish. He was deeply learned in scripture—Thomas employed him to fill the gaps in his own knowledge—but seems to have imbibed more of the spirit of the Old Testament than the New. Whenever compromise was afoot, Herbert was against it. Given Thomas's own natural tendency to meet opposition head on, Herbert was not the best confidant and intimate adviser he might have chosen. The king's party knew this, and disliked Herbert for his bluntness and intransigence. Yet these same qualities also won him their admiration, as his fellow biographer, William FitzStephen, shows.

At one stage of the struggle between Thomas and Henry, John of Salisbury and Herbert called on the king to ask for the restoration of their sequestered revenues. After John had made his plea in vain, Herbert was summoned. The king said to his men: "Look sharp now—you will see a proud man!" Herbert entered, tall and handsome like his master Thomas, and something of a dandy as well. He wore a tunic of green Auxerre cloth and an ornamented cloak of the same material, hanging from shoulders to ankles "in the German fashion." He spoke more forthrightly than John, and indicated that he had learned well the lesson Thomas had taught him on that ride to the consecration in Canterbury. "He alone is faithful to the king who does not permit the king to err," he said when his loyalty was challenged.

An exchange followed in the course of which Herbert became steadily more impudent, and the king angrier, until at last Henry exclaimed: "For shame! Is this son of a priest to trouble my kingdom and disturb my peace?" To which Herbert replied: "I do not do so at all; but neither am I the son of a priest, for I was born before, not after, my father became a priest; nor is a man the son of a king unless his father was a king when he begot him."

Henry's reaction to this bold insult (Henry's father, of course, had never been a king) is not recorded. But Henry was no despot; the manners of his court were free and easy, and his nobles could enjoy a joke at his expense. One of the barons present, Jourdain Taisson of the great Norman fief of Thury-Harcourt, blurted out: "I don't care whose son he is. I would give half my land to have him my son."

Herbert was only one of the *eruditi,* the coterie of witty and learned men whom Thomas now gathered around him at Canterbury, following the example of Theobald. John of Salisbury remained the luminary of this group whose distinction would be evidenced by the future careers of its various members: of the twenty listed by Herbert of Bosham, two became archbishops, five bishops, and one—although he joined the company in exile—ultimately reigned over the Church as Pope Urban III. With these men Thomas, who like Theobald was neither the best educated nor the most creative mind in his curia, virtually went back to school. He had never lost his taste for learning, but in the years of his chancellorship he had seldom had the leisure to indulge it. Now, amid a multitude of new administrative duties, he tried to become what his great predecessor Anselm had been: a true priest and doctor of the Church. In fact, he modeled himself on Anselm and carried about with him as a kind of manual a book of Anselm's prayers.

The majority of the *eruditi* who formed Thomas's intimate circle were English by birth. There were also several Lombards, one Welshman (the archbishop's official cross-bearer, Alexander

Llewelyn), and only one man specifically identified as Norman: Hugh of Nunant, subsequently Bishop of Coventry. It is difficult to assess the significance of this fact. Certainly it does not justify the wholly discredited theories of Augustin Thierry that Thomas was the leader of a Saxon revolt against Norman overlords. Quite the contrary, for some of the persons whom Herbert identifies as *natione Anglus* were evidently of Norman descent, like Thomas himself. The large number of Englishmen (that is, men born in England) in Thomas's circle may have been accidental; but if it was not, it suggests an incipient, probably half-conscious national bias on his part.

✠   ✠   ✠

As we read the accounts of Thomas's change of heart, and of his chastity, charity, and penitence, we must bear in mind that our authors are men writing in a long tradition of hagiography. Even so, the testimony is so unanimous (and uncontradicted by Thomas's enemies) that we must accept it as in the main true: from the moment that Thomas became Archbishop of Canterbury his thinking and habits underwent a great change. He had put on a "new man," to use the theological language of the time. If we remember the religious fervor of the age that built the great Gothic cathedrals (Notre Dame of Paris was begun the year after his consecration), we will not find his change of heart surprising. There was nothing hypocritical about it; men do not wear a hidden hair shirt, submit to flagellation, or melt into tears at Mass without a genuine conviction that they are "not worthy." In conversations with his friends, Thomas would frequently review his "sinful" past and refer to the fact that he had been transformed from "a patron of actors and a follower of hounds to a shepherd of souls."

All Thomas's actions in the early months after the consecration bespoke the change from luxury-loving chancellor to anguished convert. Before dawn every morning, after matins had been sung, thirteen poor folk were called into a lonely room in the archiepiscopal palace. There they would find a table set for them. The archbishop in person would enter, lay aside his robes, and wash the feet of Christ's poor. Then he would wait on them at table, and finally dismiss them with a present of four silver pennies each, asking them to pray for his soul. Although these acts of charity and humility were performed secretly, it was impossible that word of them should not get abroad. But it is unfair to assert that he undertook these penitences cynically, in order to court popularity. If he had been that kind of opportunist, he would have yielded to the king at the first signs of discord.

The money that Thomas had formerly lavished on ostentation, he now used for the benefit of the poor. Theobald had doubled the amount of alms given by his predecessors; Thomas again doubled it. But, as in the past, he continued to serve rare and delicate dishes to his thronging guests and retainers. He himself, however, ate sparingly, and instead of minstrels and actors for entertainment, there were readings from sacred books, as in any monastic refectory. Laymen sat at a separate table, where they could amuse themselves somewhat less solemnly. There were pages aplenty to wait on them, for by ancient custom the Archbishop of Canterbury was entitled to the service of the second sons of barons. Among those pages was the king's son, young Henry, who still remained in the household.

Thomas took very seriously the judicial duties that now devolved upon him. He held court frequently. On most days, as soon as Mass had been celebrated he left the church and entered the hall where cases were brought before him. Sometimes he called his suffragan bishops to assist him. As a judge, says Herbert, he was the fairest of men. Moreover, he introduced an innovation that stirred as much amazement as his new humility and piety: he dispensed justice without charging a fee, refusing to accept the gifts that were the universal perquisite of a lord sitting in judgment over his inferiors.

All accounts of Thomas's conduct during his first few months in the new office emphasize the hieratic solemnity and almost pedantic orderliness of his arrangements. He rose very early, devoted many hours to prayer and silent study, and nevertheless found time to fit into his schedule all of his ordinary duties as well as the extraordinary ones he had laid upon himself

as a penance for his former life. No greater contrast can be
conceived than that between the quiet regularity of the archbishop's household and the everlasting hubbub and discomfort of
King Henry's court, where no one knew what changes of mind
and place each day might have in store, since everything depended on the king's whim. As chancellor, Thomas had put up
with the chaos, and there is no record that it affected his friendship with the king; but it had clearly gone against the grain. A
man of regular habits can forgive but can never overlook sloven-
liness and disorganization.

✠   ✠   ✠

We have said little hitherto about Henry's motives in making Thomas Becket Archbishop of Canterbury. No complex explanations are in fact needed. There is no reason to assume, as so
many writers have done, that Henry had the sinister intention of
using Thomas to destroy the Church. The promotion of Thomas
seemed to Henry an altogether natural, logical step to strengthen
his rule in England, where he himself preferred not to live.
Thomas, the native Londoner, had a knowledge of English affairs that he would always lack. Henry was often unfamiliar with
the details of English social conditions and English administration, which is why he had to inquire what English customs were
and partly why he wanted them reduced to writing. But he
possessed a fine apprehension of the nature of government, and
he had instinctively grasped the great unsolved problem of the
English "Constitution": the existence side by side of two virtually
independent powers with interdependent hierarchies, jurisdictions, courts, finances, and properties. There was constant tension between the independent and the interdependent aspects of
these powers.

To a degree, the problem was shared by all of Europe; but it
was more acute in England because of the traditional isolation of
the English Church and because there were only two archbishops
in the country, one of whom was universally recognized as primate, in spite of the perennial claims of York. What more natural
then, to Henry's mind, than to assure harmony in the relation-

ships of Church and State by uniting the highest offices in both at the very top. The plan seemed to work in Germany, where the archbishops of Mainz and Cologne were archchancellors of the Empire. Given so suitable a man as Thomas Becket, whose talents lay equally in the secular and the ecclesiastical realms, the result should be a concord hitherto unknown in England. Far from plotting against the Church, in appointing Becket, Henry was attempting a reasonable method of ending the traditional conflicts between archbishop and king.

Henry, proceeding on this assumption, obtained a papal dispensation to allow his archbishop to retain the post of chancellor. But Thomas, with a haste as tactless as it was expressive of his determination to be his own master henceforth, sent a messenger to Henry, still overseas, bearing the Great Seal. *"Pur les olz Deu*—by the eyes of God!" Henry swore his favorite oath. "Doesn't he want to keep it any more?"

The messenger, Master Ernulf, replied: "He feels that the burdens of two offices are too much for him."

"He no longer cares to be in my service," Henry snapped. "I feel that."

It is scarcely surprising that in his first anger Henry took Thomas's resignation of the chancellorship as virtually equivalent to the feudal *diffidatio,* the formal renunciation of fealty which a vassal was required by custom to announce to his lord before he opposed him. Henry could scarcely believe the excuse of overwork, for Thomas still held in his hand the archdeaconry of Canterbury.[1] For his charities and his sumptuous household, Thomas needed larger revenues than his predecessor, and the archdeaconry had a very considerable income.

Partly in the search for additional sources of revenue, partly to remedy the slackness of Theobald's later years, Thomas now began to reassert Canterbury's claim to alienated property. That in itself was nothing unusual; every bishop tried to do the same—all the more so since during Stephen's reign much church land had been lost and never recovered. But Thomas laid about

---

[1] As punishment, Henry soon forced him to give up that post. The new archdeacon, Geoffrey Ridel, became one of Thomas's most determined enemies.

him with a heavy hand. He made a visitation of his archdiocese, and wherever he found an estate in the possession of a layman which he knew belonged to his see, he had his men-at-arms abruptly seize it, without troubling about litigation. If property had lapsed for some time, so that there could be reasonable doubt as to its ownership, he produced documents and the testimony of old men of the district—the traditional method for settling disputes over land. So long as the farms and manors of lesser lords were in question, Thomas was able to recover them without much difficulty. But when he began to lay claim to holdings of great lords and tenants-in-chief of the king, he met stubborn resistance. The castle and honor of Tonbridge were in the hands of Roger, Earl of Clare, who was related to most of the nobility of England. Moreover, Roger's sister was a woman of extraordinary beauty, with whom Henry had been passionately in love at one time. Thomas must have known this; he was either rash or relying too heavily on the king's friendship when he put in a claim for Tonbridge.

He was at the same time challenging another of Henry's powerful nobles, who in this case was also a tenant of the see of Canterbury. Thomas appointed a clerk named Laurence to the church of Eynsford. The lord of the town, William of Eynsford, forcibly ejected Laurence's men; an affair that was to have an ominous sequel. We shall return to this; but it is important to note now a simple fact that has been consistently overlooked in all discussions of this matter: the quarrel was essentially one over money. The ecclesiastical question—whether the priest Laurence was better suited to exercise his office than the clerk whom William of Eynsford had in mind—was not at issue. The right of presentation to a benefice—advowson was the technical term for it—was coupled with the right to collect a tax known as the first fruits, or annates, from the beneficed cleric. Since this tax amounted to a full year's revenue of the church in question, the sum was considerable. In insisting on presenting his own clerk, William of Eynsford was refusing to renounce income he had previously enjoyed. And Thomas, in presenting Laurence, was demanding money that his predecessor had failed to collect.

The affected landowners complained of these proceedings to the king, either by letter or by going overseas to the court, for

Henry was still on the Continent. But Thomas had with fore-thought obtained the king's permission to reclaim alienated church property, and Henry put off the petitioners, saying that he would soon return to England and look into the matter. For the time being, Henry ignored the whispers that the archbishop was planning to make himself more powerful than the king. Henry knew enough of courtiers and petitioners not to believe everything he heard, and he was aware that his friend Thomas had made enemies during his chancellorship. Although the resignation of that office had been a blow, he was not prepared to condemn Thomas on that score alone. The reported change in Thomas's life and character puzzled him more than the charges of avarice and pride. He resolved to cross the Channel and see for himself.

He announced that he would spend Christmas in England. Delayed by contrary winds, he tarried at Cherbourg until nearly the end of January. When at last he landed at Southampton, Thomas was there waiting to meet him, little Henry at his hand. Some of the older writers say that the king greeted Thomas with some coolness, but Herbert of Bosham, who was present, asserts that they met with mutual expressions of gladness. They exchanged the kiss of peace, and conferred frequently and privately with one another. In the face of such a show of harmony, Becket's enemies "hid themselves and dissimulated their complaints."

Together the king and archbishop traveled up to London. They were met there by the Council of the realm, consisting of all the bishops and abbots and most of the greater nobles. An expedition against the troublesome Rhys ap Gryffyd, Prince of South Wales, was projected; Thomas had already made the necessary preparations. All consented to the decision of Thomas and Henry that the vacant see of London ought to be filled promptly. Bishop Richard of Beaumais II had died the previous year, after prolonged paralysis, leaving the finances and administration of the see in disarray. Next to Canterbury, London was unquestionably the most important episcopal seat in England. Henry, now no longer certain that he had done well to place Thomas in Canterbury, decided to take out a form of insurance. He would have Gilbert Foliot, Bishop of Hereford, transferred to London.

Perhaps to Henry's surprise, Thomas raised no objection. The new Thomas Becket saw no reason not to respect Gilbert for his opposition, the previous year, to the old Thomas Becket's promotion. And Thomas could remember, although Henry seemed to have forgotten, that Gilbert had once placed his diocese under the interdict to punish the obstinacy of the Earl of Hereford. He had also threatened a royal officer with excommunication for citing the Dean of Hereford before the secular court. Where the interests of the Church were at issue, Gilbert seemed to be a man after Thomas's own heart.

The translation of a bishop from one see to another was uncommon, and required papal consent. Fortunately, Pope Alexander was in Paris where he could be reached quickly and easily. Ralph, Archdeacon of London,[2] was accordingly dispatched to Paris with letters from Henry and Thomas. Alexander readily acceded to the plan; he was more than eager at this time to keep in the good graces of Henry, and welcomed the prospect of Henry's leaning for advice on a prelate so notable for austerity and loyalty to the Church. Thomas's letter began with a pardonable tribute to his native city as well as to his "venerable brother Gilbert":

> We are all aware that the city of London is noble and famous above all the other cities of the kingdom. For much of the public business of the realm is conducted there; our lord king commonly resides there; and the notables frequently meet there. The church of London has long been deprived of her pastor. She desires a bishop whose upright life, knowledge of Scripture, and wisdom in secular affairs would match the excellence of the city itself. After due deliberation, therefore, the clergy, our lord king and the Holy See have unanimously requested that you be translated to the church of London. It will be for the common good of the kingdom and the needs of the Church that you bear the burden of pastoral cure there. We enjoin you, therefore . . . not to withhold your consent.

Thus Thomas placed in a position of power the man who subsequently, as he himself would later write, "first divided the

---

[2] Subsequently the famous historian and Dean of St. Paul's, Ralph de Diceto.

134

unity of the English church and armed the minds and hands of the king and his officials for the destruction of ourselves and of ecclesiastical liberty." Even more dangerous than possession of the see of London was the new relationship that sprang up between Gilbert and the king, for Gilbert, apparently at the pope's request and with Henry's glad consent, became Henry's confessor. In a sense, he was replacing Thomas as intimate adviser and mentor. He did not have it in him, however, to replace Thomas in Henry's affections; he was too cold and reserved a man, too much the professional churchman for that. But he had in ample measure the captious temperament, the learning, the eloquence, and the quiet belligerence to make him the leader of the opposition to Thomas when the time came. Almost immediately, in fact, he asserted his independence of Thomas by refusing to take the oath of canonical obedience. As Bishop of Hereford, he argued, he had already sworn obedience to the Archbishop of Canterbury—that is, Theobald—and therefore need not do it again. Probably his motive at this time was less the desire to antagonize Thomas than the hope that he would succeed in having London raised to archiepiscopal status. Henry of Winchester had entertained similar dreams about his see many years ago.

Old habit was hard to break, and Thomas now found himself in almost constant attendance on the king. He and Henry went together to Canterbury to attend the monks' procession on Palm Sunday. They then continued on to Dover, where they met the Count of Flanders and his son to draw up a treaty on the military and other services owed by the count to the King of England. In these negotiations, Thomas seems to have played his old part of diplomat. But the difference in the relations and the duties of the once inseparable pair became apparent with the onset of spring. In April, Henry set out on the expedition against the Welsh. It was to prove little more than an armed progress; the intimidated Welsh prince submitted without a fight. The previous year, in Normandy, Thomas had headed a picked force of knights for Henry. Now there could be no question of his personal participation. The Archbishop of Canterbury could not lead an army. Instead, Thomas stressed his transformation into an ecclesiastic by leading the bishops of England to the Council of the Church that Pope Alexander had convoked at Tours, his present residence.

Alexander's pontificate so far had been nothing if not stormy. Scandinavia, the Holy Roman Empire, Hungary, Bohemia, and much of northern Italy had recognized his rival, the antipope Victor. Alexander held the allegiance of England, France, Spain, Sicily, and southern Italy. After a brief attempt to remain in Rome against the arms of the Germans and the riotous factions of the city, Alexander had fled to the safety of France. He now called a council in order to consolidate his hold on the papacy and denounce his opponents.

In requesting the presence of Thomas Becket and the other English bishops, Alexander made a significant concession to the English tradition that high ecclesiastics might attend councils abroad only with royal permission. "We decree," he wrote in a letter to Henry and the clergy of England dated from Paris March 18, 1163—just one day *before* his letter consenting to Gilbert Foliot's translation—"that your consent is not to result in any detriment or inconvenience to yourself or your heirs; that it is not to introduce any *new custom* into your kingdom, nor diminish in any way the dignity of the realm." We may, if we will, read into this letter much of the future relationship between Alexander III and Henry II. Clearly, Alexander would not have recognized the king's right to keep his bishops from answering a pontifical summons if he had not been painfully dependent on the support of England and France.

Thomas Becket prepared to cross the Channel in his customary lavish manner. If he had been magnificent as chancellor, he must be more so as archbishop. He arrived at Gravelines in Flanders with a great train which included Herbert of Bosham, who has described his reception. Count Philip and the other nobles of Flanders came to meet him as if he were a reigning prince, vying with one another to honor the statesman-ecclesiastic whom they regarded as more powerful than ever. His journey across Normandy and Maine resembled a triumphal progress, even though this time he had no monkeys riding the backs of his horses. When word of his arrival reached Tours, the folk of the city poured out through the gates to greet him. Cardinals and other princes of the Church accompanied them in such numbers that, it was said, only two were left in attendance on the pope himself. Alexander, rather alarmed at the prospect of so many people crowding into his private chambers in the wake of the archbishop, came out into the great hall to meet him: thus giving the impression of a signal honor which he had possibly not intended. For although the faithful Herbert of Bosham declares that the pope had long desired to see Thomas, the pope's words as Herbert quotes them sound like a reproof thinly veiled as consideration for a tired traveler: "Go and rest, brother, for rest is necessary after labor."

The popular welcome at Tours cannot be accounted for solely on the ground that Thomas was primate of the most powerful king in the Western world. To be sure, in honoring the archbishop the people and the dignitaries of the Church were paying tribute to Henry. But above all they were curious. They wanted to see this phenomenon whose abrupt conversion from man of the world to paragon of religion prompted people to say: "This is the finger of God." In an age of religious fervor, the story of the seeming miracle had spread swiftly. Moreover, it was an anniversary for Thomas: the Council of Tours opened on Trinity Sunday, exactly one year after his consecration as archbishop.

Although seventeen cardinals, one hundred twenty-four bishops, and four hundred fourteen abbots had assembled at the pope's summons, the greatest honor was shown to the representatives of the English Church. Thomas and his suffragans were seated at the right hand of the pope, his old enemy, Roger of Pont l'Evêque, Archbishop of York, on the pope's left. The sermon at the first session was preached by Thomas's old acquaintance, Bishop Arnulf of Lisieux, who denounced Emperor Frederick Barbarossa as a tyrant and passionately proclaimed the unity of the Church.

The chief business of the council was the excommunication of the antipope Octavian and all his followers. Among the more important of the decrees was a condemnation of the "damnable heresy" that had lately arisen in the district of Toulouse and had "already infected vast numbers throughout Gascony and other provinces." This was the Catharist heresy, which in the following century was to be so bloodily crushed in the horrors of the Albigensian Crusade. It was already spreading north, and in three years some members of the sect (which was rapidly becoming an independent Church) would reach England, where they were mercilessly condemned to miserable deaths, being stripped of their clothes and driven out into the winter cold.

One decree of the council certainly made a deep impression on the mind of Thomas Becket, and prompted some of the conduct that so offended King Henry after he returned home. Canon VII strictly forbade bishops and other prelates to "grant to the laity the tithes and disposal of churches." This was precisely the substance of the dispute between William of Eynsford and Thomas, and the archbishop returned to England determined to enforce his right to present a priest to the church at Eynsford—with consequences that we shall shortly see.

Thomas himself conducted some negotiations with Pope Alexander. He presented a plea for the canonization of his predecessor Anselm. He likewise obtained confirmation of the privileges of the see of Canterbury—presumably a reassurance of its primacy over England and particularly over the archbishopric of York. It would be well if we knew more about the personal impression that Thomas and Alexander made upon one another; but here our sources veil everything in generalities. It is surely not speculating too far to assume that both men were struck by their similarities. Alexander, like Thomas, was a former chancellor (of the papacy), an experienced canon lawyer, a theologian who had been influenced by Abelard, a man of diplomatic skill and high executive capacity who dispatched his cardinal-legates unceasingly throughout the Christian world. The most important feature of this council was the meeting of the two men, although neither could know this at the time. Nevertheless, pope and archbishop had an opportunity to exchange views and to take the measure of each other; and it must have surprised and pleased the pope to learn that this English archbishop held an even more stiffly high-Gregorian position on the privileges and immunities of the Church than he himself. William of Newburgh relates that at the council Thomas, "unable to endure the pricks of conscience, secretly resigned into the pope's hands the archbishopric, which he had received not honestly and canonically, as it were, but by the agency and at the hands of the king. The pope, approving his action, reimposed the burden of pastoral office upon him at the Church's hand, and healed the over-scrupulous prelate of the wound of a troubled conscience."

It is a dramatic story, but probably not true; for as we have seen above, Thomas at this time felt confident that he had been canonically elected. In any case, Alexander dismissed him more graciously than he had received him, giving him his blessing and the kiss of peace. Thomas returned swiftly to England, where he was joyfully greeted by the king "as a father by his son."

IX

First Disputes

"THE ANCIENT ENEMY," says William FitzStephen, "envied so upright a pillar in the Lord's Church, so bright a candle on God's candlestick. The enemy sowed tares. . . . The king's courtiers, eager to please him and itching to gain his ears, defamed the archbishop and hated him without cause."

Any man who exerted as much influence as Thomas provided cause enough for hatred. But Thomas himself was not blameless. He fostered the hostility of the courtiers by his haughtiness and inability to remember that he was no longer the king's chief adviser in secular affairs; he fostered it further by the tenacity with which he held on to all possible sources of income. This seeming greed was the obverse of his munificence: he was constantly in need of money to sustain his lavish way of life and his generous charities.

Significantly, the first overt quarrel with Henry arose over a financial question. Shortly after Thomas's return from Tours, the king held a council at Woodstock (where in after years—so the ballads relate—he was to build a bower for "Fair Rosamond"). Henry, whose own revenues had been seriously diminished by the ending of the vacancy at Canterbury, declared his intention of collecting for the fisc a payment of two shillings per hide of land, known as the "sheriff's aid." There has been much discussion of the nature and origin of this payment which need not concern us here. It had in any case become a customary due rather than a legal tax, and was used by the sheriffs for their own benefit.

Henry's motive in demanding that the aid be paid to him directly was not only a financial one. It was part of his general policy of tightening and centralizing his administration, of keeping his officials under close supervision and seeing to it that they governed in his interest and that of his people rather than their own. Thomas's motive in opposing him sprang in part from a general concern for liberty, not just the liberty of the Church. He objected in principle to the conversion of a customary gift into a legal tax. But beyond that, he felt that Henry was making a grave political error in depriving the very men on whom he depended for honest and efficient government of an important source of income. The sheriffs would inevitably try to compensate themselves for the loss by other means: either by cheating the treasury or by illegal exactions. The outcome of Henry's inquest of 1170, when he sent out itinerant justices to investigate the financial affairs of the sheriffs, proves that they did in fact resort to such devices. When that inquest was over, Henry found it necessary to dismiss most of his old sheriffs.

It was, then, in his former capacity of informed adviser on governmental matters that Thomas told Henry to his face that he ought not to demand the sheriff's aid as revenue. "Nor will we give it to you as revenue, my lord king," he said. "But if the sheriffs and servants and officials of the shires serve us worthily, and defend our vassals, we will not withhold the aid from them."

Thomas had given similar advice to the king many times in the past, and of course had quarreled with him several times on matters of policy. Such disagreements, inevitable between two strong-minded men, had not hitherto led to any serious breach. But in the past, Thomas the chancellor had been Henry's confidential minister and had probably thrashed out most such questions in private. Now he was disputing one of Henry's proposals before the assembled nobility of the kingdom and from a different vantage point: that of the primate, whom a King of England had always to reckon with as almost an equal and half a rival. Henry's Angevin temper flared at this public rebuke.

"By God's eyes," he swore, "it will be given as revenue and inscribed in the king's roll. Nor is it seemly for you to contradict me when no one is trying to impose a burden on any of your men."

Thomas had a temper of his own, and he was no longer willing to let the king treat him like an underling. He returned oath for oath: "By the reverence of those eyes by which you have sworn, my lord king," he said, "it will not be given by all my land, and not a penny from any land under the jurisdiction of the Church."

The king fell silent, rebuffed, realizing that he had voluntarily surrendered the power to coerce Thomas. Perhaps for the first time the whispers of the courtiers acquired substantial meaning for him: Thomas as archbishop was going to give him trouble. His temperament demanded a public retort to what he regarded as a public insult. At the same time he understood that his decisions on secular matters could no longer directly affect Thomas. If he were to retaliate, it would have to be on some matter that affected the clergy. One lay ready to hand.

William the Conqueror's separation of the secular and ecclesiastical courts had been prolific of abuses. Crimes committed by men who enjoyed the status of clerics could not be tried in the king's courts; and to Henry's mind the ecclesiastical courts did not punish them with sufficient severity to deter further breaches of "the king's peace." Lawless acts by clerks and men who masqueraded as clerks were on the increase. Robert de Monte lamented: "England is at this time infested by a kind of robbers unheard of until our days. They go about under the disguise of religion; and having dressed themselves up in the garment of monks, they join travelers; and when they have arrived in some lone road or in some forest, they summon their companions by signal, murder the travelers, and plunder them of their money and goods." When such robbers were caught, they pleaded clerical immunity and demanded trial in the ecclesiastical courts. A large body of "headless" clerks (as they were called because they had no superiors) roamed about the country, and complaints against them were commonplace.

Henry had encountered the problem of these "criminous" clerks before. There had, for example, been the case of the rural dean who blackmailed a citizen of Scarborough by falsely charging the man's wife with adultery. The dean was haled into court and tried in the presence of the king, two bishops, the Archbishop of York, and the treasurer of York, John of Canterbury.[1] When the dean could offer no proof for his slander, Henry made the angry remark cited earlier that archdeacons and deans exacted more money from the people than he himself collected in revenue every year. He asked what punishment was to be inflicted on the dean. Clerical esprit de corps was very strong: John of Canterbury suggested that the man be sentenced to return the money he had extorted and be placed "at the mercy" of the Archbishop of York. In practice this meant he would pay a fine to the archbishop. Richard de Lucy, always jealous of the royal prerogatives, thereupon asked: "And what will you adjudge to our lord the king, whose ordinances the man has violated?" In effect, de Lucy was demanding that some part of the fine be paid to the king. But John replied forthrightly, with that spirit of guarding the Church's immunities which he had imbibed in Theobald's household: "Nothing, because he is a clerk." Richard retorted: "I will not sustain that sentence!" and stalked out of the room.

The ecclesiastics supported the sentence. Henry, offended, ordered that it be appealed to Archbishop Theobald. Nothing came of the matter, however, because before the date set for the prosecution of the appeal, Henry's brother Geoffrey died and the king hastened across the Channel to Normandy. Nevertheless he brooded about the matter, for when he had a moment of relaxation a year and a half later—at Falaise, Christmas 1159—he reverted to it and issued a decree that "no dean shall bring an accusation against any person without the testimony of such individuals in the neighborhood as are of good life and reputation."

At Woodstock now, with Thomas's intervention in the matter of the sheriff's aids freshly rankling, Henry raised the question of the line between secular and ecclesiastical jurisdiction and the conduct of the clergy in England. He asked for a report on capital crimes and was informed that more than a hundred mur-

---

[1] Thomas Becket's close friend John was a man with a great future in the Church. Formerly one of Theobald's clerks, he soon became Bishop of Poitiers and ultimately Archbishop of Lyons.

ders had been committed by clerks in England since the beginning of his reign. Among the cases of homicide was a former canon of Bedford named Philip de Brois who had allegedly killed a knight and been tried in the Bishop of Lincoln's court. There he had cleared himself by the ancient practice of compurgation: that is, he had found twelve honorable men willing to swear that they believed him innocent of the crime. These men did not constitute a jury in the sense that they heard evidence and decided on the basis of it; and the trial was more of a rite than a forensic proceeding. Nevertheless, compurgation was not wholly a method of thwarting justice. In the twelfth century it was not easy to persuade men to risk their immortal souls by perjury; a good many cases occurred in which criminals could not obtain compurgators. On the other hand, crimes of sudden passion committed by men of good repute might well go unpunished under such a system.

Simon FitzPeter, the sheriff and itinerant justice in Bedfordshire, either because he bore Philip de Brois an old grudge or because he genuinely believed him guilty, reopened the case. He repeated the "slanderous charge of homicide" and ordered Philip to stand trial once more. Philip, a man of high birth, responded by heaping abuse on the sheriff, who promptly reported to the king this offense against the royal dignity. Henry, so everyone believed, was delighted with this opportunity to attack the clergy. He insisted that the incident be described to his barons and bishops in the presence of Thomas Becket. Then, assuming out of hand that the murder charge was true, he demanded that Philip be punished both for homicide and for abuse of a royal official.

This case marked the first great clash between archbishop and king on the question of clerical immunities. Thomas, with his legal training, recognized at once how much was at stake. He made no attempt to divert the king. Instead, he flatly refused to allow a clerk to be tried in the king's court, and took Philip under his protection. The only concession he made was to permit some of the king's prominent laymen to observe Philip's second trial in the archbishop's court. But the court itself was strictly ecclesiastical; the judges were Thomas himself and some of his suffragan bishops.

Philip had by this time come to his senses. He realized his danger and now did his best to soften his judges. He ought not to be tried again for homicide, he argued, since he had already been tried and acquitted. On the other hand, he recognized that he had been wrong in insulting the king's officer and wished to make whatever amends the court would demand—"only let it be reasonable," he pleaded.

Thomas and his bishops saw an opportunity to placate Henry. They imposed an unusually harsh sentence for what was after all only a verbal offense. The murder charge could not be tried again, they agreed. But their sentence for abusing the king's officer obviously, although not admittedly, made some concession to Henry's view that Philip had been judged too leniently in the Bishop of Lincoln's court. "We decree," the judges declared, "that your prebend shall remain under the king's hand for two years, and your possessions and all your income distributed to the poor at his will and pleasure." In addition, Philip was "to stand naked before the sheriff after the fashion of laymen"—that is, to be flogged publicly by him.

Philip, glad to have escaped the death sentence Henry had threatened, submitted to the verdict. Nevertheless Henry remained unsatisfied. An insult to his officer ought to have been tried in his own court, he insisted. "By the eyes of God," he blurted out when he heard the verdict, "now you will swear to me that you judged a just judgement and did not spare the man because he is a clerk."

This initial clash with Thomas was followed immediately by another, for on July 22 Roger, Earl of Clare answered the archbishop's summons in Canterbury's suit against him for the castle of Tonbridge. Henry's anger was so exacerbated that Thomas did not venture to press his claim against the powerful earl. He decided, however, to make an example of William of Eynsford, a lesser magnate who held only seven knights' fees. William, we will recall, had actually laid hands on Canterbury men by forcibly expelling the priest Laurence from Eynsford Church, and Thomas possibly hoped that a dramatic counterstroke would serve as a warning to the lay nobility of England. As soon as he returned to Canterbury, therefore, Thomas resorted to the ulti-

mate weapon at the command of a churchman: he excommunicated William of Eynsford.

Excommunication was regarded as a kind of plague affect-
ing all who came into contact with the excommunicate. For that
reason, William the Conqueror had insisted that none of his
"tenants-in-chief," those who held their fiefs directly from the
Crown, might be excommunicated without the knowledge and
consent of the king. Tenants-in-chief were, on the whole, the
great nobles of the realm with whom the king daily consulted and
consorted. The Conqueror's custom was therefore necessary to
protect the king from the contagion of excommunication. Henry
promptly sent a message to Thomas demanding that he absolve
William of Eynsford. Thomas temporized. He suggested that he
and Henry meet to discuss the case. Henry angrily refused to see
him; until the matter was settled, he would communicate with
Thomas only by messenger, he declared.

At length Thomas decided to yield, to forgo the revenues of
Eynsford church in the interest of peace with the king. He sent an
envoy to Henry, who was then at Windsor Castle, announcing
that he had already absolved William. But appeasement came too
late. "I owe him no thanks for it now," Henry exclaimed.

It seemed almost as if the clerics of England were conspiring to create causes of dissension between king and archbishop.
Henry had recently procured the election of his cousin Roger, the
son of Robert of Gloucester and one of his boyhood friends, to
the bishopric of Worcester. In August, Thomas officiated at the
consecration of Roger, whom he knew and liked as a learned
and spiritual young man. Almost immediately he had to subject
his new suffragan to a first test of obedience and a choice between
archbishop and king. A clerk in the diocese of Worcester was
accused of having raped a young girl and murdered her father.
The king ordered trial in the secular court. Thomas interfered; he
commanded Roger of Worcester to put the clerk into the episcopal prison and not to allow the royal officials to touch him. What
the clerk's ultimate fate was, we do not know.

The lines of battle were already drawn, and by September of
1163 both Henry and Thomas seemed to realize that they were
facing a hard contest. The conflict Thomas had feared before his

election was coming upon him sooner than he had expected and on ground less solid than he could have wished. Defense of the property of the Church and the immunities of the clergy were good causes; but it was unfortunate that his endeavors should make him seem to be countenancing rape and murder. He tried vainly to assuage Henry's anger by imposing more severe punishments on clerks, sentencing one to branding as well as degradation for stealing a silver chalice from St. Mary-le-Bow, and another to exile.

Such acts of severity, which could scarcely be justified by canon law, suggest something of Thomas's nervousness at the time. Indeed, he seems to have passed through a psychological crisis—scarcely surprising in view of the profound change in his life and situation within fifteen months. The loss of Henry's friendship was a personal as well as a political misfortune. His agitation is plainly revealed in a letter he wrote to Pope Alexander during September. It was the first of many letters of similar tenor, so many that it would be impossible to quote them at length. But since it was the first, and representative, we shall this time reproduce it in full:

To his dearest lord and father, Alexander, by the grace of God supreme pontiff, greetings and all obedience in Christ from Thomas, humble minister of the church of Canterbury:

The letter of consolation which your Paternity has designed to address to us would certainly bring great balm to one suffering from ordinary woes; and if my troubles were single, they would give me hope of being able to breathe freely. But from day to day evil grows stronger here and injustices multiply—not ours, but Christ's, though since they are Christ's, they are so much the more our own. Storms follow one upon the other like the waves of the sea, and it seems to us that we can expect nothing but shipwreck. What remains for us but to waken Him as if he were asleep in the boat, saying: "Lord, save us, we perish!" Iniquity has chosen its moment well, having seen the precarious state of the Roman Church. For what is poured out upon the head, be it good or bad, sweet or bitter, runs down over the beard and stains the clothing. What Jesus Christ bought with his blood is wrested from him; the power of the world

147

reaches out its hand for his portion. Neither the ordinances of the holy fathers nor the statutes of the canons, whose very name is detested among us, now suffice to protect the clergy, who hitherto were exempt from lay jurisdiction by special privilege. But since it would be long and tedious to relate in writing all that we are suffering, we are sending to your Paternity Master Henry, a faithful servant of yours and mine, and have charged him to inform you by word of mouth of all that he has seen and heard here. Please believe him as if we ourselves were speaking directly to you. Know that if it were possible we should much prefer to visit you in person than by proxy. We speak to you as our father and lord; but we pray you to keep what we say strictly confidential. For nothing is safe here. Almost everything that we say in public or even in private is repeated to the king. Woe to us who are reserved for such times of calamities. *With what hard and dire a servitude we are now paying for the liberty we possessed in our former state.* Should we not have fled rather than see the patrimony of the Crucified One given over to destruction? But we do not know whither to flee, if not to Him who is our refuge and our strength.[2]

A somewhat conspiratorial bent, an almost paranoid anxiety, a profound regret at having miscalculated in accepting the promotion, speak from this letter. But along with dismay, the strength of religious feeling is unmistakable. It is impossible to read letters such as this and believe that Thomas was hypocritical, that his role as a man of religion was artificial.

The expectation of worse trouble to come, which Thomas here expressed so strongly, was soon fulfilled. Henry issued a summons to his bishops and barons for another council—he had taken to holding these "parliaments" at quarterly intervals—to meet in his palace at Westminster. Ostensibly the purpose was to settle the issue pending between Thomas and Roger of York: Canterbury's claim to the primacy and Roger's insistence on

---

[2] In the translation of this letter I have retained the ecclesiastical "we" and such locutions as "your Paternity" in order to convey something of the flavor of the Latin. But there is a danger in such archaizing translations; the conventions obscure the thought for the modern reader. In future versions, therefore, I shall use simpler modern language.

independence of Canterbury. Quite possibly Henry represented these claims as the business of the council in order to put Thomas off guard and make his sudden attack all the more effective. For when the council opened on October 1, 1163, no word was spoken about the respective privileges of York and Canterbury. (The everlasting contention between the two sees served Henry's ends too well, as it had those of his predecessors, for him to wish to see an end to it.)

Instead, Henry at the outset returned to the issue that had been broached at Woodstock: the punishment of clerics guilty of major crimes. The peace of his kingdom, he declared, was being disturbed by a host of clerics who committed rape, robbery, and murder. The episcopal courts could not impose penalties severe enough to restrain such men from further evils. Men who thought so little of their sacred orders as to commit outrages would not be likely to tremble at the prospect of spiritual penalties. He had consulted, he said, with men skilled in both the civil and canon law, and they agreed that the proper method for dealing with the problem was that followed in the time of his grandfather, Henry I.

At this point in his long opening address, the king turned directly to Thomas Becket. "I demand," he said, "that with the consent of yourself, my lord of Canterbury, and of your fellow bishops, clerks who are caught committing crimes, or have confessed them, be degraded, deprived of all protection of the Church, and handed over to my court for corporal punishment."

Thomas and the bishops had not expected Henry to go so far. In effect, the king was demanding the abolition of effective ecclesiastical jurisdiction in all criminal cases: an end, that is, to clerical immunity from lay prosecution. For if the clerk had to be degraded for a crime, he became as much subject to civil law as any layman. Quite aside from the humiliation, degradation was in itself a harsh punishment for it was equivalent to stripping a man of his means of livelihood. To then deliver him to the civil courts for further penalties meant inflicting a double sentence for the same crime. This was the point that Thomas Becket seized on.

He and the bishops withdrew to consult among themselves. Some of the bishops were not sure of their ground; they argued

that the crimes of men in sacred orders were all the more repre-
hensible and should therefore be punished more harshly than
those committed by ordinary laymen. But Thomas pointed out
that double punishment was contrary to canon law. *"Nec enim
Deus judicat bis in indipsum"* (for God does not judge twice in
the same cause) he said. And after a good deal of discussion he
convinced them that the king was attacking a principle essential
to the freedom of the Church. At last all agreed that they could
not yield to the royal demand. Thomas returned to the great hall,
followed by the bishops, with the confidence that he would be
speaking for the united Church.

"The customs of Holy Church," he began, "are fully set
forth in the canons and decrees of the Fathers. It is not fitting for
you, my lord king, to demand, nor for us to grant, anything that
goes beyond these, nor ought we consent to any innovation. We
who now stand in the place of the Fathers ought to humbly obey
the old laws, not establish new ones."

"I am not asking you to do anything of the sort," Henry
replied. "I ask only that the customs which were observed in the
times of the kings my predecessors be also observed in my time.
In those days there were holier and better archbishops than you
who saw and consented to those customs and never raised any
difficulty or controversy about them with their kings."

"Whatever was done by former kings against the rules laid
down in the canons, and whatever practices were observed out of
fear of kings, ought not to be called customs but abuses," Thomas
replied. "Scripture teaches us that such depraved practices
ought to be abolished rather than extended. You say that the holy
bishops of those times kept silent and did not complain. Perhaps
those were days for silence; but their example does not give us the
authority to assent to anything that is done against God or our
order or office in the Church that divine dispensation has committed to us. However, you shall find us always obedient and
ready to accord with your will and pleasure in everything that we
can possibly consent to, saving our order."

"By the eyes of God!" Henry swore. "Let me hear no word
of your order! I demand absolute and express agreement to my
customs!"

Henry, who had been growing more ill-tempered as the day

advanced, now turned to each of the bishops separately and asked whether they were willing to observe the customs of his realm. One by one, each answered using the same formula: that they would, saving their order. Hilary of Chichester alone, whose previous experience with the royal wrath had softened his resolve, tried to placate Henry by substituting the phrase *bona fide,* in good faith, for the *salvo ordine meo* so obnoxious to the king. But Henry, by now beside himself with rage, misread his intention. He thought that Hilary was seeking still another evasion, and shouted abuse at him. Once again he turned to Thomas and denounced the united front of the bishops against him. The phrase "saving their order" was sophistry and hidden poison, he declared. If they wanted to remain in his favor they must swear absolutely and without reservation to observe the customs of his realm.

Thomas made a last effort to soothe him. "My lord king," he said, "we have already sworn fealty to you by our life and limbs and earthly honor, saving our order, and the customs of the kingdom are included in 'earthly honor.' We cannot promise to observe them in any form other than the one in which we have already sworn."

Abruptly Henry rose and stormed out of the hall without a word. The bishops stood in silent consternation. Then Thomas turned upon Hilary and angrily berated him for having altered the agreed formula of their reply without consulting him or his brother bishops.

Thomas had stood fast, and he had succeeded in holding the support of his suffragans—no mean accomplishment. But Henry, too, had gained something besides chagrin and frustration from the course of the day's discussions. He had shifted the ground of his attack from the specific question of criminous clerks to that of general obedience and consent to his customs. Paradoxically, this shift must also have been welcome to Thomas, who knew that the general feeling of the country was outraged by criminality among the clergy. At the same time, it was more difficult for him to rally the bishops behind him in support of the vague general principle embodied in the phrase "saving my order." For the time being, nevertheless, he succeeded by sheer force of personality.

Before dawn next morning, Henry sent word to Thomas

demanding return of the castles and fiefs he had held since the time of his chancellorship. He also removed Prince Henry from the archbishop's tutelage. This done, he left Westminster and returned to London without so much as a parting word to any of the bishops. He left behind a dismayed and shaken group of prelates. They felt that it was in some respects easier to face the king in his fury than to wonder what terrible punishments he might be planning. Perhaps when they returned to their sees, they would find their homes burned to the ground. Terrified, several of the bishops hastened to London in pursuit of the king.

They found Henry in consultation with another bishop, Arnulf of Lisieux, who had previously fallen into Henry's bad graces and had now come to England to mend matters. This unscrupulous prelate, who only a few months before at Tours had so ardently preached the very cause that Thomas was now defending, is said to have advised Henry against imposing any penalties on the other bishops. Rather, he suggested, the king should attempt to win them over so that Thomas would stand isolated in his opposition.

It was a logical plan. But before taking a step that would definitely undermine the archbishop's authority, Henry resolved to make one more effort to regain the friendship that, as he conceived it, he had lost through no fault of his own. Perhaps he would be able to come to a private arrangement with Thomas. He summoned Thomas to meet him at Northampton.

If Henry had expected Thomas to come as a humble petitioner he was disappointed, for the archbishop approached the city with a large train of followers. In rebuke, Henry refused him admittance. He sent messengers to inform Thomas that he was already in the city with many men "and you nevertheless have arrived with a great multitude; there is not room enough to hold you both, so the king commands you to wait for him here."

That single act on Henry's part transformed the interview into something resembling an encounter between two hostile generals preparing to parley. Thomas turned aside with his train into a meadow, and the king rode out to meet him. Sensing that the king intended to shame him by assuming a stance of humility, Thomas raced toward him on his charger in order to pay the first salutation. But the attempt was comically ill-fated; both their high-spirited horses misinterpreted the meaning of this dash across an open field. They neighed, reared, and maneuvered into position as if on a battlefield. Thomas and Henry were forced to rein them in, trot back to their own lines, and change mounts before they could come peaceably together.

At last, on more stolid steeds, they met again and rode off apart from their followers. But by then Henry was in no mood for diplomacy. He spoke his mind bluntly:

"Have I not raised you from poverty and lowliness to the summit of honor and rank?" he asked Thomas. "Even that seemed little to me unless I also made you the father of the kingdom, placing you above myself. How is it then that after so many benefits, so many proofs of my love for you, which everyone is aware of, you have so soon been able to blot them from your mind, so that you are not only ungrateful but oppose me in everything?"

The archbishop replied: "Far be it from me, my lord. I have not forgotten your favors—which are not yours alone, for God deigned to confer them on me through you. For that very reason, far be it from me to be ungrateful or oppose your will in anything that accords with the will of God. You know how loyal I have been to you, from whom I expect only a temporal reward. How much more ought we both to do faithful and honest service to Almighty God, from whom we receive temporal and hope for eternal goods. You are indeed my lord, but He is my lord and yours. It would be useful neither to you nor to me if I were to neglect His will in order to obey yours. For on His fearful Day of Judgment you and I will both be judged as servants of one Lord. Then neither of us will be able to answer for the other and no excuses will avail; each of us will receive his due according to his acts. Temporal lords must be obeyed, but not against God. As St. Peter says: 'We must obey God rather than men.' "

This was certainly the new Thomas, in whose existence Henry had scarcely believed. But there was an easy way to bring him down to earth. "I don't want you to preach a sermon," Henry said dryly. "Aren't you the son of one of my villeins?"

Proof of a gentleman's education was one answer to such an insult. Thomas flung a quotation from Horace into the king's face. "It is true," he said, "that I am not 'sprung from royal ancestors';[3] nor was Peter, the blessed Prince of the Apostles, on whom the Lord conferred the keys to the Kingdom of Heaven and dominion over the whole Church."

"That is true," the king said. "But he died for his Lord."

Henry probably meant to say only that Peter had been loyal to the death. But Thomas seized the opportunity to score a debater's point. He replied, as if Henry had uttered a threat: "I too will die for my Lord when the time comes."

Henry tried to bring the conversation back to the benefits he had heaped on Thomas. "You rely too much on the ladder you have mounted by," he said.

"I rely on God," Thomas answered. "Cursed is the man who trusts in man. Nevertheless, whatever you will say to me and I answer you, I am as ready as in the past to serve your honor and good pleasure, saving my order. But where your honor and your soul's salvation are concerned, you ought really to have consulted me, whom you have always found a faithful and useful adviser, rather than those who are vindictive toward me although I have never hurt them. They have stirred up this bad feeling, on the pretense that they are worried about your honor. I don't think you will deny that before I received holy orders I was always loyal to you. Then how much more ought you to believe in my loyalty now that I have been raised to the priesthood?"

The argument was cogent and Henry was in fact baffled. Thomas had always been faithful. Why did he now insist on interposing those three exasperating words, *saving my order*, between them? All would be well again, Henry said, if he would only renounce those words, if he would acknowledge that he was his king's man still, without reservation. Of what sinister aims did he suspect his lord king, that he refused to promise to observe the customs—customs that were not his, Henry's, alone, but hallowed by tradition, accepted in the days of his grandfather and the kings before him. He was asking nothing unreasonable.

Henry pleaded, threatened, insisted. Thomas pleaded, placated, and remained obdurate. At last the two men parted. Neither had yielded an inch.

---

[3] *"Atavis edite regibus" Odes*, I, 1.

8

Clarendon

IF THERE were any doubt that Thomas Becket had read John of Salisbury's *Policraticus,* the interview at Northampton would lay it to rest. The whole spirit of the "sermon" Thomas preached to the king is that of the *Policraticus.* Nor is this surprising, for John was in daily converse with Becket and had opportunity to reinforce the ideas he had formally elaborated in his writings. Henry was well aware of this. He became convinced that John was a pernicious influence on Thomas, and within a few months he sent John into the penniless exile which that brilliant and high-principled intellectual had anticipated with dread during the years he had served as Theobald's chief adviser and letterwriter. Both Henry and Thomas now shared the tendency to blame the "advisers" for their disagreements. For a few months longer, neither could bear to believe fully in the other's ill will.

Henry's conviction that Thomas could be brought round if subjected to the proper "influences" inspired his next effort. He now followed up Arnulf of Lisieux's proposal, and conferred separately with the bishops. Foliot of London, Roger of York, and Hilary of Chichester were quickly won over—the first two out of personal hostility toward Thomas, the last from want of character. Hilary, as the most neutral of the three, was sent to talk with Thomas. Thomas received the news of the defections with bitterness. He accused Hilary and Roger of having bartered the liberties of the Church for the king's favor by promising to obey customs contrary to the canons, and declared that they would never have him as an "accomplice in such horrible presumption."

Thomas would soon learn the folly of such categorical assertions.

"I ask you," Hilary replied, "what is this horrible evil that you alone see, and that no one but you sees? The king is only asking us for a word of respect and honor. He has promised that if we make the concession, he will never use it to demand anything of us contrary to our order. Where is there such great evil or such terrible presumption in honoring our lord the king?"

"There is nothing wrong with honoring the king. On the contrary, it is good to do so, so long as we do not dishonor God and endanger the Church. You can rest assured that the king will demand of you what you have promised him, but you have no way of making him keep his promises."

Hilary gave up; but this was only the first of the efforts at mediation. Henry had dispatched Arnulf of Lisieux and Richard of Ilchester, Archdeacon of Poitiers, to the papal court at Sens to lay his troubles with Thomas informally before the pope. The two envoys assured Alexander that Henry was asking nothing novel for England. They presented a rather highly colored account of the archbishop's opposition. Arnulf is said to have crossed the Channel six times in the course of a few months, going back and forth between Henry's court and the Curia. Alexander was then not nearly so well informed on English conditions and traditions as he would later become in the course of the long controversy. He evidently accepted in large measure Arnulf's version of the dispute, and sent an envoy to Thomas with letters from himself and the cardinals urging the archbishop to modify his stand. The envoy was Philip, Abbot of l'Aumône, one of the great daughter houses of Clairvaux. Philip had for years been prior under Bernard of Clairvaux and he carried some of the enormous moral authority of the late saint. Associated with him on his mission were Thomas's one-time teacher, Robert of Melun, now bishop-elect of Hereford, and John, Count of Vendôme.

These were men of a different caliber from Hilary. Thomas listened to their arguments with reluctant respect. The letters

from Alexander and the cardinals pointed out the weak state of
the Church because of the schism: how dangerous it would be if
the illness that had infected the head of the Church should spread
to the limbs. Because of his delicate circumstances at the moment, Alexander urged Thomas to be moderate, and declared
that he would take the responsibility himself for any ill that might
befall the Church as a result. Moreover, Philip of l'Aumône said,
the king had taken an oath that he would not introduce any novel
customs or make any demand upon the bishops contrary to their
order. He wanted no more than abandonment of the phrase
"saving my order," because his royal dignity had been affronted.

Thomas was not so obstinate as many writers have presented him over the centuries. Shortly before, he had declared:
"If an angel came from Heaven and gave me such advice, I
would curse him!" But the paternal fondness for Henry so evident in the conversation at Northampton urged him, as strongly
as the arguments of the envoys, to give way. The pope's command reinforced his own inclinations. Herbert of Bosham, who
as we have seen was at this time particularly in his confidence,
declares that he was "moved above all by love" for the king. And
so Thomas Becket at last agreed to recant: to assent to the king's
customs without inserting the obnoxious three words on which
the whole controversy had now seemingly focused.

Accompanied by the three envoys, he left his manor at
Harrow, where the discussions had been held, and in the cold
December rains rode to see the king at Woodstock. There the
quarrel had begun; there, he hoped, it would end. Unfortunately,
he could not resist initiating the conversation by lecturing Henry
once more, this time on the virtues of some kings of England, the
vices of others who had been oppressors of the people. But at last
he came to the point and made his formal amends: "Know that I
shall observe the customs of your kingdom in good faith,[1] and as
is only proper, shall be obedient to you in everything that is
right." Certainly these were no pledges of unconditional surren-

---

[1] Thus Thomas used the very phrase, *bona fide,* for which he had
rebuked Hilary of Chichester. Some time in the interval Hilary
must have convinced Henry of the harmlessness and Thomas of
the usefulness of the formula.

der; but the king chose not to take offense at the *bona fide* and the *omnia in bono*. For his own good reasons the form of the recantation would suffice him for the present, even if he suspected hidden reservations.

"Everyone is aware," he replied, "of how stubborn you were in your opposition, and how you injured my royal dignity by contradicting me in public. If you are now resolved to honor me as you should, the retraction should be made in the presence of all, just as the detraction from my honor was done publicly. Therefore, do you convoke the bishops and abbots and all the other eminent ecclesiastics; and I for my part shall call together all my magnates, so that these words restoring my honor can be uttered in the presence and the hearing of all."

This was not exactly reconciliation, but postponement and promise of reconciliation. Yet it is clear from the king's language that Henry still regarded Thomas as sovereign over the Church, even as he himself was sovereign over the lay lords. It is just possible that if Henry had realized fully the power he already held over the bishops in their capacity as lay barons, he would not have felt so keenly the necessity of pushing his quarrel with Thomas to extremes. His own uncertainty about the traditional relationship of an English king toward his bishops led him to exaggerate the archbishop's power. That is why, at the subsequent confrontation, he insisted on a definition of his own rights that ultimately diminished rather than strengthened them.

The convening of the new council was fixed for the middle of January. Thomas now returned to Canterbury with Robert of Melun, there to consecrate him as Bishop of Hereford on December 22. Henry, meanwhile, celebrated his victory in rather bad taste by keeping Christmas at the castle of Berkhamsted, which he had taken from Becket's custody after the quarrel at Winchester and which he found very comfortable, for Thomas had recently spent large sums in repairing it.

✠ ✠ ✠

When the council at the royal hunting lodge of Clarendon opened, Henry began the proceedings by requesting that Thomas repeat in public the submission he had made in private. But the agreement as Henry phrased it evidently differed widely from the terms previously arranged with the Abbot of l'Aumône. In the meanwhile, moreover, Thomas had been having second thoughts. He now procrastinated, evaded, declared that he must first take counsel with his bishops. Whereupon Henry flew into one of his dreaded Angevin rages. The king's anger was "like the roaring of the lion." He swore that if he did not obtain an unconditional promise to observe the dignities and customs of his kingdom, he would resort to the sword. His fury infected the barons in the assemblage, and turbulent scenes followed. "The priests of the Lord stood exceedingly terrified, like a flock of sheep ready for slaughter."

The bishops withdrew to a single room to confer among themselves. Some of them, though frightened, supported Thomas's stand; others pleaded with him to yield. Bishops William of Norwich and Jocelin of Salisbury had offended Henry in the past. William, now an old man, had opposed the scutage of 1156, and Jocelin had been compelled to surrender the castle of Devizes to Henry, then still only Duke of Normandy. Using the characteristic technique of concentrating his ire upon scapegoats, Henry now threatened the two bishops with death or mutilation. They begged Thomas to take pity on their plight. But although he was plainly concerned for them, Thomas remained inflexible. Shortly afterwards, Robert, Earl of Leicester, and the king's uncle Reginald, Earl of Cornwall, approached the archbishop. "We are your friends and lieges," they said to him. "And we too beseech you to have pity. Unless you give the king full satisfaction today, we shall be compelled to commit an unheard-of crime with our own hands."

They did not state the nature of the crime, but Thomas interpreted their words in a way that shows the direction his thoughts were already taking. "It would not be so unheard of if it should befall us to die for the laws of the Church," he replied. "A host of saints have taught us that by word and example. The Lord's will be done."

The earls were followed by two Templars who repeated the earlier arguments of Philip and assured Thomas that once he satisfied the king, he would never hear mention of the customs again. Henry would then forget all his indignation and hostility and restore Thomas to full favor and love. "This we faithfully promise you and may our souls be condemned to eternal damnation if henceforth the king demands of you anything contrary to your will or your order."

We will recall that in his days as chancellor Thomas had entertained particularly close relations with the Templars. Richard of Hastings, provincial of the order in England, was a good and reliable friend. Thomas knew, moreover, that Henry held the Temple in high esteem, and he found it hard to believe that the king would violate a pledge given to the Knights Templar. Henry's lay barons were by now in a sulky and violent mood, and the bishops were wavering. The bickering had gone on for three days; sheer physical fatigue was undermining his resolution. Quite abruptly, it seems, Thomas gave way. Leading his flock of bishops, he went into the king's hall and made his recantation.

"My lord king," he said, "if the dispute between us had revolved around my personal rights, I would have yielded to your will at once, without the slightest opposition. But since it concerned the affairs of the Church, and since grave and dangerous matters have been brought forward on both sides, you should not regard it as strange or offensive that I have been so scrupulous in God's cause. For I know that I must account to God for my stewardship, and that he does not spare the wicked. Now, trusting in your prudence and your clemency, I consent to your demand, and I declare that I will observe the customs of the kingdom in good faith."

No sooner were the words spoken than Henry called out in a loud voice: "You have all heard the archbishop's promise. All that remains is for the bishops to do the same, at his command."

"I wish them to satisfy your honor as I have done," the archbishop said.

All the bishops obeyed except Jocelin of Salisbury, who only took the oath after he had pointedly asked Thomas what he ought to do. Henry reprimanded him for this; but Jocelin evidently explained his conduct afterwards, for he was soon firmly in the ranks of Henry's partisans. Possibly he provoked the little scene in order to emphasize the archbishop's own submission in a striking manner.

Such is the account of the council as given by the partisans of Thomas. Gilbert Foliot, writing two years later, offered an entirely different version of the proceedings. The bishops had stood fast behind Thomas in his refusal to consent to the customs, Foliot wrote, and it was Thomas himself who suddenly betrayed them out of cowardice. As Foliot described it:[2]

> We were all shut up in one chamber, and on the third day the chiefs and nobles of the kingdom, their rage at its height, burst into the conclave in which we sat, threw back their cloaks and shook their fists at us, exclaiming: "Listen, you who despise the laws of the kingdom and do not obey the king's commands. These hands, these arms, even these bodies are not ours; they are our lord king's, and they are ready at his nod to avenge his wrongs and work his will whatever it may be. . . . So change your minds and yield to his commands before it is too late to avert the danger that threatens you!"—Let God judge who it was that fled, who became a deserter in the battle. For surely it was not . . . Henry of Winchester, nor Nigel of Ely, nor Robert of Lincoln, nor Hilary of Chichester, nor Jocelin of Salisbury, nor Bartholomew of Exeter, nor Richard of Chester, nor Roger of Worcester, nor Robert of Hereford, nor Gilbert of London. All these stood firm. . . . It was the leader of our chivalry who turned his back, the captain of our camp who fled. Our lord of Canterbury withdrew from the counsel of his brothers and after considering by himself for a while returned to us and said: "It is my lord's will that I foreswear myself; for the present I submit and incur perjury—to do penance for it later as well as I can." We were thunderstruck to hear these words, and gazed at one another groaning in spirit at this fall from the height of virtue and constancy. . . .

Foliot's polemical distortions are easy to detect. He was certainly being disingenuous in omitting the names of Roger of York and William of Norwich, while nevertheless asserting that

---

[2] The controversy over the authenticity of the letter in question, *Multiplicem nobis,* has been definitively settled by David Knowles (*The Episcopal Colleagues of Thomas Becket,* pp. 171–80).

all the bishops stood firm. The narratives of the contemporary biographers and the subsequent conduct of the bishops, including Foliot's own, make it plain that there were other waverers. What is clear, if we combine the contradictory accounts, is that once again Thomas yielded reluctantly to pressure, to fears for the safety of some of the bishops, and possibly to threats against his own life. He may also have wished to gain time, for he knew Henry's capacity for acting rashly and repenting afterwards. But it was indeed Thomas who first gave way, and the genuine surprise of his brother bishops is certainly mirrored in Foliot's letter. This was not to be the only sudden about-face in his struggle with Henry. Thomas regarded his consent as having been extorted by violence and fear (*per vim et metum extorta*); but he gave it.

Henry immediately raised the question of what the customs were. A curious note, this: none of the contending parties was really familiar with the "customs" under discussion. As the *Saga* quaintly puts it: "The king is young, and the archbishop not old; wherefore neither knows the full certainty of the matter."

Thomas was, however, fifteen years older than Henry, and this difference in their ages was crucial. For it meant that Thomas's first experience in public life had come during the reign of Stephen, when the Church had been able to encroach steadily on the royal prerogative, and papal authority had become more firmly established in England than at any time since the Conquest. Control of the Church had slipped gradually out of the king's hand—so much so that Stephen's arrest of the bishops of Salisbury and Lincoln had very nearly cost him his throne. During this same period many churches formerly owned by laymen passed to the patronage of monasteries or bishops; appeals to the pope and visits by ecclesiastics to Rome had become common. As we have seen, Stephen had been unable to enforce his prohibition against Archbishop Theobald's attendance at the Council of Reims. And in a matter of far more importance to himself, he had failed to force Theobald to crown his son Eustace. During Stephen's reign the courts of bishops and archdeacons had succeeded in taking more and more cases away from the royal officials.

These were the conditions that Thomas Becket regarded as

natural, right, and "customary." To Henry, who considered the entire reign of Stephen an illegal usurpation, the only right customs were those that had been in force under Henry I or his predecessors—a time of far more stringent royal control over the Church. Stephen had permitted free elections in the Church because he could not help himself. Henry I had compromised on the question of investiture; but he had never allowed the real power of appointing bishops to slip from his hand. Henry II, therefore, had clearly in mind the kind of customs he wanted observed; and he trusted his loyal justiciar to draw up a list that would enable him to rule with the same unchallenged authority as his grandfather. Accordingly, Richard de Lucy and Jocelin de Balliol were instructed to make a "recognition" of the customs of his grandfather's day, and to present it to the council in writing. Proceedings were therefore adjourned for a week or so. Toward the end of January, Richard and Jocelin, whom Thomas would later denounce as "fabricators of those heretical outrages," returned to the assemblage of barons and bishops with the document that was henceforth to become the heart of the controversy: the Constitutions of Clarendon.[3]

To Thomas Becket these Constitutions, sixteen in all, were heretical, wicked, and above all novel. To Henry and his lay advisers they were a fair and honest statement of the customs of the kingdom, arrived at by the sensible procedure of "recognition," which Henry was also introducing into ordinary legal practice. Both men were right from their respective vantage points. The "freedom of the Church," which Thomas regarded as immutable, was in fact barely twenty years old; but the very freedoms that the Church had enjoyed in recent times had produced a different Church and different churchmen.

What was meant by "freedom of the Church"? The key issues were: 1. Inviolability of church property. 2. Canonical elections to high offices in the Church, which in practice meant a minimum of interference on the king's part. 3. Freedom of churchmen to leave the country at will, so that they might obey a summons from the papacy, consult with the pope, or carry appeals to the

---

[3] See Appendix, pp. 383–6, for the complete text.

Curia. 4. Freedom to fill vacant sees promptly. 5. Control of church property and church jurisdiction by the bishops. 6. Free entry into England of papal legates. 7. Recognition by the king of the pope's authority over the whole English Church. 8. Freedom from interference by the barons, which could sometimes be more troublesome than that of the king.

To Thomas Becket and to all those who had in one way or another been nurtured in the household of Archbishop Theobald, these freedoms were self-evident truths. To Henry II, nurtured in the traditions of the Norman kings, they were arrogant invasions of the royal dignities. In practice, he knew, the Church had never exercised all the freedoms it claimed, and did not really expect to. By the exercise of temperate judgment on both sides, compromises could usually be effected. And if Henry at this point had not insisted on his written record, the whole issue might well have evaporated.

Unfortunately Henry's most salient trait, the trait that made him the founder of English law, drove him forward into an impasse. Henry's great legal reforms, the abiding work of his later years, were marked by a strong desire for clarity, definition, system. The disorder of his personal life, which contemporaries liked to stress, did not extend to his conduct of cases at law. He would listen attentively to lengthy legal arguments, would patiently and intelligently examine evidence, and would display keen judgment in his decisions. And on the whole he must have rendered just verdicts, for his courts were immensely popular. His subjects were willing to pay heavily for the privilege of having their suits tried in the king's court.

His attempt to introduce clarity into the relations of Church and State by setting forth in writing the "customs" that governed those relations was on the face of it laudable. But in the given situation it was impracticable, because it eliminated the possibility of tacit compromise. The English Church in 1164 was fully acquainted with canon law as set forth in Gratian's *Decretum*. It could not subscribe to doctrines that were in flagrant violation of the canons, although it might tolerate them in practice. By producing the written Constitutions of Clarendon, and by demanding that the bishops sign and seal them, Henry rendered impossible evasion and silent toleration, adherence to principle and submission in practice.

Henry's own mother recognized that publication of the Constitutions was a great mistake. In the course of the subsequent negotiations, after Thomas had gone into exile, one of his friends went to see the Empress Matilda, on the chance that she might be persuaded to intercede. The empress asked Thomas's representatives to read the Constitutions to her in Latin and explain them in French.[4] They did so, and were disappointed to hear from her that she approved of some of them. As the envoy naïvely wrote to Thomas: "The woman is of the race of tyrants." As a ruler, Matilda knew the needs of royalty. But she was highly displeased that the customs had been reduced to writing. This, she said, was without precedent. And yet Henry's greatness lay precisely in his ability to go beyond precedent.

Thomas and the other bishops had given their word that they would observe the customs of the kingdom. But they were horrified when the text of those customs was presented to them for signature. Their reaction to the Constitutions as a whole is reflected in the terse summary of Gervase of Canterbury: "A discussion of a grave character and full of threats took place between the archbishop and the king concerning the enforcement or annulling of ecclesiastical law." This was the exaggeration of a Canterbury monk who had been consecrated by Thomas Becket in person, for the Constitutions did not in fact aim at annulling canon law, but rather at keeping it within tighter bounds. On many points, the document accurately stated the customs of England as they had been accepted by the Church in the days of Henry I. But if we compare the complete text of the Constitutions with the "freedoms of the Church," we will see that they did in fact infringe on most of the liberties claimed by churchmen.

In brief, the Constitutions provided that disputes over advowson and presentation of churches were to be settled in the king's court. (This was an obvious reference to Thomas's disputes with

---

[4] An interesting indication of the level of learning of a royal lady in the twelfth century. Evidently Matilda understood Latin but spoke and thought in French.

William of Eynsford and others.) Members of the clergy were not to leave the kingdom without the king's permission. (This clause attempted to reinstitute the conditions that had prevailed under William the Conqueror and his successors, but had lapsed under Stephen.) Laymen were not to be accused in ecclesiastical courts except under certain conditions. (This tried to meet the abuses of the archdeacons, of which Henry had so often complained.) Tenants-in-chief[5] of the king were not to be excommunicated without the king's knowledge and permission. (Here was the case of William of Eynsford again; but there can be no doubt that this had been a genuine custom of the realm.) Appeals to Rome were banned except with the king's consent. And so on.[6]

The real innovation in the Constitutions, from Thomas Becket's point of view, was the provision in Article III for the treatment of criminous clerks. Clerks charged with crimes were to be summoned to the king's court if it appeared that they had committed a breach of "the king's peace." They would then be sent on to the ecclesiastical court, where actual trial would be held. If convicted, they would be degraded and returned to the king's court for sentencing. (Such is the accepted interpretation of the rather obscure language of the clause.) Article IX provided for a jury of twelve men to decide "by recognition" whether property disputes between laymen and clerks concerned lay or ecclesiastical tenure. Thus laymen would be deciding whether such disputes were to be tried in the church or the secular courts.[7]

Herbert of Bosham records a point-by-point analysis of some of the Constitutions, and seems to imply that Thomas contested each of the controversial articles in open council. In view of what

---

[5] Great lords who held their land directly from the king.

[6] Some of the other clauses will be referred to later.

[7] The extent to which this clause laid the basis for our modern jury system is a matter of much dispute, and far too complicated to be discussed here. It should be noted that all jurors under Henry II differed from modern jurors in that they were presumed to know about the matter at issue; they were not, as modern legal theory prescribes, persons of open mind deciding an issue on the basis of evidence freshly presented to them. *Recognitio* was a statement of the facts so far as they were known to the recognitors, who were thus rather more witnesses than jurors.

had gone before, and of the statements of other sources, this seems highly unlikely. Henry would never have tolerated another public debate; his short temper had already reached the breaking point. The objections that Thomas raised must have been expressed in private discussions with members of his own household, or with the other bishops. The only public protest he ventured at this point, having already given his consent, was to evade affixing his seal to the parchment. This he did cautiously and meekly, dissembling his feelings, exerting all his old skill at diplomacy, and managing to carry off the refusal without again inflaming Henry's anger. After all, the Constitutions themselves declared that the promise had been given *viva voce,* by word of mouth. Thomas did accept a copy of the Constitutions—to have the evidence for his case, he remarked. Another copy was given to the Archbishop of York, and the third was kept for the royal archives.

Thus ended the memorable Council of Clarendon. As Thomas left the city, he rode by himself, saddened and deeply disturbed, speaking to none of his fellows—in sharp contrast to his habit. He felt that he had betrayed the Church which Anselm and Theobald had preserved intact, and what distressed him most was the conviction that this defeat would not have been inflicted on him if he had been a more religious man. The misfortune had inevitably come to pass, he told Herbert of Bosham, because he had been raised to his office from the court rather than from the Church, like his predecessors.

According to another account, there was a good deal of discontented murmuring among the members of his household as the party rode toward Winchester on the way back to Canterbury. At last Thomas's cross-bearer, Alexander the Welshman, whose native name was Llewelyn and who ranked among Thomas's *eruditi,* boldly accused Thomas of having abandoned his flock and betrayed his conscience and reputation. "When the shepherd has fled, the sheep lie scattered before the wolf." Whereupon Thomas groaned and said, sighing: "I repent, and am so horrified by my sin that I judge myself unworthy to approach as a priest Him whose Church I have vilely bartered. I will sit silent in grief until the 'day-spring from on high hath visited me,' so that I merit absolution by God and the lord pope."

Many modern critics (almost all of them taking their cue from Edward Freeman) have interpreted words such as these as proof that Thomas was playing a role, carefully fitting himself for the part of a saintly archbishop. Yet the words, self-pitying and excessively emotional though they are, scarcely justify such a view. Thomas was what he professed to be: a religious man who had recently renewed his vows after being placed in a high religious office. His sense of failure was sincere; but like many a new convert, he was also guilty of overdramatizing his falls from grace. Moreover, like Henry Plantagenet, he hated defeat for its own sake and could not reconcile himself to it. Neither king nor archbishop was a notably good loser.

When he reached Canterbury, Thomas struck back, using religion as his weapon—just as nine months later he would wield his cross as if it were a sword. He engaged in ostentatious penances and suspended himself from officiating at the altar. This was equivalent to a public declaration: Behold, the king has placed me in such a position, has forced me so ruthlessly to violate the rules of my sacred order that I can no longer in good conscience perform my religious functions. His penances caused talk, as they were meant to, and the pope wrote to Thomas gently rebuking him. "You ought to consider most carefully how grave a matter this is, especially in a person of your importance, and how great a scandal might arise from it." Alexander absolved him from whatever sin he believed himself to have committed, and commanded him to resume the celebration of Mass.

There is an ironic sequel to this story. Immediately after the Council of Clarendon, Henry wrote to Pope Alexander asking his approval of the Constitutions. It seemed likely to him that the exiled pope, who was now so dependent on the good will of England, would readily oblige. At the same time, Henry requested that Archbishop Roger of York be granted the papal legation for all of England, which would place Roger in the same superior position vis-à-vis Thomas that Henry of Winchester had once held when as papal legate he was able to dominate Theobald.

But Alexander was a man of courage as well as diplomatic pliancy. He might have tacitly ignored the exercise of customs so at variance with all the claims of the Church; but schooled in canon law as he was, he could not possibly give his written consent to them. Of the sixteen articles of the Constitutions of Clarendon, Alexander "tolerated" only six and condemned the other ten. Inevitably, the really controversial articles were among those condemned. Then, however, as a modest consolation to a powerful ruler whom he was offending, he granted Henry's request for the legation. At the same time (February 27, 1164) he wrote to Thomas informing him that he himself and the church of Canterbury were to be exempt from the jurisdiction of the new legate, and urging him therefore not to be dejected, since his rights were in no way infringed. "It has never occurred to us and never shall (God willing) to wish your church to be subject to any but the Roman pontiff."

This type of legation was not at all what Henry had in mind. He wanted Roger to be appointed Thomas Becket's ecclesiastical superior. Alexander's grant was so hedged around with restrictions that it was virtually useless, and after a while Henry returned the document to the pope in disgust. What followed testifies to the charismatic quality of Thomas Becket's personality and the infectiousness of his example. For four months later, in June, we find Thomas's old friend John of Canterbury, now Bishop of Poitiers, writing to reassure him about the legation, and informing him: "As for the legation for England, you ought have nothing to fear, if the pope's word can be trusted. For he has already atoned by grave penance for whatever concession he granted to the Archbishop of York." Thus the pope imitated the conduct he had rebuked. That was some reassurance to Thomas Becket, who had heard the news of the legation with consternation. In his first encounter with Alexander on the plane of diplomacy, Thomas had received a little more from the one hand than was taken away by the other. The pattern of their relationship over the years was thus established in the first months of the controversy.

✠   ✠   ✠

The spring of the year 1164 was marked by intrigues and negotiations on both sides, whose net effect was to make a mockery of the Constitutions of Clarendon. One of the aims of the Constitutions had been to restrict appeals to the pope, and in general to limit intercourse between the English Church and the Curia. Had this been possible, Henry would have been able to claim that he was indeed restoring the customs of his ancestors, the "kings my predecessors," as he always phrased it. But in fact Henry himself now initiated the negotiations with Alexander, through his emissaries John of Oxford and Geoffrey Ridel, the Archdeacon of Canterbury whom he had imposed on Thomas Becket. Henry, not Thomas, first brought the Constitutions to the attention of the pope. Henry, not Thomas, first made an international issue of his quarrel with the archbishop.

Thomas, in self-defense, kept an envoy at the papal court in Sens, and also enlisted his friends now on the Continent, John of Salisbury and Bishop John of Poitiers, to represent his interests at the Curia, to attempt to win support for him from Louis of France, and to look around for a refuge in case he were forced into exile. Thomas remembered only too well the remark that Henry had dropped during the Battle Abbey case, when Hilary of Chichester pointed out that a bishop could not be deposed. "Very true," Henry had said then, "but he could be expelled." And the whole court had roared with laughter. Exile, then, seemed to Thomas the inevitable outcome of the quarrel. That was the traditional method of English kings for dealing with recalcitrant clerics, and it was Henry's method—as the recent expulsion of John of Salisbury clearly demonstrated. In fact, the promotion of John of Canterbury to the see of Poitiers might also be considered a form of exile, for it was assumed that Henry had made him a bishop in order to get him out of England.

Thomas's friends warned him that he must not expect much support from the Curia. There were many factors working against Thomas at the papal court, and few for him, wrote John of Salisbury. Henry's envoys would be generous with money "which Rome has never despised," and the pope would not dare to offend King Henry. It had already become clear how much the cause of Becket and of clerical immunities depended on the position of the pope, and hope briefly revived at the news that the antipope had died at Lucca. Thomas's envoy wrote to him at length about Octavian's death, relating how the "schismatic prince of Belial" (this of a man who had until recently been a respected cardinal of the Roman Church) had been refused burial by the canons of San Frediano because they believed him already "buried in hell," and how Alexander, hearing his cardinals exulting over the death of his enemy, chided them. The rejoicing was in any case premature, for Frederick Barbarossa refused the opportunity to make peace with the Church and quickly created a new antipope in Guido of Crema, who took office as Paschal III.

Possibly encouraged by the prospect that Alexander would now be readier to support him, and eager to present his version of the quarrel and the pernicious potentialities of the Constitutions to Alexander in person, Thomas twice tried to leave England during the summer. There can be no doubt that he was recalling his voyage with Theobald sixteen years before—"swimming rather than sailing"—and hoping that the consequences of such a flight would be the same: he would be welcomed and praised by the pope, and eventually recalled with honor by the king, whose anger, he thought, would subside in his absence. Actually Henry feared his going, for he thought that Thomas might persuade the pope to impose the interdict on his lands. In any case, the attempts to reach the papal presence failed. Thomas was driven back once by contrary winds. The second time the sailors, fearing that they would be punished by the king for their part in the archbishop's flight, pretended that the winds were against them and put back into port. Thomas returned unexpectedly to his palace in Canterbury during the night. The members of his household had dispersed and the palace was deserted except for one clerk, bolder than the others, who had just come to Canterbury. He had sat up late, lost in gloomy thoughts of his master's tribulations. At length he decided to retire—in the archbishop's own room!—and sent his boy to close the outer gate so that they could sleep more securely. By the light of his candle, the boy saw the Archbishop of Canterbury sitting alone in a corner near the gate and started back in terror, thinking he had come upon a phantom. Fortunately, the monks of Christ Church were on call; the exhausted Thomas was able to obtain a bite to eat and to

171

explain what had happened. It was plainly not the will of God, he declared, that he should leave England.

These attempted flights were a direct violation of the Constitutions to which Thomas had formally assented. But Henry took no action for the present, and even pretended to know nothing of the matter when Thomas, apparently in desperation over the deteriorating situation, went to see him at Woodstock. The king received him courteously but coolly. Only toward the end of their interview did he ask sardonically whether Thomas thought the realm too small to hold the two of them.

The question betrayed Henry's own opinion of his present relationship to his former friend. England was indeed too small to hold them both, he was saying, as long as Thomas insisted on ruling the Church like an independent sovereign. During the seven months from the Council of Clarendon to the Council of Northampton, the attitudes of both men had changed. No open clashes between king and archbishop are recorded, and yet Thomas Becket's resistance had hardened once more and Henry had decided to ruin him. Possibly Henry planned to offer Thomas his forgiveness after he had humbled him—the king's partisans repeatedly claimed that this was his intention. But first he must have a complete capitulation.

There were various reasons for this radical resolve. All the contemporaries mention the courtiers who trafficked in rumor, misinterpreted the archbishop's every act and word, and invented slanders. As chancellor Thomas had made many enemies among the barons; merely by becoming archbishop he had offended some of the clergy. The backbiters called Thomas's asceticism hypocrisy, his careful management of the wealth of the Church avarice, his insistence on his views of canon law pride and wilfulness. Henry had been susceptible to influence when Thomas was his chancellor; he could also be swayed by other forceful and proud men around him who for years had been compelled to choke back their hostility to Thomas, and who could now speak freely. John of Oxford, Geoffrey Ridel, Roger of York, Jocelin of Salisbury, and Gilbert of London now had the king's ear, and there is little reason to doubt the contemporary charges that they used their opportunities to denounce the fallen favorite.

Thomas himself made a further contribution to the growing crisis. He had violated the Constitutions of Clarendon by attempting to leave England without permission, and he had violated them again in defending criminous clerks who were brought before the royal courts in accordance with Article III of the Constitutions. Because he had refused to set his seal to the document, he regarded his promise to obey the customs as not binding. His loyalest admirer, Herbert of Bosham, inadvertently convicts Thomas of breaking his oath when he comments: "He observed the good royal and ecclesiastical customs; but those that had been introduced to the detriment of the church and the dragging down of the clergy, he pruned away as bastard shoots, lest they strike deep roots."

Immediately after the promulgation of the Constitutions, Henry had begun putting them into practice. He ordered that clerks found committing crimes be "seized without mercy and condemned by their own parishioners, even shamed and maimed like any lay person." Some of the bishops murmured in protest, but only Henry of Winchester, Roger of Worcester, and Robert of Hereford dared offer some support to Thomas in his efforts to keep criminous clerks under the jurisdiction of the church courts. (Winchester and Hereford were very old men; Worcester was the king's cousin.) Thomas himself intervened on behalf of clerics whenever he could. He also took to reading aloud in public the proviso in Gratian's *Decretum* which plainly stated that bishops were the only lawful judges of ecclesiastical persons. To Henry such uncompromising opposition meant that he would not be able to govern as he desired until he had stripped Thomas of all power. His archbishop's pledge "in good faith" was evidently worthless, Henry complained. Thomas, for his part, believed with intense bitterness that he had been betrayed. Before Clarendon, he had been assured that the dispute was merely one of words, and that if he gave his consent to the "customs," omitting the restrictive clause, no more would be heard of the matter. Now he could see daily the growing aggressiveness of the royal officials. The promise had been worthless. At best, Philip of l'Aumône had been deceived; Hilary of Chichester, Thomas firmly believed, had been a conscious deceiver. But the motivating force behind these deceptions was his one-time friend, King Henry himself. Henry could not be trusted. He was infected by the disease of monarchs, tyranny, and Thomas now resolved to oppose him unflinchingly.

One further element in Henry's policy must be mentioned. Through his mother, the empress, Henry had long had intimate ties with Germany, and was already projecting the marriage of his daughter Matilda to Henry the Lion. Before the recognition of Alexander as pope, there had been, we will recall, a faction in England favoring Frederick Barbarossa's antipope; and there were English courtiers who now raised the issue once more. The advantages for England and for Henry's Continental domains of an outright alliance with Frederick were self-evident; only the schism in the Church remained a major obstacle. Alexander III had not endeared himself to Henry by rejecting the Constitutions of Clarendon and by his efforts to make peace between Henry and Thomas: efforts which had amounted to sanction of Thomas's arguments. For Henry, a possible way out of the whole problem was withdrawal of his recognition of Alexander. Henry's bishops would certainly object, and they were a formidable group when united, who could probably rally much of the country behind them. But deprived of leadership, they could be intimidated—Clarendon had demonstrated that. With Thomas removed from the scene, at any rate, Henry would have a much freer hand in determining his own policies toward the Roman Church and the Holy Roman Empire.

The sum of all the various arguments came to the same thing. Henry now acknowledged to himself that he had been fearfully mistaken in procuring the election of Thomas Becket to the see of Canterbury. But what he had done, he could undo.

He sent out writs summoning a great council of the realm to meet at Northampton on Tuesday, October 6, 1164.

XI

Northampton

IT WAS customary for high officials to be invited to councils of the realm by royal writs. These had in fact been issued to the earls, sheriffs, bishops, and abbots in due form—with the exception of the Archbishop of Canterbury. Henry would not write directly to Thomas because he was unwilling to use the conventional formula of greeting. Instead, he addressed a writ to the sheriff of Kent summoning Thomas to appear in Northampton on October 6 to answer in a suit brought against him by John the Marshal.

That suit had come about as follows: John the Marshal, a baron of the Exchequer who held the marshalcy as a hereditary office, claimed land belonging to the archiepiscopal township of Pagenham. He had sued for this land in the archbishop's court and lost his suit. John thereupon availed himself of the recourse provided for in Article IX of the Constitutions of Clarendon: alleging that he had been denied justice in the archbishop's court, he obtained a summons from the king ordering Thomas to appear on September 15 in the royal court to answer his claim. Thomas, in keeping with his consistent policy of refusing to recognize the validity of the Constitutions, did not appear. Instead, he sent four knights with letters from himself and the sheriff of Kent, setting forth the facts of the case: that John's evidence had been insufficient and that he had sworn improperly on a book of tropes (a service-book), rather than on the scriptures—presumably because he was trying to evade the technical guilt of perjury.

Henry denounced Thomas for not appearing in person, threatened his messengers, and finally appointed the opening day of the council for trial of the case. He was so angered by Thomas's defiance that he could scarcely be prevailed upon to let the four knights go, even when they had given security that Thomas would appear to answer the suit three weeks later.

Characteristically, Henry himself was late for the council, for on his way to Northampton he "went hawking along every river and stream." We may, if we will, interpret his hesitancy charitably: that some lingering sorrow over the death of friendship moved him to postpone the decisive confrontation. Thomas, for his part, came determined not to antagonize Henry further, if that were possible. On the morning of Wednesday, October 7, he waited on the king in the antechamber of the palace chapel, and when Henry came out after Mass, Thomas rose reverently "and showed a firm and calm face in readiness for the favor of a kiss, according to the English custom, if the king should offer it; but he was not admitted to the kiss." This first interview was brief and cool but not openly acrimonious. Thomas mentioned that William of Courcy had occupied part of the lodgings reserved for him and his train at the Cluniac monastery of St. Andrew's, and asked Henry to order William to vacate these quarters. Henry obliged. Thomas then requested permission to go to Sens to confer with Pope Alexander about his quarrel with Archbishop Roger of York, who would not profess obedience to the see of Canterbury. Henry declared that he would allow no one to leave England. Finally, Thomas stated that he had come to answer the summons in the case of John the Marshal. Henry said that John was still busy at the Exchequer in London, but would be arriving next day; he would then try the suit himself.

In fact, John the Marshal never arrived and his suit was not tried. It had served only as a pretext, and in the hurly-burly that followed was forgotten by everyone but Thomas Becket, who referred to it repeatedly.

When the actual business of the council began on Thursday, many of the bishops and barons of Normandy as well as those of England were seated in the *aula,* the great hall of Northampton Castle, on the lower floor of the two-story Norman structure. At once, Thomas was charged with contempt of court for having

176

failed to appear three weeks before to answer the suit of John the
Marshal, and for having offered no "essoin," that is, excuse for
nonappearance. A heated wrangle followed. Some of the sources
say that Thomas pleaded illness. William FitzStephen, who was
there, asserts that he did not. We are probably safe in following
William. Thomas's interest was in maintaining the integrity of his
own court, not in finding an excuse. The facts were clear, and the
reasons he gave for his conduct were not accepted. "It seemed to
all," FitzStephen remarks, "considering the respect due to the
king and the oath of liege homage which he had taken, and the
observance of the king's earthly honor to which he had sworn,
that he had little defense."

The court decided that for failure to appear when summoned,
Thomas should be "at the king's mercy." In theory this meant
that all his goods were forfeit; in practice, such sentences always
implied a fine, the amount being fixed by custom or the royal
discretion. But respect for Thomas and his office was strong, and
a further wrangle now arose. The barons proposed that the bishops ought to pronounce the sentence, since they were the culprit's
fellow priests. The bishops protested that the judgment was secular rather than ecclesiastical, and that in this case they were
sitting as barons rather than as bishops. "If you consider our
order," they pointed out, "you will have to consider his likewise.
As bishops we cannot judge our archbishop and our lord." Thus
the bishops themselves were the first to make the very point that
Thomas later used against them.

Henry had listened with growing irritation to this dispute,
which so plainly revealed the uneasiness of all his magnates, lay
and ecclesiastical. Now he issued an abrupt command to Henry
of Winchester to pronounce the sentence. Reluctantly Bishop
Henry obeyed, and in an undertone urged Thomas to accept the
sentence quietly. Thomas commented sardonically: "This is a
new kind of judgment, perhaps according to the new canons
promulgated at Clarendon."

Henry of Winchester and the other bishops pointed out that
no law justified refusal to accept the sentence of the king's court.
Grudgingly, Thomas acceded to their argument, and agreed to
pay the fine, whatever it was. It was set at £500. Henry demanded guarantees that it would be paid. Significantly, all the

bishops "went bail" for Thomas, promising to pay the sum if he did not or could not. In other words, at this point in the proceedings the entire body of English bishops, including those who opposed Thomas on most questions, stood by their superior—even Roger of York, it would seem. The sole exception was Gilbert Foliot, who thus made himself conspicuous by his refusal to be a guarantor.

Henry was unwilling to follow up his victory by trying the case of John the Marshal because he felt that he was on weak ground. If he attacked the decisions of an archiepiscopal court, he would be challenging the baronial courts in general and would thus risk losing the support of his lay magnates. He therefore decided to take up the question of clerical immunities, but his advisers pointed out that this would only unite the bishops behind Thomas. Thereupon Henry resorted to a series of charges so obviously trumped up that his intention to complete the ruin of his former friend became all too clear.

Where, Henry demanded, was the £300 that Thomas had received while the castles of Eye and Berkhamsted were in his charge? Thomas protested that this was a new suit, for which he had not been cited and therefore had had no time to prepare a defense. Besides, he remarked informally, the king knew perfectly well that he had used the money to repair the Tower of London and the castles themselves.

"Not on my authorization," Henry retorted. "I demand judgment."

It was probably true that Thomas had not requested Henry's permission to make these repairs, for in the past the king had always assented to whatever Thomas undertook for the good of the kingdom. Nevertheless the charge was so obviously unfair that when Thomas, for the sake of peace, agreed to pay the £300, none other than William of Eynsford—whom he had recently excommunicated and absolved—came forward to offer security for the debt.[1] The Earl of Gloucester associated himself

---

[1] Some idea of the size of the fine imposed on Thomas can be gathered from the consideration that at the present price of silver in the United States, the £800 Thomas now owed the king would be worth $8,000. In purchasing power, the sum probably represented around $32,000.

with William: fair warning to Henry that the barons did not wholly approve of the proceedings.

Next day the series of financial demands continued. Henry wanted to know what had happened to the sum of one thousand marks (a mark was two thirds of a pound) that Thomas had borrowed during the Toulouse war—five hundred marks obtained directly from Henry, and five hundred borrowed from a Jew on the king's security. Thomas protested that the money had been a gift, expended, moreover, in the king's service, and that it was unmannerly and unreasonable of Henry to ask for the return of a gift. But he could produce no evidence for his claim beyond his unsupported word, and the court therefore decided that the money must be returned. Henry once again asked for security. Thomas protested that he could easily pay the sum—whereupon Henry sardonically pointed out that all his movable goods were already forfeit. Five laymen at last came forward and offered to go bail for Thomas.

All this was only a preliminary to the major attack. Thomas was asked to account for all the proceeds of the archbishopric during its vacancy, and for the revenues of all the other bishoprics and abbacies he had held during his chancellorship. Obviously such an accounting was impossible without due preparation and Thomas said as much. He had not been summoned for that purpose, he pointed out; if the king wished an accounting, he would render one at the proper time and place. The sum demanded is variously stated, but came to at least thirty thousand marks—equivalent to some $800,000 in present-day purchasing power.

If he would not settle at once, Henry said, he must again give security. Thomas was so stunned by this latest demand that, as Herbert quaintly puts it (quoting the psalms) "all his wisdom was devoured." With sinking heart, but unperturbed dignity, he grasped at a straw. On a matter of such grave importance, he said, he would have to consult his clergy. This plea was a conscious attempt to divide the bishops from the barons, to make it clear to his suffragans that they were not "sitting as barons." Only if he succeeded in ranging the whole clergy on his side could Thomas represent the personal attack upon his honesty as an invasion of the Church's privileges. Possibly he was making a tactical error, for thereafter his friends among the secular barons no longer came to see him. William FitzStephen's statement that they ceased coming because they now understood the mind of the king does not seem sufficient explanation; Henry had made his intentions plain long before the third day of the council.

Thomas spent all the next day, Saturday, in consultation with his bishops and abbots. One by one, the bishops gave their advice. Gilbert Foliot led off: "If you recall the lowly place from which the king raised you, all the gifts he conferred on you, and if you consider that you will be ruining the Church and all of us by resisting the king, you will see that you ought to resign. Perhaps, if the king sees your humility, he will restore everything to you."

"Everyone knows that you yourself would not take such advice," Thomas replied *ad hominem*.

Henry of Winchester, his turbulent past well behind him, was now the most respected of the bishops. He took issue sharply with Gilbert, pointing out that if the primate of all England gave such an example by resigning, it would be impossible in the future for any prelate to oppose the king. Moreover, what would be the effect on canon law?

Hilary of Chichester argued that in the present disturbed state of the Church, some compromises had to be made with the letter of canon law. Robert of Lincoln—"a simple man and not very discreet"—thought that Thomas was faced with a choice between execution and resignation. "I do not see," he said, "what good the archbishopric will do him if he is no longer alive." Bartholomew of Exeter made the point that the present persecution was personal, not general, and that it would be better for Thomas to suffer than the whole English Church.

Henry of Winchester now suggested scornfully that Henry was motivated by avarice, and that perhaps a large sum of money would satisfy him. Bishop Henry generously offered to put his own vast wealth at Thomas's disposal. Accordingly, a proposal was sent to the king offering a settlement of two thousand marks. Henry refused. Whereupon Hilary of Chichester again advocated resignation as the only course that would satisfy Henry. "As chancellor you were the king's intimate," he said, "and you know

180

him better than we do. He will more readily listen to you than anyone else, whether you contend with him or yield to him. In the chancellorship, both in peace and war, you served him honorably and well, and many praised you, although some envied you. Those who envied you then are now inciting the king against you. . . . He is supposed to have said that there is not room enough in England for you as archbishop and him as king. It would be safer to resign yourself to his mercy. Otherwise (heaven forbid!), he may imprison you for embezzlement or lay hands on you—which would be harmful to the Church and a disgrace to the king."

To this speech an unnamed bishop angrily replied that it would dishonor the Church for the archbishop to consider his personal safety; that there were precedents for such a contest as this; and that none of Thomas's predecessors had given way when they were persecuted by their kings. Thomas himself was too stricken to react angrily. Later he would remark of Hilary: "He among the brothers held the place of the traitor Judas."

The discussions continued at great length all through the following day, Sunday. Thomas, apparently still stunned by the suddenness and thoroughness of the attack, had not yet decided what course to follow. Of all the bishops, only Henry of Winchester and Roger, the bishop-elect of Worcester, had clearly indicated their conviction that the principle of ecclesiastical freedom was at stake, rather than a king's determination to protect himself against a possibly dishonest official whose financial dealings he had accepted without question for nearly a decade. The Bishop of Winchester reminded all the others of the release that had been granted, at his own request, on the occasion of Thomas's election.

Agitation and uncertainty, combined perhaps with fatigue from the long discussions and the ride from Canterbury, stirred up an old illness in Thomas. He suffered from kidney stone, and that night he awoke in a cold sweat, writhing from acute renal colic. Warm pillows gave him some relief, but in the morning he was in too great pain to stand. A message was sent to the king with the news that he would be unable to appear in court that day. Henry suspected a deception, and at once sent Robert, Earl of Leicester, and Reginald, Earl of Cornwall—the highest ranking officials of the kingdom—to determine whether he was feigning. When these old friends of Thomas saw him in his bed at St. Andrew's, they realized at once that he was not malingering. Nevertheless they carried out their orders, asking whether he was prepared to present his accounts. If he were granted a respite for the day, Thomas replied, he would appear in court next day even if he had to be carried there, and would then "answer as God wills."

Touched by pity for his condition and his fall from favor, the two earls[2] warned him that some of the nobles were conspiring to kill him, and that the king was planning to have him imprisoned for life or mutilated—his eyes put out and his tongue cut off.

This report was probably an exaggeration of loose talk among Henry's more fiery knights, or possibly of some angry words that Henry himself had let fall. But in his present state of physical and mental anguish, Thomas nearly lost all courage. In his despair he consulted his confessor, Prior Robert of Merton (successor to that Prior Robert who had been Thomas's teacher in his schooldays). Prior Robert recommended the challenging religious act that caused so much talk: the Mass that Thomas chose for the following morning.

Early Tuesday morning, on what was to be the last day of the great council, some of the bishops called on Thomas. They had heard, they said, that he would certainly be condemned for treason, and advised him to resign and throw himself on the king's mercy. Thomas had recovered from his consternation and his illness; his wonted forcefulness had returned, and he answered angrily in biblical language: "My brothers, as you now see, the world is raging against me; but what saddens me more and what is more detestable is that the 'sons of my own mother' are fighting against me. Even if I were to keep silent today, future ages will someday tell how you deserted me, how you twice judged me, two days running. For although I am a sinner, I am also your archbishop and your father. . . . From what you have

---

[2] It is a reasonable assumption that Reginald and Robert were identical with the "two nobles," unnamed, who conveyed this warning (*Materials* IV, 44).

just said I infer that having already judged me in a civil suit, you are now ready to judge me in a criminal case in the secular court. By virtue of your obedience and at the peril of your orders, I forbid you henceforth to sit in any judgment upon me. And that you may not do so, I appeal to our mother, the Roman Church, the refuge of all the oppressed."

If, moreover, he added, the laity raised their hands against him, as was generally rumored, the bishops were to defend him by "ecclesiastical censure"—in other words, excommunication. And he concluded on a note that he was to strike again during the proceedings of the day: "In the midst of the world's raging, my body may tremble, because the flesh is weak; but with God's help I will not wickedly yield, nor abandon the flock committed to me."

Thomas had couched his injunction in the language of the ecclesiastical hierarchy; there was no gainsaying a command "by virtue of obedience." Nevertheless, Gilbert Foliot, who was more and more openly emerging as the leader of the king's party among the bishops, refused to accept the order. He declared that he hereby made a counterappeal to Rome against his archbishop. Thomas listened to him for a moment, and then dismissed the bishops, who hurried off to court. Henry of Winchester and Jocelin of Salisbury lingered to say a few words of encouragement to Thomas. Then they too left, and Thomas entered the church to say the Mass that Prior Robert had suggested: the Mass of the first martyr, St. Stephen, which began: "Princes also did sit and speak against me." This Mass, with its Gospel reference to "Zachary murdered between the temple and the altar," was offered like a gauntlet thrown down to the king. Thomas himself became so caught up in the emotions stirred by the words that he wept and sighed frequently. If his remark to the king at Northampton some months earlier was reported correctly—that he was ready to die for his Lord—then this celebration of the Mass of St. Stephen marks the second stage in the development of what hostile critics have called Thomas's "martyr complex," and what a friendlier observer might interpret as the growing conviction that he would not escape with his life from his conflict with the king. The idea of martyrdom obviously came hard to him;

but he spent years in accustoming himself to it, until it must at last have seemed the only fitting conclusion to his life's work.

Informers, who had been having a busy time of it all that week, rushed out of the church to tell the king that Thomas was comparing Henry and his nobles to the persecutors of the first martyr. William FitzStephen calls this interpretation "malicious," but it was in fact accurate enough.

When Thomas emerged from the church, he declared that he would go barefoot, in his vestments, and carrying his own cross, into the king's presence. His clerks and the Templar knights pleaded with him that this would only anger Henry the more, and at last he allowed them to remove some of the vestments and cover the rest with an ordinary cloak. Preceded by his cross-bearer, Alexander Llewelyn, he rode to the castle. But when he dismounted inside the gate, he insisted on taking the heavy archiepiscopal cross from Alexander. Gilbert Foliot and Hugh of Nunant, Archdeacon of Lisieux, were at the castle door, and Hugh said to Gilbert: "My Lord Bishop of London, why do you allow him to carry the cross himself?" Foliot replied: "My good man, he always was a fool and always will be."

Robert of Hereford, Thomas's former teacher in Paris, tried to take the cross from him, and Foliot actually tugged vigorously at it, this time calling Thomas a fool to his face. But Thomas was physically stronger than the two elderly men; he clung to the cross, went forward, and took his accustomed seat among the bishops. Foliot sat down beside him and for the third time tried to persuade him to give up the cross. "You are holding your cross," he said. "Suppose the king now wears his sword—what a brave show king and archbishop will make!"

"I am doing this to preserve the peace of God for my own person and the English Church," Thomas replied. And with another sharp allusion to Foliot's frustrated ambition, he added: "Say what you like, if you were here in my place, you would feel differently. But if my lord the king now takes the sword, as you say, surely that would be no sign of peace."

The last to come into the hall was Thomas's old enemy, Roger of York, who made a dramatic entrance with his cross borne before him—in violation of the pope's ban against his displaying his cross outside his own province. He had delayed his coming partly "in order to be more conspicuous," partly in order not to seem to be plotting with the king. The two huge crosses in the hall reminded FitzStephen of a line from Lucan: "Lance threatening lance."

King Henry had withdrawn to an upper chamber on hearing of Thomas's arrival, for he would have no part in dramatizing a confrontation of *regnum* and *sacerdotium*. Possibly, too, he feared his own temper. He summoned the other bishops to the upper hall, and Thomas was left alone with Herbert of Bosham and William FitzStephen. For a while the archbishop and his future biographers sat in silence. At last Herbert spoke in a low voice: "My lord, if they lay impious hands on you, excommunicate them at once." FitzStephen, sitting at Thomas's feet, raised his voice somewhat and said solemnly: "Far be it from him. The holy apostles and martyrs of God did not do so when they were seized and ill treated. If it happens, he should pray for them, forgive them, and possess his soul in patience." A little later, when FitzStephen was about to take up this theme again, he was ordered to be silent by one of the king's marshals. The marshals, rods in hand, had come in and announced that no one was to speak with the archbishop. FitzStephen communicated nevertheless by raising his eyes to Thomas and indicating that he should gaze at the image on the cross and pray. Years later, FitzStephen remarks proudly, the archbishop remembered that scene and reminded his follower of it.

The bishops, meanwhile, were talking with the king. They told him that Thomas had reprimanded them and forbidden them to judge him henceforth on any secular charge. Angrily, Henry replied that this was a clear violation of Article XI of the Constitutions of Clarendon, which bound the bishops to participate in all of the king's trials and judgments unless these involved the shedding of blood.[3] Still unwilling to go to the lower hall, where sword would have confronted cross, Henry sent several of his

---

[3] Thomas himself seems to have missed the point that the king's insistence on the bishops' participation in the judgment in itself disproved the rumors that he was to be condemned to mutilation or death. Not in his worst moments would Henry have demanded that bishops sit in a capital case, and no bishop would have accepted so outrageous an innovation.

barons to ask whether Thomas intended to abide by this appeal, and also whether he was now prepared to present the accounts of his chancellorship, as had been requested on Friday, and to provide sureties for his debts.

At this point Thomas delivered his great speech of the day. Henry was not there to hear it, but it made a deep impression on many of the barons. Seated in his chair—"in order to preserve his dignity as archbishop"—he spoke clearly and fluently, without stumbling over a single word:

Men and brothers, earls and barons of the lord king, I am indeed bound to our liege lord the king by homage, fealty, and oath; but the oath of a priest has justice and equity for its fellows to a peculiar degree. In honor and fealty to the lord king I am bound in all due and devoted submission to offer him obedience in all things, saving the obedience I owe to God and my ecclesiastical rank as archbishop. I decline this suit, since I was summoned neither to render accounts nor for any other case, but only for the case of John. . . . I admit and recall that I received many tasks and dignities from the lord king. In these I served him faithfully, both here and overseas. I gladly spent all my own revenues in his behalf and then borrowed considerable sums. Furthermore, when by divine permission and the grace of the lord king I was elected archbishop and about to be conse-crated, I was released by the king and given free to the church of Canterbury, no longer subject to secular suits of the king. Al-though in his anger he now denies it, many of you well know this, as do all the clergy of the realm. I pray, beseech, and adjure those of you who know the truth of this to remind our lord king of it. For it is not permissible to produce witnesses against the king, nor is it safe or necessary, since I am not going to enter on a formal lawsuit. After my consecration, I attempted to bear the honor and the burden I had assumed to the best of my ability. . . . If I have failed, I do not blame the lord king or any other man, but chiefly my sins. God has the power to increase grace to whom and when he wills.

I cannot give sureties for rendering an account. I have al-ready obligated all the bishops and friends who could help. Nor ought I be compelled to do so, for no judgment has been passed upon me. The only suit for which I was summoned here was that of John the Marshal. As for my prohibiting the bishops to judge me and my appealing against them—I recall saying to my fellow bishops that they condemned me more seriously than is just for a single absence, and not for contumacy. That is contrary to custom and ancient precedent. For this I appealed against them, forbidding them while this appeal is pending to judge me in any secular suit arising from the time before I became archbishop. I still appeal and place my person and the church of Canterbury under the protection of God and the lord pope.

He fell silent. Some of the magnates returned silently to the king, pondering his words. Others among the king's barons and sidekicks (*stipatores lateres*) glanced at him out of the corners of their eyes and began reminiscing in deliberately loud voices: "King William, who conquered England, knew how to tame his clerks. He arrested his rebellious brother Odo, Bishop of Bayeux."

"He condemned Stigand, Archbishop of Canterbury, to perpetual imprisonment."

"What about our king's father Geoffrey, the Count of Anjou, who had the bishop-elect of Séez and several clerks unmanned, and the excised parts brought to him in a bowl?"

These remarks were the rough jests of fighting men, and of Thomas Becket's bitterest enemies, such as Ranulf de Broc; but it is no wonder that Thomas thought his life in danger. Henry was not barbarous, but in his rages the Angevin strain of cruelty could always break out.

It nearly did so now, when the archbishop's reply was brought to Henry. Frightened clerks reported that the king at once turned upon the whole body of the bishops, his face fiery red with fury. By the homage and fealty they owed him, he thundered, they must join in pronouncing sentence. The bishops pleaded that they could not do so without violating their oath of canonical obedience. They had taken a more recent oath to sit in judgment with him, the king shouted; if they now refused, they were violating their oath to observe the Constitutions of Clarendon.

There was a great deal of bustling to and fro on the upper

floor. The noise of angry voices penetrated to the hall below every time the door of the upper chamber was flung open. Henry raged and swore so violently that even Roger of York, whose enmity toward Thomas dated back twenty years, grew uneasy. He left the council chamber and descended to the hall where Thomas, William FitzStephen, and Herbert of Bosham were still sitting, surrounded by marshals. "Let us go," Roger said loudly to his clerks. "It is not fitting that we should watch what is soon going to be done to the Archbishop of Canterbury."

But even on Roger's own staff there were sympathizers with Becket. Master Robert Grand, Roger's clerk, boldly answered his superior: "I shall not leave until I see what God's will is in these matters. If he should spill his blood in fighting for God and His justice, what finer or better end to life could there be?"

Bartholomew of Exeter had come in, and now fell to his knees before Thomas. "Father," he pleaded weeping, "spare yourself and us, your brother bishops. The king has let it be known that he will treat all who oppose him as traitors."

The disgraceful behavior of his fellow bishops had only hardened Thomas's resolution. He looked straight into Bartholomew's eyes and said: "Go. You do not understand the will of God."

Even Henry of Winchester, who had supported him throughout, briefly left the king's council chamber to beg Thomas to resign, on the chance that this would pacify the king. "I did not take office on condition that I resign it, but to spend myself for it," Thomas answered. As the turbulence rose around him, he appeared more and more imperturbable; the only time he betrayed his inner tension during the whole long day was at the very end, when he stumbled on his way out of the hall.

Timidly, the bishops returned to Henry and reported that the archbishop would not release them from the ban. If they participated in the judgment now, in violation of their duty of obedience, they risked excommunication by Rome. In any case they would prejudice their case in the papal court. It was dangerous to say this to Henry, in his present temper, for they were assuming that the case would have to go to the papal court. But at last they succeeded in persuading the king to agree to a compromise. Probably the suggestion came from Gilbert Foliot, who was extremely concerned to remain within the letter of canon law.[4] Henry agreed to allow them to obey the archbishop's prohibition, provided that they appealed against it to the pope. Whereupon the bishops now went down in a body to confront Thomas. Glib Hilary of Chichester acted as spokesman.

"My lord archbishop," he said, "forgive us, but we have much to complain about. You have gravely injured us, your bishops. You have placed us between the hammer and the anvil by this ban of yours. If we reject it, we are disobedient; if we accept it, we break the law and offend the king. For recently, when we met with you at Clarendon, the king required us to observe his royal dignities, and so that there would be no doubt about them he presented to us in writing the royal customs under discussion. At last we pledged our consent and promised to observe them; you led the way and we, your suffragans, followed at your command. When, furthermore, the lord king exacted an oath from us as security, and required the impression of our seals, we told him that our oath as priests to observe his dignities in good faith, lawfully and without guile, ought to be enough. The lord king accepted our argument and agreed. You now compel us to act contrary to our word by forbidding us to take part in this trial, as he demands. From this grievance, and lest you add anything more to our injury, we appeal to our lord the pope, and for the present we obey your prohibition."

According to several writers who were not present at the proceedings, and who tend to portray Thomas as a silent sufferer, he replied only: "I hear." But William FitzStephen gives a longer and more formal response which shows Thomas at his worst and his best: at his worst in being a stickler for legal punctilio when it suited his purpose, in making use of escape clauses in a way that justified King Henry's rage; and at his best in standing by principle even at the cost of humiliation and danger, in defending principle for the king's sake as well as his own, and so abiding by

---

[4] Dom David Knowles has shrewdly suggested that the idea behind the compromise originated with the German canonist Gerhoh of Reichersberg (*The Episcopal Colleagues of Thomas Becket*, pp. 82–4).

his concept of a higher loyalty to his sovereign, which might often involve saving Henry from his own rashness; at his best also in having the courage to change his mind and break his word when he saw that he had been led into a trap.

"I hear what you say," he replied, according to FitzStephen, "and, God willing, I shall be present to answer your appeal. But at Clarendon I made no concession, nor did you through me, except saving the honor of the Church. For you yourselves say that we made these three reservations: in good faith, without guile, and lawfully. These preserve for our churches the privileges they have by papal law. . . . Besides, it does not accrue to the dignity of a Christian king that ecclesiastical liberty, which he has sworn to defend, should perish. The lord king sent these same articles which you call royal dignities to the pope for confirmation, and they have been returned with disapproval rather than approval. Thus the pope has given us a lesson. We should be ready to accept what the Roman Church accepts, reject what it rejects. Moreover, if we fell at Clarendon—for the flesh is weak—we ought to regain our courage and with the strength of the Holy Spirit strive against the ancient enemy who forever seeks to make one who stands fall, and to keep the fallen from rising again. If we yielded or swore unjustly, you know that an illegal oath is not binding."

Thomas's language at the end of his speech contained a strong allusion, which would not be lost on the bishops versed in scripture, to the passage in Romans 14:4: "Who are you to pass judgment on the servant of another? It is before his own master that he stands or falls. And he will be upheld, for the Master is able to make him stand."

The bishops returned to the king and reported Thomas's answer. Henry now permitted them to absent themselves from the judgment, and they again came down to the hall and sat with Thomas. The lay magnates then pronounced their verdict and sentence. Since shouts of "traitor" could be heard even in the lower hall, presumably Thomas was condemned for treason. But we do not know. The curious feature of the whole story is that neither judgment nor sentence was ever reported. From a subsequent letter of Henry, it is clear that the verdict was in fact

190

treason. But none of the sources ever states what the sentence was. Since all the barons had deliberated together, the nature of the sentence must have been widely known; biographers and chroniclers alike report with eagerness all of Henry's real and alleged villainies, so this silence perhaps suggests that the actual sentence, despite all the turmoil, may have been surprisingly mild—designed more to humiliate Thomas than to inflict any harm upon him. And there is a curious evasiveness in Herbert of Bosham's explanation that because of the archbishop's refusal to listen at Northampton "we do not know for certain what was adjudged."

After some delay, the barons descended to the lower hall—again without the king. Thomas remained seated, holding his cross as they approached; and awe of his spiritual office and his charismatic personality fell heavily upon them. Robert of Leicester, highest ranking of the earls, commanded some of his following to pronounce the sentence, but all were unwilling. At last Leicester reluctantly took the unpleasant task upon himself. His sympathy for Thomas was manifest, and he found it difficult to come to the point. Instead, he went back over all that Thomas owed the king, over the discussions at Clarendon, and at last said that the archbishop must now hear his sentence.

Thomas interrupted him: "I will hear no judgment, for I have appealed to the pope."

Taken aback, Robert of Leicester tried again; then he gave up the unwelcome task and asked the Earl of Cornwall to speak. Reginald, too, began and stopped. Hilary of Chichester interposed: the treason was manifest to all, he said, and the archbishop must hear his sentence. At this, Thomas burst out: "What do you think you are doing? Have you come to judge me? Judgment is given after a trial. I have done no pleading today. I was summoned for no suit except the suit of John, who did not come to contest it with me. You cannot sentence me for that. I am your father; you are chiefs of the palace, lay powers, secular persons.[5] I will not hear your judgment."

---

[5] This sentence contains the key to Thomas Becket's thought; it expresses the fundamentals of the Gregorian position. Cf. John of Salisbury, *Policraticus,* Bk IV, Chap. 3.

Brandishing his cross as if it were truly a weapon, he rose and moved with dignity toward the door, making his way through the noisy, excited crowd. Some of the sheriffs and lesser barons threw rushes at him. Near the hearth in the center of the hall he stumbled over a bundle of faggots, but quickly regained his balance. Ranulf de Broc shouted "Perjurer!" and Earl Hamelin, the king's illegitimate half brother, taunted him with cries of "Traitor!" Abruptly, Thomas turned on Hamelin and called him a lackey and a bastard. "If I were a knight, my own hands would give you the lie," he said. Then he went out the door.

The horses were tethered by the locked gate of the bailey. As Thomas mounted, one of his clerks took down the bunch of keys, which was hanging unguarded, and opened the gate. It was afterwards accounted a miracle that he had so swiftly found the right key.

Outside the castle Thomas was hailed by an enthusiastic crowd. The townsfolk had thought him already killed; now they swarmed around him, asking his blessing, so that he had difficulty controlling his horse and keeping a hold on his cross. The multitude grew greater and their cheers louder as he rode through Northampton to his lodgings at St. Andrew's. Once Thomas was in town, he was safe from insult; there was no need of the crier whom King Henry sent out to proclaim that no one was to molest the archbishop.[6] King Henry was well liked, but Thomas was loved; and in the clash between the two, the populace was undoubtedly on Thomas's side.

The crowd was composed of the poor and the infirm; among the latter were sufferers from "the King's Evil," the name given to scrofula (a form of tuberculosis of the bone and lymph glands) which in popular belief could be cured by the royal touch. The practice of "touching for the Evil" had been initiated by the recently canonized King Edward the Confessor, at whose Translation Thomas had presided in October of the previous year. Historians and later biographers have oddly overlooked this casual remark by Alan of Tewkesbury that the scrofulous thronged around Thomas demanding his blessing. For if the people be-

---

[6] At the entreaty of Bishop Robert of Hereford, says FitzStephen.

lieved that Thomas could cure the King's Evil, they were according him royal honors. There is no evidence that the popular adulation in any way stirred Thomas Becket to secular ambitions, but it does help to account for the king's suspicions of his ultimate aims.

There were, of course, reasons for the archbishop's popularity which have nothing to do with Thierry's wild notions of a Saxon rebellion against the Normans. Thomas was still admired for the feats of his secular career, and was given much of the credit for the era of prosperity and domestic peace that had begun with Henry's reign. His style, as we have seen, was more kingly than the king's. His largesse had always been princely, and as archbishop his opportunities for generosity were far greater than they had been during his chancellorship—partly because charity was the business of the Church, partly because he was at home in England all the time, whereas previously he had so often been overseas with the king, and partly because he had greater means at his disposal. Even now, after the most harrowing day in his life, the impulse of liberality did not desert him. When he arrived at the monastery of St. Andrew's, he gave orders that the motley crowd who had followed him were to be fed.

Thomas Becket's popularity was also nourished by his opposition to the Constitutions of Clarendon. The last article of the Constitutions provided that "Sons of villeins ought not to be ordained without the consent of the lord on whose land they are known to have been born." This clause, to which the pope had made no objection, directly interfered with one of the principal avenues of social mobility in twelfth-century England. The barons naturally favored it, for a villein's son who entered the clergy ceased to be available to his lord for labor and services, and at the same time acquired clerical immunity. If he had scores to settle with his former lord, a baseborn clerk enjoying the protection of the Church might be a dangerous enemy. By the same token, a refractory villein could both escape possible punishment and raise his station in life if he were free to enter the Church. Thus Article XVI of the Constitutions affected a privilege precious to the common folk, the rustics who were, indeed, mostly Saxons. Insofar as Thomas opposed all the Constitutions, the common people regarded him as their defender. In this sense, then, Thomas enjoyed the support of Thierry's "Saxons": but they were a class rather than a nation. Certainly at this time they had no thought of rebelling against their anointed king; but they applauded the spiritual leader who advocated their rights and lavished bounty upon them.

There was even greater opportunity than usual for the archbishop's bounty that night. For after waiting on him at the refectory table, many of the knights and pages of his household tearfully requested that he release them from his service, lest the king's anger also fall upon them. As laymen, Herbert of Bosham remarks, their conduct was excusable; but there could be no excuse for the forty-odd clerks who likewise deserted. Thomas ordered that their places at the board be filled by the beggars and townsfolk who had gathered outside. Then he ate his supper, showing a "cheerful and affable" mien. He was already regretting the words he had spoken on striding out of the hall of the castle. The admonition he now gave to his followers was directed as much to himself as to them and shows him, as so often, wrestling with the contradiction between his worldly impulses and his religious faith. When William FitzStephen remarked to him: "This has been a bitter day," he replied: "The Last Day will be more bitter." And after a short silence, he added: "Let each of you hold to silence and peace. Let no bitter words fall from your lips. Do not answer; let them taunt you. It is the mark of a higher character to bear insults, of the lower nature to inflict them. They command their tongues, but we our ears. Insults touch us only if we recognize in ourselves the evils they allege."

During supper there was reading as usual, this time from the *Historia Tripartita* of Cassiodorus—a sixth-century compilation of the *Antiquities* of Josephus and several ecclesiastical histories. In the course of the reading a sentence from the Bible was quoted: "If they persecute you in one city, flee to another." Thomas raised his eyes and exchanged glances with Herbert of Bosham. At that moment, Herbert conjectures, the thought of flight was born.

But the day's negotiations were still far from over. While the company was at table, Gilbert Foliot and Hilary of Chichester arrived, saying that they had found a way to make peace. "On what terms?" Thomas asked. "It is only a question of money between you and the king," they replied with truly monumental disingenuousness. "If you turn over two of your manors, Otford and Wingham, to him as a pledge for the time being, we think he will be pacified." Furthermore, they argued, he would remit the sum Thomas owed and probably would soon restore the manors anyhow. What prompted the bishops to make this foolish suggestion it is impossible to say. They did not pretend that Henry had made any such offer, and it is obvious that he would not. Possibly they merely hoped to clear themselves before their fellow bishops and the public by playing the part of unwearying peacemakers. Thomas sensibly rejected the proposal. He pointed out that Henry already held one of the manors, and that the property of Canterbury belonged to the Church, not to its archbishop.

After the meal, Thomas sent Walter of Rochester, Robert of Hereford, and Roger of Worcester to the king to ask his permission to leave Northampton,[7] and to provide a safe-conduct for the journey—a request that indicates Thomas's fear of being attacked by some of the king's more hotheaded retainers, who might take the opportunity offered by the royal disfavor to settle old scores. The bishops found the king in good humor—Henry evidently felt that he had gained his ends—but unwilling to give a definite yes or no. He would let them know next day, he replied.

Thomas felt that the answer boded ill. The talk of mutilation and imprisonment had affected him more than he had shown. Until Henry revealed his intentions more plainly, it might be wise for him to take sanctuary in the church. There was a bit of play acting in his instructions to the monks to carry his bed into the chapel and place it between two altars. When the monks later came into sing compline, they saw him there, apparently asleep. But in the meanwhile, other arrangements were going forward.

---

[7] There is disagreement among the sources as to whether Thomas asked leave to return to Canterbury or to go abroad to prosecute his appeal to the pope. But he probably would not have dared, at this juncture, to suggest that he wanted to go overseas in person.

PART THREE

Exile

XII

Flight

RAIN streamed down upon the city and the autumnal countryside that night; but storm and darkness were welcome to Thomas Becket. Toward midnight he rose from his bed between the altars and stole out of church and monastery, accompanied by two canons from Sempringham and his personal servant, Roger. His only baggage was the pallium and the archiepiscopal seal. Horses had been placed in readiness outside the walls of St. Andrew's. The four riders passed safely through the deserted streets of Northampton and out the unguarded northern gate— symbol of a realm at peace. Reasoning that the royal officials would expect him to make for Canterbury and the coast, Thomas instead rode straight north toward Lincoln. The driving rain so thoroughly soaked his thick woolen cloak that he had to stop twice to cut off a piece of it to lighten its weight. Nevertheless they made good speed, for they traveled some fifty miles to Grantham before snatching a brief rest. Before dawn, they continued on their way, and reached Lincoln that morning. A ride of seventy miles (Herbert of Bosham later inaccurately reckoned it as fifty) in the rain and dead of night was quite a feat for a man who had only just risen from a sickbed.

At Lincoln, they lodged with a fuller named James. Here Thomas adopted ordinary monastic dress and the name of Brother Christian. The following day he continued by water down the Witham toward a lonely spot in the fens known as the Hermitage, which belonged to the canons of Sempringham: the order

199

founded by St. Gilbert, who was subsequently to attain a fame almost equal to Thomas's own. Thomas rested there for three days while couriers went forward to prepare an escape route for him.

Slowly, traveling mostly by night and partly by water, he worked his way southward for the remainder of the week until he reached Eastry, near Sandwich, a manor that belonged to the monks of Christ Church, Canterbury. Here he remained for another week, awaiting an opportunity to cross to the Continent. It testifies to the tight organization of the Church that a man of such prominence and striking appearance, whose face and tall stature were known everywhere in England, and particularly in Kent, could remain hidden so successfully for a full two weeks. None of the many monks, priests, and canons who aided his escape, or necessarily knew of his whereabouts, betrayed him. It is also true that Henry's officers seem not to have searched very diligently for him. Henry confined himself to having the ports watched; but he evidently had little hope of keeping Thomas from leaving the country. "We have not done with the man yet," he remarked. The comment of the other Henry, the Bishop of Winchester, differed significantly. When he heard of the archbishop's escape, he said: "May God's blessing go with him."

On All Soul's Day (November 2, 1164), Thomas set sail from Sandwich before dawn in a small boat manned by the two canons and his servant Roger. Despite the rough sea, they made the coast of Flanders before evening. Fearing the Count of Boulogne, whose marriage he had opposed, and unsure of the attitude that Philip of Flanders would take toward a fugitive from his sovereign, Thomas avoided the ports and landed on the beach near Gravelines. Unaccustomed to walking, hampered by the long robe and the clumsy shoes that were part of his monastic habit, he repeatedly tripped and fell in the slippery sand. The rough crossing of the Straits of Dover might well have weakened a man more used to privation than Thomas, and at last, after another fall in which he scraped his hands severely, he lay on the sand in despair, declaring that he could not take another step. His companions, seeing a boy some distance up the beach, ran to him and pleaded with him to hire a mount. The boy returned with a sorry beast (a horse in some versions, an ass in others) without saddle or bridle and with only a rope halter around its neck. The canons spread their cloaks on the animal's back and had to lift Thomas into this improvised saddle. But he felt so uncomfortable, and above all so undignified, that after a few miles he decided to walk again.

Thomas had managed to remain incognito for weeks in England, where he was well known. In Flanders, however, the secret could not be kept so well. Rumors of his flight had preceded him, and he himself must by now have become impatient with his game of hide-and-seek. He nearly betrayed himself by looking with too keen an interest at a hawk that a knight was holding on his wrist. At an inn in Gravelines, the landlord recognized him by his manners but promised to keep his secret. Nevertheless, by the time Thomas stopped at the Cistercian abbey of Clair-Marais, near St. Omer, the whole countryside knew who he was. Richard de Lucy, on his way to see the Count of Flanders, heard of his presence there and stopped to see him.

De Lucy had not participated in the trial and judgment at Northampton. He had been on pilgrimage to St. James of Compostella, the great shrine of Christendom in that era, whose fame was soon to be outstripped by the shrine of Thomas himself. De Lucy was not only a capable administrator, a shrewd judge, and a man of unswerving loyalty; he was also a deeply devout Christian who would end his life in a monastery that he was to found in honor of his king's great adversary. Now, at Clair-Marais, he tried to persuade that adversary to return to England. What began as a courteous conversation between two old friends ended in an unseemly wrangle. De Lucy held land in fee from the Archbishop of Canterbury, and was therefore formally Thomas Becket's "man." He now offered a *diffidatio,* warning Thomas that he would henceforth be his enemy if he persisted in opposition to the king.

"You are my vassal and ought not to talk to me like that," Thomas said. Precisely because he was a burgess, he was given to harping on the feudal code.

"I give you back my homage," Richard replied.

"You did not receive it as a loan," Thomas said sharply.

Thomas had sacrificed one more friendship to principle.

Other and more welcome visitors hastened to Clair-Marais at the news of Thomas's safe arrival there. Herbert of Bosham had not traveled with Thomas, for those two towering figures would surely have been recognized if they had been together. Instead, he had gone straight from Northampton to Canterbury and there gathered what money he could—it amounted to no more than a hundred marks and some silver plate—before crossing to the Continent with some of Thomas's other clerks and servants. Their reunion was joyful, although Herbert brought the disturbing information that a party of envoys from King Henry had crossed from Dover on the same day that Thomas left from Sandwich, and had arrived at the abbey of St. Bertin at the same time that Thomas reached nearby Clair-Marais. The party was a large one, consisting of the Archbishop of York, the bishops of London, Worcester, Chichester, and Exeter, the Earl of Arundel (Henry's great-uncle by marriage, for he had married the widow of Henry I), and a considerable number of clerks of the court. They were on their way to see King Louis of France, Herbert had learned, to ask him to lend no support to Thomas, and were then charged to proceed to the pope at Sens and present to him their own appeal and the king's case.

These envoys left the abbey after three days, and Abbot Godescalc of St. Bertin then invited Thomas to stay with him—an invitation that Thomas accepted all the more gladly since St. Bertin was a traditional resort of exiled English archbishops. There Anselm had stayed sixty-seven years before; and Theobald, with Thomas at his side, had likewise found refuge there after the Council of Reims. At St. Bertin, a vast and ancient congeries of buildings set in an area of flat, well-tilled fields and completely surrounded by a stout wall, Thomas was able to rest comfortably at last from the hardships of the fugitive life he had been leading. He at once set in motion the intense diplomatic activity that was to occupy the remaining years of his life. Herbert of Bosham was ordered to follow the king's envoys secretly, keeping a day's journey behind them.

Here was as assignment dear to the heart of that impetuous young man, and Herbert describes with zest his part as espionage agent and representative of his master. He tracked the envoys for three or four days, until they reached Compiègne, where King Louis was staying at his castle—since Merovingian times the Frankish and French kings had loved to hunt in the forest of Compiègne. Herbert entered the town the day after the envoys left, and almost immediately learned to his relief that their mission had failed.

The English envoys had brought a letter from Henry to Louis, a letter that reveals how badly Henry stood in need of a chancellor who possessed the diplomatic skills of Thomas Becket. For it was a lame, impolitic, and self-betraying plea that Henry addressed to Louis:

> To his lord and friend Louis, illustrious King of the French, from Henry, King of the English and Duke of the Normans and Aquitanians, and Count of the Angevins, greetings and love.
>
> Know that Thomas, who was Archbishop of Canterbury, has been publicly judged in my court by a full council of the barons of my realm as a wicked and perjured traitor to me, and under the manifest name of traitor has wickedly departed, as my envoys will tell you more fully. Wherefore I entreat you not to permit a man infamous for such crimes and treasons, nor his men, to remain in your kingdom. Please do not let this great enemy of mine receive any aid or counsel from you or yours, as I would not give or allow any to be given to your enemies in my realm. Rather, please help me effectively to avenge myself for the disgrace inflicted upon me by this great enemy of mine, and to regain my honor as you would wish that I would do for you if the need arose.

Thomas, as chancellor, would never have allowed his sovereign to take so whining, egocentric, and unstatesmanlike a tone, or to ask for help from one who, it could easily be foreseen, would be disinclined to give it. For it was elementary common sense to assume that policy and piety would combine to urge Louis to support the archbishop. After all, Thomas's opposition was weakening Louis's greatest rival on the Continent.

Along with the letter the envoys were supposed to deliver a verbal request for the return of the fugitive. But Louis scarcely gave them the opportunity, for he interrupted as soon as he heard the first words of the letter. "Who *was* Archbishop of Canterbury?" he repeated. "Who has deposed him? Tell me that now, my lords, who has deposed him? Who has deposed him?" And as the abashed envoys still did not reply, Louis added: "Certainly I am as much a king as the King of the English; but I do not have the power to depose the least of the clerks in my realm."

William, Earl of Arundel, then reminded Louis that Thomas as chancellor had devastated his lands and seized his towns during the Toulouse campaign, and by his shrewdness had "lopped off a not inconsiderable part of your kingdom and power." Louis replied generously that such conduct on Thomas's part seemed to him good and honorable. He had been serving his lord faithfully, and it ill became Henry to return evil for good.

In the presence of the discomfited envoys, Louis then called for the papal chamberlain, who happened to be present at Compiègne: "Tell my lord Pope Alexander from me," he said, "that I hope he will receive the Archbishop of Canterbury with kindness, and not heed any unjust accusation against him."

Herbert, entering Compiègne next day, at length obtained an audience with Louis, who did not know him. "He asked us repeatedly, as was his wont, whether we were of the archbishop's household and family," Herbert comments, alluding to Louis's habit of repeating the same phrase over and over. When Herbert had convinced him that he was in fact an intimate of the archbishop, the king listened graciously to the tale of their woes, labors, and perils. "Then the bowels of the royal compassion were vehemently stirred." Louis related what had passed between himself and Henry's envoys, and then added: "Before harrying so harshly so great a friend, archbishop, and personage, the Lord King of the English ought to have remembered that verse, 'Be angry but do not sin.' " Whereupon Herbert's companion, who was possibly the quick-tongued Alexander Llewelyn,[1] replied: "My lord, perhaps he would have remembered the verse if he had heard it as frequently in the canonical hours as we have."[2] Louis smiled at this, and dismissed the messengers with the promise

---

[1] I follow here a suggestion of Dom L'Huillier (*Saint Thomas de Cantorbéry*, I, 369).
[2] The verse (Eph. 4:26) would be heard at least once a day at compline: "Be angry but do not sin; do not let the sun go down on your anger."

that Thomas would have peace and security in France. It was an ancient prerogative of the Crown of France to shelter exiles, especially ecclesiastics, he added, and he intended to abide by that tradition.

Comforted, Herbert and his companion continued on their way to Sens, where the pope received them at once. Herbert described with devotion and long-winded eloquence "the archbishop's hardships, difficulties, and griefs, his perils in that fight with beasts at Northampton, perils among false brethren, perils in his flight, perils en route, perils in the sea and even in the harbor, his labors, poverty, and distress, his change of clothes and name in order to avoid the snares of his enemies." The pope listened, Herbert avers, with fatherly compassion, was moved to tears, and said: "Your lord still lives in the flesh as you say; but while still living he can claim the privilege of martyrdom." Certainly Alexander himself was even now experiencing the tribulations of exile in the flesh, as Herbert well knew. Nevertheless, he must soon have tired of Herbert's loquacity, and as he had done at Tours with Thomas Becket, he availed himself of the lateness of the hour and the supposed weariness of the travelers. "After giving us his apostolic blessing and consolation, he quickly dismissed us to our lodging," Herbert records.

Next day His Holiness found that Herbert was not the only loquacious Englishman. Alexander had announced a public audience, to which Herbert and his companion were invited, to hear the envoys from King Henry. Gilbert Foliot, as leader of the delegation, opened the proceedings with a lengthy speech in which he harped once again on his notion that Thomas Becket was a fool—a notion that none of the other enemies of Becket shared. It was the pope's task to rebuke those who acted foolishly, Gilbert declared. The dissension between *regnum et sacerdotium* had arisen over a minor matter and might easily have been settled by moderation. But the Archbishop of Canterbury had insisted on having his own way, had rejected the advice of his brother bishops, and had pushed matters to extremes. "Had we consented to his proposals, matters would have become worse. . . . To shame us, his brothers, he has fled, although no violence was used or threatened—as it is written: 'The wicked flee when no man pursues.' "

At this the pope interrupted: "Do not be unkind, brother."

"My lord, I shall not be unkind to him," Foliot answered.

"I do not say you are unkind to him, brother, but to your-self," Alexander said.[3]

Alexander had shrewdly rebuked the bishop for a weakness of character that Foliot himself was aware of: his spitefulness toward his superiors. Confused and ashamed, Bishop Gilbert fell silent, to the relief of Hilary of Chichester who had been waiting for the opportunity to display his eloquence in the presence of His Holiness. Hilary took up Gilbert's theme that Thomas Becket had rejected the counsel of his fellows, and added to it the threat that such actions might well create schism in the Church. But in his enthusiasm he soon slipped into grammatical mistakes in his Latin, someone came up with a feeble pun about his solecism, and the whole assembly dissolved in laughter. Dashed, Hilary also fell silent.

Forewarned by the experience of the other two, Roger of York and Bartholomew of Exeter limited themselves to a few words. York reminded the pope that he had known Thomas Becket from the beginning of his career, and had found that "he cannot easily be turned from an opinion he has once formed." Bartholomew asked for legates to hear the suit between the king and archbishop and decide it.

The Earl of Arundel had probably understood most of the Latin proceedings, for all that he pretended ignorance; and although he certainly missed the fine point of grammar that had stirred such hilarity, he could gather that the bishops were not doing well in their presentation of the case. He asked permission to speak, and tried to mend matters by taking a softer line. He spoke in his native Norman French:

"My lord, we unlettered men know nothing whatsoever of what the bishops have said. We ought therefore to explain as well as we can why we have been sent. We have not come to contend or to slander anyone, especially in the presence of so great a person, to whose will and authority the whole world bows by

---

[3] It is difficult to convey the sense of this in translation. *"Parce, frater." "Domine, parcam ei." "Non dico, frater, quod parcas ei, sed tibi." Parco* means spare, be merciful, forbear.

right. But we have undoubtedly come to assure you, in your presence and that of the whole Roman Church, of the devotion and love which our king has always borne and still bears toward you. There is no one more faithful or more devoted to God within the unity of the Catholic Church which it is your task to govern. There is no one more anxious to preserve peace. Nevertheless, the lord archbishop also is equally well versed in his rank and order, prudent and discreet in the things that concern him, although somewhat too sharp, it seems to some. If it were not for this dissension that has arisen between the lord king and the lord archbishop, the State and Church would together enjoy peace and comfort under a good king and the best of pastors. This, then, is our plea: that your Grace will take careful heed to remove this dissension and restore peace and love."

In the discussion that followed, the envoys pressed the pope to declare judgment at once on the issue between Thomas and the king. Alexander refused on the ground that Thomas was not present to defend his case. If the envoys would wait until he arrived—it was reliably reported that he was on his way to Sens—he would be glad to try the suit. But the envoys informed the pope that they had been strictly commanded to remain only three days, and then return to King Henry. Could not Alexander order the Archbishop to return to England?

That would be like ordering a prisoner to return to his jail, Alexander said.

Then would he appoint cardinal-legates to try the case?

"Since you have asked for legates, you shall have them," Alexander replied.

The king's envoys were relieved; they had already distributed lavish presents among the cardinals—"whose nostrils the smell of lucre had infected"—and were convinced that silver would do its usual work. They kissed the pope's foot and withdrew. But Gilbert Foliot took the precaution of returning to ask the pope what authority would be given the legates.

"Due authority," the pope replied.

"But," said Foliot, "we ask that they be able to settle the case so that it cannot again be appealed."

"That is my glory, which I will not give to anyone else," the pope replied. "And in truth, when he is judged, we and no one else will judge him, for it would be contrary to reason to send him back to England to be judged among enemies and by his adversaries."

The ambassadors could get no more out of the pope. Secretly, they made extravagant offers: if Alexander consented to depose Becket, the king would guarantee Peter's pence in perpetuity; moreover, he would collect it from every house in England "from which smoke issued," instead of only from the villeins as heretofore. But Alexander refused; he badly needed the thousand pounds per annum, but he was not venal like his cardinals.

Their three days up, the envoys took their leave. It was typical of Henry's impatience that he had given them so short a time for negotiation. But it was also indicative of his scorn for the slow machinery of the Curia and his suspicions of his own bishops. He did not want them out of his control and subject to the influences of the papal court for any length of time. Unfortunately for him, he did not consider that his virtual ultimatum necessarily prejudiced his case, and that the man who had challenged the Emperor Frederick to his face was not likely to yield to pressure from a king, even the richest and most powerful king in Europe and one on whom Alexander was just then peculiarly dependent. For that matter, Alexander was even more dependent on Louis VII, who was after all his host.

The English envoys traveled as swiftly as possible, for they had heard rumors that some French knights, eager to avenge past insults to their monarch and the present harassment of Thomas Becket, whom they admired, were planning to attack the party and plunder it.

Meanwhile Thomas was approaching Sens, not as a humble suppliant accompanied by a few clerks, but with a magnificent train of three hundred mounted men. He had been met at Soissons by King Louis, who had promised him full support and had insisted on providing him with a retinue befitting his station. Louis had good reason to remember Thomas Becket's fondness for display. The returning English party and the arriving archbishop's party caught a glimpse of one another across the river Yonne. The English ambassadors might at this point have disobeyed the letter of their instructions and returned to argue the case against Becket before the pope, since Alexander had made it a condition that the archbishop must be present, and they could now see that he would be. But either they were too fearful of Henry's wrath if they lingered or, more likely, they did not welcome the prospect of another confrontation with Thomas. In any case, they continued their return journey, only detaching one of their number to go back to Sens and see how the pope received the archbishop.

Thomas Becket himself was certainly as anxious as the envoys about the nature of his reception. He understood that Alexander, his fellow exile, would be caught between the hammer of the King of England and the anvil of the King of France; and he had already been informed that many of the cardinals inclined toward Henry's side, out of conviction or self-interest. Yet by accepting Louis's gifts of money and men, Thomas was lending color to charges that he had betrayed his sovereign. On the other hand, he was a proud man; his recent collapse on the beach near Gravelines had been prompted perhaps as much by humiliation as by physical exhaustion. He was also a man of the world who knew that although powerful ecclesiastics might pity poverty and commend lowliness, they would not respect it. Thus both inclination and policy moved him to temper the humility of a persecuted churchman with the ostentation of an eminent statesman. He had therefore accepted King Louis's offer, and arrived at Sens more like a victor than a victim. So impressive was his equipage that a large number of cardinals came out to meet him as he approached the city, even though many of them had already been won over to Henry's cause.

But what happened thereafter? The contemporary sources betray us when narrating the crucial meeting between Pope Alexander and Archbishop Becket. Not that they fail to give a fulsome account of the external details: how Alexander embraced him, gave him the kiss of peace, expressed sympathy for his trials, and insisted on seating him at his right hand. We even have the account of a miracle that Thomas unwittingly performed in the pope's presence. When Thomas and Alexander were at table together, it seems, Alexander asked a waiter to bring him water.

When it was served, he passed the pitcher to Thomas. "Bless it and drink," he said. Thomas thereupon blessed the water, which was changed to wine, and after drinking passed it to the pope. When Alexander realized that it was wine, he called the waiter and asked in a whisper: "What did you bring me?" "Water," the waiter replied. "Bring me more of the same," the pope said. This was done, and twice more Thomas blessed the water and drank wine, without knowing the power of his blessing. Whereupon, we are told, the pope was "sore afraid."

But although the superficial and apocryphal details are plentifully supplied, each of the accounts we have contains internal contradictions, and among the various narratives there are irreconcilable disagreements on what actually passed between the two men. Several sources allege that Thomas confessed "with sighs and groans" that he was not canonically elected, but had been forced upon the Church by the secular power. He would not resign at the instance of the king and his fellow bishops, he supposedly declared, for fear of setting an evil precedent, but: "Now, however, lest I involve in my own ruin the flock to which I, such as I am, was given as shepherd, I resign the archbishopric of Canterbury into your hands, father." The pope and the cardinals then withdrew to consider the resignation, and although some cardinals favored acceptance, the pope and the majority decided that Thomas was "fighting for all of us, and ought therefore to be supported in every possible way."

William FitzStephen is somewhat doubtful about the resignation. He declares tersely: "It is said that he resigned the archbishopric into the pope's hands." Guernes, the French biographer, who would have been likely to know about things that happened on the Continent, says nothing about it. Edward Grim, in relating the resignation, adds the scarcely reassuring phrase—"as was told me for certain." Herbert of Bosham says not a word about resignation or admission of noncanonical election, though he was present throughout the proceedings.

These expressions of doubt and this silence on the part of so many of the biographers, together with the absence of any mention of the matter in the letters or pamphlets of the opposing party, suggest that the whole story of the resignation as Alan of

Tewkesbury gives it may be founded on a misunderstanding. For it is known that Becket asked the pope for a confirmation of his primacy—meaning, in particular, of his superiority to the Archbishop of York, with whom he had wrangled from the moment he was consecrated. Possibly Alan confounded primacy with primateship, and then decided to dramatize the whole story.

There is, of course, the alternative possibility that Herbert of Bosham, the biographer most in a position to know, deliberately suppressed his knowledge. Herbert never thought highly of humility, and he would certainly have advised his master against any such reckless step as resignation of Canterbury into the hands of a pope whose temper had not been tried and who was surrounded by cardinals hostile to the archbishop's cause. Herbert would have viewed any such concession or confession as a terrible moral weakness and tactical error. He might therefore have chosen to say nothing about it, or might easily have repressed his memory of it in the twenty years between the event itself and his description of the interview at Sens.

The strongest objection to the story of the resignation, however, is that it is inconsistent with Thomas's character. Thomas Becket, as we have seen, had convinced himself that he had been canonically elected. Even if he had not believed that, moreover, he was too astute to offer such a handle to his enemies. Only a few weeks before, at Northampton, he had declared that he had not taken office in order to resign it; his recent privations had undermined neither his pride nor his intellect. To offer resignation now, even to the pope, would have been to concede the material victory to Henry if it were accepted, and to permit doubt of his fitness for office to enter the pope's mind, even if it were not accepted. There seems every reason for us to believe, therefore, that Thomas Becket did not resign his archbishopric into the pope's hand even though almost every writer on the subject since the twelfth century has unquestioningly repeated Alan of Tewkesbury's account.

To say that Thomas would not have resigned at this time does not mean that he would never have contemplated such a step. On at least one occasion he actually did consider resigning, and Herbert of Bosham does not hesitate to report it. But this was a year and a half later, when circumstances had greatly changed. After many disappointments, austerities, and penances, after all attempts at mediation and all direct appeals to Henry had failed, Thomas began to believe that the whole Church would continue to be troubled as long as he remained archbishop. He suffered "many vacillations of the soul," and called his learned men together to consult with them on the wisdom of resigning. Herbert describes, with a satisfaction that betrays his own advice, how the *eruditi* exhorted Thomas to remain at his post. It may well be that garbled accounts of this incident gave rise to Alan of Tewkesbury's story.

One thing that did definitely take place at Sens was a thorough discussion of the Constitutions of Clarendon in a formal papal consistory. Herbert, either for dramatic effect or because he had actually forgotten, tells us that the pope now saw the "chirograph" of the Constitutions for the first time. This, of course, is a mistake; as we have seen, King Henry himself had sent a copy of the Constitutions to the pope shortly after the Council of Clarendon, and Alexander had already expressed his opinion. Nevertheless, in lieu of the gift of gold or silver customary on such occasions, Thomas Becket dramatically spread his parchment of the Constitutions at Alexander's feet.

"Holy father," he said, "this is the reason for my exile, and if you give me leave, let me read it to you, and submit it to your decision. For I did not think I had the power to consent to the novelties written here."

The pope ordered the Constitutions to be read and analyzed by Thomas. Cardinal William of Pavia, "dearest friend of the king at the pope's court," appointed himself defender of the document in the absence of Henry's envoys. There followed a scholastic debate that the one-time schoolmaster Alexander must surely have enjoyed. Cardinal William unfortunately had believed Gilbert Foliot's slanders of Thomas's intelligence; he thought of the former chancellor as ignorant in canon law and unskilled in logic-chopping: a secular who borrowed his ecclesiastical ideas from such aides as John of Salisbury and Herbert of Bosham. It would be an easy matter, he imagined, to put this layman in his place.

Thomas listened quietly to the whole of the cardinal's long speech, to the defense of each of the Constitutions, and the charge that he was disturbing the peace of the Church over trivia. Then Thomas replied *par bel latin,* taking up each point in turn, quick-wittedly responding to the cardinal's ill-tempered interruptions, and presenting his cause so eloquently that William of Pavia was "confounded." After answering the cardinal's arguments for an entire morning session of the consistory, he returned to his own analysis of the Constitutions and explained in detail to these Italian clerics, who naturally did not understand the whole of the situation in England, the import of the various clauses and how they diminished the "honor of the Roman Church." If he did not draw the obvious parallel between Henry's claims and those of Frederick Barbarossa, he refrained only because it was implicit in all that he said. Alexander understood only too well the nature of the conflict between *regnum* and *sacerdotium* in which he himself was caught.

The pope indicated his agreement with Thomas in a backhanded way, by rebuking him for ever having consented to the customs, then praising him for having risen again after falling. He thanked him for his present defense of the Church and promised to help him "where reason permitted." For although Alexander's sympathies clearly lay with Thomas, the Angevin empire was still the mainstay of his shaky hold on the pontificate. If Henry withdrew support, the German emperor and his antipope would triumph—and that this was a real danger, subsequent events were to show. For the present, Alexander could only think that he must let tempers cool. He had by now taken the measure of Thomas's imperious nature, and he recommended a course in humility. Let Thomas retire to a monastery for a time, live quietly and meekly among the brethren, with only a few of his clerks accompanying him, and wean himself from the good living he had hitherto enjoyed. Herbert of Bosham asserts that Thomas chose the Cistercian abbey of Pontigny for his refuge; Alan of Tewkesbury presents the matter as if the pope virtually sentenced the archbishop to Pontigny as punishment, ordering him to remain there "until the day of consolation nears and the time of peace descends from on high." Meanwhile, the pope allegedly told him, "keep up your courage and manfully resist those who disturb the peace." Whether by the latter the pope meant the agents of Henry or such advisers as Herbert of Bosham, he did not say.

Accompanied by Herbert and Alexander Llewelyn, among others, Thomas Becket set off with the Abbot of Pontigny, who had been present at the consistory. He may have reflected, as he journeyed toward the monastery where he was to spend the next two years in retirement, that the pope had not said a word concerning the appeals: the bishops' appeals against his prohibition of their sitting in judgment upon him, and his appeal against the judgment of the king's court in a suit over revenues that he allegedly owed to the king from his days as chancellor. Alexander had condemned the Constitutions, but he had reserved decision on the legal issues between the archbishop and the king. Yet in effect Thomas had already won his major point, for Henry had accepted the authority of the pope as arbiter.

For Thomas at Pontigny, as he donned the monastic habit of "thick and coarse woolen cloth" which the pope had personally blessed and sent to him, this must have been some small consolation—if he realized it. But he seems to have been unaware that the larger cause was already won. He blamed himself and his sins for his failure, and resolved on a penance that he kept secret from his friends. Underneath his habit, he took to wearing a hair shirt from neck to knees.

XIII

Humility and Pride

THE EARLY BIOGRAPHERS describe with enthusiasm Thomas Becket's penances at the Cistercian monastery of Pontigny. He spent night after night on his knees praying, they say. When he slept at all, it was on the cold stone floor. He ordered his chaplain to flog him regularly. He did not change his hair shirt, so that he might suffer the more from the bites of innumerable fleas (Thomas with his passion for cleanliness). He punished the flesh by standing for hours in icy streams. And so on. These stories, if they are true at all, are probably embroideries on single instances. Any twelfth-century Christian might occasionally seek out extreme penances. King Henry himself wore a hair shirt once, and submitted to flagellation, as we shall see.

The import of the stories is clear: in the early part of his stay at Pontigny Thomas was in a mood of contrition, not to say depression. He had counted heavily on his personal interview with Pope Alexander. He had expected His Holiness to denounce the English bishops for betraying their ecclesiastical superior, and to condemn the secular power for daring to judge a minister of God. Instead, Alexander had temporized, and had also humiliated him. The proper place for a man of Thomas Becket's attainments and ecclesiastical dignity was at the Curia. Alexander might have taken Thomas into the papal service, thus making use of his skill in diplomacy, his familiarity with the leaders of Europe, and his administrative abilities. But Alexander made no move to give Thomas a place in his court. That must have been a bitter blow to the exiled archbishop.

Life in a Cistercian monastery was in itself penitential. Thomas Becket, who was oversensitive to cold, might have been grateful to his hair shirt for its warmth, since the monks were allowed only two tunics, even in the coldest weather, and no breeches. Thomas himself seems to have violated this rule, for he had hair drawers. In fact on one occasion, when they needed mending and he did not know how to have this done without revealing the secret of his penance, the Virgin Mary came to him, sat down beside him, and deftly stitched them up. In general, however, he tried to abide strictly by the Cistercian Rule. This included sharing the diet of his hosts, which consisted largely of gruel (meat and lard were reserved for the sick in Cistercian monasteries). Since Thomas arrived at Pontigny on November 30, he found the menu even sparer, for between September 13 and Easter of each year the monks ate only one meal a day.

The vitamin-poor diet took its toll. Thomas fell ill. A swelling developed on his cheek; tissue and bone necrosed; soon he was suffering from a case of acute osteomyelitis.[1] During the course of this painful and protracted disease he suffered from terrifying deliria. Once he dreamed that a quarrel had arisen between himself and the king. He was standing all alone in the presence of the pope and the cardinals to argue his case, with the cardinals taking the king's side. Suddenly they rush upon him, their fingernails clawing at his eyes like great talons. The pope cries out, but in the noise and uproar the cardinals do not even hear him. Then the cardinals vanish and he sees approaching "men terrible to behold," who seem to be his executioners. Advancing upon him, they draw their swords and cut off the crown of his head, which falls forward over his eyes.

The Cistercians, like most monks, had some skill in medicine; but Thomas's disease would not yield to ordinary remedies. At last an operation was risked: an operation in the manner of the age, without anesthesia, with no attempt at antisepsis. Two ne-

---

[1] I gratefully acknowledge the kindness and acuity of Eric Adler, M.D., of Greenfield, Mass., who has diagnosed Becket's illness from the description of the symptoms given by the contemporary biographer Edward Grim.

crotic fragments of bone were successfully removed, and Thomas then recovered completely. Herbert of Bosham, who believed that poor diet had caused the illness, rated him for "immoderate abstinence." He had succumbed, said Herbert, to a temptation the devil used upon those who could not be overcome by gluttony. Thomas at length took advice; he returned to his habitually delicate foods, although he continued to eat sparingly.

With improved health his spirits revived also, and he plunged into the struggle for vindication. To his last hour, pride and humility warred in the soul of Thomas Becket, but until his last hour humility seems to have nourished his pride. This, perhaps, is why he was so often accused of hypocrisy. His penances were genuine; but he returned from them with renewed courage and belligerence, and often with self-righteousness.

Like a prisoner who studies law to draw up his appeal, Thomas spent the long days and nights at Pontigny preparing his case. Pontigny was close to Sens, where the pope still resided, and also to Auxerre, at whose celebrated school of law Thomas had studied some twelve years before. Now he sent to Auxerre and to monasteries and churches all over France for books bearing on canon and civil law and the history of England. He applied also to the pope for copies of Canterbury privileges that might be found in the papal archives. Within a short time, he had at his disposal in the library at Pontigny a complete collection of the Fathers of the Church, the letters and sermons of Yves of Chartres, the works of Anselm, Lanfranc, and Geoffrey of Monmouth, as well as Bede's *Ecclesiastical History*. Above all, of course, there was Gratian's *Decretum*. The works of the Fathers and of Bernard of Clairvaux would naturally have been in a Cistercian library; and since the Cistercian order had been founded by the Englishman Stephen Harding, a number of books on English matters would probably have been available also. But it is probable that many of the works listed in the monastic catalogue were brought to Pontigny by or at the instance of Thomas Becket.

We have direct evidence of the nature of his reading during this period of enforced inactivity in a remonstrance addressed to him by his friend John of Salisbury:

I wish, advise and pray you above all that you turn your mind to the Lord and the refuge[2] of prayer. . . . The laws and canons are useful, but believe me, there is no need of them now. . . . Spiritual exercise and the cleansing of conscience avert the scourge and win the mercy of God. Who rises up with conscience stirred from a reading of the laws, or even the canons? Rather, I say: scholastic exercise swells the pride of knowledge, but rarely or never kindles devoutness. I would prefer you to ruminate on the Psalms and peruse the blessed Gregory's Moral Books than philosophize in scholastic fashion. . . . God knows in what spirit and with what devotion I make this suggestion; you will take it as you please. But if you do as I say, God will be your aid, so that you need not fear man's intrigues. He knows that in our present troubles we cannot hope for anything mortal, so I think.

Thomas Becket prized such freespokenness in his friends; but he was readier to hear advice than to follow it. If we may judge by the innumerable letters that poured from his pen during the six years of his exile, he by no means abandoned his studies of the laws and the canons. He tried to satisfy the demands of his friends by reading the Psalms frequently, with Herbert of Bosham, a competent Hebrew scholar, to explicate them for him, and he quotes assiduously from them in his letters. But he also read the works of Bernard of Clairvaux and Hugh of St. Victor for their insistence on the superiority of the spiritual to the secular power. Rather than the *Moralia* of St. Gregory, he applied himself to the imperious letters of Gregory VII. Above all he studied Gratian's *Decretum,* quarrying it for quotations that he could use in his letters, discussing it with his *eruditi,* finding in it buttresses for his arguments and his convictions. He availed himself of the presence of many of his clerks in Pontigny, employing them to search the scriptures and canons for useful citations.

The pope had ordered Thomas to limit himself to a few attendants at Pontigny. Thomas's financial straits likewise recommended such a course, for he was dependent entirely on the

---

[2] Reading *suffugia* rather than the printed *suffragia* (*Materials* V, 163).

charity of his hosts and on such assistance as Louis of France was able and willing to provide. Nevertheless his retinue swelled enormously after Christmas, although the increase was not of his own doing.

What had happened was this. Gilbert Foliot, Hilary of Chichester, William of Arundel, and the other envoys that Henry had sent to the pope returned to England at the end of December. Since the Northampton Council, Henry had been making a progress through southern England, and on Christmas Eve the envoys found him at Marlborough. He responded to their tale of a fruitless mission with one of his characteristic outbursts of rage. On the day after Christmas he issued an order to his bishops forbidding them to pay any revenues to clerks of Thomas of Canterbury who might hold prebends within their sees. Simultaneously, he issued a writ to his sheriffs that amounted to a declaration of war upon the archbishop and, very nearly, the Church of Rome:

> If any clerk or layman in your bailiwick has appealed to the Roman Curia, I command you to seize him and keep him firmly in custody until you learn my will. Seize also all revenues and possessions of the archbishop's clerks for the Exchequer [*in manum meum*], as Ranulf de Broc and my other officers shall inform you. And the fathers and mothers, brothers and sisters, nephews and nieces of all the clerks who are with the archbishop you shall put under safe pledges, as well as their chattels, until you learn my will concerning them.

Henry went out of his way to be offensive in choosing Ranulf de Broc to execute this order. Among Becket's partisans the Broc family had the reputation of being "the greatest ruffians in England," and Ranulf possibly went beyond the king's intentions in the harshness with which he carried out the king's mean revenge upon Thomas Becket's dependents. For Henry decided that all the archbishop's household, together with all their relations, were to be sent into exile after taking oaths to present themselves to the archbishop at Pontigny so that he might see the misery his intransigence had inflicted upon so many innocents. Hilary of Chichester had the courage to protest, vainly, that such an act would earn the king universal execration—as it did—and that in addition it would provide Becket with the very staff of able servants he now lacked.

Ranulf de Broc showed no mercy. Hundreds of persons of every age and sex, "the woman sick with child and the suckling baby lying in the cradle," were stripped of their possessions and forced to leave England in the dead of winter. A forlorn procession of destitute exiles, all the more wretched because they had been in comfortable circumstances, wound its way along the roads of France throughout the winter of 1164–5. The sight of them grieved Thomas, as it was intended to, and he wrote desperately to friends and acquaintances as far away as Sicily in the effort to find refuges for these unfortunates. Among the exiles were his own sisters: Mary, later to become Abbess of Barking; Rohesia, to whom Henry in later years penitently granted the income from a mill; and Agnes, who married a man named Thomas and later endowed a hospital on the site of their father's home. One of the sisters and her children found refuge at the abbey of Clair-Marais; a letter from Pope Alexander is extant thanking the abbot for his kindness to them. The pope also acted to check the flow of refugees to Pontigny by absolving the involuntary exiles of their oath to present themselves to Thomas.

Among all these new exiles one was conspicuously absent. William FitzStephen succeeded in making peace with the king by presenting to him an intricately rhymed prayer in verse. It is perhaps this defection that explains the curious silence about him observed by all the other biographers, none of whom mentions his name—as if they regarded him as banished from their company. Yet Thomas himself forgave him; and William's own account suggests that he later joined Thomas in exile, presumably of his own free will. Moreover, both Herbert of Bosham and John of Salisbury subsequently attempted to make separate peace with the king. Clearly an effort to retain or recover revenues and perquisites in England was not regarded as betrayal by the Becket party. On the contrary, in demanding that the king return what he had taken, the clerks of the archbishop's household were seeking simple justice. William FitzStephen reports tersely but without the slightest embarrassment that he "had peace," and he proudly sets down the poem that gained it for him. His pride was justified, for the rhymed prayer was an admonitory assertion of divine supremacy:

Rex cunctorum saeculorum, Rex arcis aetheriae,
Rector poli, rector soli, regum Rex altissime . . .
Tu creasti, Tu formasti, coelos, terras, maria:
Quae fecisti, condidisti, Tu gubernas omnia.[3]

Henry, like everyone else in his age, could only assent; but William had found a clever way to remind him that there was a king above him, and that he did not govern all things. The poem contained a further admonition that was meant as a direct reference to the current controversy:

Cum in ira mente dira interdum efferveo,
Deus care, moderare in me quod non valeo.[4]

If the poem had the desired effect of persuading Henry to moderate his rages, it did not lessen his determination to win the contest. The subsidence of anger only brought out the calculating aspect of his character; and he began laying plans to deliver a decisive blow against Thomas Becket and the pope who, as he saw it, had betrayed him. The threat that his envoys had dropped in passing during their interviews with the pope had not been altogether idle. Henry was seriously considering the possibility of withdrawing his recognition of Alexander. To that end he initiated negotiations with the Emperor Frederick. Rainald (Reginald), Archbishop of Cologne, Frederick's chief minister, set out for Rouen accompanied by a number of other distinguished envoys. Henry, in spite of a threatening situation on the Welsh border, crossed to Normandy during Lent in order to meet them. He also had in mind an interview with Pope Alexander, which

---

[3] King of all the ages, celestial monarch, ruler of heaven and earth, highest king of kings . . . you created and shaped the heavens, the earth, and the seas. You govern all that you made, all that you founded.

[4] If now and then I seethe in terrible rage, dear God, cool this anger that I myself cannot control.

prospect caused great alarm in Becket's entourage. John of Salisbury wrote to Thomas:

> On turning the whole matter over in my mind and trying to judge what we may hope for, I cannot anticipate much advantage from an interview in which our king meets the pope in person. He will state much in his own favor, much against you, and as is his custom he will alternate threats with promises and bargainings, and will be able to influence compliant and vacillating minds.

Thomas took this advice to heart, and wrote to Alexander begging him not to consent to an interview with Henry unless he, Thomas, were present. Alexander, who was now feeling more secure because he had heard that the new antipope, Guido of Crema, was being rejected everywhere in Italy, took a firm stand. He wrote sternly to Henry:[5]

> You have written to us to say that, by the advice of good men, you would consent to have a conference with us if our brother, Archbishop Thomas, were not present. This procedure seems to us neither lawful nor kind; and surely the Roman Church would stray far from the path of duty if we in any way joined in fellowship with those who shun the archbishop. Who is to answer for the church of Canterbury if Archbishop Thomas is to be banned from a conference where her rights and needs are discussed? God forbid that we should . . . grant you or any other secular lord to impose absence or to shame him who for the right of God and steadfast zeal for the law is already banished and held in contempt by others.

Henry's response to this letter was a whirlwind of diplomatic activity. He went to Gisors and held a conference with King Louis, whom he tried to persuade to abandon Becket. This effort failed; but his clear warnings of his intentions shook the French king. Louis was horrified at the prospect that Henry really meant to abandon Alexander, for that would involve the political as

---

[5] This letter is extant only in an Icelandic version but appears to be authentic.

well as the religious encirclement of France. When John of Salisbury subsequently called on Louis to speak with him on Becket's behalf, he found the king as sympathetic as ever to Thomas personally, but unwilling to press the pope in his favor for fear of driving Henry into the arms of the emperor and his puppet pope.

This small success in hand, Henry returned to Rouen, where he gave an excessively friendly reception to Count Philip of Flanders, as prophylaxis against his veering toward the cause of Becket. This was followed by his welcome to Becket's German counterpart—after a fashion, for Archbishop Rainald of Cologne had been Frederick Barbarossa's chancellor and had been rewarded with an archiepiscopal see in the very year of Becket's promotion. Rainald, however, had gone along with his sovereign in breaking with the Church of Rome; in fact, he was believed to have led rather than followed, and by now generally enjoyed the reputation of "pope-maker." A German Iron Chancellor eight hundred years before Bismarck's day, Rainald remained until his death from "Roman fever" in 1167 the moving spirit behind Frederick Barbarossa's ecclesiastical policy. We will recall that he had clashed with Pope Alexander, then Cardinal Roland, at the Diet of Besançon in 1157. As archchancellor of Italy, he guided Frederick's Italian policy, and was responsible for many of the harsh measures and crushing taxes that ultimately led to the rebellion of the north Italian cities and the formation of the Lombard League. Rainald has been blamed for urging the utter destruction of Milan, which Frederick caused to be razed to the ground except for the cathedral and a few churches. That act of savagery in no small measure contributed to the detestation in which the German emperor was held throughout western Europe. But it had also made Frederick the most feared monarch of his age.

The emperor with whom Henry II was now about to contract a virtual alliance had come to his throne only two years before Henry himself, and was to occupy it for almost the same length of time (he outlived Henry by less than a year). As vital and contradictory a personality as Henry himself, to whom he was distantly related, Frederick had succeeded in uniting the quarreling dukes of Germany and raising the medieval Empire to its greatest power since the days of Charlemagne. A lover of history and learning like Henry, devoted to his judicial and administrative work, Frederick could be a mild, generous, dutiful prince. He could also, like his English cousin, sometimes act with surpassing cruelty. At the siege of Crema, Frederick had hung captured prisoners by ropes to the fore part of a great siege engine—the "cat"—so that the people of Crema were forced to kill their own kinsmen when they attempted to destroy the engine.

Frederick admired above all his putative ancestor Charlemagne, and he tried to pattern himself upon the great Frankish sovereign in military exploits, careful administration, patronage of the arts, and policy toward the Church. He was even now planning to have Charlemagne canonized, and seems to have been awaiting only the support of the King of England. Frederick's conception of the respective roles of emperor and pope was that of Charles, who had once written to Pope Leo III:

> It is my duty, by the Grace of God, to defend the Church of Christ against the assaults of pagans or the ravages of infidels which may threaten her from without. . . . It is your duty, most holy father, like Moses to lift up your hands in prayer to God for the success of my arms.

Frederick took a similar tone, giving the famous doctrine of the two swords his own imperialistic interpretation:

> On earth God has placed no more than two powers: above there is but one God, so here one pope and one emperor. Divine providence has specially appointed the Roman Empire as a remedy against continued schism.

But despite these brave words, Frederick lacked the objective means and the subjective stature to put such a program into effect. Unlike his great predecessor, he did not possess Gaul. Italy was far stronger, and far more urbanized, than it had been in Charlemagne's time; and the Church with which Frederick had to contend was the post-Gregorian Church. The consequence was that while he ruled Germany wisely, if sternly, he wasted the substance and blood of his people in the fruitless effort to subdue Italy and to dominate the Church.

The parallel between Frederick's struggle with Alexander and Henry's struggle with Thomas was obvious to both rulers, who shared an extreme jealousy of their regalian rights. Frederick had apparently solved his problem by installing a subservient pope on the Chair of St. Peter. Henry could solve his by securing from Frederick's pope the consecration of a subservient archbishop. Frederick's envoy, Archbishop Rainald, scarcely needed to indicate other, political advantages that would accrue to Henry from an alliance—he made those clear by pointedly omitting a visit to Louis VII when he passed through the territory of France.

Henry and Rainald discussed marriages to cement the revival of old ties between England and the Empire. They agreed on the betrothal of Henry's eldest daughter Matilda to Frederick's cousin, Duke Henry of Saxony, and of his daughter Eleanor to the emperor's infant son.[6] Henry then sent the emperor's envoys to Queen Eleanor in England, who was to convoke a council at Westminster to confirm the arrangements. The arrival of "the schismatics" caused a tremendous stir. Henry now received the first clear hint that England would not tamely submit to his plans for a change of religious allegiance.

Earl Robert of Leicester, the aged justiciar, forcefully demonstrated his outrage at the presence of the Germans. He refused the *pax*, the kiss of peace, to Rainald, and ordered that the altars at which the archbishop had officiated be purged of the contamination. The English bishops were equally perturbed. Most of them probably would not have followed Henry into schism. But as Gilbert Foliot later wrote to the pope:

"There will not be wanting some to bow the knee to Baal and, without regard to religion and justice, receive the pallium of Canterbury at the hands of their idol [i.e., the antipope]. Nor will there be wanting persons to occupy our sees and, seated in our seats, they will obey him devotedly."

---

[6] Matilda was actually sent to Saxony two years later to be married to Duke Henry. The betrothal of Eleanor came to nothing; she ultimately married Alfonso of Spain.

For the time being, Henry ignored murmurs of opposition and went ahead with his plans. He ordered John of Oxford and Richard of Ilchester, two stalwarts of the anti-Becket party, to accompany the imperial envoys back to Germany. There they attended Frederick's Diet of Würzburg.

The great Council of Würzburg held its opening session on May 22, 1165. It was attended by almost all the lay and clerical magnates of the Roman Empire, to which Frederick had recently attached the epithet Holy. For Frederick was determined to convince the Western world that he was a devout son of the Church—his Church, of course, not that of "the schismatic Roland" (i.e., Alexander). But although Frederick had made his intentions clear, there was still a small and in the circumstances not very vocal party at the council who hoped that, with Victor IV now dead, a compromise could be effected, Paschal III dropped, and the schism in the Church ended. The leader of this small group of "Alexandrians" was Conrad, the archbishop-elect of Mainz. Conrad was that friend and correspondent whom Thomas Becket had called "the half of my soul"; he was held in highest esteem by Pope Alexander, and was regarded as spiritually and intellectually the foremost personage among the German clergy, next to Rainald himself. His presence at the council was an indication that the Alexandrian party had not yet given up all hope. On the first day of the council—Rainald had not yet returned from his mission to Henry II—Conrad appeared to be gaining adherents among the German prelates. There seemed at least a dim possibility that he might organize a faction strong enough to urge compromise upon the emperor.

These hopes were dashed at the second session, when Rainald arrived at the assembly with John of Oxford and Richard of Ilchester. Dramatically, he announced the success of his efforts to convert the King of England from the cause of "Roland" to that of the only legal and canonically elected pope, Paschal III. Under the impact of this news, the forty archbishops and bishops present at the council consented to follow Frederick and the secular leaders in taking the unprecedented oath that Rainald proposed: henceforth never to recognize Alexander or any member of his party as rightful successor to the throne of St. Peter, and to receive Paschal as their "universal and Catholic Father" whom they would hold "in obedience and honor and reverence." According to Frederick's own account: "The honorable envoys of our friend the King of England swore in the presence of our entire court on the relics of the saints, in behalf of the King of England and his barons, that he also and his whole kingdom will faithfully stand on our side and hold with the Lord Pope Paschal as we do."

The Diet concluded its sessions by decreeing that within six months a similar oath must be exacted of all Germans throughout the Empire. Any cleric who failed to take it would lose his post, any layman his freehold or fief. Many of those who consented to the oath were troubled by this brutal crushing of freedom of conscience; but only one man, so far as we know, resisted the coercion. Conrad of Mainz chose to follow the recent example of his friend Thomas Becket. Secretly, he escaped from Würzburg at night and fled to Pope Alexander in France.

Exactly to what, and to what extent, the English envoys had sworn, whether they exceeded their authority or acted on instructions that Henry preferred later to disavow, cannot definitely be ascertained. Certainly Henry continued to entertain the notion of abandoning Alexander, for he would later write to Rainald: "I have long wanted the right opportunity for withdrawing from Pope Alexander and his perfidious cardinals who presume to support that traitor to me, Thomas, former Archbishop of Canterbury." And as late as the end of the year 1165, Frederick Barbarossa was in correspondence with Henry over the canonization of their common ancestor, Charlemagne. The canonization was finally undertaken by the antipope, and the imperial manifesto that Barbarossa issued at the formal ceremony on December 2, 1165, stated unequivocally that in promoting the elevation of the "most holy emperor" to the company of saints, Frederick had been "encouraged by the urgent request of our dear friend Henry, King of England."

Nevertheless, all through the months that followed the Diet of Würzburg, Henry in person, or Gilbert Foliot for him, persistently denied that he had any intention of recognizing the antipope. He maintained that his envoys had sworn no oaths to the "schismatics," and that he himself had no thought of abandoning Alexander III, for all that the pope so ill requited his fealty. Yet he had conveyed an altogether different impression to Frederick Barbarossa. Frederick would scarcely have made public proclamations of their friendship if he had not been convinced that Henry really intended to adhere to Paschal. And, in fact, few persons in England, France, or Italy believed Henry's disavowal of his envoys. There was a curious clumsiness and naïveté about the double game that Henry was attempting to play. He enjoyed a reputation for subtlety and deviousness, and his contemporaries were only too willing to attribute to him the cunning of the serpent. But to the modern eye his policy looks unstable and indecisive rather than shrewd. Without Thomas Becket at his side, he stumbled in his efforts at foreign policy, and embroiled himself in many embarrassments.

In all fairness, of course, it must be granted that Thomas himself caused some of these embarrassments. While Henry had spies everywhere, as Thomas and his friends often complained, Thomas also did not lack for informants. Every promise that Henry's envoys made, every interview they had with either side, was almost immediately published abroad by Becket's partisans. All correspondence passed through the hands of clerics, since it was conducted in Latin; and there were many more admirers of Becket among the lower than the higher clergy. The consequence was that the king could keep few of his plans secret from Thomas. No wonder that the conflict often reduced Henry to baffled, frustrated fury.

The fact was that Henry had chosen the worst possible moment for his adventure in ecclesiastical politics, and he soon realized this. For the fortunes of Guido of Crema (Paschal III) appeared to be declining rapidly. Italy invited Alexander to return. The pope left Sens in April 1165, and after a slow, adventurous, and roundabout journey by way of Sicily reached Rome, where he was welcomed with great enthusiasm. Although Frederick's archfoe, Milan, had been destroyed, the imperialist party seemed weaker than ever in Italy.

Alexander's new strength manifested itself in renewed support for Thomas Becket and the principles of ecclesiastical independence. In June, even before Alexander left the soil of France, he finally decided the issue that had been the immediate cause of Thomas's flight. The Northampton sentence was declared null and void in terms that must have seemed to Thomas a complete vindication of the high-Gregorian position he had taken. Alexander wrote:

> That the less cannot judge the greater . . . is declared by laws both human and divine, and is clearly set forth in the statutes of the holy fathers. It is our task to correct errors and to amend those things which, if not corrected, would leave a pernicious example to posterity. Accordingly, we have pondered these matters with anxious care, and have concluded that the Church ought not to sustain loss or injury through the fault of any individual. We therefore adjudge to be utterly void the sentence presumptuously passed on you by the bishops and barons of England because you did not obey the king's first summons. In that sentence the aforesaid bishops and barons declared the forfeiture of all your movable goods. In so doing they violated the form of the law and the custom of the Church, especially since you have no movable goods except those of the Church. We therefore quash the sentence by our apostolic authority, ordering that for the future it shall have no force, nor shall it avail to prejudice or harm you or your successors hereafter, nor the church committed to your authority.

Possibly Thomas was stung by the phrase "through the fault of any individual," but he could only rejoice at the tenor of the letter. He had won his case; his appeal had been successful. If Henry refused to accept the pope's decision, he would lay himself open to excommunication or interdict. The powerful weapon of ecclesiastical censure had, so Thomas thought, been returned to his hands.

But his triumph was shortlived. Alexander had no wish to push matters to extremes, and in an accompanying letter he ordered Thomas to refrain from action:

> Since the days are evil and many things must be tolerated because of the nature of the times, we ask you to be discreet . . . doing nothing precipitately or hastily. . . . Bear with the king until next Easter, and take no measures against him or his

land until that date. For by then God will grant better times, and both you and we may safely proceed further in this matter.

That last sentence was the clue to the pope's conduct. Until he was safely re-established in Rome, he wanted to hold the thorny problems of England in suspension, neither surrendering Thomas's cause to Henry nor alienating Henry entirely. He therefore dispensed his rebukes evenhandedly, for at the same time he wrote a sharp admonition to Henry, couched as a letter to Gilbert Foliot. The king, he pointed out, had of late "turned his mind and soul" away from his previous devotion to the Church, had communicated with schismatics, forbidden appeals, exiled the Archbishop of Canterbury, and was oppressing the churches and the clergy of his kingdom. "Unless he repents his evil deeds," Alexander concluded, "God will surely visit harsh vengeance upon him and his, and we ourselves will no longer be able to endure them with patience."

Gilbert's reply to the pope was virtually an official statement of the king's case. Henry had not heard that the emperor was excommunicated. He had not exiled the Archbishop of Canterbury; Thomas had left England of his own accord, and no one would prevent him from returning—only he would have to answer certain charges. If the king had injured any churches or churchmen, he would render satisfaction as judged by a full council of the English Church. This reply, Bishop Gilbert added, "seems to us in the main to justify his cause."

Thus Gilbert supported Henry's conduct with the weight of his own prestige and with that of Robert of Hereford, who had accompanied him to the interview with the king. Such a stand was expected from Gilbert Foliot. But it caused consternation in the camp of Becket's partisans that Robert of Hereford now associated himself with the king's party. Robert, the former Paris master who had taught the youthful Becket, had been thought a strong advocate of the rights of the Church. Alexander had looked to him to remonstrate unflinchingly with the king. But Robert, old and perhaps already suffering from the illness that brought on his death less than two years later, evidently "feared man before God," as Alexander wrote to him in rebuke.

Thomas had consecrated Robert, and had counted on him for support. It was Robert, we will recall, who had begged the king at Northampton to send a herald into the streets to proclaim that no one was to molest the archbishop. But when Robert, conceiving his role as that of mediator, wrote to Thomas urging mildness, he received a sharp reprimand. "You are preaching humility, even abject submission . . . when you ought to be strengthening the constancy of my vacillating mind and, with me, sustaining the attack in order to defend our inheritance of the cross and crush the enemies of the Church," Thomas wrote to him, and urged him "more firmly and more boldly to perform the duties of your office." Yet in spite of this strong language, there was an undercurrent in this letter to Robert that betrayed the psychological crisis through which Thomas was passing in his enforced inactivity at Pontigny. When Thomas brooded upon his wrongs, he became filled with an uncharitable hatred and was capable of referring to Henry as "the animal." But when, during hours of meditation which the monastic life provided in such abundance, he remembered his friendship with Henry, he grieved. At such times he could write, as he did to Robert:

> Further—there is one thing which I am not able to endure without the greatest bitterness of soul: verily, I weep for my most beloved lord the king. For fear and trembling have come upon me, and the shades have overwhelmed me since I have seen that tribulation and difficulties are threatening my lord the king.

Henry's troubles at this time were by no means solely connected with Thomas Becket, although some of them may well have been due to the absence of Becket's counsel. The king had decided to flee from the perplexities of ecclesiastical policy and the potential embarrassments of his envoy's commitments at Würzburg by campaigning personally in Wales. The call for another punitive war against the Welsh, who had been ravaging the marches, had already gone out at the Council of Northampton. After thorough preparations—the Pipe Rolls are full of references to purchases of arrows and provisions—Henry marched a large army into Wales during the summer. Even there, he could not entirely escape his problems with Thomas Becket, for Gilbert Foliot and Robert of Hereford caught up with him at Oswestry, bringing the pope's letter of admonition quoted above, and soon afterward John of Oxford arrived with a report on the events at Würzburg.

To make matters worse, nature seemed to conspire with the Welsh against Henry. He camped in a valley at the foot of a high mountainside with his huge and unwieldy army. The light-armed Welsh clung to the high ground, like the Gascons at the Pass of Roncesvalles, and harried the English by guerrilla tactics. Soon the Welsh succeeded in cutting the English supply train. And then the work they had begun was completed by the weather.

The month of August had been threatening, for two comets had appeared in the sky, one in the south and the other in the north. A comet, as a contemporary chronicler explained:

is a star which is not always visible, but which appears most frequently upon the death of a king or the destruction of a kingdom. When it appears with a crown of shining rays, it portends the decease of a king; but if it has streaming hair, and throws it off, as it were, then it betokens the ruin of a country. There was a great tempest . . . during that same month. Many people saw the Old Enemy taking the lead in that tempest; he was in the form of a black horse of large size, and always kept hurrying towards the sea, while he was followed by thunder and lightning, and fearful noises, and a destructive hail. The footprints of this accursed horse were of very enormous size, especially on the hill near the town of Scardeburch, from which he gave a leap into the sea; and here, for a whole year afterwards, they were plainly visible, the impression of each foot being deeply graven in the earth.

The torrential rains that accompanied the storm formed flash floods that rushed down the steep sides of the mountain and washed out the English camp. Hundreds of men were drowned, the army's supplies were carried off by the raging waters, and Henry was forced to retreat ignominiously within the great walls of Chester. He then decided to invade Wales from the sea, and waited for ships from Ireland, which he had hired. But there was no Thomas Becket to plan campaigns for him, no Thomas Becket to keep a navy in shape for him, and when the ships arrived they proved insufficient for the task.

The Welsh expedition had been a total failure. Overcome by another of his uncontrollable rages, Henry pitilessly ordered the mutilation of his hostages, the sons and daughters of the Welsh princes Owen and Rhys. The boys' eyes were put out, the ears and noses of the girls cut off. No wonder that Thomas Becket feared for the soul of his beloved lord.

As if these were not enough disasters for a single month, on August 22, 1165, a son was born to Louis VII of France—the long-desired heir whom Louis had almost given up hoping for. The child was baptized Philip, and with his birth vanished all the plans that Henry may have cherished of some day uniting the kingdoms of France and England under his firstborn son Henry, the "young king." Henry could not foresee the grief and humiliation that this child would inflict upon him when grown to manhood; but if comets portended anything, he must have had forebodings. And these could scarcely have been quieted when he learned of the wild rejoicing that spread throughout France at the news that the kingdom had a prince at last. The news, in fact, reverberated through Europe; even the Saracen kings of Spain sent ambassadors with royal presents.

The story that Gerald of Wales tells about the birth of the prince who was to be the great Philip Augustus has often been quoted, but it has not lost its freshness. As a young man, Gerald happened to be studying in Paris at the time the boy was born. The news was received with such great joy that no language can express it, he writes.

> Through the extent of the whole city, such a noise and clang of all the bells burst forth, and so great a number of wax-lights were blazing through all the streets, that those who were ignorant of the cause . . . thought that the city must be on fire. The author of this work, being in the city, and then a young man in the twentieth year of his age, immediately leaped to the window from the couch on which he had stretched himself and

fallen into his first sleep; and looking out, he saw two very poor old women in the street bearing torches before them in their hands, and exulting with joy in their countenances as well as their voices. . . . And when he had inquired of them the cause of such commotion and exultation, one of them immediately looked up at him and replied: "We have now a king given to us by God, by whom disgrace and loss, punishment and grievous shame, confusion and sorrow in abundance, shall come upon your king." . . . For the woman knew that he to whom she was speaking, and his companions, were sprung from the kingdom of England, and, therefore, against them and their king the old woman bitterly uttered this speech, which was as if poured forth by a prophetic spirit, and which in reality was fulfilled within a short time, with too much truth.

Four years later Henry saw this boy in Paris, and Thomas Becket describes in a letter how he looked at Philip "with some sadness, talked briefly and superficially with him, and hastily dismissed him."

✠ ✠ ✠

At this time, it may be, Henry sought solace from many set-backs in the arms of a beautiful young girl with whom he fell so deeply in love that he flaunted his intimacy with her before the entire court. She was Rosamond Clifford, the "Fair Rosamond" of ballad, for whom at Woodstock the king "builded such a bower, the like was never seen." The stone-and-timber bower with its hundred and fifty doors and the famous maze may be legendary, but Rosamond was real enough. Certainly the king spent much of his time at Woodstock during the following months. Queen Eleanor was out of England, staying at Angers as regent for Anjou and Maine. No paragon of virtue herself, Eleanor apparently avenged herself by conduct similar to the king's. John of Poitiers suggests as much in a letter to Thomas Becket in which he warns Thomas not to hope for any intervention by the queen, since she is wholly under the influence of one of his enemies, Ralph de Faye. John speaks of the relationship of

234

the two as subject to "conjectures which grow day by day, and which seem to deserve credence."

Whatever may have been in Queen Eleanor's mind at this time, thoughts of firm administration were not. Revolts had flared in Maine and Brittany, and early in the spring Henry was forced to leave the delights of Woodstock and cross the narrow sea to subdue William Talvas, Count of Séez, and his son and grandson. Henry successfully reduced the castles of Alençon and La-Roche-Mabile in Maine, and made preparations for an invasion of Brittany in force. He also seems to have effected some kind of reconciliation with Queen Eleanor (at any rate their fourth son, John—the future King of England—was born at the end of the year, on the day before Christmas). Henry lingered in his Continental domains, to repair the ill effects of Eleanor's lax governance. The chronicles note that he celebrated Easter, which fell on April 24 that year, at Angers.

This was the Easter of 1166, the date by which Pope Alexander had promised to "proceed further" in the matter of the conflict between Thomas Becket and Henry Plantagenet.

XIV

Vézelay

FOR NINE MONTHS Thomas Becket had chafed under the restraints imposed upon him by the pope. He had written to powerful personages all over Europe, had sought the intercession of the king's mother, the Empress Matilda, the queen, Louis of France, the King of Scots, Arnulf of Lisieux, and his own suffragan bishops in England. At times rumors had reached him that the king was on the point of making peace with him at the instance of this or that personage; but these rumors soon proved to have no substance. Henry continued obstinately to maintain that no one had exiled Thomas and that he could return any time he pleased.

All the negotiations of this period had been slow, cumbersome, and indirect, conducted by letter and messenger, always through intermediaries. Thomas and Henry had neither seen nor communicated directly with each other since the beginning of the Council of Northampton. Now Thomas resolved to approach personally the man whom he loved and hated more intensely than anyone else in the world. He addressed three fervent appeals to Henry, each more severe than its predecessor. As he himself subsequently characterized these letters: "We admonished him often with the affection of a father, pleaded with him with the loyalty due to a lord, reproved him with the authority of a pastor."

For the bearer of his first letter, Thomas chose a Cistercian abbot named Urban—"Urban in name, urbane in fact, urbane also in speech." The letter began with a long preamble on the difficulty of frankness: if he spoke freely, he risked the anger of his lord; if he remained silent, he would surely incur the wrath of God, who says, "If you do not warn the wicked from his wicked way, and he shall die for his sin, his blood will I require at your hand." In equally biblical language, Thomas went on to speak of the situation of the Church in England:

> In your land is kept in captivity the daughter of Zion, the spouse of a great king, oppressed by many, insulted by those who have long hated her, and by whom she ought rather to be honored than afflicted, and especially by you. . . . Believe me, most serene prince, my much-loved lord, the Almighty is slow in retribution, long-suffering in His patience, but most severe in His vengeance.

This rather monkish vein must have taxed Henry's patience. Whatever specific proposals Thomas made for the settlement of the differences between himself and Henry were evidently to be imparted orally by Urban. The letter ended with a plea, touching in its humility, for "the condescension of an interview with you," and concluded with the assurance that Thomas regarded Henry as "once and always, my lord."

That first letter must have convinced Henry that the worldly chancellor whom he had loved had become for good and all a religious fanatic. Henry dismissed Urban with rude words, whereupon Thomas dispatched a second, longer letter that was much more a cry from the heart and mind than the first. If the first letter had been a pious exercise, the second (see page 239) was to show the fruit of Thomas's studies at Pontigny. At the same time it also laid bare the anguish he was undergoing, cut off from the active life on which he throve and the friendship of the man whom he had served happily and well.

Much had happened between the composition of the first and the second letters, and in consequence Thomas Becket was confronted with a momentous decision. On Easter Day, April 24, 1166, Pope Alexander redeemed his promise to "proceed further" by appointing Thomas legate of the Holy See for all of England except the province of York. In announcing the legation to Thomas, Alexander recommended that he use his new powers "with prudence and discretion," but he also ordered him to "endeavor to root out vice and plant virtue in the vineyard of the Lord." Simultaneously, Alexander wrote to the clergy of England announcing the appointment, praising Thomas's devotion to the Church and papacy, and ordering them to obey him humbly in all matters. An accompanying letter to Roger of York warned him that the crowning of kings of England was the sole privilege of the Archbishop of Canterbury. Thus early arose the issue which was to be a contingent cause of Thomas Becket's death.

The office of legate carried with it the important power of suspending all the bishops in the legate's province. When that office was granted to other than its traditional holder in England, the Archbishop of Canterbury, the archbishop might well find himself helpless to compel the obedience of his suffragans. Such had been the case during Bishop Henry of Winchester's tenure of the legateship under Archbishop Theobald. Thomas himself knew only too well the importance of the office, for he had been instrumental in securing the legation for Theobald. And although Pope Alexander had hedged his bets, as it were, by excluding Roger of York from Thomas's jurisdiction, there was good technical precedent for that. Roger was already legate for Scotland, and legates were ordinarily not subject to one another.

On that same Easter Sunday, King Henry had held a conference with Louis of France at Angers. Thomas had half expected to be invited, and had made preparations for leaving Pontigny; but the invitation was not forthcoming. News of the legateship had not, of course, reached either Thomas or the English bishops as yet. When it did come, some time in May, Thomas wrote to his friend Nicholas, Master of the Hospital of Mont St. Jacques, near Rouen, asking him to urge the empress to intervene if she possibly could. For he was, he declared, on the point of "unsheathing the sword of the Spirit, which is sharper than any two-edged sword" against her son and his land. Yet even now, with his powers restored, Thomas held open the door to reconciliation. He instructed Nicholas:

> Assure her that if her son . . . should take his mother's advice and listen to the voice of God, he will find us ready both to honor God and do his will. Meanwhile, we mourn sincerely

for him as for a dying son, and as God is our witness, we wish
and pray likewise for his honor and his health.

This message was conveyed to Henry at Chinon, where he
had convoked a council to prepare for his invasion of Brittany
and to deal with the problems raised by the archbishop's legateship. Henry was beginning to feel that his difficulties were becoming, in the phrase of John of Salisbury, an "inextricable laby-
rinth." At the council the king complained to his barons and
ecclesiastics "with sighs and groans" of Thomas's machinations
against him. With that ready emotionalism that was admired by
his contemporaries, he burst into tears at the news of the impending excommunication or interdict. "The archbishop would deprive me of my body and soul alike!" he cried. Then his mood
veered abruptly; his eyes flashed fire, as they always did in his
rages, and he shouted at his counsellors that they were all traitors
for being unwilling to take care and pains to deliver him from the
trouble caused by one man.[1] Henry was to use similar but
stronger language, with graver consequences, four years later.
On this present occasion his outcry was a shot aimed at his
learned advisers, Gilbert Foliot, Roger of York, and John of
Oxford. These men, he felt, had led him into the mazes of canon
law and there abandoned him.

His anger was scarcely appeased when the same "urbane"
messenger arrived at the council bearing Thomas's second letter,
Desiderio desideravi.[2] Thomas wrote:

> With desire have I desired to see your face and speak with
> you; greatly for my sake, but even more for yours. For my sake
> that when you saw my face you might recall to mind the services

---

[1] *Tandem dixit quod omnes proditores erant, qui eum adhibita
opera et diligentia ab unius hominis infestatione nolebant expedire.*
R. H. Froude's translation, "who had not the zeal or courage to rid
him from the molestation of one man," has been widely adopted,
and has given rise to the misconception that on this occasion also
Henry spoke "murderous" words.

[2] This letter is generally considered to have been the third—an
identification based largely on its being given in most manuscripts,
but not all, without salutation. See *Materials* V, 269, footnote *a*.
I am, however, persuaded by the arguments of R. Foreville, who
demonstrates from internal evidence that the letter was in all
probability the second rather than the third. Cf. Foreville, 218–22.

I rendered faithfully and devotedly to the best of my conscience
when I was under your obedience . . . and that you might be
moved to pity me, who am forced to beg my bread among
strangers. Yet, thanks be to God, I have enough to sustain me.
. . . For your sake for three reasons: because you are my lord,
because you are my king, and because you are my spiritual son.
In that you are my lord, I owe and offer you my counsel and
service, such as a bishop owes his lord according to the honor of
God and holy Church. In that you are my king, I am bound to
you in reverence and regard; in that you are my son, I am bound
by reason of my office to chasten and correct you.

After this appeal to former friendship and reminder of the
public as well as the personal relationship that had obtained
between himself and the king, Thomas turned to a brief statement of formal doctrine. He pointed out that kings received their
power from the Church and possessed none of the rights that
Henry had arrogated to himself in the Constitutions of Clarendon. He admonished Henry to "abstain from all communion with
schismatics" and reminded him of his coronation oath to protect
the Church and preserve her liberties. Then he stated his conditions for ending the quarrel: restoration to Canterbury of the
see's former rank and status and all possessions, return of what
had been taken from his dependents, and permission for himself
to return. If these conditions were granted, Thomas wrote:

I are ready faithfully and devotedly to serve you as my
dearest lord and king with all my strength in whatsoever I am
able, saving the honor of God and the Roman Church, and
saving also my order. Otherwise you may know for certain that
you will experience the divine severity and vengeance.

The threat in the last line was clear enough to Henry.
Interdict and excommunication were in the offing; Thomas had
warned his mother and was now warning him directly. Henry had
already seen that the temper of his people and his bishops would
not allow him to abandon Pope Alexander. Yet how was he to
avoid the paralyzing blow of ecclesiastical censures?

Bishop Arnulf of Lisieux, who had been so busy before the

Council of Northampton, and who had been trying to keep on good terms with both sides, suggested a resource. An excommunicate could not appeal because he was already outside the fold of the Church. But appeal against an impending excommunication could procure postponement for another year. Arnulf therefore proposed that he deliver to Thomas a formal notification of the appeal, that being the necessary legal preliminary. Henry accepted the suggestion although, as John of Salisbury shrewdly observed, the king himself was thus resorting to the very measure of appeal to Rome which he had sought to avoid by promulgating the Constitutions of Clarendon.

As soon as the Council of Chinon ended, Arnulf set out for Pontigny, accompanied by Bishop Froger of Séez and Archbishop Rotrou of Rouen—the latter, a close friend of Thomas Becket and John of Salisbury, averring that he was joining the mission in the hope of acting as mediator. Arnulf had had a good many quarrels with Froger of Séez in the past, and the three must have made an uncomfortable party. When the bishops reached the monastery, they found Becket gone. Thereupon they gave a public reading of their appeal, but failed to follow the prescribed form of civil law by posting it on the gates of the monastery: a technicality that Herbert of Bosham noted with a somewhat gloating satisfaction. They then returned as rapidly as possible to Chinon to inform the king that they had been too late. Henry promptly fell ill from sheer rage and frustration. All that he could do now was to order the ports of England closely watched to prevent any anathema that Thomas might pronounce from being published in the country. At the same time he warned his English clergy not to obey any such measures, since he had already appealed to Rome.

Thomas's absence from Pontigny had not been accidental. An unnamed member of the archiepiscopal household at the king's court had informed Thomas of the impending visit from the bishops, and its purpose. An appeal lodged at Pontigny would be valid whether or not the archbishop were there, since he was temporarily domiciled there; and Herbert of Bosham's remarks show that he, at least, was aware of the legal points involved. Thomas, however, told Herbert that he wished to have no intercourse at all with the king's envoys, and would avoid meeting them by going on a pilgrimage to the shrines at Soissons and Vézelay. Having made his decision, Thomas concealed his true intentions even from his closest confidant.

Soissons boasted shrines to the Blessed Virgin, to St. Gregory, "founder of the English Church," and to St. Drausius, a seventh-century Bishop of Soissons "who, so the Franks and Lorrainers believe, makes invincible those combatants who watch through the night in his memory." Thomas spent a night in vigil before each of the shrines, commending himself to his patroness, the Virgin, and to the two saints before the coming struggle. Then he set out for Vézelay, where the great monastic church prided itself on possession of the body of St. Mary Magdalene. As if this were not wealth enough, two years before—in 1164—a great miracle had taken place at Vézelay: precious new relics had been found by chance inside a hollow wooden statue of the Virgin. These (evidently carefully labeled) included some hairs of the Virgin herself, a bone of St. John the Baptist, fragments of Christ's purple robe. Such items were conventional relics of the day. What stirred Thomas's imagination was that the find included bits of clothing worn by Shadrach, Meshach, and Abednego (the three companions of Daniel who defied Nebuchadnezzar and were thrown into the fiery furnace for refusing to worship the king's golden image). To Thomas Becket, their reply to the King of Babylon: "Our God whom we serve is able to deliver us from the burning fiery furnace, and he will deliver us out of your hand, O king," might serve as the paradigm of his own stance toward Henry of England. As they had passed unharmed through their ordeal, so he, by courage, might survive his, in spite of the forebodings of death that came to him in recurrent dreams.

Thomas Becket was not yielding to banal superstition in cherishing such thoughts. He had been living for two years amid the intense piety of a community of Cistercian monks, and had naturally been influenced by his surroundings. The worldliness and perhaps the cynicism of his days as chancellor had long ago been left behind; illness, frustration, and suffering had refined his zeal. But in any case, a devoutness bordering on fanaticism was always close to the surface in almost any man of the twelfth century. This was the age of increasing devotion to the Virgin, of crusading ardor, of rededication of the Church in the face of heresies and schism, of passionate cathedral-building. In fact, the fabric of Vézelay itself was new: the massive Romanesque structure had been almost entirely rebuilt since the great fire of July 1120 had consumed it, immolating more than a thousand persons in a fiery furnace. It had risen more beautiful than ever from its ashes; and it was on the hillside below Vézelay's church of St. Mary Magdalene that St. Bernard had preached the ill-fated Second Crusade in 1146, twenty years before.

The religious motivations for a pilgrimage to Vézelay, then, were so strong that Thomas Becket could unhesitatingly choose the abbey church as the site of his first major counterstroke against King Henry. To St. Mary Magdalene was attributed the faculty of striking off the chains of prisoners. Thomas Becket would see the saint, carved in stone, her full face and compressed lips at once enigmatic and kind, looking down upon him as he attempted to throw off the fetters of exile. But there were also good political reasons for his choosing Vézelay for his dramatic pronouncement. The monastery enjoyed the privilege of being subject only to the pope. This meant that it would be relatively immune to any revenge that Henry might try to inflict upon the abbot and monks. As a direct dependency of Rome, Vézelay could be considered "extraterritorial." Any action that Thomas undertook there would not embarrass his host, King Louis of France. For Louis could easily answer any reproaches from Henry by pointing out that he had no jurisdiction over the monks of Vézelay.

Thomas was only one of a multitude of pilgrims "from divers kingdoms and many nations" who streamed up the steep road into Vézelay to keep the feast of Pentecost there, attracted by the fame of old and new relics. But he was, of course, the most important ecclesiastic present, and the Abbot of Vézelay invited him to celebrate High Mass on Whitsunday, June 12. After the Mass, Thomas ascended the pulpit and delivered "an elegant and fruitful sermon to the people." He followed this with a statement —to which the audience and his own intimates alike listened

243

thunderstruck—of the causes of the quarrel between himself and the king.

Then he moved to the narthex, one of the most beautiful church porches in Europe. There, standing before the central pillar that divides the great portal, beneath the richly sculptured curved tympanum, Thomas solemnly lit candles, one by one, inverted them, and dashed them out on the ground. In rapid succession he excommunicated John of Oxford and Richard of Ilchester for taking a sacrilegious oath to the emperor and dealing with the schismatic Archbishop of Cologne; Richard de Lucy and Jocelin de Balliol for their part in formulating the Constitutions of Clarendon; and Ranulf de Broc, Hugh of St. Clare, and Thomas FitzBernard for laying hands on the possessions of Canterbury. He denounced the Constitutions, itemizing those he regarded as intolerable and absolving the bishops of England from their oath to observe them. Then, his voice breaking with tears, he publicly warned King Henry to repent and change his ways, lest he also incur sentence of anathema.

Thomas had, in fact, intended to excommunicate Henry also, although his friends had long advised against his going so far. But two days before, a messenger from King Louis had reached him, informing him that Henry was so ill he had been unable to attend a planned conference with Louis. Thomas seized upon this pretext for refraining from the fatal step. He limited the dread sentence to those courtiers whom he regarded as instigators of Henry's anti-clerical policies, and contented himself with addressing to Henry a long and impassioned plea, desperately urgent, that wonderfully reflects the agitation in his own mind. The letter, the famous *Expectans expectavi,* runs to ten pages (in the printed text) and is a strange, highly emotional medley of exhortation, denunciation, theory, warning, and supplication. It expresses at one and the same time Thomas's longing for the contest to be ended, and his inflexible resolution to fight on at all costs if he could not gain his point.

The letter begins with a renewed assertion of his conviction that Henry was the prey of evil advisers:

I have waited expectantly for the Lord to turn toward you, so that you would change your way, repent and depart from the path of iniquity. I have hoped that you would break with those wicked friends whose instigation and advice, so I believe, caused you to fall into the abyss. Hitherto we have delayed in vain, meditating in silence and waiting with the greatest affection for a messenger to come from you and say: "The king, your son and your lord, has long been led astray by deceit and lured to the destruction of the Church. But now, inspired by divine mercy and filled with the utmost humility, he hastens to liberate the Church, to redress and correct all wrongs."

Day and night, Thomas continued, he had prayed for the king. He reminded him of the other letters he had addressed to him, pointed out again that to consent to evil was to participate in it. He quoted, from the *Policraticus* and Gratian, the example of Constantine who had refused to consider charges against priests; and he once more urged the superiority of the priesthood over the secular ruler:

Who can doubt that the priests of Christ must be regarded as the fathers and teachers of kings and princes and all the faithful? Would it not be lamentable insanity for the son to attempt to dominate the father, the pupil the teacher?

This was a direct quotation from a letter of Pope Gregory VII, as was a further statement of theory:

For there are two principles by which the world is ruled: the sacred authority of priests, and the royal power. The authority of priests is the greater because God will demand an accounting of them even in regard to kings.

Here Gregory himself was quoting from Pope Gelasius I—and Thomas in all probability had derived both quotations from his readings of Gratian's great compendium of canon law.

But after allusions to examples of kings and emperors whom popes and saints had excommunicated, Thomas returned to supplication. He urged his "most beloved son, most serene highness, most revered lord" to follow the example of King David who returned to God with a contrite and humble heart after he had sinned. Then followed a solemn warning of impending excom-

municication, couched in language that equally outraged Henry
and the bishops of England, and prompted the bishops to refer to
Thomas's "terrible" letter:

> If you do not listen to me, I who am wont to pray for you
> before the majesty of Christ's body with overflowing tears and
> sighs, then I shall cry out against you and say: Arise, O God,
> judge Your cause [Ps. 74:22]. Remember the outrages and the
> injuries that are being done to You and Yours by the King of
> England and his followers continually. Forget not the ignomi-
> nies inflicted upon Your Church, which You established with
> Your blood. Avenge, Lord, the blood of Your servants which
> has been spilled. Avenge, Lord, the afflictions of Your servants,
> which are infinite in number. The pride of those who hate and
> persecute You and Yours has grown so great that we can no
> longer endure it.

Once again, at the end of his long letter, Thomas adverted
to the theme of the wicked advisers. He did not say these things
to Henry to provoke him to greater anger, as would no doubt be
suggested by those malignant persons who day and night whis-
pered insidiously to him. Rather, Thomas wrote, he wished to
persuade his lord to take care for the sake of his soul, and to
avoid the peril that was at the gates.

In conclusion, he called upon Henry to think of the conflict
in historical perspective, and to remember his mortality:

> Consider, where are the emperors, where the kings and
> other princes, and where the archbishops and bishops who
> preceded us? In truth, they toiled and suffered, and now others
> have entered upon their labors. What more is there to say? The
> glory of this world passes away. Therefore remember your last
> hour.

246

XV

The Paper War

IMMEDIATELY after the excommunications, a spate of justificatory letters poured from the pens of Thomas Becket and his followers—and were answered, verbosely and passionately, by the king's partisans. Thomas wrote to Pope Alexander to ask confirmation of the sentences. He appealed to cardinals and other members of the Curia to support him in the aggressive course he had chosen. He dispatched haughty and imperious messages to Gilbert Foliot and the other bishops of England, charging them on their obedience to restore the sequestered property and benefices of Canterbury clerks and to hold no converse with the excommunicates. He informed Bishop Jocelin of Salisbury that he had suspended him for yielding to the king's wish that John of Oxford be appointed Dean of Salisbury. To all his correspondents, Thomas gave lists of those he had excommunicated by name and specified the articles of the Constitutions of Clarendon that he had condemned as particularly obnoxious (Articles I, II, III, VII, and VIII; see Appendix).

In spite of Henry's orders to his officials to guard the ports closely, these letters reached their destinations in England. We do not know by what means they were delivered; but the strength of Thomas's party in England may to some extent be judged by the speed and efficiency of his courier service. Within twelve days of the Vézelay excommunications, the bishops and abbots of England were meeting to consider their course. They were bound by canonical obedience to respect the wishes of their archbishop—

all the more so now that he had been appointed papal legate. Yet they had all sworn to accept the Constitutions of Clarendon, and none was prepared to join the archbishop in exile and poverty.

If the bishops as a body were perplexed, Gilbert Foliot was tormented. By temperament and monastic training he believed firmly in the principle of ecclesiastical obedience. Furthermore, he was the king's mentor, adviser, and confessor at the request of Pope Alexander himself. He had been repeatedly urged to use his influence with Henry to heal the quarrel. Moreover, Gilbert was highly orthodox; he hated schism and acknowledged Alexander's authority. At the same time, he knew Henry only too well, and therefore feared him; and he hated Thomas Becket. Throughout the dispute, but especially during this period, Foliot suffered the anguish of a man who was trying to serve two masters.

His only hope lay in procrastination and in attempting to bring the king and pope together, while at the same time thrusting the troublesome archbishop into the outer darkness. He therefore formally appealed against Thomas Becket's past, present, and future actions, and fixed the "term of the appeal" as it was called (that is, the date at which the parties were to meet in the papal court to try the case) as far ahead as he dared: May 18, 1167.

The appeals were justified in long letters to the pope and the archbishop, written in the name of all the bishops of England. We cannot determine with certainty which among the bishops actually subscribed to the sentiments in the letters, which were opposed, and which neutral. But from the first Thomas and his supporters recognized that no matter who had signed the letters, Gilbert Foliot was the author of them. Sometimes ingenious and sometimes ingenuous statements of the king's side of the dispute, they were in effect pamphlets, and they received wide circulation. They reveal, as do no other documents, the mind of the man who was Thomas Becket's most formidable adversary among the bishops of England who had refused to stand by their natural leader.

Gilbert Foliot has been described as a sincere ecclesiastical statesman who stood for the cause of moderation against Thomas Becket's extremism, and as a man of true piety and unblemished probity. Yet it is difficult not to accuse him of lying outright when he wrote, in his letter to the pope of June 24, 1166, that King Henry was "most Christian in faith and most virtuous in the bonds of conjugal chastity."[1] Possibly Henry failed to tell the whole truth to his confessor; but can we believe that Gilbert was so saintly as to be sheltered from all knowledge of the king's adulteries? That he took the trouble to make the point implies his awareness of the common gossip.

For the pope's benefit, Gilbert draws a portrait of the king as a most dutiful son of the Church who so willingly submits to divine laws that there is no need to threaten him with ecclesiastical censures, as the archbishop has unjustly done. Henry, he writes, is animated solely by the desire to preserve peace and justice and to remove all scandals and sins from his kingdom. For this reason he wanted to judge in his own court the "enormous excesses of certain insolent clerks," since he regarded deprivation of orders as insufficient punishment for their atrocious crimes. Thus "a holy contention arose which, we believe, is excused before the Lord by the single-mindedness of both parties." When Henry drew up the Constitutions of Clarendon, he did so not out of love of dominion, nor with any intention of crushing the liberties of the Church, but solely from a desire to establish peace in his realm. But still, if he has done anything wrong, he is always willing to be corrected by papal authority. In fact, the king's anger was almost extinguished, but the Archbishop of Canterbury has now stirred it afresh.

Gilbert does not seem to notice the illogical twist his argument has taken. Or perhaps he hopes that others will not notice how the mild and humble sovereign has suddenly become an angry one whose devotion to the Church may not survive the unprovoked assaults of the terrible archbishop:

> This [i.e., the excommunications] is the shortest way to the entire destruction of religion, and to the subversion and ruin of both clergy and people. Wherefore, do not let the Church be thus subverted in the time of your apostolate; let not our lord the king and the people, his servants, be turned from their

---

[1] *Rex namque fide Christianissimus, in copula castimoniae conjugalis honestissimus. . . . (Materials* V, 404).

obedience to you; let not the irascibility of the Archbishop of Canterbury trouble our lord the king, or us, or the churches committed to our care.

In his letter addressed to Thomas himself, which likewise purported to come from all the bishops, Gilbert alleged that the news of Thomas's fasting and spiritual occupations[2] had begun to soften the king. "Your friends and well-wishers were received graciously by His Majesty as long as such things were heard about you." But now Thomas is hostile and threatening; he has drawn the sword and the fight has begun again. Patience and humility would heap coals of fire upon his enemies. Everyone remembers what kindness the king once displayed toward him, exalting him from poverty to glory and admitting him to friendship, so that all his dominions were in Thomas's power.

> The king wished to anchor you fast in the things which belong to God and His Church. Despite his mother's efforts to dissuade him, despite the complaints of the kingdom, and although the Church itself sighed and groaned as far as it was able, he sought every means to raise you to your present eminence, hoping henceforth to be able to reign happily, enjoying maximum security because of your ability and advice.

But Thomas had disappointed these hopes; the king has found only strife where he hoped for support. Many efforts are being made to persuade him to desert Pope Alexander. The emperor's envoys have offered great gifts and many promises; but Henry has so far "stood firm as a rock." How terrible it would be if his own anger were to prompt him to change sides after all.

Both Herbert of Bosham and Master Lombard of Piacenza, Thomas's teacher of canon law at Pontigny, wrote long and learned replies to this pamphlet—*libellum*, as Herbert calls it. Lombard discussed the question of the appeal legalistically, arguing that appeals were meant as a resort for the oppressed, not the oppressors. Herbert wrote in his usual insufferably diffuse

---

[2] A valuable confirmation from a hostile observer that the tales of Thomas Becket's change of heart and way of life are not mere hagiographic myths invented after his martyrdom.

manner. His reply is notable chiefly because it begins with the same initial words as Thomas's third letter to King Henry, *Expectans expectavi*—perhaps this was Herbert's way of claiming some influence on the style and tone of that letter. It may also be that he was merely imitating his master. He did not, however, succeed in imitating Thomas's incisiveness and clarity. The one forceful and direct reply was that written by Thomas himself.

Thomas begins by exposing, with stinging scorn, the pretense that the bishops are united in protesting against his measures: "Your joint letter which we cannot easily believe to have proceeded from your joint wisdom." He reminds them that in attacking him, who has taken the whole danger of opposition to the king upon himself, they are betraying their own vital interests. Then he reviews carefully the origins of the quarrel and the reasons for his "voluntary" exile:

> Although the divine mercy has sometimes allowed the Archbishop of Canterbury to be exiled unjustly, who ever heard of his being tried and condemned and compelled to give bail in the king's court, above all by his own suffragans? . . . I was unable to submit with a clear conscience to these great injuries to God and His Church, nor to remedy them without risk of my life, or dissemble them without endangering my soul's salvation. For that reason I chose to turn aside for a while. . . . I was forced to keep my departure secret if I did not wish it to be prevented entirely. But the Lord . . . was concerned for the honor of the king and his party, that nothing might be done against me which would redound to his dishonor. . . . It turned out well for those who were eager for my death and thirsted for my blood. . . . Do not, my brothers, confound the rights of the monarchy and the Church. Their powers are distinct, and one of them derives its authority from the other. . . .

Then Thomas proceeds to answer the charges, in words we have already quoted (see pages 115–16), that his election had not been canonical. And he lashes out directly at the one man who had opposed it for a while, Gilbert Foliot:

> If anyone was truly troubled by it, let him not say that his own injury was suffered by the whole kingdom and the Church.

> . . . If anyone felt envy, or was actuated by ambition; if so peaceful, lawful, and unanimous an election grieved anyone and led him to intrigue and to wish to upset everything, may God induce him to confess his error.

The charge that the king had raised him from low estate stung Thomas, perhaps because he knew that Gilbert was only repeating Henry's own words. He answers that he would rather have nobility of mind than noble ancestry, and reminds the bishops that David had been taken from among the goats to become ruler of God's people, Peter from fishing to become head of the Church.

But Thomas was not quite satisfied with his reply. He addressed another long letter directly to Gilbert Foliot, repeating his arguments in even stronger language, and placing the blame for perpetuation of the quarrel squarely (and somewhat unjustly) upon the Bishop of London:

> It is cause for wonder, indeed for extreme astonishment, that a man of prudence, well versed in Holy Scripture and wearing the habit of religion, should lay aside the fear of God and so openly, not to say irreverently, oppose truth, stand against justice, and confound right and wrong; that such a man should seek to overthrow the establishment of Holy Church, which the Most High founded.

Thomas compares Gilbert's letter to a scorpion, gentle at the mouth and stinging with venom at the tail, for the bishop begins by promising obedience and ends by appealing against it. Gilbert has appealed before and the pope has rejected his appeal, Thomas reminds him. And then the worldly pride of the man who has been chancellor reasserts itself. In his previous letter, Thomas tacitly accepted the charge of lowly origin. Now, addressing Gilbert in person, he points out that his beginnings were, after all, neither so lowly nor so poor as Gilbert implies:

> You speak of my having been elevated from a lowly state to the highest position. . . . What lowly state is it you are thinking of? If you look at the time at which he placed me high

in his service, I held the archdeaconry of Canterbury, the prior-ship of Beverley, many churches, several prebends and quite a few other benefices.[3] In regard to the things of this world, my position was by no means so low. And if you look at the origin of my family and my ancestors, they were citizens of London who dwelt in the midst of their fellow citizens without reproach, and by no means of the lowest station. . . .

There was no need for you to take the trouble to remind me of the benefits the king conferred on me. For I call God to witness that there is nothing under the sun I prefer to his favor and welfare, except for those things that belong to God and Holy Church. . . . I received many more favors than you mention from him. But even if they were multiplied a hundred-fold, ought I to imperil the liberties of the Church of God in return for them?

Referring to his promotion to Canterbury, Thomas now bluntly accuses Gilbert of ambition:

I heard no complaints, no exclamations on the part of the kingdom, but rather acclamations. . . . It may possibly be that some ecclesiastics did sigh about that promotion, as aspirants generally do when they find themselves disappointed in the hopes they have entertained. And possibly those same persons are now the authors and advisers of the present dissension, by way of revenge for their misfortune. . . .

You say that the king is and always has been ready to give me satisfaction. This you assert you can confidently maintain. Then pause a moment and answer these questions. When you say he is ready to give satisfaction, in what sense do you mean it? You see those of whom God says that He is the father and judge—the orphans, the widows, the fatherless, the innocents, and those who are entirely ignorant of the matter in dispute—you see them proscribed, and you are silent. You see clerics banished, and do not protest. You see others despoiled of their property and insulted, and you do not object. You see my servants arrested and bound in chains, and you remain mute.

---

[3] This passage is conclusive evidence that "pluralism"—the holding of several benefices by one ecclesiastic—was regarded at the time as altogether normal and honorable.

You see the goods of your mother church of Canterbury seized, and you do not resist. You see me, your father, barely escaping the swords at my throat, and you do not sorrow. Worse still, you do not blush to stand with my persecutors, who in me persecute God and His Church; and you do so openly. Is it giving satisfaction not to correct evils already perpetrated, and day after day to go from bad to worse?

Gilbert Foliot had to answer in his own defense. He was also the one ecclesiastic in the king's party who possessed the eloquence, the command of Latin style, and above all the personal bias that were essential for a full presentation of the king's cause. He was not the most logical of controversialists, but neither were his opponents. Gilbert drifted off into subsidiary matters and inapposite quotations when he tried to present his side of the issue; but still he was the only man who could make a halfway convincing argument for the regalists. He now did so in the noted and notorious manifesto *Multiplicem nobis*.[4] This polemic states the case against Thomas by subtle distortions of fact, by blackening his character, by lines of reasoning whose inconsistencies do not appear at first glance. It contains a number of assertions which cannot be checked against any other evidence and some statements that are patently improbable. Above all, it conceals beneath a bland surface bitter personal malice toward Thomas Becket. Involuntarily we are reminded as we read *Multiplicem nobis* of Pope Alexander's admonition to Gilbert Foliot at Sens: *"Parce, frater."* [5] Gilbert had learned nothing; he continued to be unkind to himself when he attacked the archbishop.

Gilbert begins by protesting the injustice of Thomas's having singled him out as the object of abuse. He vows before God that he has never coveted the power and office of the archbishop. He opposed Thomas's election not because his own hopes were thwarted, but because he saw the privileges of the Church undermined, "the spouse of Christ shamefully deprived of the liberty which she has always enjoyed." Thus Gilbert, not Thomas, was the defender of the Church's liberties—the same Gilbert who

[4] See footnote 2, p. 161.
[5] See footnote 3, p. 206.

now sees nothing irregular in the king's forcing the church of Salisbury to grant John of Oxford a deanery as a reward for his diplomatic endeavors.

There follows the charge, which has given rise to much pointless discussion, that Thomas bought the chancellorship. "If we look back at the beginning, who in all our world is unaware, who is so dull as not to know that you obtained the dignity of chancellor by bidding several thousand marks, and on that favoring breeze found a haven in the church of Canterbury?"

Here Gilbert adroitly contrives to create the impression of a formidable accusation where in fact there was none. To purchase an ecclesiastical office was, of course, simony, and as such condemned by the Church. On the other hand, some secular offices were regularly for sale; and when they were, no shame attached to paying for them. The shame, then, would lie only in lack of merit and ability. But Gilbert himself had earlier written that the king was utterly dependent on Thomas Becket's ability as chancellor.

The above passage is the only indication that Thomas may have paid for the chancellorship. The office, however, was indubitably purchasable. Geoffrey Rufus bought it from Henry I in 1122; Geoffrey, Archdeacon of York, paid Prince Henry 1,100 marks for it in 1176; and William Longchamp gave Richard £3,000 for the privilege of being his chancellor in 1189. Nevertheless, merit also mattered; for Richard refused another offer of £4,000. There is, therefore, nothing intrinsically improbable in the allegation that Thomas Becket had to make a large payment to Henry when he entered upon the duties of the chancellorship, nor is there anything intrinsically disgraceful in such conformity to custom. The real venom of the accusation is contained in the logical ellipsis by which Gilbert succeeds in imputing malpractice to Thomas. For the suggestion is that he wanted the chancellorship in order to use it as a steppingstone to Canterbury. In other words, Thomas was guilty of simony at long range; he had paid for the chancellorship in the expectation of being rewarded (seven years later!) by promotion to Canterbury. This is patently absurd. At the time he became chancellor, Thomas was already Archdeacon of Canterbury. If he had been ambitious to succeed Theobald, the logical course would have been to remain in the service of the see of Canterbury, not accept a position in which conflict with the Church was almost inevitable, as he well knew. To the modern mind, it may be added, ambition to be Archbishop of Canterbury does not in itself seem discreditable. But here we must try to understand the twelfth-century view. To aspire to be a bishop was indeed discreditable, for no man ought to think himself virtuous enough to be shepherd of a multitude of souls. To strive for such office, therefore, was to be guilty of the sin of pride.

The difficulty for Gilbert was that he actually suffered from that sin and in his better moments reproached himself for it. Hence the passion with which he disclaims ambition; hence also his projection—as we would call it today—of his own ambitions upon Thomas. Thomas's reluctance to accept the office of archbishop is amply documented. Yet Gilbert describes the circumstances of Thomas's election in these words:

Our good father, the late Archbishop Theobald of pious memory, had ended his days; and you, who had your eyes open to this contingency, immediately rushed back from Normandy to England.[6] The king speedily sent that able nobleman and guardian of his kingdom, Richard de Lucy, whom you have now so meritoriously excommunicated. His instructions were that the monks of Canterbury and the suffragan bishops of that church should elect you for their father and pastor without delay. Otherwise they would anger the king, and quickly find that he regarded them as enemies.

Thomas himself, and all his "creatures," Gilbert continues, were likewise using threats, promises, and blandishments to secure the election. He, Gilbert, raised his voice against it "in a

[6] Theobald died on April 18, 1161. The see remained vacant, and Thomas apparently stayed on the Continent, for more than a year. If Thomas did rush to England immediately after Theobald's death, he must have done so on business for the king. The events that Gilbert describes as happening so "speedily" took place in the late spring of 1162.

256

manner," but only succeeded in having himself and all his friends and relations threatened with banishment. Thus Thomas had invaded the sheepfold of the Lord like a wolf, and so taken away the liberty of the Church.

Foliot now proceeds to give his own account of the events at Clarendon already cited.[7] Then he reviews the Council of Northampton, and performs a remarkable feat of turning the circumstances upside down by simultaneously blaming Thomas for disobeying the original summons in the case of John the Marshal and condemning him for accepting the king's sentence and fine without considering the canon: "No bishop shall be cited before a civil or military judge in any case, either criminal or civil." In the next breath, apparently unaware of the contradiction, Gilbert reproaches Thomas for not having agreed to the king's demands for money.

Similar contradictions occur in Gilbert's presentation of the king's character and motives. Henry "was actuated not by avarice but by anger"; this same Henry is exemplary in patience, and although deeply wounded by the archbishop's carrying the cross like a weapon into the hall at Northampton, he contained his rage. Gilbert has quite forgotten the shouts of fury in the upper chamber at Northampton. He again forgets the mild and temperate king when he charges Thomas with cowardice for having escaped while leaving his bishops behind to face death if they ventured to oppose Henry. Yet here, strangely, he writes as if he understood Thomas's inmost thoughts about martyrdom:

> It is the cause that makes the martyr; to suffer persecution for holiness is glorious, for obstinacy or perverseness is ignominious. It is praiseworthy and victorious to suffer the sword for Christ, but to provoke death is madness; and if we weigh our deeds as well as our words, we shall not hastily provoke martyrdom. For you bent the knee at Clarendon and took flight at Northampton; you disguised yourself and secretly fled beyond the confines of the kingdom. What did you gain by this? Why, you showed your anxiety to escape that death with which no one

---

[7] See p. 161.

deigned to threaten you. What effrontery, then, father, to invite us to meet death when you showed everyone, by the plainest signs and in the most glaring light, that you were terrified of it and seeking to flee it?

In these words, Gilbert unconsciously knows more than he consciously admits. He is projecting once more when he alleges Thomas's terror; but when he speaks of the impulse to provoke martyrdom he is seeing more deeply than he knows, and uttering a reproach that will be repeated by Thomas's dearest friend, John of Salisbury, at the very end.

Gilbert continues his argument by insisting that the whole dispute arose over an insignificant issue—certain customs that the king wanted observed, not even his own customs, but those of his ancestors. It is Thomas who has taken up arms and holds his sword over that hallowed head, a head anointed with the chrism, which makes the king another Christ. (In fact, the chrism had not been used at Henry's coronation; reforming popes had stopped that practice. The "oil of catechumens" was used instead.) After all, the king could hardly hope to profit from the Constitutions, for he was no longer interested in the glory of this world:

> To tell you the truth, this is the kind of man you are attacking. His dear children, his exceptionally noble and good wife, the many kingdoms subject to him, the company of his friends, the multitudes of people under his sway, the riches of the world—all these scarcely dissuade him, scarcely restrain him from spurning all, stripping himself bare, and setting off after our Lord Jesus as He carries His cross.

Gilbert Foliot seems to have been one of the very few persons in Europe who discerned, through all the trappings of worldliness, concupiscence, pride, anger, and such lesser sins as chattering and doodling at Mass, the essential saintliness of Henry of England. Henry, Gilbert alleges, has responded well to the admonitions from the pope and the prayers of others. In his natural goodness of heart he was already on the point of altering the Constitutions, and would have surely done so if

Thomas had remained humble and not challenged him again. But while he was engaged in his troublesome preparations for a campaign against the rebellious Bretons, Thomas had "sent him those terrible letters, savoring neither of the affection of a father nor the modesty of a bishop; and all that had been done was at once destroyed by your threats."

✠　✠　✠

Thomas himself never answered this manifesto, so far as we know. But he sent the entire correspondence to his friend, John of Salisbury, who commented: "Does he think anyone in Europe will swallow that?" John made fun of the allegations that the king "thought compliance sweet" when he was admonished about his errors. If it were true, he remarked, how despicable his present advisers were to allow him to offend so enormously, instead of correcting him.

But John warned Thomas again, as he had done often before, not to place too much reliance on the court of Rome. He believed in the pope's good will, but also understood his difficulties. "So great are their necessities, so formidable the dishonesty and cupidity of the Romans, that he [the pope] sometimes uses the license of power and gives himself by dispensation what may benefit his secular government but is not advantageous to religion."

XVI

Legates

EVER SINCE his consecration as archbishop Thomas Becket had baffled and angered his sovereign, but he had not really undermined the king's power. The excommunications of Vézelay, however, raised the conflict to another plane. Henry partly lost the services of some of his principal officials; he had to avoid meetings with them, lest the contagion affect him also; and their thoughts were now turned more upon their personal dilemma than upon his business. In addition he now had to face the grave possibility that the entire Church of England would soon be opposing him, with the full support of the papacy. At the same time he was beset by revolts against his overlordship in Brittany and by the increasing menaces of France. In the circumstances, he concluded that these new troubles were due to the machinations of Thomas Becket. This was outright treason—*proditor* became his favorite epithet for the archbishop—and Henry began to entertain the wild notion that Thomas meant to wrest control of England from him.

Given these fears, Henry could not be content to answer the archbishop's fulminations with nothing more than the Bishop of London's paper thunderbolts. Henry's conception of royal dignity involved retaliating for every slight; and no form of revenge seemed to him too petty or too demeaning of that dignity. He vented his wrath upon all who showed the slightest sympathy for Thomas, insofar as he had power over them. English students at Paris were ordered to come home unless they wished to lose all

260

hope of preferment. A byproduct of this order was a large influx of scholars into the existing schools at Oxford; and while the actual origins of Oxford University still remain a matter of controversy, there can be no doubt that Henry's quarrel with Becket made the town a much more important center of scholarship than it had previously been.

Henry also demonstrated ingenuity in devising forms of pressure against those who were outside his reach, such as the Cistercian monks of Pontigny. At the Council of Chinon Henry had already protested bitterly that Cistercian monks were lending moral and material support to the archbishop and were also smuggling his letters into England. He had warned the Abbot of Cîteaux to put a stop to these practices. In September 1166, a general chapter of the Cistercian order was held at Cîteaux— the *Carta Caritas,* the Rule of the order, made it obligatory for all abbots to attend an annual meeting of the mother church once a year. Henry seized the opportunity to address a stern warning to the Cistercians, threatening confiscation of the order's vast possessions within his domains and expulsion of the monks from England if Pontigny continued to harbor his enemy, Thomas Becket, "my former chancellor."

Frederick Barbarossa had already carried out a similar threat against the Cistercians in the Empire, and the monks were terrified. Some had courage: the Abbot of Pontigny passionately invoked the duty of hospitality, and others proclaimed that it would disgrace their vows for them to be swayed by the loss of worldly possessions. But the English abbots observed that the burden of their support would fall upon the French members of the order. Gilbert, Abbot of Cîteaux, was no St. Bernard; he placed the interest of his order above principle and the fate of an individual. As soon as the session ended, he set out for Pontigny to inform Thomas Becket of Henry's letter: these were King Henry's words, but of course the lord archbishop must decide for himself what he wished to do.

Thomas had no real choice. He did not want the entire order injured for his sake, he declared, and would leave as soon as he found somewhere to lay his head. But although the Cistercians thus managed to save face, all Europe knew that Henry of

England had procured the archbishop's expulsion from Pontigny. The exile was to be exiled twice over.

If we may believe the self-pitying speech that Herbert of Bosham attributes to the archbishop, Thomas was stunned by this news and cried out in despair: "Let God provide for us now, for we have no other refuge." But if we read carefully and note the archbishop's references to "this solitude" and to the monks as "those dead to the world," we may, if we will, see in these traditional formal phrases (ostensibly intended only as compliments to the brethren) a measure of discontent with the loneliness of Pontigny. Thomas, who fought on almost every issue, suddenly proved to be amenable when he was asked to leave Pontigny. Far from being dead to the world, he longed to escape from the monotonous rounds of monastic life to the more hectic urban atmosphere that was his native element. He naïvely betrayed his own feelings when Herbert of Bosham reminded him of King Louis's promise to provide him with funds sufficient for him to establish himself in any city in France. "I remember," Thomas replied to Herbert, "but it seems to me now, brother, that you are again longing for the magnificence of a court and the delights of a city, which in these times we who are fettered by the chains of the Gospel ought to abandon." When Thomas rebuked his followers, he was often rebuking himself.

Nevertheless he succumbed to temptation. Herbert was sent to ask Louis for help. And Louis, who at this juncture in his long and tense relations with Henry II was once more on the verge of a rupture with his powerful vassal (he had hoped in vain to thwart Henry's conquest of Brittany), gladly offered to aid the man who was capable of causing the King of England as much anguish as all the armies of France. "Greet the archbishop in my name," he answered Herbert, "and tell him to choose any city or castle in our domain, and he will find it ready for him."

Thomas chose Sens, close enough to Pontigny to make the moving easy, and above all identified with Pope Alexander, who had spent so much of his own exile there. In November 1166 Thomas left the monastery of Pontigny. He was escorted part of the way by weeping monks, but was not spared a parting remark by the abbot that he had eaten and drunk too well. But if the leavetaking was dispiriting, the reception at Sens was heartening. Archbishop Hugo, surrounded by his clergy and the cheering populace of that lively city, welcomed him warmly and supplied him liberally with money and provisions in the name of King Louis. The Benedictine abbey of St. Columba, just outside the city, offered him hospitality, and was to remain his home until his return to Canterbury. It was a pleasanter refuge than Pontigny. Herbert of Bosham plainly speaks for his master when he praises the city of Sens, set in the midst of a fruitful plain bounded by hills, with the lovely Yonne River flowing between steep banks. In the heart of the city rose the great cathedral newly built by William of Sens, who after Thomas's death was to undertake the rebuilding of Canterbury cathedral. Herbert and Thomas found the inhabitants of Sens open-handed, cultured, friendly, and sociable.

Unwittingly, Henry had eased the pain of exile for Thomas by driving him from the isolation of Pontigny to Sens, where six great highways intersected. The king had also aroused public opinion against himself, and angered the pope. In an effort to repair the situation, he dispatched envoys to Pope Alexander. Either out of calculated insolence or a desire to employ his most skilled diplomat, he chose as head of the delegation to Rome none other than the excommunicated Dean of Salisbury, John of Oxford.

In spite of Thomas Becket's cries of outrage to the pope, and pleas to cardinals in the Curia, John of Oxford was received graciously by Pope Alexander. For after all he carried credentials in which King Henry requested the pope to treat him with absolute confidence, as if he were the sovereign in person. John's first request, of course, was that he personally be absolved—and to this end he cheerfully swore to Alexander that he had made no promises to the "schismatics" at Würzburg. ("That swearer," John of Salisbury henceforth called John.) He also distributed presents liberally among the members of the Curia. A veritable espionage story unfolded. By bribery, John succeeded in obtaining copies of all the letters that Thomas and his friends had sent to Rome. On the other hand Thomas, though his purse was leaner, was himself not ill-informed; his own letters show again and again that he knows his antagonists' plans and the contents of their letters. A copy of the pope's letter to Henry, announcing the appointment of a legation, was promptly put into Thomas's hands.

Advance information did not help, however, because Pope Alexander's political predicament had changed radically for the worse in the six months that had elapsed since the excommunications at Vézelay. Rumors sped across the Alps that Frederick Barbarossa was already raising a vast army for an invasion of Italy. Alexander could no longer afford to offend the King of England, and he desperately tried to make peace between Thomas and Henry. Failing that, he knew he must delay any decision as long as possible. Although Thomas bitterly accused him of vacillation, Alexander in fact yielded to necessity. He lifted the ban of excommunication from John of Oxford, confirmed him in his holding of the deanery of Salisbury, and sent him back to England with the promise that papal legates would be appointed to settle the dispute.

The message that John of Oxford brought with him promised Henry everything he had asked. The legates would have "full powers to examine and judge the ecclesiastical disputes that have arisen between you and our venerable brother, the Archbishop of Canterbury; also the case relating to the appeal between the archbishop and the bishops of your kingdom." In the meantime the archbishop was forbidden to "molest, disturb or disquiet either yourself, your people or your kingdom until these matters in dispute have been brought to a conclusion." Any sentences that Thomas might pronounce were declared null and void in advance. If necessary the king was to show the letter. "But otherwise we beg your Serene Highness and urgently request you not to let anyone know of this letter or the tenor of it, but to keep it strictly secret."

Alexander also promised that his legates would absolve the members of the king's household whom Thomas had already excommunicated. Thus the excommunicates would have to wait until the arrival of the legates, meanwhile suffering all the anxieties and disadvantages of excommunication. But then Alexander inserted an escape clause. "If in the meantime any of them is in fear of death, we allow any bishop or member of the clergy to absolve them." This was a provision that King Henry interpreted with the greatest liberality, and availed himself of with a goodly measure of wit. He ordered the excommunicates to Wales or to the Continent. On the grounds that men who risked turbulent Wales and the turbulent Channel were *in metu mortis,* all the excommunicates were absolved. Thus the Vézelay sentences were annulled.

Unfortunately for the pope's reputation, and heartbreakingly for Thomas Becket, Alexander's situation forced him into an undignified double game. Writing to Thomas on the same day, he announced the legation in entirely different terms. His beloved sons, William of Pavia, Cardinal of St. Peter's, and Otto of St. Nicholas, were to try to effect a reconciliation between Thomas and Henry. There was no mention of their full powers to judge the issues. Instead, Alexander urged Thomas to "dissemble for the present if everything is not in accord with your wishes," and to "trust fully the aforesaid cardinals." Foreseeing Thomas's reaction, he enjoined him: "You ought not be suspicious of William [of Pavia], for we have firmly and strictly ordered him to do all in his power to make peace for you." And then Alexander suggested to Thomas one major cause of his change of front by defining a highly important aspect of "the perilous state of the present time":

> For the rest, we request and advise you, our beloved brother, to apply to the illustrious Count of Flanders on our behalf, and earnestly request him, in view of the Church's needs and our own, to supply us with generous support. For we do not believe that he can give alms more acceptable to God than by providing us at present with financial aid to enable us to defend the liberties of the Church.

Far from being reassured, Thomas was alarmed and horrified when he read the names of the legates. Cardinal Otto had a good reputation but was considered venal—"a Roman and a cardinal," as John of Salisbury remarked succinctly. William of Pavia was a known partisan of Henry, and his appointment was the direct result of pressure from Henry's envoys. He looked, commented John, "rather to the fear of God than to the honor of the Church."

✠   ✠   ✠

John of Oxford returned triumphantly home by way of France, magnifying his accomplishments at the Curia and declaring that he now had the cardinals in his pocket. His boasts angered King Louis and distressed Thomas Becket to the point of despair. For a time Thomas passed through a dark night of the soul. His faith wavered; he ceased to be a suffering churchman and assumed the role of irascible secular. The succession of blows wholly unsettled him. He had thought the pope firmly behind him, his cause almost won, his enemies on the retreat before the terrible fact of excommunication and the threat of interdict. Now Pope Alexander had betrayed him. The self-discipline that had sustained him for two years at Pontigny abruptly deserted him. He became moody, querulous, irate. He lost the judiciousness and address that under Theobald and Henry had made him the foremost diplomat of his age. In astonishingly intemperate language, he wrote to the pope warning him that his reputation was at stake. He insultingly admonished the Holy Father to dispense evenhanded justice. Bitterly, he quoted to his clerks Gilbert Foliot's exultant exclamation when the pope's letters were shown to him at Winchester: "From now on Thomas will no longer be my archbishop."

To one of the two legates, William of Pavia, Thomas addressed a curt, offensive note: "You tell me that you have come to these parts to settle the questions between the King of England and ourselves as shall seem expedient to you. We do not believe that you have come for this purpose, nor do we accept you as intermediary for many reasons which we will show at the proper time and place."

Fortunately this letter was never dispatched. In spite of his hysterical moods, Thomas retained a grain of good sense. He submitted the draft to John of Salisbury, who was appalled by the tone and content. After all, John protested, Thomas was writing to a cardinal-priest and a legate of the Holy See in language that would not do for the pope's footman. Although Cardinal William's sentiments were well known, he had not yet done anything to provoke such rudeness. "If he sends his and your letters to the pope, the king's case will appear to be justified, and you convicted of contumacy by the evidence of your own writing."

Thomas tried again, with results scarcely more diplomatic. "I do not like the first or the second draft of the letter you have decided to send to Cardinal William," John wrote bluntly, "because it seems to me excessively full of suspicions and biting sarcasms." John succeeded in restraining Thomas, and himself wrote far more diplomatically to the cardinal, expressing pleasure at his coming to settle the quarrel and indicating that although William's intimacy with King Henry had aroused suspicions, he trusted that the prelate would use that intimacy well to promote the liberty and peace of the Church.

But the admonitions of well-meaning friends could not long subdue the recklessness and wild indignation that had taken possession of Thomas. His worst side came to the fore; the letters he wrote during this period are filled with cries of anguish, extravagant threats and denunciations, imperious demands. He declared that he would refuse to all eternity to accept the judgment of Cardinal William. He constantly referred to his enemies as thirsting for his blood and seeking his life.

Writing to a friend like Conrad of Mainz, who had himself voluntarily assumed the burden of exile, Thomas could express the full measure of his dilemma:

Caught between a clear conscience and the hardest of misfortune, I do not know whether to indulge my feelings or submit to the times. The bitterness of my soul torments me to say what I feel at any risk; the harshness of the times urges me to keep silence at the risk of the Church. Good God, where shall

I turn? Certainly, danger is everywhere. . . . The renowned
city is captive which once subdued the whole world, is subverted
by the craving for human favor; and what could not perish by
the sword has succumbed to the poisonous allures of the West.
What shame! The Church's liberty has been exchanged for
temporal gain. She goes to her ruin by the crooked paths of
riches; she has been prostituted like a whore who is accessible to
the lust of the many in the street; princes have fornicated with
her at will. . . . Woe to us! What shall we do?

Such was the note Thomas struck again and again, while
Cardinals William and Otto slowly made their way up through
Italy and into France. The two cardinals consumed nearly half
a year in the journey from Rome. Their dilatoriness was not
entirely their own fault; Louis of France, who believed that
they were coming to depose Thomas Becket, hesitated for
some time to grant them a safe-conduct. Then they lingered
for a while in Provence in order to remain aloof from the
desultory war that had broken out between France and England.[1] The cardinals were also slowed by their efforts to raise
money, for Pope Alexander had charged them with the additional task of obtaining funds in the Continental domains of
Henry, and in France. The Curia was truly in desperate straits;
Alexander had had to write to the Archbishop of Reims begging him to raise a hundred marks of silver for the papal
treasury. Knowledge of this reached Thomas Becket and his
friends, and added to their forebodings. In such circumstances,
how could the Curia resist the lure of more English silver
pennies?

While the cardinals were en route, Alexander's difficulties
were mounting. Frederick Barbarossa and his redoubtable
archbishop-chancellor, Rainald, had decided to solve the "Italian problem" by force of arms. In the spring of the year,

---

[1] Henry had attacked Count William of Auvergne, who held land
of both kings. Count William appealed to Louis, who responded
by ravaging the Vexin border. Henry returned from Auvergne to
Normandy, and early in June of 1167 held a conference with
Louis. But the two kings were unable to come to an agreement,
and the war continued as a series of raids and counter-raids.

Frederick led a vast German army across the Alps into Italy. Archbishop Rainald advanced on Rome by way of Pisa, while Frederick himself in a pincer movement closed in from Ancona, on the eastern coast of the peninsula. At the Battle of Tusculanum (present-day Frascati), Rainald with a few men crushed a much larger force of Romans; and when Frederick's troops joined his, the fall of Rome became inevitable. At the end of July, Frederick's knights broke through the Porta Viridaria and drove the fleeing Romans before them to the gates of St. Peter's. Fighting raged to the high altar of the basilica itself; the floor of the central church of Christendom was stained with blood, and the holy edifice nearly burned to the ground.

Pope Alexander escaped from Rome disguised as a pilgrim. He made his way to Benevento, where he was received with acclamations. But his cause seemed lost. Frederick Barbarossa had seemingly attained the supreme moment of his life. Paschal III entered Rome with the victorious Germans, and on August 1 the antipope solemnly crowned Frederick's wife Beatrice with the imperial diadem. Although Frederick himself had been crowned twelve years before by Pope Adrian IV, Paschal repeated the emperor's coronation in a glittering ceremony.

At this moment Frederick could justly feel himself a second Charlemagne. He had united *imperium* and *sacerdotium* as only his illustrious predecessor had done. He had installed a subservient pope on the throne of St. Peter, and apparently held all of Italy north of Rome securely in his grasp. But then the hand of God intervened—so the matter was viewed by Thomas Becket, whose fortunes were so closely linked to those of Pope Alexander; so it was viewed by the papal party, by many among Frederick's adherents, and perhaps for a time even by Frederick himself. The day after the coronation, bright sunshine suddenly gave way to a terrible downpour. Then the rain ceased, the clouds vanished, and sultry, oppressive heat descended upon Rome. Mists rose from the marshes, and with them the dreaded Roman fever. The disease ran its course in a single day; men were "in perfect health in the

morning, dead before evening." Frederick lost twenty-five
thousand men, including two thousand of his notables. The
greatest blow of all was the death of Rainald of Cologne. The
Germans broke camp at once, and fled from the pestilential
vicinity of Rome. But they did not want to leave Rainald's
body behind, for they were convinced, or pretended to be, that
their warrior archbishop had been a saint. Accordingly, they
boiled the whole body in water to separate the flesh from the
bones, so that they might take his relics with them.

A much diminished German army made its way north to
Pavia, where Frederick spent an uneasy winter, for all of
Lombardy now rose against his rule. Most of the major cities
of northern Italy banded together against the Germans; and
although the antipope continued to hold Rome, it was evident
that imperial policy in Italy had suffered an almost total collapse. Alexander III stayed in Benevento for the time being;
but the increased security of his position was manifested in the
stronger tone that he took toward the adversaries of Thomas
Becket. He warned his legates not to be lured into visiting
England, and he now instructed them that their task was to
bring about a reconciliation between King Henry and Archbishop Thomas, not to decide the issue onesidedly.

Thomas exulted when he heard the news that, as he put it,
"the schismatical Frederick has been ignominiously humiliated." But his own humiliations had so robbed him of judgment that he indulged in the wildest exaggerations. "If we
rightly consider what has happened, never since the world
began has God made plainer his power, shown his justice more
justly." John of Salisbury, too, saw in the fate of Frederick a
warning to King Henry. "God scatters the people who seek
war, and those who withdraw from the peace of God will
undoubtedly perish. What persecutor of the Church has ever
been heard to escape the avenging right hand of God?"

It was, then, in a mood of far greater confidence than he
had felt at the beginning of August that Thomas, in October,
awaited the arrival of the legates. Cardinal William and Cardinal Otto stopped off at Sens to see him on their way to Normandy, and made a good impression on him. Cardinal William

proved to be a man of persuasive eloquence. The two legates explained that the purpose of their journey was solely to effect a reconciliation. Thomas, although still doubtful of William, began to feel more sanguine, and after the departure of the legates he waited impatiently for further news from them.

He had to wait some time, with growing anxiety, for the two cardinals neither returned to him nor informed him of their activities. At last, on November 1, they sent Thomas a peremptory summons to a conference on St. Martin's Day, November 10, to be held on the border of France and Normandy.

Thomas found it no easy task to raise money for the journey, assemble his scattered advisers, and obtain horses—he had no more than three in his stables. Money was constantly a problem for him, dependent as he was upon the bounty of King Louis; moreover he was convinced that his enemies followed a deliberate policy of trying to force long and expensive journeys on him and his followers in order to make his maintenance more costly to Louis. He obtained a week's respite from the cardinal-legates, informed them that on no account would he set foot inside the domains of King Henry, and on November 18, 1167, arrived with his party of fellow exiles at the field between the castles of Gisors and Trie where the dukes of Normandy had traditionally met with the kings of France. It was characteristic of Thomas that although he made a great point of his poverty in all his letters, and used it as one of his arguments against indulging in further litigation, he was too proud to appear without a retinue befitting his station. He turned up with a sizable following. John of Salisbury, Herbert of Bosham, Lombard of Piacenza, Alexander of Wales, and Alan (probably Alan of Tewkesbury, his future biographer) are mentioned among "many others." Thomas later expressed to the pope his gratitude to King Louis for "munificent entertainment."

On the way to the conference in the morning, Thomas revealed to his friends that he was expecting the worst. In a dream during the night someone had offered him poison in a golden cup, he told his fellow exiles. ("And so," Herbert of Bosham remarks, "it fell out.")

Cardinal William of Pavia opened the session. He enlarged upon the kindness of the pope in sending them, the legates; he spoke of the perils and difficulties of the journey from Rome. (That was more than mere rhetoric; he was hinting to the two kings that secular princes ought to see to the safety of the roads.) He then referred to the greatness and inflexible character of King Henry, the sovereign's former favors to the archbishop, the possibility that humility and moderation might appease the king's anger. Then he turned to Henry's grievances against his archbishop. A somewhat exaggerated list of complaints culminated in the charge that Thomas had only recently, by intrigue, involved Henry in a war with the King of France—a war that was still unsettled, although a truce until Easter had recently been arranged.

In his reply, Thomas heatedly denied this allegation; and the first day's negotiations ended with the decision to submit the question to King Louis himself. Louis, on the following day, supported Becket's denial by taking an oath in the presence of the legates. The cardinals then tried another approach. William of Pavia appealed to Thomas himself for assistance. He said that Henry had angrily denounced them, the legates, when he learned that they did not have the power to pass sentence—as John of Oxford had boastfully led him to suppose—but only to mediate. Thomas, surely, knew Henry's character better than anyone else; would he tell them the best way to placate the king? After all, Henry had long loved and honored the Roman Church; he was a great and powerful sovereign; and he was asking of Thomas no more than the rights and customs his predecessors had enjoyed from the archbishop's predecessors. Did Thomas claim to be better than his forefathers?

Thomas recognized the cardinal's language as a borrowing from Bishop Gilbert of London. But he replied circumspectly that none of his predecessors had ever been required to make any such promise; that the pope, in the presence of the two cardinals themselves, had at Sens mercifully absolved him of his previous pledge to observe the "wicked constitutions"; and that he would sooner bow his neck to the executioner than consent to them again. Once more, Thomas had the Constitutions of Clarendon read out, and asked whether a priest could ever dissemble agreement with them without risking his salvation.

In that case, William suggested, would it not be better for him to resign than to continue to make such trouble for the Church? Thomas replied: "I will not yield in this cause because that would mean setting a pernicious example that would result in the destruction of ecclesiastical liberty and perhaps the ruin of the Christian faith itself. For who would dare raise his voice henceforth? If other pastors similarly gave way, who would rise in opposition and stand as a wall to protect the House of Israel? Has our present pope or his predecessors given any such example to the Church?"

This argument revealed the fanaticism to which Thomas Becket had been driven. Refusal to compromise for fear of setting precedents is the classical folly of revolutionaries, weak rulers, and schoolmasters. Thomas Becket had known this well in his days as a secular diplomat. He had not hesitated to tax the Church when that was necessary, for he knew then, as every diplomat must, that expediency will always find some means for overriding precedent. He had constantly before his eyes the adroit maneuverings of Frederick Barbarossa and Pope Alexander, both strong men, both determined to gain their ends, but both flexible enough to shrug away the implications of their past acts when necessity counseled a change of front.

The legates, however, could find no dignified way to meet Thomas's fanatical argument directly, and so they shifted ground. Would he accept their judgment of the dispute, they asked. Thomas sensed a trap. If he refused, he would seem to justify the king's case; if he accepted, he would be allowing the cardinal whom he regarded as his enemy to become his judge. He therefore replied evasively that he had been deprived of his see and all his worldly possessions, so that he could not afford expensive litigation. If he received full restitution, he would be willing to submit to the judgment of Pope Alexander or anyone the pope pleased to appoint. When they asked whether he would accept their judgment solely in regard to the bishops' appeal against him, he gave a similar answer, adding that he had received no instructions from the pope on that score.

The point was, of course, that Thomas did not dare to trust William of Pavia, and was not sure how far Cardinal Otto would go in his behalf, although he believed in Otto's good faith. Yet it was difficult for him to avoid the appearance of obstinacy when the two cardinals together proposed that the whole question of the royal customs be simply dropped. The king, they argued, could not be expected to accept conditions inconsistent with his dignity. But if he granted peace without any mention of either keeping or abolishing the customs, it would be understood that the Constitutions of Clarendon were null and void. So long as Thomas did not bind himself to observe the customs, everyone would understand that he had won, while at the same time the king would not be humiliated by express abandonment of the issue on which he had fought for so long.

There followed one of those scholastic arguments so beloved of ecclesiastics. Thomas replied that on his part silence would indicate consent to the customs, and quoted canon law: "He who does not object when he can is assumed to consent," and, "He who openly ceases to protest against misdeeds incurs the suspicion of hidden consent." The cardinals in their turn argued that when a bishop promoted a man to sacred orders, he did not explicitly speak of celibacy, but it was tacitly understood that the candidate consented to the state of continence. They adduced many other examples, but neither side succeeded in convincing the other.

With that, the negotiations ended. "And so," Herbert of Bosham concludes "with no peace made, or rather without any hope that the cardinals would be able to make peace, we took our leave, and they returned immediately to the king."

Thus the first legation had ended in failure. Thomas Becket left the conference with mingled feelings of disappointment and elation, as his subsequent letters to the pope reveal. He was pleased that he had escaped the pitfalls set by the cardinals, proud that King Louis had supported him unconditionally, and relieved that the legates had not held a mandate to decide the issue as he had feared. But on the other hand he was downcast that the pope would not give him firmer support, and instead permitted the dispute to run on from year to year, from appeal to appeal. Were not things already bad enough, he cried out to the pope:

> Must we, by the authority of this legation (which never should have been sent) be dragged on and on from year to year, from sorrow to sorrow, from misery to confusion? Must our right and justice be converted into our ruin and the ruin of our miserable fellows? Good God, what will be the end of this grief? Rise up, O God, and judge thy cause, avenge the blood of thy servants who have been vilely slain, and of others who faint under intolerable afflictions; for there is no one to deliver us from under the hand of our enemies except our lord pope and a very few others like him.

But if Thomas was discontented with the outcome of the meeting, the cardinal-legates had reason to be even more so. They now had to face the wrath of King Henry; and after lingering at Gisors for a day or two, apparently to confer with Louis of France, they set out for Caen, where Henry was staying. William of Pavia in particular had desperately wanted to bring him some concession; now they were returning to the king empty-handed.

Henry, still unaware of their failure, surprised them by courteously coming to meet them some two leagues outside Caen. He greeted them blithely, and conducted them to their lodgings. Henry had assembled many of his clerics from England and Normandy to pay honor to the papal legates. On the following day, Cardinals William and Otto were invited to wait on the king after Mass. A large company of archbishops, bishops, and abbots assembled in the royal audience chamber with Henry to hear the cardinals' admission that they had been unable to persuade or overawe Thomas Becket, and had not been given the power to force him to yield. The conference took place behind closed doors. After some two hours, the cardinals came out, followed by the king as far as the outer

275

door of the chapel. There Henry turned, and while the cardinals were still within earshot exclaimed: "I hope to God I never set eyes on a cardinal again!"

Returning to the council chamber, Henry furiously berated his churchmen; late that evening they emerged looking thoroughly shaken. Early next morning the king went hunting, deliberately avoiding the cardinals and leaving his ecclesiastics to deal with them. The bishops conferred among themselves, and later in the day went to the church near the cardinals' inn. Of the English clergy, the Archbishop of York and the bishops of Worcester, Salisbury, Chichester, and London were present. The legates were invited to join their discussions, and as usual Bishop Gilbert of London acted as spokesman for the English clergy. His agitation, remarks the anonymous friend at court who reported on these events to Thomas Becket, was betrayed by his "insipid and hardly elegant" speech. Becket's friend reported it in full:

> You have heard that we received letters from our lord the pope, and we have them in our hands at this moment. In them he indicated that we should meet you when you sent for us, so that the dispute between the king and our lord of Canterbury might be settled, as well as the suit between us, the bishops of England, and the archbishop. We were told that you had been given full powers. For that reason, as soon as we heard of your arrival in these parts, we came to meet you, wholly ready and prepared to await your judgment, and to initiate an action or respond to it. Our lord king likewise offers to accept whatever sentence you decide to pronounce between him and our lord of Canterbury. Since, therefore, neither the king nor you nor we have failed to obey the pope's mandate, let the blame rest where it ought to rest. But since the archbishop does everything suddenly and precipitately, striking without warning, suspending and excommunicating before he even issues an admonition, we have forestalled such sudden sentences by appeal. We appealed previously and we now renew the appeal, and all England joins in it.

Gilbert Foliot then reviewed the grounds of the quarrel, which as he saw it had nothing to do with principles, with liberty of the Church, right of appeal, immunity of the clergy from trial in lay courts, or anything of the sort. Rather, the king demanded of Thomas Becket forty-four thousand marks of silver for revenues he had received during his chancellorship, while the archbishop claimed that he had been absolved of such debts at the time he was promoted. "The archbishop thinks," Gilbert attempted to joke, "that promotion cancels debts as baptism remits sins."

Gilbert then launched into a tirade on the archbishop's dangerous conduct, which might even lead the king to abandon the Roman Church. He propounded a remarkably disingenuous explanation of the royal ban on appeals to Rome (Article VIII of the Constitutions of Clarendon): the king had issued this prohibition solely in order to save poor clerics the expense of appeals to the Holy See. Since he had thus acted in the interests of the clergy, he was naturally vexed to find members of the clergy ungrateful. As for the courts at home in England, he was perfectly willing to let clerks take all church matters to ecclesiastical courts, so long as they would accept civil judges in civil suits.

Finally Gilbert complained that Thomas kept demanding services that were not legitimately due to an archbishop from his suffragan. "He requires me to deliver so many letters that if I had forty couriers at my disposal they would not suffice." In addition, Thomas had withdrawn nearly sixty churches (with, of course, their revenues) from his jurisdiction. "He blames everything on me, and keeps hounding me more than any other bishop." Against all these actions, Gilbert now appealed.

Thomas's friend at court did not describe the two cardinals' reaction to this eloquent lament. Apparently neither was shaken in his preconceptions. As they were leaving on December 3, the king came to them and humbly pleaded with them to intercede for him with the pope. His Holiness could, if he would, free him from his troublesome foe, he said. Suddenly Henry burst into tears. Cardinal William of Pavia pretended to be deeply affected; but Cardinal Otto barely restrained his laughter.

Nevertheless, Henry gained something by this show of submissiveness to the papacy. The cardinals sent a formal message to Thomas acknowledging him as legate of the Holy See, but forbidding him to place an interdict upon the kingdom of England or its clergy. Thus, after a year of intense anxiety, Thomas Becket was left in the very position in which he had stood at the beginning. Henry, too, had gained nothing but further delay and the prospect that his kingdom would continue to be disturbed, his clergy divided, and his reputation impaired at home and abroad. His mood was summed up by the friend at court: "As for the king, he seems to want nothing but your head on a platter."

XVII

Montmirail and Montmartre

WITH BOUNDLESS INDIGNATION, Thomas Becket learned that he had been stripped of his powers over the English Church. The empty title of legate was still his; but his hands were tied. In his anguish, he threw pleas, accusations, and bitter denunciations in all directions. To William of Pavia, he wrote: "I did not think I was to be put up for sale, or that you would reap a profit from my blood." To Pope Alexander he protested in language almost threatening: "Your legates have acted with equal iniquity and presumptuousness toward us and the Church. . . . Going to the very limits of their powers, they have suspended us from all authority over the English Church. . . . Lord, lord, our eyes are turned to you, lest we perish. Aid us, my lord, and keep your promises, which I hope did not lift our hearts in vain! . . . Pity us, my lord, that God may pity you in the Last Judgment." He accused the entire Roman Curia of venality, bewailed again and again the condition of the Church in England, and warned Alexander that King Louis of France deeply resented the papacy's compliance toward Henry. Louis was, in fact, so vexed that he for his part toyed with projects for an alliance with the Germans.

Alexander, beset by a succession of delegations from Henry and from Becket, still fearing the power of Frederick Barbarossa, anxious to retain the good will of King Louis, resorted to further temporizing. In his desperate eagerness to make peace between archbishop and king, he offered concessions to

279

both parties. In May 1168 he confirmed the decision of the cardinal-legates and granted Henry exemption from ecclesiastical censures until such time as he should take the archbishop back into his favor. Simultaneously—with what seemed on the surface arrant duplicity but was really evidence of his determination to mediate rather than decide the dispute—he wrote to Thomas that the suspension of his powers to excommunicate was to last only until the Lent of 1169.

At the same time, the pope appointed two new legates: Simon, Prior of Mont Dieu, and Brother Bernard of Corilo, whose instructions were to persuade the king "to receive our venerable brother Thomas, Archbishop of Canterbury, back into his grace and love, and recall him to his see and to the church committed to him." Thomas might take it as a hint of some change in Alexander's intentions that he chose two monks, rather than worldlier cardinals or bishops, to be his emissaries this time. Moreover the envoys carried with them two letters to King Henry, one *commonitory* (i.e., warning) and the other *comminatory* (i.e., threatening), which they were to present successively if Henry would not make peace.

By now peace had begun to seem sweet and highly desirable to Henry. His truce with King Louis had expired at Easter, 1168. In spite of Thomas's protests of loyalty and Louis's disclaimers, Henry firmly believed that Thomas was inciting the French king to make war upon him. Perpetually troubled by rebellious vassals, Henry had all he could do to keep his far-flung domains in order. He appealed for peace, but could secure only a prolongation of the truce until July. Then he arranged a conference with Louis at La Ferté Bernard, across the river from Chartres. But the conference broke up in angry wrangling, and desultory campaigning was resumed for the rest of the year. At last, at the beginning of January 1169, Henry and Louis met at Montmirail near Chartres and concluded a treaty of peace. The agreement was sealed by the betrothal of Prince Richard of England to Louis's daughter Adela. In the warmth of good feeling engendered by these successful negotiations, Henry acceded to Louis's request that he meet with Thomas Becket and the papal envoys, whose arrival had been delayed by the hostilities between the two powers.

Thomas Becket accepted the invitation with high hopes. The papal envoys hinted at assurances from Henry that he would grant everything Becket desired, once his honor was satisfied. The new treaty was precious to Henry: he was known to be eager for a stable peace. And Thomas himself was willing to make large concessions. His own supporters, the exiled clergy, were longing to return to their homes and secure employments. Five years of charges and countercharges had somewhat obscured the original causes of the quarrel. They urged Thomas to make an end of it by throwing himself entirely on the king's mercy. Prudence certainly recommended such a course; for Thomas could not afford to offend Louis, his sole support, by appearing intransigent. He felt unsure of Alexander, feared that the pope might yield to the new solution Henry was urging: his translation to a Continental see. And above all, he was weary of exile, of living on charity, of seeing so many others suffer for his sake. He yearned, too, for reconciliation with the man who had been his friend, whose good opinion he still valued, and whose good will he craved. The charges of "traitor" stung; and although they might not be true in the literal sense, he knew that his dissension with the king encouraged Henry's enemies and weakened the position of England in her relationships with foreign powers. The whole concept of an English foreign policy was something that Thomas Becket himself had virtually created during his chancellorship; now he was foremost in undermining it.

Under these inner and outer pressures, Thomas agreed to the formula proposed by the papal envoys: that he would submit the whole question to the king's will and pleasure. In prolonged discussions with the mediators, Thomas at last consented to do so "saving God's honor." This was the formula that Thomas had devised as a substitute for his former phrase, so obnoxious to the king, "saving my order." But the mediators insisted that the use of either formula would destroy all chance of reconciliation. Alone among his advisers, Herbert of Bosham persistently warned Thomas that he was falling into a trap as he had done at Clarendon; that the king could not be trusted to keep his promises; and he would surely regret it if he surrendered unconditionally.

In the discussions that raged on the eve of the conference, Thomas was drawn this way and that; he seemed no longer to know his own mind. While the two kings sat together, waiting for the archbishop to decide, the mediators plied him with arguments until at last he seemed to give way, and perhaps thought himself that he meant to yield. At the last moment, as Thomas was being brought forward toward the kings by the papal envoys and other distinguished men, Herbert of Bosham pushed his way through the crowd and managed to whisper a few words into his ear: "Be careful, my lord, walk warily. I tell you, speaking from conscience, that if in this compromise you suppress the words 'saving God's honor' as you formerly suppressed in England 'saving my order' when the question of observing the royal customs was involved, your sorrow will be renewed." Even in these "few words" Herbert could not refrain from quotation: "You will immediately recall the sad words of the psalm: 'I was dumb with silence, I held my peace even from good, and my sorrow was renewed.' "[1]

Thomas turned and looked into his fellow exile's face; but there were so many persons thronging around him and trying to speak to him that he could not answer. With the papal envoys and Archbishop William of Sens accompanying him, he was escorted into the presence of the kings. At once he rushed forward and threw himself at Henry's feet. Henry, obviously as moved as Thomas himself, caught him by the hand and raised him to his feet.

The moment of emotion was brief. Thomas then began a long, carefully prepared formal speech that was directed as much to King Louis and public opinion as to King Henry. He pleaded for mercy upon the English Church, blaming himself and his own sinfulness for all that the Church had hitherto suffered. But even as he thus indicted himself, he was careful to specify some of the grosser offences that Henry had commit-

---

[1] Ps.39. R.V. and A.V.: "My sorrow was stirred."

ted against the Church. Finally he wound to the conclusion that all were waiting for: "On the whole matter which is in dispute between us, my lord king, in the presence of our lord the King of France and the archbishops, princes and others who stand around us, I throw myself on your mercy and your pleasure. . . ." But then, to the astonishment equally of his friends and of all those who had labored so hard to mediate the dispute, he added: "Saving the honor of God!"

At these words Henry immediately burst into a furious denunciation of Thomas. He accused him of pride, vanity, and ingratitude. Had he wholly forgotten ten years of royal gener-osity? But he was ambitious, that was it; he hoped to unseat his own liege lord and become sovereign in his stead. "Did you not, as chancellor, take oaths of allegiance from my subjects on both shores of the sea, in order to disinherit me?" he preposterously asked Thomas. And turning to Louis, Henry added: "For the same reason he lived so luxuriously and acted with so much liberality in his chancellorship."

"My lord, you reproach me for my actions as chancellor," Thomas replied in a tone that combined humility and firmness. "But it is only your anger that leads you to rebuke as a fault what ought to have earned your gratitude. All who stand around here know what I did in your service, the loyalty with which I served you. . . . It would be degrading and improper for me to recall the advantages my services brought to you, or to taunt you with them. The whole world saw and knows the truth. . . ."

Henry interrupted. Turning to the King of France, he said: "My lord, this man foolishly and vainly deserted his church, secretly fleeing by night, although neither I nor anyone else drove him out of the kingdom. Now he claims that his cause is that of the Church and that he suffers for the sake of justice. He has deceived many influential men by his arguments. I have always been willing and am now to allow him to rule over his church with as much freedom as any of the saints who preceded him. But please take note of this, my lord, that whenever he disapproves of something, he will say it is con-trary to God's honor, and so always get the better of me. Let me propose this to him, so that no one shall think me a despiser of God's honor. . . . Let him behave toward me as the most holy of his predecessors behaved toward the least of mine, and I will be satisfied."

It was the same proposition that Cardinals William and Otto had earlier made in their negotiations with Thomas. Now, spoken in public, it made a favorable impression upon the audience of notables. Everyone cried out: "The king has humbled himself enough." Louis, too, was impressed. He turned to Thomas and asked in a harsh and insulting tone: "My lord archbishop, do you wish to be more than a saint?"

Thomas answered with composure that he was ready to resume governance of his see on those terms, but that he would not admit any new customs harmful to the Church. And he added, in effective peroration: "It is true that there have been archbishops better and greater than I, and every one of them had to root out some of the abuses in the Church. But if they had corrected them all, I would not now have to face this ordeal by fire."

The pope's envoys and the nobles of both kingdoms thronged around Thomas, urging him to omit the offensive phrase, "saving the honor of God." Even now, they said, after all the harsh words that had been exchanged, he could still have peace if he would. But Thomas had taken his decision, perhaps involuntarily, and he remained obdurate. He did not even answer the reproaches that were flung at him from all sides until his intimate friend, John of Canterbury, now Bishop of Poitiers, warned him that his obstinacy might mean the destruction of the Church. Then he said mildly: "No, brother, take care that you do not cause the destruction of the Church. God willing, it will never be destroyed by me."

The resentment among his own clerks, who saw their hopes of returning home dashed, was expressed in outright insolence. As they departed, one named Henry of Hocton was riding directly in front of the archbishop. Suddenly his horse stumbled. "Gee up!" he said loudly enough for Thomas to hear. "Saving the honor of God and the Church and my own order."

Thomas pretended not to have heard, as he pretended to be

unperturbed that King Louis coldly ignored him and stopped sending provisions to his party, so that he became dependent on the charity of William of Sens and of John of Poitiers, whom he had just insulted. But his resistance to the king stirred enthusiasm among the common people of France, as of England. When he passed through the streets of Chartres, the populace lined the way, cheering him loudly. Nevertheless it was a doleful procession that returned to Sens. Without further support from King Louis, the exiles would find themselves in a hopeless situation in France. Thomas was already contemplating dismissing all his clerks, so that they would not suffer the consequences of his obstinacy, and withdrawing alone or with one companion to Burgundy. In the midst of his discussions of this, a message arrived from Louis requesting his presence at court. "They mean to drive us out of the kingdom," one of the clerks predicted gloomily. "You are no prophet, nor a prophet's son," Thomas replied in biblical language, as he prepared to answer the summons.

As soon as the message arrived, Thomas had guessed its meaning. His confidence sprang from insight into the volatile character of the French monarch, whom he had known for more than twenty years. When he entered the king's presence, Louis gazed at him for several minutes without a word. Then, as he had once abased himself to St. Bernard, Louis fell to his knees before Thomas and tearfully begged forgiveness for having abandoned his cause at Montmirail. Thomas had been right all along about the perfidious character of King Henry, he acknowledged. For in Louis's presence at Montmirail Henry had solemnly made peace with the nobles of Poitou and Brittany; and now he had broken his word, violated the pact, seized the possessions of some of these nobles, despoiled the lands of others, thrown the lords themselves into prison where he was keeping them in chains. Louis could now only praise Thomas's prudence, discretion, and foresight.

Simultaneously, the papal commissioners seem also to have come around to the archbishop's view. They delivered to the king their second letter, the comminatory one threatening ecclesiastical censures. Thus, within little more than two months

285

after the conference at Montmirail, which seemingly had ended in a signal defeat, Thomas Becket returned to the fray fortified by assurances of papal support. Lent began early in March that year of 1169; his suspension was automatically lifted and once again he wielded the weapon of excommunication. He spared the king, as he had done in 1166, out of sentiment and policy. He issued one more warning of his intention, and Gilbert Foliot reacted at once with a fresh appeal against the blow. But Thomas this time ignored the appeal. On Palm Sunday, April 13, 1169, he reimposed sentence on most of the men whom he had excommunicated at Vézelay three years before.

Like a summons at law, the sentences possessed no legal validity until they had been served upon the offending parties. All the ports of England had been closed, travelers' baggage was carefully searched, and dire penalties were threatened against anyone who dared to carry messages from the Archbishop of Canterbury. Nevertheless Thomas found a courageous young Frenchman named Berengar to deliver the formal notices of excommunication. By unknown methods, no doubt aided by Thomas's many partisans in England, Berengar crossed the Channel safely with his bundle of letters, and on Ascension Day, May 29, 1169, entered St. Paul's cathedral in London during High Mass. He knelt before the priest and held out his letters as if he were making an offering. When the priest took them, Berengar commanded him in the names of God, His Holiness, and Archbishop Thomas to open the package, deliver the letters at once, and stop the Mass. Then Berengar shouted the news to the people of London that their bishop was excommunicate, darted under a cloak held for him by a friend, and in the ensuing confusion made his escape.

Among the letters he had thus successfully delivered was the following addressed to the dean and clergy of London:

You know, as does the entire Latin world, how perversely our brother Gilbert, Bishop of London, has taken advantage of the schism and done his utmost to disturb the peace of the Church. Hitherto we have endured his conduct with great patience; but he has continually abused our patience, has stubbornly refused to accept correction, and has heaped disobedience upon disobedience. Therefore . . . we have publicly excommunicated him, and command you by your obedience, at the peril of your orders and your salvation, to withhold all communion from him. We similarly command you to avoid as excommunicate the persons whose names are appended.

The names of the excommunicates included Geoffrey Ridel, Archdeacon of Canterbury; Richard of Ilchester; Richard de Lucy; Jocelin, Bishop of Salisbury; Robert de Broc, and others.

Another letter in the bundle was addressed to Gilbert Foliot in person. It was curt, bitter, and similar in language to the general notice of excommunication. It ended with the sharp injunction: "We therefore command you to refrain, as the forms of the Church prescribe, from all communion with the faithful, lest by coming in contact with you the Lord's flock be contaminated to their destruction, whereas they ought to have been taught by your instruction and guided by your example to the Life Eternal."

Bishop Foliot promptly gathered the clergy of London and presented to them elaborate arguments to justify his not obeying his archbishop's commands. But in spite of his brave front, the monastically trained bishop was in an agony of doubt. He wrote desperately to the king, to Arnulf of Lisieux, and to friends on the Continent begging their intercession with the pope. His letter to Henry is significant for its citation of Pope Sixtus from the False Decretals, that famous ninth-century forgery which the Carolingian Archbishop Hincmar of Reims had called "a mousetrap for metropolitans." Gilbert wrote, in a letter meant for wide publication:

> Your excellency, my lord, undoubtedly knows how heavily his lordship of Canterbury has laid his hand upon us and others of your loyal servants, and with the right hand of iniquity aimed his spiritual sword against us, in defiance of justice. The canons clearly provide that no one shall be condemned unsummoned and unconvicted, that no bishop can excommunicate a man until his guilt is proved. Since, then, his lordship has thus acted

unjustly, we trust in God that his sword may smite nothing but
the air. For we anticipated the blow by appealing to the pope,
and an appeal made at the beginning of Lent must nullify a
sentence passed on Palm Sunday. Pope Sixtus ordained that
when a bishop considers himself unjustly treated by his metropolitan, he may appeal to the Roman see, which must hear the
case, and in the meantime he cannot be excommunicated.

In spite of these brave words, Gilbert was persuaded by his
friends and his own uneasy conscience to render obedience to
the excommunication, at least to the extent of refraining from
exercise of his priestly office. He let Henry know that he would
prefer to set out for Rome in person in order to present his
appeal to the pope. Henry, of course, was pleased by his
scrupulous acknowledgment of the Constitutions of Clarendon, and readily granted Gilbert permission to leave England:

I have heard of the outrage which that traitor and enemy
of mine, Thomas, has inflicted on you and other of my subjects,
and I am as much displeased as if it had fallen on my own
person. You may rest assured that I will do my best through our
lord the pope, the King of France, and all my friends, that
henceforth he shall not have it in his power to injure us or our
dominions. It is my will and advice that you do not suffer this
matter to prey upon your mind, but defend yourself to the best
of your ability. . . . If you wish to proceed to Rome, I will
furnish you with everything necessary for your journey. . . .

Gilbert availed himself of this opportunity and crossed to
Normandy, intending to present himself before the pope in
person. He was, however, an old man, unused to the strenuous
conditions of travel. Moreover he feared to pass through the
domains of the King of France, which he regarded as swarm-
ing with enemies—although Louis would certainly not have
permitted anyone to harm so distinguished a churchman. Gilbert
therefore made slow progress through King Henry's Continental territories of Poitou and Aquitaine. He required many
months to make his way as far as Milan, suffering as only a
devout priest could from his inability to participate in Mass
and from the necessity of warning good Christians not to
contaminate themselves by contact with him.

Pope Alexander, to save the aged bishop further hardship and himself an awkward personal confrontation, sent Foliot word to Milan that he had empowered Archbishop Rotrou of Rouen and Bishop Bernard of Nevers to absolve him, provided that he swear to obey the papal instructions on the matters in dispute. This tentative forgiveness was an adroit stroke of policy on Alexander's part, and contributed materially to the ultimate compromise. The pope had succeeded in making it a matter of acute personal concern to the leader of the anti-Becket party to bring about a reconciliation between archbishop and king. For Gilbert did not take excommunication lightly, as did some other of the royal partisans, notably John of Oxford. To be cut off from the Church preyed on Gilbert's mind, even though he sincerely believed that his archbishop had no legal right to impose so terrible a sentence upon him.

In the meantime Alexander had redoubled his efforts to resolve the conflict by compromise. He wrote to Thomas, in tones of regret tinged with rebuke, that it was a pity he had employed the weapon of censure while negotiations were still in progress. In the hope that new men would bring new solutions, he had appointed two new mediators, members of the Curia of somewhat lesser rank and hence, presumably, lesser pretensions than the cardinals. They were Subdeacon Gratian, a nephew of Pope Eugenius III, and Vivian, Archdeacon of Orvieto, distinguished as a canon lawyer. These men were already on their way to France.

Meanwhile Henry had received two rebuffs. He had proposed in vain to the Holy See that Becket be transferred to some other church; he had even offered to pay all the pope's debts and ten thousand marks in addition if Alexander would grant him permission to fill all vacancies in the English Church, including Canterbury, at his discretion. To Louis VII Henry had sent Geoffrey Ridel, Archdeacon of Canterbury, and the Bishop of Séez, requesting the Most Christian King (for so the King of France was even then known) to expel the archbishop from his dominions. But Louis had replied that the right of asylum for exiles had always been customary in the kingdom of the Franks.

Gratian and Vivian made far better speed than had William and Otto. As Herbert of Bosham remarks, they were less hampered by baggage and the importance of their own station. The legates paid their respects to King Louis, and then lingered in Sens for protracted conversations with Thomas Becket while waiting for Henry to return from Gascony to Normandy. Thomas succeeded in winning over Gratian; he was less successful with Vivian. Once again Pope Alexander had neatly balanced his legation by sending a pair whose sympathies leaned in opposite directions.

The conferences with King Henry in Normandy went ill. Henry found that these legates were not so pliant as he had hoped, and he put on his usual displays of fury, which were half tactical, half real. At one point Henry swore: "By God's eyes, I'll do it another way." But this threat of resorting to schism did not make so deep an impression as it had four years earlier. The orthodoxy of England's clergy and people seemed secure beyond a doubt; and even Henry's tame bishops now remonstrated with him when he addressed the papal legates insultingly. Gratian himself replied imperturbably: "Do not threaten, my lord. We fear no threats, for we have come from a court that is accustomed to command emperors and kings."

For a full week, from August 24 to September 1, the legates followed the king's train from Domfront to Bayeux to Bures, patiently continuing the discussions and seeking to extract concessions from both sides. The excommunications were a sticking point; at Bures Henry stalked away from the legates in a towering rage, shouting back at them: "Do as you like; I don't think you or your excommunications are worth one egg." Finally Gratian consented to absolve all those excommunicates who were then at the king's court; Vivian was to be sent to England to absolve the others. With many setbacks, terms of settlement were hammered out, until at last it seemed that the mission of this third team of legates would prove successful. But at the last the negotiations collapsed over a seeming matter of words. Henry's passion to repay Thomas Becket for having publicly humiliated him led him to devise an imitative formula: he would concede all of Becket's demands "saving the dignity of the kingdom." Thomas, for his part, believed "dignity" to be an evasive synonym for "customs." His representatives countered with the demand that the formula of peace also contain the parallel phrase, "saving the dignity of the Church." Neither side would budge, and at last Gratian gave up in disgust and returned to Rome.

His fellow legate, Vivian, lingered, to the annoyance of Thomas Becket, who did not trust him. Nevertheless Vivian alone proved a more successful negotiator than had the two legates together, possibly because the king had reason to believe in his good will. Vivian pointed out that Thomas Becket's next step would be to impose the interdict upon all of England, with the pope's sanction. What that would mean, Henry could imagine only too well: the unnatural silence throughout the country as all church bells ceased to ring; the cessation of all public worhip; the bowed heads of priests and monks unable to say Mass; the postponement of marriages; the awesomely quiet holy days, without the usual processions and festivals. The people would not soon forgive a king who brought interdict upon them; and Henry sensed that they would blame him rather than the archbishop who imposed the sentence.

Grudgingly, bitterly, perhaps remembering another Henry barefoot in the snow at Canossa ninety years before, Henry consented to give way on all the points at issue. He would abandon the "customs," would permit churchmen freedom of appeal to Rome as often as they wished. He would even cede all the property that Becket claimed for the church of Canterbury, even though—and here lay the great difficulty—some of it had passed through several hands in the interval, so that to restore a given manor would involve a whole chain of restitutions and in effect would mean punishing some men for their loyalty to him while rewarding those who had traitorously rebelled against him.

In return for these remarkable concessions, all that Henry asked of Thomas Becket was omission of "saving" clauses. This seemed reasonable enough, since the archbishop was not being asked to assent to any customs. In substance, the compromise that Vivian had arranged amounted to abandonment of all claims on both sides.

Thomas agreed. He could not very well continue the contention when everything that he had demanded was being granted.

When the preliminary questions had been settled, Vivian and King Louis arranged another conference between Henry and Thomas at the Chapel of the Martyrdom on Montmartre—the supposed site of the martyrdom of St. Denis. Here, at the brow of the hill, with the orchards and gardens of the Parisian suburbs spread out below on the south side and the abbey of St. Denis visible in the plain to the north, the king and archbishop met once more. Henry had just come from a pilgrimage to the shrine of St. Denis, where he had inspected the great new abbey church on which Abbot Suger had expended so much intelligence, treasure, and intense concern. As an offering, Henry had placed a splendid pall and eighty gold pieces (probably "besants," coins of Byzantium) upon Suger's golden altar. The English king was in good humor when he arrived on Montmartre. The King of France, his clergy, and his knights had given Henry a splendid reception, and had been duly impressed by the gold coins—rarities in France and England. Henry was looking forward to the end of the long struggle with Becket. Somewhat nettled, he discovered that the archbishop had not yet arrived, and a messenger was sent to urge the approaching Becket to hurry. Thomas retorted pridefully that it was unfitting for a priest to make haste.

The somewhat belated conference nevertheless got off to a relatively smooth start. Cardinal Vivian presented to Henry a petition whose wording had been carefully worked out in advance:

> By the order and counsel of the lord pope, for the love of God and the lord pope, for the honor of Holy Church and the well-being of the king and his heirs, we petition our lord king to receive us into his grace. We ask him to grant peace and full security on the part of himself and his men, without artifice, to us and all those who quitted the realm with us and for our sakes. We ask him to return to us our church of Canterbury in all the fullness and liberty which we had it in the best times after we succeeded to that see; and all our possessions which we had after our promotion to the archiepiscopate, to have and to hold

as freely, honorably, and peacefully as we did then. And we ask the same for all our followers. We ask the king to restore to us all the churches and prebends belonging to the archiepiscopate which fell vacant after we left the country, so that we may deal with these as if they were ours.

Even at this late date, with the text before him of an agreement that had already been the subject of endless negotiation, Henry attempted an evasion. He replied suavely—"changing the words," as Cardinal Vivian put it—that the archbishop should have his church and his possessions as his predecessors in the archiepiscopate had had them. Cardinal Vivian had by now had enough experience with Henry to appreciate the significance of this alteration, which would exclude all the possessions that Thomas had reclaimed for the church between the time of his consecration and his exile, and all the dependent churches and prebends that had fallen vacant during the exile. Above all, such a version of the agreement would have omitted the castle and honor of Saltwood, now occupied by Ranulf de Broc. Saltwood had previously been held by Henry of Essex as a fief of Canterbury. When Henry of Essex was convicted of high treason,[2] his property escheated to the Crown; but Saltwood, since it had been a Canterbury fief, should presumably have reverted to Canterbury.

Vivian therefore insisted on the original wording, and the discussions turned to the amount of compensation for seized movable goods. The archbishop's need of ready money was acute, and he now put in a claim for thirty thousand marks. King Louis urged that "so necessary and desired a peace" ought not to be impeded over a matter of money, and Henry

---

[2] Henry of Essex, the constable, had dropped the royal standard and fled the field, crying that the king was dead, at the Battle of Consilt in Wales, in 1157. Or so Robert de Montfort charged six years later. Nevertheless the constable fought well beside Thomas Becket in the Toulouse campaign two years after his allegedly disgraceful behavior. In 1163, however, he was forced to engage Robert de Montfort in the ordeal of battle, was defeated and disgraced, and would have been executed if Henry had not clemently permitted him to retire to a monastery.

finally consented to pay whatever sum was eventually determined by appraisal.

The settlement seemed complete. There remained only one
question: what sort of guarantee would the king give that he
intended to keep his promises? Not that he had reason to
distrust the king himself, Thomas said peaceably, but he knew
that many of the king's vassals hated him and would do all in
their power to violate the terms of the peace—especially those
who owned property that rightfully belonged to the Archbishop of Canterbury or his fellow exiles. Therefore some
security ought to be given. The pledge he asked for was the
pax, the kiss of peace from the king. Such had been the advice
of Pope Alexander, whom Becket had consulted when the
prospect of an early settlement appeared. A priest could not
legitimately ask for oaths or substantial secular guarantees,
Alexander had written Thomas. The kiss of peace must suffice
him.

The mediators had throughout the day carefully averted any
prolonged confrontation between Thomas and Henry, for fear
that the old recriminations would break out. Now King Louis
himself, accompanied by the cardinal and other mediators,
went to Henry with the archbishop's request for the pax. It was
already close to nightfall, and Henry was preparing to leave,
for quarters had been prepared for him and Louis at Mantes,
thirty-six miles away. It would have been simplest for him to
go back to the chapel and give the kiss; but he could not bring
himself to do so. Although a long hard day lay behind him,
and a hard ride ahead, he answered suavely enough that nothing would please him more than to kiss Thomas, but he could
not do so. He no longer bore the archbishop any grudge, but
he had one day sworn in anger that he would never grant
Thomas the *pax,* even if he some day made peace with him.
This solemn oath he could not break.

Louis and most of the other mediators listened to this reply
with apprehension. They returned to the chapel, where Becket
was waiting, and reported Henry's exact words without attempting to give the archbishop any advice. He knew the
king's mind better than any other man; let him decide for

himself. They suspected, says Herbert, "that beneath the honeyed speeches which had previously passed between them they had imbibed some hidden poison."

As soon as the king's words were quoted to Thomas, he replied that he would not make peace unless Henry granted the kiss of peace. This was not sheer obstinacy. In his boyhood, in his days of hunting and fowling with Richer de l'Aigle, and in his years of secular life as chancellor of England, Thomas had grown accustomed to the feudal mode of sealing agreements with the *osculum pacis.* He understood Henry's conception of honor: the king's unwillingness to kiss him seemed a clear proof of dissimulation.

The mediators now after all began urging Thomas to give way on this last remaining obstacle to peace. Thomas remained adamant, and the conference broke up. Both kings set out for Mantes, Henry repeatedly cursing the archbishop and telling over to all who would listen the endless troubles Thomas had caused him. Thomas and his friends did not have nearly so far to ride. They were lodging once more at the Temple, where Thomas had stayed ten years earlier as an honored chancellor of England plotting a diplomatic stroke for his king against the King of the French. As they descended the hill toward the bank of the Seine, one of the archbishop's companions came up to him and said rather sourly: "The peace of the Church has been discussed today in the Chapel of the Martyrdom, and I believe that only through your martyrdom will the Church ever obtain peace."

Thomas turned around and answered laconically: "Would to God she might be delivered even by my blood."

XVIII

The Reconciliation

BLAME for the failure of the Montmartre conference fell this time upon Henry, whose refusal of the kiss of peace was generally regarded as proof of insincerity. Archdeacon-legate Vivian denounced the king, whom he had previously supported so stoutly; and Pope Alexander was sufficiently convinced by his reports to take a much stronger stand. He appointed another pair of legates who did not have to travel all the way from Italy, Archbishop Rotrou of Rouen and Bishop Bernard of Nevers on the Loire. Rotrou was a subject of King Henry, Bernard of King Louis. Although Rotrou had once denounced Thomas as motivated chiefly by "pride and passion," and believed that Thomas ought to admit the "royal dignities," he was personally well liked by members of the Becket party.

Alexander was by now as impatient as King Henry for settlement of the long quarrel. He wrote directly to Henry informing him that "by the authority of St. Peter" he absolved him from his vow never again to kiss Thomas; and he strongly urged the king to remove this one remaining obstacle to peace. To Rotrou and Bernard, the new commissioners, Alexander dispatched orders to threaten all of Henry's Continental lands with interdict unless the king showed clear signs of readiness to restore Thomas Becket to favor.

The restriction of the threat to Henry's territories on the Continent was the statesmanlike measure of a practical pontiff. Poitou and Anjou, Maine, Normandy, and Aquitaine, could not be successfully sealed off from letters of anathema which in the circumstances might never reach England. But the nature of the two prelates' instructions in other respects reflected that vacillation on Alexander's part of which Thomas Becket had so often complained. Rotrou and Bernard were to inform the king that the interdict would be laid down unless Becket were granted the kiss of peace, restored to office, and compensated by an immediate payment of one thousand marks. But if the king were obstinate, they need not insist on the money, and if Henry conceded everything but the kiss of peace, the legates were to persuade Thomas to accept the kiss from Henry's son. Even the time limit wavered; if reconciliation seemed in prospect, the legates might extend the time on their own initiative. Meanwhile, as a gesture of conciliation, they were to confer temporary absolution on the men whom Thomas had excommunicated.

These absolutions, and particularly that of Gilbert Foliot—which was separately performed by the Archbishop of Rouen on Easter Sunday (April 5, 1170)—roused in Thomas all the passion and pride of which Rotrou had accused him. He complained bitterly of the double-faced policy of Rome: "Our most recent messenger seemed to have received some consolation from the Apostolic See in the lord pope's letters; but they have been nullified by accompanying letters sent so that Satan might be loosed to the destruction of the Church." He denounced the Bishop of London as "the inciter of schism and the author of all malice." He compared the fate of the two parties: "You condemn the wretched and innocent exiles . . . while you absolve the sacrilegious, the man-killers, the predators, the impenitents." The funds that Henry's men used so lavishly for bribery in Rome, he pointed out, had been accumulated by despoiling the Church. He recalled his comrades who had died of hardships on wearisome travels to Rome—"if only the road to Rome had not destroyed so many wretched innocents"—and declared that he would look no more for justice there: "I have made up my mind no longer to trouble the Curia." His cause was lost: "Who, moreover, will dare to resist that king whom the Church of Rome encourages and arms with such triumphs, leaving a pernicious example to posterity?"

Henry's own interpretation of the absolution of Gilbert Foliot resembled that of Thomas. Convinced that he had at last bent the Curia to his will and need no longer fear the Archbishop of Canterbury's fulminations, he proceeded with the plans he had so long cherished for the coronation of his eldest son. Prince Henry was now fifteen. Thomas Becket had been sent over from England, we will recall, to prepare for that coronation eight years before. Since at that time the see of Canterbury was vacant, Thomas himself had obtained permission from Pope Alexander for Roger of York to perform the coronation.[1] Such permission was essential because it was generally agreed that the Archbishop of Canterbury alone had the right to crown kings of England. The custom had been breached on occasion in the past, but only when the Archbishop of Canterbury was for some reason not available for the coronation.

Thomas had long been aware of Henry's determination to crown his son. After August 15, 1169, when Frederick Barbarossa crowned his son Henry at Aachen, Thomas realized that the danger of Henry Plantagenet's following the emperor's example was growing acute. He asked the pope to forbid Roger of York or any of the other bishops of England to crown and anoint young Henry. Alexander replied with a diplomatically ambiguous epistle: "We order you by our apostolic authority not to presumptuously undertake anything whatsoever that will invade the ancient privileges and dignity of the church of Canterbury."

Thomas himself interpreted this vague language as he wished and issued a strict injunction to the bishops of England, ordering them by virtue of their obedience and in peril of their orders not to participate in the crowning of young Henry. But the pope's generalities seemed to him altogether inade-

---

[1] *Materials* VI, 206, where the letter is wrongly dated 1167 instead of 1161. For a discussion of this issue, see Foreville, *L'Eglise et la Royauté en Angleterre sous Henri II Plantagenet*, pp. 280 ff.

quate, and when he heard that King Henry was about to depart for England, he pressed Alexander for a more specific prohibition. On February 25, 1170, at about the time that Henry was actually crossing the Channel, Alexander at last dispatched an unequivocal mandate:

> We have been informed on the testimony of many persons that the right of crowning and anointing the kings of England has by the ancient custom of his church been reserved to the Archbishop of Canterbury. Therefore, by our apostolic authority and these present letters, we issue the following command to you, our brothers. If the illustrious King of the English should wish to have his son crowned and anointed king while our venerable brother Thomas, Archbishop of Canterbury, remains in exile, let none of you presume to lend your hand to this act or take any part in it. If any of you does so presume, let him know that he is risking his office and his order. We will deny all appeals in this matter, and accept no excuse for such wickedness.

This letter certainly sounded a note of determination rare in the correspondence of Alexander III, and Thomas Becket should have been satisfied with it. But how was he to put it into the hands of the Archbishop of York and the other bishops of England? At Michaelmas (September 29), five months before, Henry had issued the sternest of all his decrees intended to seal off England from the Continent. Anyone bearing letters from the pope or archbishop was to be arrested immediately and treated as a traitor—that is, put to death. Everyone who departed from England had to obtain a license from the justiciar, and in order to return he needed a writ from the king in person. This stringent measure applied to all persons, but particular care was taken with clerics. In anticipation, moreover, of possible interdict, Henry had provided that if such a sentence was passed upon his land, any bishop or abbot observing it was to be driven into exile with all his kin.

Cross-Channel communication had nevertheless continued precariously. But with the king now in England, preparing at last for the coronation of Prince Henry which the quarrel with Becket had delayed for so many years, the isolation of the country was certain to be maintained with the utmost rigor. Henry, on the spot, would see to the enforcement of his orders. It seemed unlikely that any of Becket's clerks, or even some friendly French monk, would succeed in smuggling the pope's letter to York.

In this dilemma, Thomas turned to a nun named Idonea. Nothing is known about her, but the letter of encouragement that Thomas addressed to her has been preserved. It is a revealing letter, especially in its references to the faltering Apostles who denied their Lord, despaired, and went into hiding. The reference is hardly obscure if it is remembered that Thomas and his contemporaries usually referred to the Holy See as the Apostolic See. Even now, when the papacy appeared at last to be emerging from hiding, Thomas could not refrain from expressing his disappointment with its past vacillation. But the letter is remarkable also for the intensity of faith and the tenderness for the emissary that shine through the formal scriptural examples with which it opens. We may, if we will, read into the lines a note of guilt. Thomas seems to have been not altogether happy to expose a woman to possible torture and death at the hands of Henry's sheriffs:

Thomas, by God's grace Archbishop of Canterbury and legate of the Holy See, to his beloved daughter Idonea. Greetings, and may you preserve the virtue of obedience and vigorous zeal for justice.

God has chosen the weak of this world to vanquish the strong. The pride of Holofernes was put down by the courage of a woman when men failed, leaders were terrified, and priests had fled. Esther was chosen to bring salvation to the exiles and the condemned of the Church. When the Apostles faltered, fled, and what is more, fell to denying the Lord, women followed him to his Passion, faithfully stayed with him even unto his death. For this they were rewarded with the vision and the consolations of angels, and with the firstfruits of the Resurrection. While the Apostles lay hidden, nearly overwhelmed with despair, the glory of Redemption and the grace of the Evangel was announced to the women. I hope that, with the help of God, you will join that company kindled with zeal for Christ. May the spirit of love drive fear from your heart and render not only possible but light the task that seems hard, and that the needs of the Church make imperative. . . .

I therefore order you and enjoin you for the remission of your sins to hand over the letter from our lord the pope, which I am sending you, to my venerable brother Roger, Archbishop of York—if possible, in the presence of several of my brother-bishops. If they are not with him, deliver the letter in the presence of whoever happens to be there. And to prevent him from suppressing the original by subterfuge, give a copy to the eyewitnesses so that they may read it, and explain to them what it is about, as our messenger will instruct you. A great reward is offered you for your toil, my daughter: the remission of sins, the fruit that never decays, the crown of glory which in spite of all the stains upon their previous lives the blessed sinners Mary Magdalen and Mary of Egypt received from our Lord the Christ. May Our Lady of Mercy be with you and persuade her Son, whom she brought forth as God and man for the salvation of the world, to be your guide, companion, and guardian. He who broke the gates of hell and shattered the power of the demons will know how to hold back the hand of those impious men who would wish to harm you. Go, spouse of Christ, and remember that he is always with you.

Idonea successfully delivered her message; but in spite of all the precautions Roger of York succeeded in suppressing it. Roger was only too willing to invade the privileges of his old enemy, Thomas Becket; he had been trying to assert the equality of York ever since the elevation of his rival. With advancing years, Roger of York had increasingly given way to his two chief vices: hatred of Becket, and avarice. He used every opportunity to increase the revenues of his see, and was so successful in this respect that upon his death he left the finances of York in better condition than those of any other English diocese. While in other sees bishops and their archdeacons were often at odds, Roger worked in fullest harmony with his own archdeacon, John, whom so impartial an observer as William of Newburgh calls "a crafty and avaricious man." Instead of appointing eminent churchmen to benefices, Roger and John preferred youths or even boys, so that they could keep them under wardship and pocket the revenues.

The coronation offered Roger the dual opportunity of profiting—for Henry was sure to reward him handsomely—and striking a blow at Becket, thus gratifying both his vices at once. On June 14, 1170, therefore, Roger anointed young Henry and crowned him King of England. The bishops of Durham, London, Salisbury, and Rochester assisted—with what feelings we do not know. The young king was not required to take the usual oath to preserve the liberties of the Church; if the partisans of Becket may be believed, he swore rather to preserve and obey the "customs" of the kingdom, that is, the Constitutions of Clarendon.

Immediately after the coronation, Henry recrossed the Channel to Normandy. There, outside Falaise, he was met by his cousin Roger, Bishop of Worcester. The conversation that took place between them[2] reveals the extraordinarily outspoken tone that Henry's nobles could take with him, the fickleness of his temper, and the pridefulness he so fully shared with his antagonist, Thomas Becket.

Roger of Worcester had been invited to attend the coronation, but Henry had concealed from him the fact that it was to be performed by the Archbishop of York. Assuming that a reconciliation with Thomas was in the wind, Roger proceeded to the port of Dieppe to make his crossing. By this time Henry was already in England. While Roger was waiting for transportation, he received a letter from Thomas warning him of the king's intention to have York crown the young king, and commanding him to stop this sacrilegious injury to the rights of Canterbury. The spies of Queen Eleanor and of Richard of Le Hommet, constable of Normandy, learned of Becket's injunction. Convinced that Roger would obey it, they immediately dispatched letters to Roger forbidding him to cross, at the same time warning the port authorities not to let the bishop take ship. Thus Roger never left Normandy.

Henry knew nothing of these events. When, therefore, he met Roger outside Falaise, he immediately broke into angry

---

[2] William FitzStephen records this conversation so vividly, and in such detail, that we may assume his presence at the scene (*Materials* III, 103 ff.).

denunciations: "Now it is plain that you are a traitor. I ordered you to be present at my son's coronation and named the day. You refused to come, proving that you do not love me or desire my son's advancement. The truth is that you favor my enemy and hate me." He threatened to deprive Roger of the revenues of his bishopric. "Truly, you were never the son of good Earl Robert, my uncle, who brought us both up in his castle and taught us there the rudiments of good conduct and learning."

The bishop told the king about the orders he had received, but Henry refused to believe him. "The queen is in the castle of Falaise, and Richard of Le Hommet is probably there also or will be tomorrow," he retorted to his boyhood friend. "Are you naming them as the instigators of this?"

Roger availed himself of his intimate knowledge of Henry's relations with his wife. "Not the queen," he said, "because out of fear and respect for you she might suppress the truth, and then you would be still more furious with me; or if she confessed it to be true, you might rage madly against that noble lady. I would sooner lose a leg than have her suffer one harsh word from you about it. But I am glad that this happened, for I would not have liked to be present at the coronation. It was unjust and contrary to God's will—not because your son does not deserve to be crowned, but because the man who crowned him acted presumptuously. If I had been there, I would not have allowed it."

Roger went on to remind Henry of what had been done for him by his father—"Earl Robert, your uncle, who brought you up honorably and fought for you against King Stephen for sixteen years, and was at last taken prisoner fighting for you." He accused Henry of ingratitude toward his younger brother, whose fief he had cut down to a quarter of its former size. "This is how you confer benefactions on your own kindred and your friends," he said bitterly. "This is how you reward those who have deserved well of you."

The bold allusion to Thomas Becket was plain, and Roger made it plainer by reproaching the king for having confiscated the Peter's pence and the revenues of six vacant sees, as well as those of Canterbury. One of the sycophants in Henry's retinue immediately began to abuse Bishop Roger. Henry abruptly turned on him and swore violently at the man. He himself might say what he chose, but let no one think he could dishonor the king's kinsman. "I can scarcely keep my hands from your eyes," he threatened the terrified courtier.

By this time they had wound their way up the serpentines to the thick-walled Norman castle that had been the birthplace of Henry's great-grandfather, William the Conqueror. After dinner, Henry was relaxed and good-natured. He drew Roger of Worcester aside and talked amicably with him about the possibilities for peace with Thomas Becket. Henry, with his sharp awareness of the symbols of power and the importance of prerogatives, could fully measure the impact of his latest blow against the Archbishop of Canterbury. In this case the traditional rivalry between the two archiepiscopal sees was compounded by the personal enmity between Roger of York and Thomas of Canterbury. By having Roger crown his son, Henry had attacked Thomas's primacy and his pride. But the coronation had also been an affront to the pope, risked in defiance of Alexander's direct prohibition, and Bishop Roger's anger now warned Henry that he was in danger of alienating a majority of his English bishops. After a victory, moreover, it was easy for Henry to make concessions. Thus the sudden shift in his mood toward Bishop Roger presaged the imminent reconciliation with Thomas Becket.

There were three overriding reasons for Henry to compromise now, if he possibly could. The threat of interdict had grown very real; the bishops of Rouen and Nevers had actually been ordered to impose it if peace were not made. There was also renewed danger of war with Louis of France, whose daughter Margaret had not been crowned along with her young husband. This omission—result of precautionary second thoughts on King Henry's part, for royal robes had been prepared for the young queen—had added another to Louis's long list of grievances against the King of England.

Henry's third reason can be deduced from his subsequent conversation with Thomas Becket at Fréteval. Henry had just left England in the hands of a fifteen-year-old boy who throughout his life had seen little of his father and had scant reason to love him. Young Henry, now that he bore the title of king, would need a mentor with a commanding personality if he were not to prove a troublesome subject. No man was more suitable to that part than the boy's former "nourisher," Thomas Becket, whose ability to restrain a headstrong young man Henry knew so well from his own youth. Precisely because Thomas had now so many enemies in England, his presence would serve as a check on possible cabals among courtiers who might otherwise exert undue influence upon young Henry. Even now, after all that had intervened, Henry had not abandoned hope that Thomas would consent to assume secular as well as ecclesiastical duties. His dream of an archbishop-chancellor had not entirely faded. For in spite of his reiterated charges of "traitor," Henry sensed that if he could persuade Thomas to undertake secular tasks, these would be carried out with all the former chancellor's efficiency and flair.

Five weeks after the coronation of the young king, Henry met with Louis of France at Fréteval, between Tours and Chartres. Archbishop William of Sens persuaded Thomas Becket to attend. On the third day of the conference—July 22, 1170—Thomas and King Henry met once more. To the surprise of the courtiers, who had seen so many previous meetings break up in recriminations, and who only that morning had heard the king swear that he would never grant Becket the kiss of peace, the two men made peace.

From the first moment, Thomas was struck by the change in the king's manner. As soon as Henry saw Thomas approaching, accompanied by the Archbishop of Sens, he ran forward with head bared. He saluted the two prelates first, before they had the opportunity to greet him, and drew them away from the crowd. William of Sens, seeing that all was going well, left the two alone, and for a long while Henry talked to Thomas "with such intimacy that it seemed as if there had never been any discord between us"—as Thomas himself reported in his triumphant letter to the pope. Thomas also was friendly, but he could not manage to be as gracious. Almost at once he dropped into his old habit of lecturing the king, warned him to repent, reminded him of all the offenses he had committed against the Church. But he offered Henry, as he had always done, the excuse he himself preferred to believe: that the king had been misled by evil counselors.

Thomas had already agreed to abide by the settlement of Montmartre, so that he could not well raise again the old points at issue: the liberties of the Church, the sums due to the exiles in compensation, the ecclesiastical lands that had fallen into secular hands, and the many matters comprehended under the head of the "customs" or Constitutions of Clarendon. But a new issue had arisen since Montmartre, and this Thomas broached, for it was not only the latest but the sorest of his grievances. He rebuked Henry for having had his son crowned by York, and denounced Archbishop Roger as blindly ambitious and impudently presumptuous.

In spite of his desire to be conciliatory, Henry protested this. He made no attempt to deny that the pope had forbidden the coronation, but he contested the claim on which the prohibition was founded. In a tone of moderation and persuasiveness, he invoked the precedents of the past hundred years. "Who crowned King William, who conquered England for himself and the succeeding kings?" he asked. And what of his grandfather, King Henry? Had either of these been crowned by the Archbishop of Canterbury?

Thomas had the facts of Church history at his finger tips. There were special reasons in each of these two cases, he replied. Stigand, in the time of William, had not been recognized as the lawful archbishop, and Anselm had been in exile when Henry I was crowned. All other kings had been crowned by the Archbishop of Canterbury, and Henry I had in fact been crowned a second time upon Anselm's return.

This argument cut both ways, for Henry might properly have replied that his present archbishop was in exile at the time of the recent coronation. But he merely smiled and heard his old friend out as Thomas went on to say that in making this protest he was concerned only for the rights of Canterbury and did not wish to diminish the young king's glory, but rather to augment it in every way he could. To this Henry replied amiably: "If you love my son, you do so by a double right. For I gave him to you as a son, and you received him at my hand, as you remember. And his love for you is such that he cannot endure the sight of any of your enemies. I know that he will avenge you, and even more severely than he ought, as soon as he has the opportunity.[3] Nor do I doubt that the church of Canterbury is the noblest among the churches of the West, nor would I deprive her of her rights. Rather, with you to advise me, I wish to take measures to relieve her and restore her to all her ancient dignities. But as for those who hitherto have betrayed both me and you, I will, with God's help, so answer them as the merits of traitors deserve."

These words gave rise to a fatal misunderstanding. The construction that Thomas put upon them is indicated by Herbert of Bosham: "Among other things, the archbishop begged the king to allow him, without the king's taking offense, to avenge by ecclesiastical censures the injury that his suffragan bishops, along with the Archbishop of York, had inflicted on him and the Church by crowning the king's son. *And the king assented.*" By his remark about traitors Henry certainly did not intend to consent to further excommunications. On the contrary, he must have hoped that ecclesiastical censures would now cease; and Thomas himself, in his own account of the interview, nowhere states that he directly promised not to take offense at such censures. Nevertheless Thomas read some such meaning into Henry's words, for he sprang from his horse to kneel at his sovereign's feet. Again his own account differs from that of Herbert, who says that he actually prostrated himself. In any case, Henry promptly dismounted, seized his stirrup, and held it for him so that he might remount. Then, tears in his eyes, the king said: "Need we go on? My Lord Archbishop, let us renew our old affection; let each of us show the other what good he can and forget former hatreds. But I beseech you, show me honor in the sight of those who are watching us from a distance."

They continued their talk, and Henry grew expansive. He

[3] These words have a strangely prophetic ring. If they occurred in a chronicle or biography, we would certainly assume that they had been added by the writer with benefit of hindsight. But Thomas himself quotes them in a letter to the pope written almost immediately after the reconciliation. They must, therefore, stand as evidence for Henry's acute insight into the character of his son— insight which did not help him to guard against the consequences of young Henry's lack of filial regard. A desire to avenge Thomas was, however, only a pretext, not a factor in the complex of motives that led to young Henry's revolt against his father in 1173.

informed Thomas that he was considering taking the cross. Would Thomas once again be the boy's tutor and adviser, holding in his hand all the affairs of the kingdom? Thomas replied that he would always be ready to aid with advice, as the Archbishop of Canterbury ought; but he could not again assume a secular post. This offer sounds almost incredible, but Henry probably meant it in all seriousness. It may seem to the twentieth-century observer that there was a curious muddle in Henry's thoughts, for he had frequently accused Thomas of aspiring to rule the kingdom in his stead. Why, then, should he offer him the chance to do so now? But for a man who thought in the context of feudal relations, there was no lack of logic. To Henry's mind, Thomas would only prove his loyalty if he accepted a secular charge from his sovereign's hand. Henry still felt that he had lost the will and intelligence of his former second-in-command to an independent power within his kingdom: the Church. If he were to restore all losses to the Church, he felt entitled to ask restitution of the loss he in his turn had suffered. There were not many men of Thomas Becket's ability in his lands.

Much that passed between king and archbishop on this occasion remained unrecorded. Twice they dismounted and remounted. At last they rode back to the impatient crowd in evident harmony, and Henry announced that the reconciliation had been effected: "Since I find the archbishop well disposed toward me, I would be the worst of men if I were not well disposed toward him, and would prove true all the evil things that are said of me." Someone suggested that the kiss of peace be exchanged, since the pope had absolved the king of his oath. But at this Henry balked; later, he declared, he would gladly kiss the archbishop on his mouth, his hands, or his feet; but to do so at this time would comport ill with his honor, for the kiss would seem to have been the price of settlement. Thomas said no more about it, evidently because in spite of his wariness he was filled with delight that he and Henry had not lost the habit of intimate talk.

Uneasiness remained, nevertheless, and plainly stronger on Thomas's side than Henry's. For as an exile Thomas's lot had been hard, but he had been free; and now he was committing himself physically to Henry, was voluntarily abandoning the

safety of France for the perils of Henry's dominions, where by
now, he well knew, he had so many irreconcilable enemies. All
those who had profited from the spoils of Canterbury and the
property of the other exiles would attempt to thwart the settlement. All those who had committed themselves against him, by
sycophancy, invective, and action, would fear for their position
in the king's good graces. All those who held high office would
dread the restoration of his one-time influence over the king. The
king might mean well, but could he enforce his will? Would he
continue to mean well in the face of malignant whispers, lying
tales, intriguing courtiers? That question must be tested. Accordingly, it was Thomas who made demands and Henry who, in the
subsequent discussions of details, made one concession after another, gave guarantees that he begrudged, and received little in
return. Carefully, the two old friends avoided speaking to each
other about the many substantive matters, for fear of losing their
tempers again. But when Arnulf of Lisieux came forward with a
"subtle" proposal that all the excommunicates be absolved, since
the king was forgiving all the exiles, Thomas would not consent.
Distinctions had to be admitted, he declared, for there were men
of very different conditions among those excluded from the communion of the Church. Some had been condemned by papal
breves, and these he did not have the power to absolve.[4] On the
other hand, William of Sens presented to Henry a scroll on which
were punctiliously listed all the confiscated possessions of the
church of Canterbury, petitioning the king to right these wrongs.
As Thomas wrote to Pope Alexander: "Because you did not
order that he restore to us and ours what has been taken away,
we could not order it, but neither can we, God willing, yield that
point. According to your command, the request is deferred, not
abandoned."

Thus there were reservations on both sides. But Henry and
Thomas talked easily together until evening, and agreed that
Thomas would not depart for England at once. He must pay his

---

[4] Thomas would later employ this same argument with the king's
officials after his landing in England, and again with the four
knights.

respects to Louis and his other benefactors on the Continent, must settle his affairs, and then would stay with Henry long enough for everyone to see plainly that he was once more in the king's good graces.

Privately, Thomas explained to the pope: "I shall wait in France until our envoys bring word that retribution is being made. . . . I do not fear that the king will not keep his promises, but that evil advisers may again mislead him."

Pope Alexander had not yet succeeded in re-establishing himself in Rome, but his situation in his own long struggle with the secular power had slightly improved during the past two years. Paschal III, the antipope, had died in September 1168. Although his own cardinals promptly elected a successor, a relatively unknown abbot who took the name of Calixtus III, support for the line of antipopes was dwindling throughout Europe. By sheer longevity, as well as by the incessant activity of his legates, Alexander was consolidating his position as supreme pontiff of the Western world. He entered into negotiations with the Emperor Manuel, with a view to healing the schism between the Eastern and the Western churches. Probably Alexander never seriously intended to return Italy to Byzantine rule, as Manuel hoped; but the threat served well as an additional form of pressure upon Frederick Barbarossa. And Frederick, faced with danger from the East when he already found himself unable to control rebellious Lombardy, showed a disposition to negotiate. He was not committed by oath to the new antipope, as he had been to Paschal. Calixtus, moreover, had no power in Rome proper; he was forced to take up residence in stoutly walled Viterbo, north of Rome, where Pope Adrian had once compelled Frederick to hold his stirrup. On the other hand, Alexander himself likewise could not secure admittance to Rome. He moved closer to the city than his rival, however, settling in the salubrious air of Tusculum, fifteen miles from the ancient capital. From the citadel on its dominating crag he could look down upon the one-time villa of Cicero, and across the Campagna to Rome herself. Thus Rome lay between the two popes, one to the north and one to the south, an unwilling bride who yielded to neither suitor. Close though he was, Alexander could not take the final step that would bring him back to Rome as master. By playing off the imperial against the papal party, the Roman Senate, whose functions had been revived by Arnold of Brescia, preserved a precarious independence.

In promoting peace between Thomas Becket and Henry II, Alexander was, among other things, suggesting to Frederick Barbarossa the possibility of compromise between the imperial and the papal power. Frederick had, indeed, observed the negotiations closely; his envoys, the Archbishop of Mainz and Henry the Lion, were present at the conference of Montmirail.[5] Frederick took the hint, invited the abbots of Cîteaux and Clairvaux to a council of the realm at Bamberg, and then sent them to Alexander with a German bishop to discuss conditions for peace. For some time these negotiations prospered, but ultimately Frederick refused to make the personal submission that Alexander demanded, just as Henry II refused to grant Thomas Becket the kiss of peace. Alexander's bitterness—a natural outcome of his disappointment—was shortly afterwards reflected in his sterner attitude toward Henry II of England, and led to those threats of interdict that so notably influenced Henry's change of heart. Still, Alexander now had reason to hope that Frederick would not remain forever hostile to the Holy See. Hence he consistently refused to go as far in severity toward the English king as Thomas Becket and his friends thought necessary and just. Thomas rarely concealed his contempt for the pope's vacillating temper; in his letter announcing the reconciliation he had sharply rebuked the pope for his excessively politic conduct: "If you had commanded as forcibly as the tone of your recent letters, no doubt he [Henry] would have rendered satisfaction and thus given an example of great value to posterity, to the Church of God, and especially to the Apostolic See."

Rumors of the pending rapprochement between emperor and pope reached Thomas Becket's ears in somewhat distorted form. Thus even after the reconciliation he could not be sure of

---

[5] Henry the Lion, who had recently become the son-in-law of Henry II of England, was partly responsible for the peace concluded on that occasion between Henry II and Louis VII.

Alexander. The dreary years of exile had taught him that what the pope gave with one hand he might take away with the other. Thomas therefore hesitated for four long months before he ventured to return to England, where he would be altogether at the mercy of Henry's savage lieutenants. Some of the other exiles impatiently hurried home, only to find "empty houses and demolished barns," and the revenues of their prebends already garnered into the coffers of the sheriffs. The king's officials had stripped the properties bare before the rightful holders returned. The woods had been cut, the livestock removed, all valuables carried away; and the major estates of Canterbury, such as Saltwood and Rochester castles, were still firmly in the hands of Thomas Becket's enemies.

Thomas protested, complained, denounced, repeatedly represented to Henry that the royal underlings were frustrating the royal will. From Sens, he sent John of Salisbury and Herbert of Bosham to the king to press his claims upon the castles and other properties still withheld. If John and Herbert succeeded, they were to continue on to England; otherwise return to Sens. In choosing these particular envoys, Thomas showed poor judgment. Henry's distrust of John dated back to the last years of Archbishop Theobald, when John was virtually administering the see of Canterbury. And Henry had not been allowed to forget Herbert's thrust that he was not the son of a king; only recently, at the banquet after the coronation, his own son Henry had repeated the barb.

Herbert and John had to wait longer than they had expected, for the king was severely ill, suffering from a bout of "tertian fever." When at length they were admitted to see the king, Henry, "as was his way, put off, put off and again put off"; he would not commit himself. Finally he turned to John and said: "John, I shall by no means hand over the castles to you until I first see you acting differently toward me from the way you have acted in the past." Herbert and John were left with no alternative; in keeping with their instructions, they returned to Thomas at Sens.

Thomas had spent the interval writing to friends all over Europe to announce the reconciliation, in language that often suggested his doubts of its durability. After two months, he resolved to go in person to wait upon the king. In the last days of September he saw him at Tours, at Amboise, at Chaumont. He had by now become convinced that the kiss of peace was essential to his safe return. It alone would serve as a visible sign to the king's retainers that Henry intended to honor the terms of the reconciliation. That view was confirmed by King Louis, to whom Thomas said wryly at their parting: "I am going to England to play for heads." Louis replied: "So it seems to me. Believe me, my lord archbishop, never put your faith in the king unless he gives you the kiss of peace. Stay here; as long as King Louis lives, you will never lack the wine, the food, and the riches of Gaul." But Thomas replied, "God's will be done," and set out for Tours. According to William FitzStepehen, he told the Bishop of Paris: "I am going to England to die."

Henry had come to Tours for a conference with Count Theobald of Blois. When he learned that Thomas was approaching, he sent his men out ahead to salute the archbishop, and then himself rode out. But in spite of these honors, "certain things went along which made Lord Thomas think that he had sometimes seen King Henry in a sweeter mood than he was now." The kiss of peace was not offered, and Thomas did not request it; but he seems to have hoped to gain it by trickery. For next morning he followed the king to Amboise, twelve miles from Tours, where the conference with Theobald was to take place in the castle that stood, and still stands, on a high rocky platform above the Loire. The king went to hear Mass in the chapel. Nigel de Sackville, the king's chaplain, who held one of the archbishop's prebends— which he would lose if restitution were carried out in full— warned Henry that Thomas was already in the chapel. Perhaps he had come so early, Nigel suggested, so that he could offer the kiss of peace at Mass, when the king could hardly refuse it. For the two men would be kneeling side by side. But Nigel had a suggestion: if the king were determined to abide by his oath never to give Thomas the kiss of peace, there was a way out of the dilemma.

"What way?" the king asked.

"Let the priest say the Mass for the dead," Nigel proposed—for the *pax* is omitted from a Requiem Mass.

Henry gave the order. After the Mass, the Introit in honor

of the Virgin Mary was sung: *Salve, sancta parens*. The priest kissed the Gospel and handed it to the archbishop, who likewise kissed it and passed it on to the king to kiss. Then, again thwarted in his hope of extracting the kiss without asking, Thomas spoke up.

"Lord," he said, "I have now come into your land; for the sake of the time, the place and our agreement, give me the kiss of peace."

"You shall have it as much as you wish another time," Henry said. And with that the matter was dropped.

They proceeded together to the conference with Theobald of Blois. On the way, there was an exchange of reproaches between them—the old, wearisome reproaches that each man had repeated so many times. Henry declared that Thomas had forgotten all the favors he had formerly received, the honors that had been showered upon him. Thomas replied that Henry did not remember how well he had served him in the past. The tedious dispute ceased when they met Theobald. And Thomas, now once again present as Henry's counselor in a diplomatic negotiation, displayed all his old adroitness. The matters at issue between the Count of Blois and the king were swiftly settled; and Theobald returned Thomas's good offices by attempting to arbitrate between the king and the archbishop.

That incident again sharply reminded Henry of what he had lost; and on the occasion of their next meeting, at Chaumont near Blois, he alluded to it. After chatting with Thomas in their old tone of familiar intercourse, he reverted to his obsession: that Thomas should serve him in a secular as well as a spiritual capacity. "Why is it that you will not do as I wish?" he asked. "If you did, I would certainly put everything into your hands."

Afterwards, telling Herbert of his offer, Thomas remarked: "And when the king said that to me, I immediately remembered the words in the Gospel: 'All these things will I give thee, if thou wilt fall down and worship me.' "

At this last meeting, Thomas and Henry also discussed plans for his return to England. Henry was impatient; he had long since realized that his power over Thomas, for good or ill, would be far greater if the archbishop were at Canterbury. On

314

the Continent, Thomas always had the protection of Louis of France, and the pope was closer to hand. Henry urged Thomas to proceed to Rouen, where he would meet him, settle all his debts, and either accompany him to England or send the Archbishop of Rouen with him. But, as was his way, the king almost immediately unsaid what he had just promised. His parting words were: "Go in peace; I will follow you and see you in Rouen or in England as soon as I can."

"My Lord," Thomas replied, "my mind tells me that when I leave you now I shall never see you again in this life."

"Do you think I am a traitor?" Henry retorted sharply.

"Absit a te, domine," Thomas replied (far be it from you, lord).

At this parting, Henry consented to dispatch to England the long-delayed official notices of the reconciliation. He issued a general writ declaring that "for the love of God and the Lord Pope, and for the salvation of ourselves and our heirs," he withdrew his anger and displeasure from the Archbishop of Canterbury and granted him "true peace and firm security from me and mine." The church of Canterbury was restored to Thomas "in the fullness in which he had it when he was made archbishop, and all the possessions which the church and he himself had and held." Similarly, Henry declared that he was returning all the churches and prebends which had belonged to the archdiocese before Thomas left the country. All these Thomas was to govern as he saw fit, "saving the honor of my royal authority."

That last thrust, that last echo of the long controversy— *salvo honore regni mei*—probably sprang equally from political caution and spitefulness. Similarly, in the writ to his son— extracted from him by the Archbishop of Rouen at Chinon a few days later—he ordered the peace as agreed, but could not bring himself to concede out of hand Thomas's claim to Saltwood Castle, where the de Broc family was now so firmly entrenched. Instead, Henry provided that the rights of the matter were to be determined by inquest. The writ read:

Henry, King of England, to his son, Henry the king, greeting. Know that Thomas, Archbishop of Canterbury, has made peace with me according to my will. I therefore command that he and all his men shall have peace. You are to see to it that the archbishop and all his men who left England for his sake shall have all their possessions as they had them three months before the archbishop departed from England; and you will cause to come before you the senior and more important knights of the honor of Saltwood, and by their oath you will cause recognition to be made of what is held there in fee from the archbishopric of Canterbury; and what the recognition shall declare to be in the fief of the archbishop you will cause him to have. Witnessed by Rotrou, Archbishop of Rouen, at Chinon.

Two of Thomas's own clerks were immediately sent over to England with these letters, and on October 5 presented them to the young king at Westminster. Thomas himself meanwhile returned to Sens to complete his preparations for departure. He lingered only long enough to receive from Pope Alexander the fateful letters he had requested in order to have some weapon in his hands when he returned to England: letters suspending the Archbishop of York, and placing the bishops of London and Salisbury once more under ban of excommunication. Alexander authorized Thomas to make use of these letters at his discretion if Henry failed to carry out the terms of the settlement. The papal epistles traveled from Segni in Italy to Sens with extraordinary speed, reaching Thomas two weeks after they were written.

Alexander, and seemingly a majority of the cardinals at this time, had at the critical moment come round to far more forthright support of Thomas Becket than at any previous time in the past six years. Partly, as we have seen, this stronger stand was due to the failure of Alexander's negotiations with Frederick Barbarossa. Partly it sprang from the conviction in the Curia that Henry had already given way, and must now be forced to carry out his commitments. In addition, Alexander's strong sense of hierarchical discipline had been aroused. Archbishop Roger of York and the other English bishops who had participated in the coronation of young Henry had violated the pope's express prohibition. For such flagrant insubordination the pope was not unwilling to see them punished.

With these letters of censure in his possession, Thomas set out for Rouen, where he expected to see King Henry once more.

He traveled slowly, reluctantly, beset by forebodings and dispirited by the bad news from his agents in England: the promised restitutions had not yet been made, and Roger of York, Gilbert Foliot, and Jocelin of Salisbury were doing all in their power to undermine the settlement. They were trying to persuade the king that the reconciliation would be useless and dishonorable unless grants to other of Thomas's churches were confirmed, and unless the archbishop agreed to observe the "customs."

At Rouen, Thomas found awaiting him a letter from Henry, brusque in tone, with a barbed allusion to the company his archbishop had been keeping: "Know that I have been unable to come to meet you in Rouen as agreed because I have been informed by friends of mine in France that the King of the French is preparing to attack my vassals in Auvergne." The implication was that Thomas, who had so recently seen Louis, should have been the first to pass on this information. Henry urged Thomas not to delay his return to England any longer, and offered as amends: "I am sending you John, Dean of Salisbury, a clerk of my household, to go with you into England; he will inform my son Henry, King of the English, that you are to receive all your possessions honorably and in peace."

The irony of being escorted by John of Oxford, whose right to the deanship of Salisbury he had contested, whom he had denounced, excommunicated, and charged with heresy, was not lost on Thomas. "How things change," he remarked to John. "The Archbishop of Canterbury ought to be providing you with safe-conduct to England—a little safer than you can provide for him."

Privately, Thomas expressed his resentment to Archbishop Rotrou of Rouen, who had received no instructions to accompany him, as Thomas had been led to expect. "Why has the king really not come in person?" he asked. "What about our kiss of peace? What about the money he promised? I have brought my creditors here with me. The king is not keeping his word."

The embarrassed Rotrou lent Thomas £300 to pay his debts, and offered to accompany him out of affection, although he had no orders to do so. But Thomas proudly refused. If the king expected him to cross the Straits of Dover under the eye of John of Oxford alone, he would do so.

Accompanied by Herbert of Bosham and a sizable retinue, he proceeded from Rouen to Wissant, on the coast between Boulogne and Calais. There he learned that his secret was public knowledge. Roger of York, Gilbert Foliot, and Jocelin of Salisbury had already heard about the papal letters he had with him, and were preparing to cross to Normandy to appeal to the king against the sentences. Moreover, they had persuaded Thomas Becket's bitterest enemies, Ranulf de Broc, Reginald de Warenne, and Gervase, Sheriff of Kent, to place armed bands in all the ports. These men were to search Thomas's baggage as soon as he landed, and confiscate the papal censures.

Already angry, doubtful of the king's good intentions, and convinced that even with the best will in the world Henry could not control his own henchmen, Thomas took rash action. The day before he himself was to cross, he sent the pope's letters to England by a trustworthy messenger, who succeeded in evading the guards, although his companion was turned back. The suspension of Roger of York, the reimposition of excommunication upon Gilbert of London and Jocelin of Salisbury, were duly delivered to the three prelates at Canterbury, where they had been waiting—perhaps to confer with Ranulf de Broc, perhaps to meet their primate and plead or remonstrate with him.

Meanwhile, at Wissant, Thomas received several warnings not to cross the sea. A clerk named Milo, in the service of the Count of Boulogne, and the pilot of an English vessel, sought him out to tell him of the savage temper of the king's retainers in England. Herbert of Bosham, perhaps with benefit of hindsight, quotes the pilot as saying: "O miserable men, what are you seeking, what are you doing, where are you hastening? Certainly to your deaths." But some such warnings were surely given, for Thomas's companions urged their master to reconsider. Herbert quotes himself as delivering a long speech, characteristically truculent and verbose, urging upon Thomas the peculiar felicity of martyrdom, if that were to be demanded of him. Thomas answered his flood of words and biblical references with terse, sober consciousness that the flesh is weak: "Your speech is loyal, but hard, and who will fulfil it?"

But he had already determined not to turn back, come what might. Next day he put to sea. His one concession to the warnings was a change in destination: instead of Dover, where so many armed men were said to be preparing a warm reception for him, he sailed for Sandwich, the port situated within his own diocese of Canterbury. As his ship neared land, he ordered the archiepiscopal cross raised, to apprise the people of his coming, and also to claim once more the protection that cross had afforded him at Northampton.

Somehow, his altered destination had become known to friend and foe alike. A vast, cheering crowd waited on shore, and many enthusiasts rushed into the icy water to welcome him. But his enemies were there also. Gervase, Sheriff of Kent, Ranulf de Broc, and Reginald de Warenne stood in arms at the dock to prevent his landing. Thomas, in describing the scene, declares that John of Oxford "saw with sorrow and shame the armed men hastening toward our ship to do violence to us." The king had after all done wisely to choose John of Oxford as the archbishop's escort. For when John came forward crying out that anyone who harmed Becket would be guilty of treason, the royal officers laid down their arms. John was too well known as the king's intimate, and as Thomas Becket's enemy, for them to doubt his word. Sullenly, they permitted the exiles to land. Gervase and Reginald attempted to extract an oath to the king from the Archdeacon of Sens, the only foreigner in Thomas's entourage. They were justified in their demand by the new decree, promulgated at Michaelmas, since the French archdeacon did not have a writ from the king sanctioning his landing in England. The archdeacon had no objection to the oath "that he would obey the King of England against all men," but Thomas refused to allow him to swear, for fear that the precedent might be used to compel the English clergy to take similar oaths. The royal officers did not dare to insist, for by this time the townspeople of Sandwich were thronging too closely around them. But the Sheriff of Kent burst into an angry denunciation of Thomas.

"You have come back bringing fire and the sword," he said. "You want to take away the king's crown.[6] You have excommunicated the Archbishop of York and the other bishops for serving

---

[6] It is worth noting that the sheriff referred to young Henry simply as "the king."

the king. Unless you look for good advice on this matter soon, something will happen that would be better not happening."

"I have not the slightest intention of undoing the king's coronation," Thomas replied. "If I could, I would gladly give him four more kingdoms. But I have punished those who defied God and the prerogative of the church of Canterbury by usurping the right to consecrate him. Why is it bringing fire and sword to inflict due justice on the sins of bishops? You will get nowhere threatening me with death; I have come to risk my neck for justice and truth."

In any case, Thomas added, he had received permission from the king to punish the bishops. If they wished to discuss the matter further, they could come to him at Canterbury.

Next morning he started out for Canterbury along a road lined with wildly enthusiastic crowds. Swarms of the common people—"Christ's poor," as Herbert of Bosham calls them—hailed him with cries of: "Blessed is he that cometh in the name of the Lord." Some prostrated themselves before him, others tore off their clothes and strewed them along the way, so that he need not touch the dust of the road. Parish priests came out with their entire villages, bearing crosses in procession. It took most of the day for him to make his way the few miles to Canterbury. There the townspeople had decorated the cathedral, dressed themselves in silks, and prepared a public banquet. The city's bands greeted him with trumpets, the choirs with hymns, the cathedral with peals of organ music.

When Thomas first entered the cathedral, says Herbert, "some saw and marveled at the face of this man, for it seemed as though his flaming heart burned in his very countenance."

In Canterbury cathedral that evening, Thomas preached a sermon on the significant text: "Here we have no abiding city, but we seek one to come." Then, in a scene of tearful rejoicing, he admitted all his followers to the kiss of peace. Toward the end of the day, Herbert came up to him and offered the lugubrious sentiment: "Lord, now we need not care at what hour you depart from this world, since today, in you, Christ's spouse the Church has won the victory. Or rather, Christ has won, Christ reigns, Christ rules."

Herbert himself records that Thomas made no reply to this outburst, as inaccurate as it was tasteless. In silence, Thomas retired to his palace "to ponder the events of that joyful yet solemn day."

Thomas Becket might be resigned to martyrdom, but he was not as eager for it as his chosen confidant. Not yet.

PART
FOUR

Martyrdom

XIX

England in 1170

DURING his six years of exile, Thomas Becket had been entirely cut off from the governance of the realm of England. He had devoted his energies entirely to the struggle for restitution, to assertion of his rights, raising money for himself, and making provision for the unfortunates who had been expelled from England for his sake. He had written hundreds of letters, engaged in endless discussions with his *eruditi,* conducted negotiations. But he had been barred from doing what he was best fitted for: governing. All his activity festered within himself for lack of outlet. By nature shaped for the great world, he was confined to a microcosm. That above all was what he meant when he complained, in letter after letter, of his terrible sufferings.

His antagonist, by contrast, had had a far easier time of it. While Henry also grieved at the loss of a friend and squandered a disproportionate amount of his time in devising new attacks or petty revenges upon Thomas and his partisans, he remained throughout those years in his proper place. While Thomas could think of little else but Henry, Henry of necessity had many other concerns besides Thomas Becket. Henry's Continental and English dominions had to be administered, his barons held in check, his taxes collected, his judiciary reformed, his foreign relations conducted, his castles repaired and enlarged, his sons and daughters married suitably and their inheritances arranged, his wife's tendencies to independence restrained—and so on. Even a man of Henry's prodigious physical endurance and mental agility could not possibly have managed all his tasks alone, and he was fortunate in having a large corps of able civil servants. But he had lost the best of them, and the question must now be asked: How much difference had it made?

One of the foremost students of Norman and Angevin England has concluded that Thomas Becket's "prolonged absence abroad seems to have made no difference in the working of the government. In spite of the position which he had occupied in previous years, he seems to have been very little missed." Historical might-have-beens cannot be definitively proved, of course; but there is evidence that the contemporaries of Henry II and Thomas Becket would have thought differently. In fact, the evidence would be virtually conclusive if it were not for the perturbing factor of the conflict itself: that is, an England not racked by the struggle between Church and State might have been easier to govern, so that it would be unfair to attribute all of Henry's difficulties to his mistakes and the absence of his chancellor from the helm. Moreover the antagonism of Louis of France, which sprang partly from the quarrel with Becket, necessitated Henry's presence on the Continent throughout most of the period. England was largely governed by his representatives, Richard de Lucy or Queen Eleanor; and Henry could personally do little more than overhaul the machinery of administration from time to time.

One such major repair was undertaken during his brief stay in England in February 1166, while Thomas Becket's hands were still tied by the pope's decree. At Clarendon, where the Constitutions had been promulgated two years before, Henry convoked another council of the realm to which he presented the document known as the Assize of Clarendon. A rather ill-organized series of instructions to sheriffs and justices dealing mainly with procedures in criminal law, the Assize was passed "with the assent of the archbishop [of York], bishops, abbots, earls and barons of all England."[1]

[1] The traditional text of the Assize has been challenged by Richardson and Sayles (*The Governance of Medieval England*, Appendix IV), who regard it as a forgery. They do not, however, suggest any plausible motive for such forgery. While their comparison with the Assize of Northampton of 1176 points up some startling discrepancies, these can still be explained as the result of deliberate revision. Until more convincing arguments are forthcoming, it seems wise to accept the general tenor if not the exact wording of the text as printed by Stubbs.

The Assize begins by making provision for an inquiry to be conducted "throughout the several counties and the several hundreds, employing twelve of the more lawful men of each hundred and four of the more lawful men of each vill." These "recognitors" are to certify on oath "whether there be in their hundred or vill any man accused or notoriously suspect of being a robber or murderer or thief," or a receiver of such. All such men are to be subjected to the ordeal by water; if convicted, their goods and chattels are forfeit to the king. But even those acquitted of a particular crime must leave England within a week "if they have been of ill repute and openly and disgracefully spoken of by the testimony of many and that of lawful men." The declarations of the recognitors are to be taken by itinerant justices. In fact, during the spring and summer of 1166 Geoffrey de Mandeville, Earl of Essex, and Richard de Lucy traveled through eighteen counties holding "assizes," or sessions of the circuit court.

The striking feature of the Assize of Clarendon was not its mention of jurors or itinerant justices—the latter had been in use for generations, and the "twelve lawful men" are mentioned in the Constitutions of Clarendon (Article VI). Under the Constitutions the jurors had functioned as a sworn inquest bound to testify to the truth of an already presented charge. The Assize of Clarendon, however, was a device for general denunciation, and as such was bound to arouse resentment and to lead to miscarriages of justice. At its worst it initiated what today would be called a witch hunt; at its best, it was a clumsy and inadequate attempt to deal with the multitude of criminals who were evidently at large in England. The very language of the Assize testifies to the general state of lawlessness, and to a tendency to institute tyrannical rule.

The Assize had its economic functions. Like most of Henry's extensions of the royal writ, it enormously increased the number of "pleas" heard in the king's courts—and pleas were a prime source of revenue. In addition, the royal coffers were filling with the proceeds from the confiscated chattels of reputed criminals. The common people grumbled that the new system merely disguised a scheme for raising money. Some of that money, to be sure, returned to the locality in the form of new jails built at the king's expense—but that particular kind of boom in construction could scarcely have aroused popular enthusiasm.

It would lead us too far afield to trace the itinerant justices to the Carolingian *missi dominici,* or the sworn inquest to its more dubious antecedents in the remote past. Although many of the items in the judicial reform went back to Henry I, the general advance in the codification of England's law must certainly be credited to Henry II. His contemporaries, however, had less reason than posterity to be grateful to the king. The system devised at Clarendon for ridding the country of criminals failed to accomplish its purpose. In counties where the cumbersome summonses were issued, men with criminal records fled in good time. In many counties, no attempt at all was made to enforce the law. Much of the revenue that Henry had expected flowed into the pockets of the sheriffs. These officials likewise turned the Assize of Clarendon into a source of profit for themselves by accepting bribes and extorting hush money. Sheriffs compounded with men who had concealed treasure trove (which belonged to the king, as did stranded whales). Infringements of the Forest Law were neglected. The harsh provision against vagabondage[2] proved unenforceable; strictly applied, it would have stopped all traffic throughout England. Moreover, there were only two or three itinerant justices available—or at any rate appointed—to make visitations.

After the enactment of the Assize of Clarendon, Henry returned to Normandy; he did not see England again until a month before Easter of 1170, when he came to prepare the coronation of his son. At the Council of the realm held in London at that time, petitioners besieged him, bitterly complaining about the intolerable exactions of the sheriffs. The enforcement of the Assize in 1166 had been followed the next year by a

---

[2] "And the lord king forbids that any vagabond, that is, a wanderer or unknown person, shall be given shelter anywhere except in a borough, and even there he shall not be given shelter longer than one night, unless he become sick there, or his horse, or can show an evident excuse. And if he remain longer than one night, let him be arrested and held until his lord shall come to give surety for him, or until he himself shall procure safe pledges; and let him likewise be arrested who gave him shelter."

survey of the forests, and in 1168 by the collection of an "aid." Some of this money had never reached the king, some of it had been squandered on heavy bribes to the papal chancery and the cardinals of the Curia for favorable rulings in the Becket controversy. Much of it was hoarded, to be subsequently wasted in the wars between Henry II and his sons. But the ultimate destination of the silver pennies concerned the people less than the fact that the demand for them seemed never to cease. England was prosperous, trade and agriculture were flourishing; but the royal levies fell heavily upon all ranks of society. The nobility borrowed from the Jews for the expenses of campaigns in Wales and France; and the common folk of their estates had to pay their debts for them.

In response to the complaints, Henry ordered an inquiry into the affairs of the sheriffs. A body of itinerant barons went about the realm investigating the receipts of the sheriffs and their bailiffs. As the barons moved from county to county, the local lords, knights, and freemen appeared before them to testify under oath to how much they had paid out "by judgments and without judgments." The accounts of all royal officers were thoroughly checked in regard to their ordinary affairs and the extraordinary revenues that had been collected during the four years of the king's absence from England. The very language of the Inquest of Sheriffs, as it was called, betrays the true workings of the Assize of Clarendon:

> Concerning the chattels of those who have fled on account of the Assize of Clarendon and the chattels of those who have been undone through that assize, let inquiry be made as to what has been done and what has issued from it in the several hundreds and the several vills, and let it be accurately and carefully written down. And likewise let inquiry be made whether anyone has been unjustly accused in that assize for reward or promise or from hatred or other unjust cause, and whether any accused person has been released or any accusation withdrawn for reward or promise or love, and who received the reward for it, and likewise let this also be written down. And let inquiry be made whether the sheriffs or any of their bailiffs, or the lords of the vills or their bailiffs, have restored any of the

things which they have taken, or have made any peace with their men, since they have heard of the coming of the lord king, in order to prevent any complaint thereof reaching the lord king or his justices.

The results of the Inquest proved to be a devastating indictment of the administration. The reports were full of stories of unjust seizures, of accounts that did not balance; and before Thomas Becket returned to England, King Henry had found it necessary to remove from office three quarters of his sheriffs. Unfortunately for the people of England, the few who were allowed to remain took their revenge for the heavy fines and humiliations to which they had been subjected "by imposing even heavier exactions than before."

It is impossible to prove, of course, that such deplorable conditions might not have developed under a continuing administration by Thomas Becket. We can observe only that no such crass malfeasances are reported during the years of Becket's chancellorship, although Thomas had become virtual regent of England only after the long period of anarchy and civil war under Stephen. It would seem that Thomas Becket's removal from a share in the government of England had indeed made a difference.

Another of Henry's major administrative acts of 1166 has been attributed to his "genius for organization," but seems to have resulted more from his ignorance of English affairs and his need for larger revenues (a need that directly resulted from the peculations of the sheriffs), as well as from nervousness about the allegiance of his subjects. It cannot be stressed too often that Henry was a foreign king who had spent most of his life out of England. William the Conqueror, another foreign king, had ordered the making of Domesday Book primarily in order to have on record the conditions of tenure and the fiscal obligations of every hide of land in England. Henry II now ordered a similar though far less comprehensive survey of his tenants-in-chief. By the first Sunday in Lent of 1166 they were to supply the sheriffs with statements "carrying the seals on the outside"—so that the sheriffs might not be tempted to alter the returns—answering the following questions: 1. How many knight's fees were there on the estates in the time of Henry I? 2. How many had been enfeoffed since the death of Henry I? 3. How many knights were "on the demesne" of the tenant, that is, how many additional knights did the tenant owe the king for knight service? 4. Had these knights performed their allegiance to the king? (If not, they had to do so by the first Sunday in Lent.)

The knight's fee had become as much a unit of taxation as an actual fief held by a knight. Some tenants held twelfths, thirteenths, and even twentieths of a knight's fee, others two, three, and four or more fees. Moreover not all holders of knights' fees were actually dubbed knights. The purpose of the inquiry, then, was to determine the relationship between theoretical assessment and actual conditions. If a tenant had enfeoffed more knights than he owed the king for service, the amount of the service—and hence of scutage—could be increased; if less, the *servitium debitum* ("owed service") could be left as it was. Either way the royal purse profited. Henry did not want more actual knights for his wars; he preferred hiring mercenaries.

The insistence that all knights who had not taken oaths of allegiance must do so immediately suggests a certain nervousness on Henry's part that no doubt sprang from his quarrel with Thomas Becket, who was waiting only for the coming of Easter to pronounce his excommunications. But the inquiry as a whole can also be viewed in relation to Thomas Becket. Henry lacked assurance in dealing with the affairs of England. He had leaned on Thomas Becket's knowledge of English conditions. Thomas had, after all, held administrative offices in England—under Osbern Huitdeniers and Archbishop Theobald—since his youth. Information that he had at his finger tips was not so readily available to Henry. Moreover, Henry had trusted his chancellor as he trusted no one else afterwards except possibly Richard de Lucy. Most of his other major office-holders were great lords in their own right, whose interests usually conflicted with his. That natural disparity of interests between a great lord, ecclesiastical or secular, and his sovereign, appears plainly in the return to the inquiry of 1166 sent in by Roger, Archbishop of York. The language of the return also illuminates the character of Roger.

Roger's *carta* differs from that of others in its full statement of the scope of the inquiry, and in its peculiar obsequiousness. Roger speaks of himself as "one of those subjected in all things to your orders"—a phrase intended to call to the king's mind the difference between his two archbishops. Roger might well feel some embarrassment, for he owed the king only twenty knights' fees in service and had more than twice that number of enfeoffed knights. At the end of his return he tried to indicate that he was not rolling in wealth, as the king might well suspect and as his vast building program at York might likewise suggest:

And since, my lord, I claim from some of these men more service than they are now performing, whereas others are keeping back services which are said to be due, not to themselves but to the table and the demesne of the archbishop, I humbly beg that this my return may not be allowed to do harm to me or to my successors by preventing the Church from recovering or preserving its legal rights.

Most of the barons of England shared Roger's alarm at the new inquiry. For eighty years, with but few updatings, Domesday Book had served as the guide to the barons' obligations to the Crown. The Conqueror's survey was regarded as so precious that it was kept locked up in the chests of the Treasury, sealed with the treasurer's seal and accessible only during the daily sessions of the Exchequer. In the meantime the taxable worth of manors and fiefs had changed greatly, and the barons feared that this new survey would soon be followed by new demands from the Crown. It was. During the next two years, Henry sent his commissioners around the country to collect the feudal aid *pur fille marier,* for the marriage of his daughter Matilda to Henry the Lion, Duke of Saxony.

Thus, during the years of Thomas Becket's absence from England, Henry had been inadvertently alienating his barons. The secular magnates of England had loyally supported the king in his struggle with the Church throughout these years. Henry, who had begun his reign by pulling down the unlicensed castles built under Stephen and by crushing the great lords who resisted his authority, found himself ever more dependent upon these lords because of his quarrel with the Church. They had supported him against the Church possibly—as Arnulf of Lisieux believed—in order subsequently to be free to deal with the king alone. Now, instead of rewarding them for their fidelity, he chose to increase their taxes, to encroach upon their authority in their own shires, and to introduce what they regarded as innovations into the intricacies of feudal homage, wardship, reliefs, and aids.

The smoldering resentment of the barons was to break out ultimately in the rebellion of 1173. But by 1170 there was already sufficient hostility toward the highhanded monarch for the barons to risk independent action. The coronation of young Henry in June of that year provided them with an opportunity to sway the mind of the fifteen-year-old boy. They began those whisperings, to which young Henry listened so gullibly, that since he was now king in name he ought to be king in fact. Young Henry's treatment of Thomas Becket in December, only six months after the coronation, would reflect susceptibility to his advisers rather than obedience to his father. For to the angry barons, the peace with Thomas Becket seemed a final betrayal on the part of their sovereign. The king, wily and ungrateful as always, would once more employ Becket to crush them, as he had done in the early years of the reign when he subdued Hugh Mortimer and the earls of Norfolk, Hereford, and Yorkshire.

This fear and antagonism, this atmosphere of intrigue and tentative conspiracy against the Crown, explain the unfriendly reception accorded Thomas Becket when he at last reached England on December 1, 1170. Thomas had to some extent been informed by friends in England of the sullen temper of the magnates; but he could not be sure whether it sprang from their own feelings or whether they were responding to secret orders from Henry. That uncertainty had informed his moving letter to the king before his departure, the last letter he was to address to his former friend:

> Christ, the examiner of hearts, the judge of souls and the punisher of the guilty, knows how sincerely and affectionately I have made peace with you, believing that good faith and guile-

333

lessness were being shown to me and mine. What other conclusion could I draw from your words. For whether you were
agreeing or disagreeing with me, your speech expressed kindness
toward me. And what other note, if not one of benevolence,
peace, and security, is sounded in the letters you sent to my lord
the king, your son, ordering restitution to me and my men of all
we held before we departed from England? But the guilelessness
and good faith I have heard in your words is not apparent in
deeds. And this, God knows, grieves me less for the disadvantages to me than for the possible slur upon your honor.

What has come of the restitution you ordered? It was put
off for ten days on the pretext that your son's advisers had to
consult Ranulf. Ask yourself, if you will, who these advisers are,
and by what loyalty they act in this way. I am convinced that
their acts will be harmful to the Church and detrimental to your
well-being and honor, unless you take pains to rebuke them. For
in the meanwhile Ranulf is destroying the property of the
Church. He is openly collecting the provisions meant for me and
storing them in the castle of Saltwood. Moreover, he has
boasted publicly that I shall not long enjoy the peace you have
granted us; that he will deprive me of life before I have eaten a
whole loaf of bread in England. The persons who informed me
of this are willing to prove it to you, if you wish.

You know well, Most Serene Lord, that one who has the
power to correct and fails to use it becomes the accomplice to a
crime. What power would Ranulf have if he did not rely on your
will and were not armed with your authority? . . .

It is plain that the holy church of Canterbury, the mother
in Christ of the Britons, is perishing because of the hatred
directed at me. Rather than let her perish, I shall expose my
head to the blows of Ranulf and his fellow persecutors. I am
ready not only to die for Christ, but to endure a thousand deaths
and all manner of torments, if he by his grace will grant me the
strength to suffer. I had wished, my lord, to call upon you once
more; but necessity draws me, afflicted as I am, to my afflicted
church. With your permission and grace, I shall return to it,
perhaps to perish that it may live, unless you in your goodness
come swiftly to my rescue.

But whether I live or die, I am yours and always shall be in
the Lord; and whatever happens to me and mine, may God bless
you and your children.

334

XX

Twenty-nine Days

IT WAS DIFFICULT to restore the habits of peace. Battle was joined afresh on the morrow of Thomas's arrival at Canterbury, when Ranulf de Broc, Sheriff Gervase, and the chaplains of the bishops came to take up the matter of the suspension and excommunications. What Thomas had done to the bishops redounded to the injury of the king and infringed the customs of the realm, they argued. But if he would absolve the bishops, York, London, and Salisbury would come to him voluntarily and make their submissions—*salvo honore regni*.

Here Thomas made the decision that cost him his life. If he had immediately agreed to absolve the bishops, he would have disarmed his enemies for the time being. Tempers would have subsided, the tensions of a seemingly imminent civil war would have relaxed for a while, and he would have had time to establish himself securely in Canterbury and perhaps begin the slow work of rebuilding his position, recovering his lands, reassuring the royal officials. He would have had time, within himself, to recover from the strains of years of exile and strife, to put aside the harsh, fanatical mien of a priest half bent on martyrdom and become once more the great prelate whose multifarious concerns necessarily make him worldlier, less unrelenting, more diplomatic, than the monk in his cell.

By now Thomas regarded Gilbert Foliot and Roger of York with less than saintly charity. He referred to them savagely as "priests of Baal and sons of false prophets." Yet he was happy to be home, eager to get on with the tasks of repairing the ravages to his church and his diocese, and more conciliatory than he had been for years. Probably, therefore, he would have compromised, had it not been for the reference to the "customs" and for those terrible words "saving the honor of the kingdom." But if he consented to absolution of the bishops on such terms, the whole long fight had been for nothing. He would be accepting the Constitutions of Clarendon, acknowledging royal rather than papal supremacy. That he could never do again. He had given way once, at Clarendon, and had believed ever since that all his troubles were traceable to that one concession. At Fréteval nothing had been said about the "customs"; and Thomas had understood the silence to signify the king's willingness to let the matter drop. But now the question was being raised again, and he knew that he could not permit his suffragan bishops to swear any oath "saving the honor of the kingdom."

Some day the matter would have to be thrashed out between himself and the king. There was little point in making an issue of it with these lesser officials and clerics; and so Thomas tried evasion. He had not himself imposed the sentences on the bishops, he declared; the pope, by his letters, had passed judgment, and it was impossible for an inferior judge to undo the verdict of a superior. The Holy See was the supreme court of appeals, and its decrees final. Nevertheless, for the sake of peace and out of reverence for the king, he would take the risk and responsibility of anticipating the pope, and would absolve Bishops Gilbert and Jocelin. He would restore them to the communion of the Church if they would swear in his presence to obey all future commands of the pope. Carefully, in making this statement, Thomas omitted the "saving" clause; he did not think that the secular officials would notice, and he hoped that the ecclesiastics would recall their obligations as churchmen and would accept his formulation. He also omitted to promise that he would lift the suspension of Roger of York. That forgiving he could not be; moreover, he could legitimately allege that he had no authority over Roger, his fellow archbishop, either to bind or to loose.

The bishops must have been waiting nearby, for his reply was carried to them immediately. Roger—who a year later was to swear solemnly that he had never promised to observe the Constitutions of Clarendon in writing or by oath—immediately took his stand on Article V of the Constitutions. It was contrary to the authority of the king and the "customs" of the kingdom, he argued, for oaths of this kind to be demanded without the king's consent. Gilbert and Jocelin, the excommunicates, were all for giving way to Thomas's demand, but Roger—"that enemy of peace and disturber of the Church"—persuaded them to continue the struggle. The words the Icelandic *Saga* attributes to him are so characteristic of the man that they may be taken as based on a firm tradition: "I have eight thousand shining pennies of gold[1] lying in my treasury, God be praised. But I will gladly spend most of that hoard to reduce the obstinacy and wilfulness of Archbishop Thomas, and put down his pride and presumption. And therefore I beg you, my brothers, do not let him weaken your determination. Ignore his threats; let us instead go all together to see the old king, who has splendidly sustained us all along against our enemy."

Roger mingled cajolery with threats of his own. If the bishops abandoned the king now and went along with his former enemy, Thomas, they would never enjoy his friendship again. "Rather will he call you what you are, faint-hearted deserters and evil traitors. He will drive you both out of his realm, as the law provides, and confiscate all your goods. Tell me, in what country would you prefer to live as homeless wanderers, stripped of everything and shamefully put down?"

Roger's argument persuaded the wavering bishops; they agreed to cross to Normandy with him to present their case to the king. Meanwhile, to prevent Thomas from ingratiating himself with young Henry, Roger sent a messenger to the fifteen-year-old sovereign warning him that Becket intended to depose him. Geoffrey Ridel, the Archdeacon of Canterbury and long one of the leaders of the anti-Becket faction in England, was entrusted with conveying this outrageous lie to young Henry.

Within a week after his return home, Thomas believed that

---

[1] Gold pennies did not exist. Roger must have had a hoard of besants, each worth about twenty-four silver pennies.

he had grasped the situation. Truth could not penetrate the wall of hostile courtiers surrounding the young king. The terms of the reconciliation, Thomas's own attitude toward the coronation of his former page, his reasons for excommunicating the bishops and suspending the Archbishop of York, the activities of the Becket clerks, who were going about the country reclaiming churches and prebends—all such matters were being presented to young Henry in a distorted light. Yet a word from the fifteen-year-old king could effectively check the intrigues. Thomas decided that he must see the boy and explain to him face to face that the long quarrel was over, that he welcomed the coronation even though he condemned the ecclesiastics who had performed it, and that he still loved the young man with whom he used to walk hand in hand through the halls of the archiepiscopal palace.

Royalty and children delight in presents. Before setting out to see the young king, Thomas sent to him a messenger, Richard, Prior of St. Martin's at Dover,[2] with three destriers, warhorses "of wonderful swiftness, elegant stature, handsome form, high-stepping, supple-gaited, with quivering ears and trembling limbs, scarce willing to stand still, their saddle blankets, and harness bright with flowers and rich colors." Impoverished though he was, Thomas still had the will and the means to be lavish. But Geoffrey Ridel and the boy's guardians had done their work well. Richard was received graciously for his own sake, he was told, because he had performed the marriage of young Henry's sister Matilda to Henry the Lion, Duke of Saxony. But he could obtain no answer to his request that the young king grant an interview to Thomas.

Nevertheless, Thomas set out for Woodstock, where young Henry was staying. He was eager in any case to see for himself the condition of his domains, and planned to undertake a circuit of the province of Canterbury after his audience with the young king. He was warmly welcomed at nearby Rochester by Bishop Walter, Theobald's brother and Thomas's defender against the intrigues of Roger of Pont l'Evêque more than twenty years

---

[2] Richard ultimately succeeded Thomas as Archbishop of Canterbury.

before. Walter had taken part in the coronation of young Henry; but Thomas preferred to assume that this old friend, now nearing eighty, had acted under duress.

Three miles outside London, the clergy and poor scholars of the city's churches awaited the archbishop's coming, along with a vast crowd of the laity. Cheering and singing hymns, the people of London hailed the returning native; and with the princely habits of his days as chancellor, Thomas distributed largesse— although now it was called alms. He dismounted at the Church of the Blessed Mary in Southwark, for he had arranged to stay at Winchester House on the bank of the Thames as the guest of Henry of Blois, the aged Bishop of Winchester. A procession of the canons of the church met him at the door, and the whole crowd joined in singing, "Blessed is the Lord God of Israel." But suddenly, rising high above the din, the voice of a woman rang out. She was well-known in the city, "a foolish, immodest and sharp-tongued woman who thrust herself into courts and public meetings, one Matilda." Again and again she cried out her warning: "Archbishop, beware the knife!"

No one who listened to the talk of courtiers needed a prophetic spirit to sense the dangers threatening the archbishop. The antagonism of the camarilla around young Henry came into the open the following day. The morning after Thomas's arrival, Jocelin of Arundel, King Henry's great-uncle, came to Thomas with a message. The young king did not wish to see him; he was to cease his visits to cities and castles, return at once to his own see of Canterbury, and stay there.

Thomas refused to believe that these orders actually came from his foster son. "Does the king mean to withhold from me all share in his peace and confidence?" he asked Jocelin.

"What I have said, he commanded you," Jocelin replied haughtily, and strode off. On his way out he met a wealthy citizen of London coming to call on Thomas. "Have you too come to the king's enemy?" he asked the man, whom he knew well. "Turn back, I advise you." But Londoners were as well informed as any in the kingdom, and they naturally sympathized with Thomas Becket of Cheapside. "If you think him the king's enemy, we know nothing about it," the man replied bravely. "We have heard and seen the king's letters from overseas, granting peace and restitution to the archbishop. If there is any hidden meaning in them, it is a secret from us."

A burgess could scarcely speak more boldly to a high official of such noble lineage, a kinsman of royalty as well as a great baron. This unidentified wealthy Londoner obviously belonged to that class of burgesses known as *barons de la cit,* among whom Gilbert Becket had once been reckoned. These men, in any case partisan to a burgess's son of their own city, a signatory witness to their Charter, additionally welcomed the return of Thomas Becket because harmony between Church and State promised prosperity and the expansion of peaceful trade. The twelfth century, it must be remembered, was peculiarly the great age of burgeoning towns in England as well as on the Continent. In the struggle between royalty and the baronage, which repeatedly passed from latent antagonism to active warfare, the townsfolk usually proved the natural allies of kings, from whom they secured protection and the charters that made separate communal jurisdiction possible. The Londoners were no exception. They had in the past stood by King Stephen when so many others had deserted him; they would remain loyal to King Henry in the coming struggle with the barons and Henry's rebellious sons.

Some of the barons, out of principle or self-interest, would not swerve from their fidelity to the old king. Among the barons who throughout King Henry's reign displayed consistent loyalty were such magnates as Earl Reginald of Cornwall. Reginald, who six years before had been unwilling to pronounce sentence on Thomas Becket at Northampton, had been present among the young king's advisers on October 5, when Thomas's clerks brought news of the reconciliation. The clerks noted his exclamation of "Thank God!"—a sentiment in which many courtiers failed to join him. Reginald now lay ill in his London town house. Thomas, in desperation, sent a messenger disguised as a physician[3] to ask Reginald to intervene at court, so that he might

---

[3] Probably the monk William of Canterbury, who subsequently wrote a biography of Thomas.

be allowed to see and talk to his foster son, young Henry. In Earl Reginald's hall the messenger was recognized as a Canterbury monk, and the sick nobleman, helpless to oppose the courtiers' plots, hastily sent him away with a warning to Thomas that his life was in danger.

If not even Earl Reginald dared to support him, the order to return to Canterbury must be obeyed. Otherwise Thomas would be openly defying the young king's authority. Thomas saved face; he declared that the command alone was not weighty enough to deter him from making the rounds of his diocese, but that he had decided to return home anyhow, since Christmas was drawing near and he did not wish to be absent from his church on so festive and solemn a day. Even so, he did not take the direct road to Canterbury at once. Instead, he set out along the highroad to Oxford and Woodstock, as if he meant to force his presence on the young king. But he went no farther than Harrow-on-the-Hill, that Canterbury manor a few miles from London to which he had first come as a stripling applying for a post in Archbishop Theobald's household. There he assured himself that a priest appointed by Nigel de Sackville still held the church of Harrow and had refused to surrender it to Canterbury's bailiff. There, too, he heard that a shipload of wine sent to him from France as a gift of King Henry had been confiscated by Ranulf de Broc; it was even said that de Broc had killed some of the sailors and imprisoned others.

Lingering at Harrow, Thomas sent Prior Richard of Dover and the friendly Abbot of St. Albans to Woodstock to protest this outrage, and to plead once more for an interview with young Henry. The prior and abbot returned with a royal writ commanding Ranulf to return ship and wine; but the young king still refused to grant Thomas an audience. Whether or not the fifteen-year-old had a will of his own, there was obviously no way of gaining access to him.

In view of the many warnings he had received, Thomas took with him a bodyguard of five knights on his return journey to Canterbury. Certainly the continued persecutions of Ranulf de Broc argued the need for some kind of guard. Ranulf de Broc was waylaying Canterbury men on the highways, interrupting the flow of provisions to the archiepiscopal palace, and giving every indication that he meant to carry out his threat sooner or later—for by now Thomas had, in spite of Ranulf's vow, lived long enough to eat a whole loaf of bread in England. There could be no doubt that Ranulf still considered himself administrator of the Canterbury estates; he hunted deer in the archiepiscopal woods with dogs from the archbishop's own kennels.

Thomas had left Canterbury in order to sound out the situation in England, to look into the truth of his clerks' allegations that much Canterbury property had not been restored, and to renew the ties of affection that had formerly bound young Henry to him. He had found sullen officials and a welcoming populace. He had found alien incumbents, such as the Vicar of Harrow, still refusing to relinquish their livings to his control. And he had found the young king inaccessible. While the common people and the burgesses lined the roads to hail him and ask his blessing, men of rank avoided him. Small wonder that he expressed the gloomiest forebodings. He still did not know for certain whether in returning to England he had walked into a trap set by King Henry, or whether the clique around the young king was independently "thirsting for his blood" (to use one of his favorite phrases). But after this brief journey from Canterbury to London, he could no longer doubt that many were athirst.

Characteristically, he determined to fight back; and characteristically, he began his counterattack on the annual festival of peace. By then he had also been goaded to fury by a seemingly trivial incident. On Christmas Eve Robert de Broc, Ranulf's brother, had prompted his nephew John to dock the tail of a Canterbury sumpter-horse. What to the boy was a prank,[4] to the uncle a calculated insult, was to Thomas symbolic emasculation. He retaliated next day.

On Christmas Day Thomas ascended the pulpit and delivered the sermon before High Mass. Taking for his text the good tidings as they are given in the Vulgate, "On earth peace to men

[4] It was the time of year for the Feast of Fools, which came to a climax on Innocent's Day (December 28), when children were permitted all sorts of practical jokes.

of good will," he began in a natural and traditional way by speaking of the glorious Nativity. Behold, he said, how much a Christian owes his Lord for such humility, that the King of kings should submit to being wrapped in swaddling clothes and laid in a manger. Then Thomas addressed himself to the morals of the people, urging them to shun sin and love virtue, and to honor the Church and her ministers. Not always were the ministers of Holy Church vouchsafed the reverence due to their sacred calling; he himself had suffered in his own person the mockery and spite of those who feared man more than they feared God. Although he had now returned to his see from a long and dreary exile, he still had to endure insults and intolerable abuse. It was even possible that he would be with them no long time. The church of Canterbury already had one martyred archbishop, St. Alphege, and perhaps she would soon have another.

At this point in his sermon Thomas's voice broke with tears. He paused, and the people, also sobbing, cried out: "Father, why do you desert us so soon, and to whom would you leave us desolate?"

But after these showers of tears, "it was as if there arose a sweet south wind ridding the air of all darkness." For when Thomas resumed, his voice rising with authority, hard, indignant, fiery, he took up the text for the day ("on which he was wont to ponder"). There is no peace except for men of good will, he declared. Since his return, men whose evil ways he had long known had done their utmost to destroy the peace which at long last had been attained between himself and the king, and to show their contempt for the servants of Holy Church. Only last night their outrages had culminated in the disgraceful insult committed by a member of that family who were foremost among Satan's minions, the de Brocs. And Thomas concluded his Christmas sermon by dashing candles to the ground as he excommunicated Robert de Broc for the crime of docking the tail of a horse "belonging to a poor peasant of his in the service of the church of Canterbury." At the same time Thomas renewed the ban on Ranulf de Broc and likewise "handed over to perpetual anathema" the present holders of the churches of Harrow and Throwley for refusing to let his men take possession. As he extinguished the candles, he proclaimed a curse upon all those "who sow hatred and discord between me and my lord the king." But this declaration of loyalty was lost upon his hearers.

Thomas has been much criticized for intemperate vengefulness in employing the most dreaded weapon of the Church to answer a petty slight. But the circumstances must be remembered: he had been home for twenty-five days and was finding his authority flouted most by those nearest to Canterbury. For more than three weeks he had waited, hoping that the hostility would subside, the insults diminish; but instead he sensed an increasing viciousness. In his present circumstances, the ultimate weapon was his only weapon. He dared not—not now—use the armed force of a feudal baron, which he after all was. His knights would scarcely have obeyed if he had commanded them to punish royal officials or the brothers and nephews of such officials; and any effort on his part to play the secular lord would have justified the king's suspicions. The lesser censures of the Church could not sway such men as the de Brocs; in fact, even excommunication did not intimidate Robert de Broc, an apostate Cistercian monk. "If I am excommunicated I shall act like an excommunicate," Robert had replied to a warning of the impending sentence.

Thomas followed these harsh measures by strokes of diplomacy. He tried to placate one of the leaders of the barons' party, old Hugh Bigot, Earl of Norfolk, by sending two of his clerks to grant provisional absolution to some Norfolk priests who had celebrated divine offices while under the ban. Possibly he hoped by this favor and demonstration of leniency to win access to the young king through Hugh's intervention. Simultaneously, he parted with his two most devoted followers, those uncompromising firebrands Herbert of Bosham and Alexander Llewellyn. Thomas ordered them to go to the King of France, the Archbishop of Sens, and other dignitaries of France "to tell them what you have seen and heard of our peace, that it is a peace which is no peace, but turbulence." Herbert pleaded that he might be allowed to stay: "Why have you done this? . . . It seems to me that you are seeking to cheat me of the fruit of your consummation." But Thomas insisted that he go—all the more so since "the king holds you in greater suspicion than others where the cause of the Church is concerned." These words are plainest proof that three days before his death Thomas was by no means bent on martyrdom. He was still hoping to reassure King Henry, still eager to justify his actions to his patrons and allies in France, still assuming that there was room and time for negotiation. At least this was his ostensible purpose. On some deeper level of his mind he must have known that he was sending Herbert and Alexander away to save their lives. For they surely would have been among the first victims of any attack upon himself. Herbert, certainly, was in constant peril at Canterbury or anywhere in England.

Herbert, writing fourteen years later, quotes himself as saying to Thomas: "I know for certain that I shall see you no more in the flesh." Thomas, he says, gravely repeated his words: "What you say and lament is true, that you will no longer see me in the flesh." We need not accept this prophecy as the actual words that passed between the two men; but some forebodings must have been expressed by both. Nevertheless, Herbert set out. For fear of being waylaid, he departed under cover of darkness on December 27, the Feast of St. John the Evangelist. "With much lamentation, shedding tears," he took leave of his master. Thomas, too, showed his emotion by repeating "again and again his permission to go and his paternal blessing."

✠　✠　✠

It is curious that Thomas dispatched messengers to the King of France, sent Gilbert de Glanville to the pope, but made no attempt to communicate directly with King Henry. Had he done so, had he sent two or three of his clerks in pursuit of the three English bishops, to answer their charges and insinuations at the king's court, the outcome might have been different. But he did not complain to the king about the menaces and insults he was receiving in England because he thought these might have been inspired by Henry himself. (In fact they were not; Henry "thought himself now at peace with the archbishop.") Herbert and Alexander might easily have stopped to see Henry on their way to Louis of France, but they had no orders to do so. And so they passed by Bures, where their presence might have prevented utterance of the fatal words, or departure of the knights.

For in the meantime the three bishops, Roger of York, Gilbert of London, and Jocelin of Salisbury, had crossed over to Normandy and met the king at Bures. Henry was celebrating Christmas, so that there was a great gathering of barons and prelates; but the atmosphere was by no means festive. Henry had already heard of the excommunications of Gilbert and Jocelin, the suspension of Roger; but he asked the bishops to repeat the story. They did so, and Henry exclaimed: "If all who crowned my son or were present at his coronation are to be excommunicated, I am not likely to escape either."

Because Gilbert and Jocelin dared not contaminate the king by associating with him, it fell to Roger of York, the most malignant and least scrupulous of the three, to be spokesman for them all. Roger magnified Thomas's bodyguard of five knights, and the cheering crowds that had lined the roads to greet him, into a strong force of armed men and a savage rabble with whom he was making a circuit of the kingdom, terrorizing the country-side. And when the king asked what he ought to do, Roger replied with disingenuous evasiveness: "Seek counsel of your barons and your knights; it is not for us to say what must be done." Almost beyond a doubt it was Roger (although the sources speak only of "someone") who added: "I assure you, my lord, while Thomas lives you will have no good days, nor quiet times, nor a tranquil kingdom."

These words precipitated the customary Angevin rage. The king's eyes flashed, his face and gestures expressed his indignation, bitterness, and mental turmoil. He cried out: "The man ate my bread and mocks my favors. He tramples on the whole royal family. What disloyal cowards do I have in my court, that not one will free me of this lowborn priest!"[5]

Henry's fits of passion were only too well known to his entourage, and might be directed against his closest associates.

---

[5] Each of the contemporary writers gives this speech somewhat differently. I have exercised traditional license in putting several versions together. William FitzStephen alleges that the king said nothing, that his look alone conveyed the message to the four knights. But all the other writers attribute to Henry various denunciations of Becket. Perhaps, as the *Thómas Saga Erkibyskups* suggests, there were several outbursts of rage at different times.

As we have seen, Thomas Becket had sometimes—in his days as chancellor—delayed execution of Henry's orders until the king's rage had time to cool. Even Henry's highest officials and closest associates might become the objects of his anger. Once at Caen, where he had come to discuss business concerning the King of Scotland, Richard of Le Hommet, Constable of Normandy, happened to say something that sounded favorable to the Scots. Henry flew into a passion, called him a traitor, ripped off his own clothes, and began to gnaw stalks of straw. How many times had he not denounced Thomas as a traitor and troublemaker, and how many times had he not cursed his entourage for not finding a ready solution to the problem of an archbishop who would not do his will? But this time the archbishop was within reach, and this time four barons of his household too eagerly seized the opportunity to translate the sovereign's wrath into the subject's act. The four came to an agreement with one another and slipped away from court. A contemporary writer declares that they did so "having seen the king's agitation and wishing to please him." But if this were the case, they behaved rather oddly both before and after for men who presumably expected to be rewarded for their deed.

The four barons—Reginald FitzUrse, William de Tracy, Hugh de Moreville, and Richard le Breton, or Brito as he is usually called—certainly acted like men in fear of pursuit. They stole away without asking the king's leave, and they took ship from different ports. Even before their act, that is, these four evidently believed that they would be stopped if their intention were known. And as we shall see, their conduct afterwards was not that of men who confidently assumed that they had pleased the king. Nor is their anxiety surprising, for these were not rough, ignorant, illiterate ruffians, but high officials, courtiers, substantial landowners, versed in law and diplomacy. They were the king's familiars, and Henry was a cultivated man. They had known both the king and Thomas Becket for a long time; in fact, FitzUrse, Tracy, and Moreville had all become vassals of Thomas Becket during his days as chancellor. They had rendered him the oath of fealty, and had probably been among that large force of knights he had brought to France to fight in the Toulouse campaign. Richard Brito, the only one of the four who had not been thus closely associated with Thomas Becket, had been an intimate of the king's brother, Prince William, and was possibly related by ties of blood to Gilbert Foliot.

As men of discernment and substance, the four barons must have realized that they would be impugning Henry's honor by violence, and possibly endangering the gains he had made in his long contest with the Church. Good fighting men though they naturally were, the four barons were not brawling brutes. Nor can it be said that they acted out of passion, with no time to reflect. A whole day and the always sobering Channel crossing intervened between the king's words and the assault of armed men upon the archbishop's palace at Canterbury. The four knights had had plenty of time for second thoughts.

At a distance of eight hundred years, and with so many documents lost forever, it is impossible to prove beyond a reasonable doubt that the four barons were acting on their own, as representatives of their class, and as part of an inchoate conspiracy which was to break out three years later in open war against Henry II, when the malcontent barons ironically enough alleged vengeance for the death of Thomas Becket as one of the reasons for their revolt. But at least two of the four murderers were associated with centers of the rebellion of 1173–4. Reginald FitzUrse, one of the king's tenants-in-chief, held estates in Leicestershire; the young Earl of Leicester was to take a leading part in the revolt.[6] Hugh de Moreville, a man of much greater consequence than the other three, was itinerant justice for Northumberland and Cumberland, the two northern counties that would be the center of the rebellion. He was also related to Richard de Moreville, one of the rebel leaders; and he seems to have been partly responsible for the untimely surrender to the rebels of vital Appleby Castle during the campaign of 1174.

[6] The Earl of Leicester's father, who died in 1168, had been a close friend of Thomas Becket's; but the young earl had taken great care not to communicate with the archbishop from the moment that Thomas left England in 1164. That is, hostility toward Thomas was the accepted spirit among the barons who were to become the active supporters of the young king against Henry II—and in fact young Henry's manipulators rather than his instruments.

At the royal court, Roger of York's lie about the archbishop's troop of armed men had stirred far more excitement than news of the suspensions and excommunications. Anathemas concerned the Church, but armed uprising was business for knights. Henry took the supposed situation seriously enough to call a council of his barons. He opened the proceedings by complaining that Thomas had invaded his land like a tyrant (a curious choice of word), that he had suspended *all* the bishops and the Archbishop of York for serving their king, had excommunicated some of them, was troubling the whole realm, intended to deprive himself and his sons of their crowns, had acquired the legation over the kingdom, and had obtained from the pope certain privileges in regard to advowson (the right of presentation to churches) which diminished the rights of the barons and even of the king himself.

Henry was still angry; he felt betrayed and believed all the charges he was making; but he was far from ready to condemn Thomas Becket to death. Some of his barons thought him on the brink of such a condemnation, however. The speeches at this council, of which William FitzStephen gives samples, suggest that the viciousness of the four barons who had left for England was shared by some of their fellows still at court. Engelger de Bohun, uncle of the excommunicated Bishop Jocelin of Salisbury, suggested that the only way to handle Becket was with rope and gibbet. William Malvoisin, nephew of the Count of Brittany, offered a historical parallel into which he managed to slip a boastful mention of his crusading past: "When I was passing through Rome on my way back from Jerusalem, I heard that a certain pope was killed for intolerable insolence."[7]

King Henry was not thirsting for Thomas's blood. Nevertheless, he did not not rebuke the speakers, and he chose to accept the rumors flying around the court: that Moreville, FitzUrse, Tracy, and Brito had set out of their own accord to arrest

---

[7] William was probably alluding to Lucius II, who while attempting to retake the Capitol from the rebellious Romans in 1145 had been stoned to death. Very probably William had heard this tale in Rome twenty years before, when he was returning from the Second Crusade. It would naturally have made a deep impression on the mind of a man who had just endured the hardships of a disastrous crusade for religion's sake.

Thomas Becket. Very well, the barons must show initiative in defense of the realm. Obviously outright revolt could not be permitted to continue. Arrest of the seditious archbishop was an essential precaution, Henry agreed—but the wily Thomas had escaped from England once before and might do so again. Accordingly three high officials, among whom was Richard of Le Hommet, Constable of Normandy, were sent out after the four knights to make sure that Thomas was seized. The three took great pains to post a screen of guards all along the coast of Normandy and England. But their care was needless, for in the meanwhile the four barons had made certain that Thomas Becket would never again depart from England.

XXI

☉ Mors Inaudita

ALTHOUGH they had sailed in different vessels, the four barons—"guided by the devil"—arrived at Saltwood Castle within the same hour. The time is variously given, but was probably toward dusk on December 28. Their fair wind and speedy passage seemed to them proof that God and the right were on their side; and a hearty welcome from Robert and Ranulf de Broc gave them assurance that man also favored their intent. Whether that intent was only to seize Thomas Becket and bring him for justice to the young king, the old king, or a council of barons; or whether it was to order him out of the country; or whether from the first they meant to kill him, only the Inspector of hearts knows (to use a favorite phrase of Thomas Becket's). Very likely the four barons themselves had not definitely settled their course of action and were screening the confusion in their minds behind some such phrase as "take him dead or alive." Surely there is stretching of the truth in the story that the four laid their plans in the darkness of night, with candles snuffed, so that they might avoid seeing each other's faces. In fact, their behavior was hardly conspiratorial; they certainly made little effort to conceal their presence at Saltwood or their hostility toward the archbishop.

Thomas himself received ample warning that they were on their way from, curiously enough, two namesakes of FitzUrse and Brito. A knight who had accompanied the barons across the Channel told one Richard, the archbishop's cellarer, that the four

PLAN
CANTERBUR
AT THE TIME
Chiefly from the W

*(The portion of the Cathea
conjectural restoratior*

A. The Nave
B. Lady Chapel
C. Chapel of St. Benedict with St. Blaise above
D. Chapel of St. Michael
E. Choir
F. Presbytery
G. Chapel of St. Anselm
H. Chapel of St. Andrew
K. Trinity Chapel with the Crypt underneath

1. High Altar
2. Altar of St. Alfage
3. Altar of St. Dunstan
4. Patriarchal Choir
5. Altar of St. John Baptist (in the Crypt)
6. Altar of St. Augustine (in the Crypt)
7. Door of the Cloisters
8. Door of the Cathedral
9. Staircase to the roof
10. Staircase to the Crypt
11. Staircase to the Choir
12. Pillar where the Archbishop stood
13. Spot where he fell
14. Spot where the body lay during the night
15. Spot where the body was buried in the Crypt
—— The course of the Archbishop
----- The course of the Knights

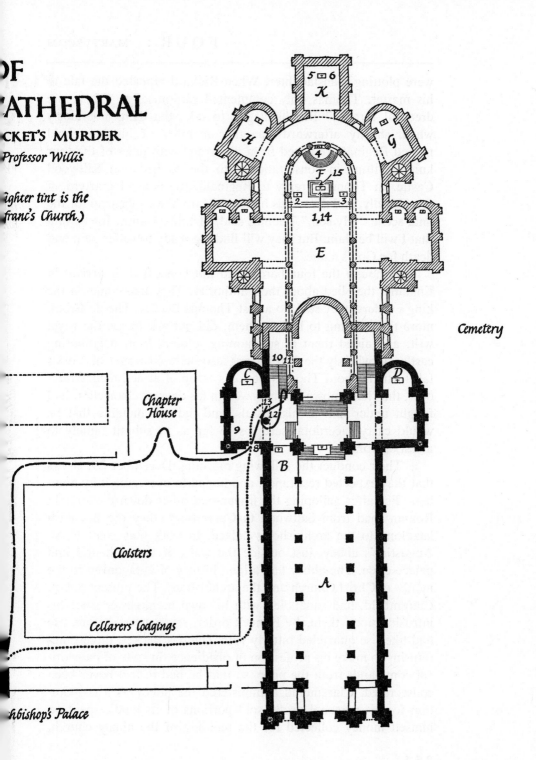

OF

ATHEDRAL

CKET'S MURDER

Professor Willis

ighter tint is the
rancs Church.)

Cemetery

K

5 6

H

G

4

F 15

2 3

1,14

E

C

D

Chapter
House

10 11

13

12

9

8

B

Cloisters

A

Cellarers' Lodgings

rchbishop's Palace

were plotting manslaughter. When Richard repeated the tale to his master, Thomas only commented sardonically: "These are dreadful threats." But he began to take the danger seriously when, shortly afterwards, another member of his household named Reginald returned from an errand with news of the four knights sitting in consultation with the de Brocs at Saltwood Castle. In Thomas's reply to Reginald, the note of martyrdom sounds fully, and the words he chooses are like a rehearsal for the final scene. "My son," Thomas said, "I think I know for certain that I will be slain. But they will find me ready to suffer pain and death for God's name."

Although the four barons did not conceal their arrival in England, they lied about their authority. They had come on the king's orders, they said, to arrest Thomas Becket. The de Brocs, more than willing to believe them, did not ask to see the royal writ, and aided them in summoning soldiers from neighboring castles. Obviously the four barons also believed Roger of York's fabrications about Thomas Becket's troop of armed men. More-over, they had known Thomas well in his days as chancellor, had fought under him as his vassals, and did not imagine that he would carry sacerdotal scruples so far as to submit tamely to arrest or worse.

Their conduct the following morning, December 29, shows that they expected resistance, and hoped to overcome it by num-bers. For after galloping the fifteen-odd miles down the straight Roman road from Saltwood to Canterbury, they did not dash headlong to the archbishop's palace. Instead, they went to St. Augustine's abbey, just outside the walls of the cathedral and palace close. The abbey had a long history of antagonism to the monks of Christ Church and the archbishops. The present abbot, Clarembald, had squabbled with his own monks ever since his intrusion upon them, by Henry's order, seven years before. He had likewise quarreled bitterly with Thomas Becket, three times refusing to make his profession of obedience, in spite of categori-cal commands from the pope, so that he had in fact never been consecrated. Clarembald administered the abbey as a corpora-tion for his personal profit, sold portions of its lands, spent on himself money collected for the building of the abbey church,

354

and whiled away the routine of monastic life by collecting bed-mates among the serfs of abbatial estates. On a single farm in the vicinity he was said to have fathered no less than seventeen bastards. God, so the monks believed, had already punished them for the wickedness of their abbot by allowing a disastrous fire to destroy many of their buildings.

This high-living abbot readily lent the four barons his retain-ers, invited them to dinner, and plied them with drink. After dinner, the four sent the majority of their fellows into the streets of the town to bid the citizens arm themselves and come to the archbishop's palace ready to serve the king. Even if the burgesses as a class had not been sympathetic to the archbishop, such a request here in Canterbury, his own city, was on the face of it absurd. Most of the citizens showed astonishment and resisted the demands. In such cases the recruiters did not insist on the levy, but merely warned the recalcitrants not to interfere and to keep the peace no matter what they saw and heard. These bold tactics prevented the townsfolk from rushing in a body to the aid of their archbishop.

FitzUrse, Moreville, Tracy, and Brito did not wait for the full force to be mustered. Acting out their part of royal officers sent on an official mission, they went first to see whether Thomas Becket would surrender to them voluntarily. Accompanied by only a dozen retainers, they rode around the circuit of the wall between Christ Church and the monastery of St. Augustine, and entered the court of the palace through the main gateway. Leav-ing their armed men to guard the gate, they strode on into the great main hall of the palace, which was filled with a motley crowd of domestics, clerks, and retainers. The time was shortly after three o'clock in the afternoon. The short winter day was drawing to its close; Thomas Becket had already finished his dinner and retired to his room with his clerks to transact busi-ness. The members of the household were still eating, however. They recognized the four knights as royal officers and invited them to table. But the four refused, and asked to see the arch-bishop. William FitzNigel, the seneschal, guided them up the stairs to Thomas's room. On the way he evidently had some words with them about their mission.

355

When the four entered, they saw Thomas sitting on his bed, deep in conversation. They went forward and sat down on the floor among the monks and clerks, but did not interrupt. For a good while Thomas continued dictating instructions and receiving reports, while outside the shadows deepened and the air grew unusually sultry for a midwinter day. At last Thomas looked up and greeted William Tracy by name.

FitzUrse answered for Tracy: "We have brought you a message from King Henry oversea. Do you wish to hear it in the presence of these men, or in private?"

Thomas answered courteously the rude tone and angry stare: "That is for you to say."

"Alone, then," Reginald said.

Thomas signed to his attendants to leave. They went out, but the doorkeeper left the door open. It occurred to Tracy, he afterwards confessed, that they could have tried to kill Becket then with the shaft of the great cross which lay at his feet. But unarmed as they were, the risk would have been great, and the open door also deterred them. Perhaps their looks betrayed their thoughts—or Tracy's thought—and Thomas became aware of the danger; or perhaps Thomas realized that they had come with no confidential message, but with angry charges. In that case he might need advice and restraint. For suddenly he said: "These are not secret matters," and he called out to the doorkeeper to send in his scholars. William FitzStephen came back into the room, along with John of Salisbury, Thomas's confessor Robert of Merton, Henry of Auxerre, a visiting Saxon monk with a considerable literary gift, one Edward Grim of Cambridge, and several others. Since the four knights were still sitting in glowering silence, Thomas said: "Now, my lords, say what you will."

FitzUrse began with what weighed heaviest on his mind: Thomas's conduct toward young Henry, as he supposed it to be.

"The king commands that you go at once to the young king and pay him honor, as you are bound to do to your king. You have been plotting against him since his coronation, have excommunicated and suspended all who helped to crown him. By now it is clear to everyone that if you had the power you would deprive him of his crown. Will you absolve the bishops, lift the suspensions, and answer for your conduct in the young king's court?"

Wearily, Thomas gave the answer he had so often repeated. Would these officials never see that denouncing the manner of a coronation did not necessarily mean opposing the fact of the coronation? "As God is my witness," he said, "I have never wished to deprive him of his crown. I would rather that my lord, the king's son, had three crowns. And I did go to him—not to answer for my conduct, because I have nothing to answer for— but to pay my respects. He would not see me, which I regret. When I was in London he ordered me to return to my own see, and has forbidden me to enter any of his cities and towns, or even villages. As for the bishops, it was the pope, not I, who suspended them."

"It was done through you; you absolve them," FitzUrse retorted in baffled fury. He knew that he was no match for a churchman in argument; but he had known Thomas as chancellor and still thought of him as a man of the world, not an authentic ecclesiastic. The ready replies "fanned the flames of his rage."

"I have already offered to absolve them," Thomas said. "It was they who refused to ask forgiveness or to pledge that they would accept the judgment of the Church. Besides, the king gave me his permission to punish them."

"Listen, listen to that!" FitzUrse roared to his companions and the audience. "Have you ever heard such deceit? He accuses the king of betraying his closest friends by allowing their excommunication. This is beyond endurance."

"Reginald, Reginald," Thomas said, "you yourself were present at that interview. You were there on the day of St. Mary Magdalen, when the king received me into his peace and favor. You know what happened."

"I never was, I know nothing about it!" Reginald said.

"You were there, for I saw you there," Thomas replied.

John of Salisbury, observing that the interview was degenerating into a senseless bicker, interrupted: "My lord, won't you discuss this with them in private." Perhaps he realized that Thomas was alluding to the words Henry had spoken on the field

357

at Fréteval, and that Reginald FitzUrse might honestly deny ever having heard them. Reginald might have seen Thomas kneel before the king, but he would not have known the reason. Or he might have been present and seen nothing; the attention of many of the onlookers must have wandered during the long talk between Henry and Thomas.

"No," Thomas replied to John. "It will not do. I cannot and ought not to consent to their demands and proposals."

FitzUrse took another tack. "From whom do you hold your see?"

"The spiritualities from God and my lord the pope," Thomas replied. "The temporalities from my lord the king."

"So you not recognize that everything you possess you have received from the king?" FitzUrse asked.

"Not at all; but I have to render to the king what is the king's, and to God what is God's. I will not spare anyone who violates the laws of Christ's Church."

The knights sprang to their feet, waving their arms and gritting their teeth. Thomas had reasserted the principle so long at issue in a tone of scorn and defiance, which up to now he had held in check.

"Threats, threats!" FitzUrse shouted. "Do you mean to excommunicate us all?" One of his companions called out: "He has excommunicated too many already." FitzUrse, who had up to this point remained at a respectful distance, took a step closer to the archbishop. "I warn you, you speak in peril of your head."

Thomas also leaped to his feet from the bed on which he had been sitting. Bulky in the many robes and wrappings he needed in winter, he towered over them. "It is useless for you to threaten me," he said. "If all the swords in England hung over my head, you could not turn me from God's justice and my obedience to the pope. You will find me ready to meet you eye to eye in the Lord's battle."

"Very well," FitzUrse (or perhaps one of the others) retorted. "Then the king commands that you leave his kingdom and his lands with all your men; from this day forward there can be no peace between him and you or your people, because you have broken the peace."

358

"Never," Thomas said. "Once I behaved like a timid priest and left England. I have returned to my church on the lord pope's advice and in obedience to him; I have not come back in order to flee. If I am allowed to perform the duties of the priesthood in peace, I shall be glad; if not, God's will be done with me."

An uproar of shouts and curses followed, in which it was impossible to make out who was saying what. Thomas's voice cut through the noise with an allusion to the feudal fealty that Moreville, FitzUrse, and Tracy had sworn to him in his days as chancellor: "Besides, you know what there is between me and you—which makes it all the more amazing that you dare to threaten the archbishop in his own house."

The others answered furiously: "There is nothing between us that is against the king." And Reginald FitzUrse added: "We not only dare to threaten, but to do more." To his fellows he called: "Let us go."

At the sound of the raised voices, more members of the household, clerks, servants, and a few soldiers, poured into the room. Reginald called to them: "We tell you in the king's name that if you are loyal to him you must abandon your fealty to this man. Guard him so that he does not flee."

He and his fellows thrust their way through the throng. Thomas called after them: "I am easy to guard; I shall not run away. You will find me right here!"

On their way out the knights came upon William FitzNigel, Thomas's steward, who had shown them in and then apparently departed. He was now coming, seemingly in all innocence, to present the day's reckonings. They seized him, saying, "Come with us."

FitzNigel shouted above the babble of voices to Thomas: "My lord, do you see what they are doing with me?"

"I see," Thomas replied. "They have the force and the power of darkness."

Consciously, somberly, Thomas was half quoting: "This is your hour and the power of darkness." All his clerical hearers would recognize the allusion to the words that Jesus addressed to those who had come to arrest him, immediately after he had received the kiss of Judas. (Judas, of course, kept the accounts of the little community—like FitzNigel.) It would have been blasphemous for Thomas to have repeated the exact words of Jesus (in Luke 22:53); but the paraphrase did not offend the twelfth-century sense of propriety. William FitzStephen, who relates this incident, is bent on presenting Thomas's suffering and death as an *imitatio Christi,* not an assumption of the role of Christ. But he was in the room at the time, and is not likely to have invented the reference to the Passion chapter from which Thomas had read so often that he commonly wove phrases from it into his speech and writing.[1]

John of Salisbury, of course, understood instantly the implication of "the powers of darkness." As soon as the doorkeeper closed the door behind the knights, and Thomas, calmer, had sat down again, John spoke reproachfully to him. "My lord," he said, "it is strange that you will take no one's advice. You always say and do what seems right to yourself alone. Was there any need for a great and good man like yourself to exasperate those wicked men still more by following them to the door? Would it not have been better to have returned a softer answer to men who are plotting to do you all the harm they can?"

"We must all die," Thomas replied. "We should not let fear of death swerve us from the right way. I am more ready to endure death for the sake of God and justice than they are to inflict it."

"We are sinners," John answered sharply, "and not yet ready to die. No one here wants to die for the sake of dying except you."

"God's will be done," Thomas said.

"I hope to God it may end well," John said, sighing.

While this exchange was going on, the other clerks were babbling excitedly about the knights. "They've come here drunk; they'll sing a different tune when they sober up," one said. "There is nothing to be feared; it is Christmas time, and besides we have been promised the king's peace." Others disagreed: "We've seen time and again how brutal those men can be."

---

[1] For example, the words *Desiderio desideravi* with which the famous letter to King Henry opens (see above, p. 239) are taken from Luke 22:15.

The discussion was interrupted by cries from the monks that the barons were donning their armor. "Let them arm," Thomas said.

✠ ✠ ✠

The four knights had in fact dashed down the stairs again, out through the great hall, and onto the porch which gave on the courtyard of the palace. As soon as they emerged into the open, they began shouting: "To arms, to arms, men!" Their men, who had been waiting in the house of someone named Gilbert, near the palace gate, came rushing out, bellowing as if they were going into battle: "King's men, king's men!" They shut the main gate promptly, to keep out the townsfolk, and assigned William FitzNigel ("at dinner the archbishop's liegeman and knight, now against him") to stand mounted guard at the small wicket-door in the gate. This they dared not close, for they might need it to retreat. A soldier borrowed from Abbot Clarembald kept FitzNigel company.

Reginald FitzUrse, who had gone no farther than the porch of the hall, forced one of Thomas's household to help him with his armor. This was quite a procedure, for it involved lacing on steel *chauces* to cover the legs, donning fifty or sixty pounds of hauberk reaching to the knees, putting on the helmet with its long bar to protect the nose—the "nasal"—and perhaps even slipping the hands into mailed gauntlets. By the time the four knights had finished casing themselves in steel, two of Thomas's servants had succeeded in shutting and barring the doors of the hall. For a while the assailants battered in vain against these doors. Then Robert de Broc, who had lived in the palace while his brother was administrator of it, called out to them that he knew another way.

The great hall of the palace was on the first floor, above a vaulted basement, with an outside staircase leading up to it—like Harold's hall at Bosham as shown at the beginning of the Bayeux tapestry. Robert de Broc led the knights around through an orchard to a wooden staircase which ascended to the solar, where

Thomas had his bedroom. Carpenters had been at work on the steps; for although it was deep winter, Thomas had been unwilling to delay repairs on his dilapidated palace. The carpenters had left their tools, and FitzUrse snatched up an axe, the other men hatchets. They broke through a window and chopped down a partition, only to find themselves in the great hall rather than the archbishop's bedroom, as they had hoped. Invulnerable as they were in their armor, they drove away the servants who were guarding the main doors, wounding some of them, and opened the heavy bars so that the rest of their retainers could enter. Then they began forcing their way toward Thomas Becket's private quarters. Bellowing orders to one another, shouting defiances, they battered at the by now locked doors.

In the archbishop's bedroom, the thud of hatchets and cries of men heated by their own efforts terrified the monks. Many scurried from the room, leaving only William FitzStephen, Edward Grim, John of Salisbury, William of Canterbury, Henry of Auxerre, Robert of Merton, and some few of the more courageous monks. These last begged Thomas not to stay there: "Lord, come to the church; these men mean to seize you or kill you."

"You monks are always cowards," Thomas said roughly. "I am not afraid of them—I shall wait here to see what is God's will."

His friends pleaded with him to come with them; he refused, and remained sitting on his bed. He had told the knights they would find him here, and here he meant to stay. The clerks began to drag him; he resisted. Someone said that vespers were beginning—it was now five o'clock—and he ought to be present at the service. Even as some argued, some were half pulling, half carrying him. The affront to dignity was too much for him to bear. Rather than be dragged unceremoniously to the cathedral, Thomas consented to walk if his cross were borne before him; surely he was recalling how it had overawed the angry barons at Northampton. Alexander Llewellyn was in France with Herbert of Bosham; Henry of Auxerre took up the cross, and a small procession formed. The din of the armed man could be heard in orchard and court; therefore the monks made their way by a little-used passageway toward the cloisters, followed by Henry of Auxerre with the cross, then Thomas, then the clerks. One monk ran ahead to force open the normally locked door to the cloisters; but as soon as he touched it, it flew wide. Richard the cellarer, who had delivered the warning to Thomas, had heard the tumult and clash of arms; his lodgings were located at the western end of the cloisters. He had rushed toward the palace and opened the door just as the party from the archbishop's room approached it. Many of those who hurried through the door did not even notice the cellarer, and later accounted the open door a miracle.

Thomas was still lagging behind. The monk who had flung the door open shouted: "Seize him and carry him!" Again an undignified struggle ensued as the party made slow progress down the north cloisters and then turned into the eastern side— Thomas protesting all the while. He broke free three times, but at last they got him through the door of the north transept and fully inside the cathedral. The monks were already singing vespers, but interrupted the service and rushed to the door. Others were still out in the cloisters, and at this moment the knights and their followers broke through into the cloisters, FitzUrse in the lead. Only he and his three companions were in full armor, but the retainers and the few townsfolk who had joined them all carried weapons. "King's men, king's men!" FitzUrse shouted, charging along the southern side of the cloisters.

The monks flew to close the double doors and put up the iron bars that would seal the church off from the cloisters. There was a loud knocking from outside; a large group of men from Thomas's household, and some monks, fleeing from the knights, were pounding in terror on the doors. Even now, all believed that the cathedral was safe. What men who proclaimed themselves the king's would have the hardihood to violate sanctuary?

Thomas turned back toward the door. "Christ Church is not a fortress," he called out. "Open the door. I command you on your obedience. Let anyone enter who wishes."

When no one moved, he pushed his way through the group at the door, slid back the bolts, and reached out to pull his monks and attendants into the cathedral. "Come in, come in, faster!" he called to them.

363

Outside it was by now almost dark, and inside the church still darker. From the dim interior, the band of armed men could only just be seen, but distinctly heard, hard on the heels of those who now came running in and who carried panic with them as they entered; everyone dashed for a hiding place. Now, with the doors open, even John of Salisbury abandoned his master. A few minutes before he had told Thomas that he was not ready for martyrdom. There were plenty of hiding places; in the dusk it would have been easy to disappear into the crypt, or up the winding stairs to the chapel of St. Blaise in the vaulting of the roof. But Thomas would not hide, even though only William FitzStephen, Robert of Merton, and the visiting monk, Edward Grim, remained at his side now. They urged him toward the choir, and he did not resist so violently, for the high altar and the archbishop's high seat were his proper place.

At this moment the four knights burst into the cathedral. Although the door from the cloisters had been barred, then thrown open by Thomas, the other doors of the cathedral had remained open all the time, and townspeople were now streaming in, some to attend vespers, some in awareness of trouble brewing. In the darkness, amid this increasing throng, the knights could not see Thomas. One of them, or possibly one of the de Brocs, called out: "Where is Thomas Beketh, traitor to the king and realm?"

Thomas, now composed, did not respond to the double insult—the allusion to his burgess birth and the charge of traitor. Reginald FitzUrse, who knew him better, cried out: "Where is the archbishop?"

Thomas answered immediately: "A priest as well as archbishop. If you seek me, you will find me here." He descended the steps he had mounted, moving toward them with dignity. By the great pillar between the Lady chapel and the chapel of St. Benedict, he stopped. Three of the knights gathered around him, while Hugh de Moreville flashed his sword to keep inquisitive townsfolk from approaching too closely. The three knights were joined by Robert de Broc's chaplain, Hugh of Horsea, who went by the name of Hugh Mauclerc. "Absolve the bishops you have excommunicated," this Hugh cried.

"I have already said what I will and will not do," Thomas answered.

"If you do not, you are a dead man," one of the four threatened.

"I am ready to die for God and the Church," Thomas replied. "But in the name of Almighty God I forbid you to harm any of my men, lay or cleric."

Even if they had come only to kill, the knights might have hesitated to commit sacrilege in the mother church of all England, upon an archbishop who had just reminded them that he was a priest. But they seem to have been still uncertain of their own intentions, for at this juncture they tried to take Thomas prisoner. Had he surrendered, they probably would not have been able to kill him in cold blood. But although he had refused to hide from them, he was by no means willing to give way. As John of Salisbury had seen, he was now bent on martyrdom. He resisted undignifiedly, like a secular; and at the same time he maddened the men with insults. For when FitzUrse dropped his axe and seized hold of his cloak, Thomas twisted away. Brito, FitzUrse, and Hugh Mauclerc tried to lift Thomas off his feet and place him on Tracy's shoulders, so that he could be carried out of the church. A scuffle began in which Thomas was helped only by Edward Grim; all the other clerics had fled; even William FitzStephen did not come to his master's aid, although he was standing near enough to hear the exchange between Thomas and FitzUrse. Thomas, his back to the pillar, gripped FitzUrse by his coat of mail and threw him to the floor. "Let go of me, Reginald, you are my vassal, you owe me fealty. You are acting like madmen, you and your accomplices. Let go of me, you pimp."

Beside himself at the insult, FitzUrse brandished his sword. "I owe you no fealty against the king!" he cried for the second time that afternoon. He whirled the sword in a great circle over Thomas's head, barely grazing it. Thomas attempted no further resistance. Bowing his head, he joined his hands in prayer and said firmly and loudly: "I commend myself and my church to God and the Blessed Mary, to St. Denis and St. Alphege." Tracy sprang forward and brought his sword down toward Thomas's head. Courageous Grim threw up his arm to intercept the blow;

the blade cut deep into his arm, was only partly deflected, and sliced into the crown of Thomas's head with such force that blood gushed over his eyes and face. "Strike, strike!" Tracy called to the others as he raised his sword again and once more brought it down on the bleeding head. Still Thomas could speak and still he stood unmoving. "Into thy hands, O Lord, I commend my spirit," he said. At a third blow he fell to his hands and knees. Grim, crouching against the pillar, clutching his nearly severed arm, heard him murmur his last words: "For the name of Jesus and the defense of the Church, I embrace death." As he lay there, Richard Brito gave him the deathblow, striking with such tremendous force that he cut off the crown of Thomas's head and shattered his blade in two on the pavement.

"The blood whitening with brain and the brain reddening with blood dyed the floor of the cathedral with the white of the lily and the red of the rose, colors of the Virgin and Mother, colors of the life and death of the martyr and confessor."

Hugh Mauclerc, de Broc's chaplain, to complete the horror placed his foot on the dead man's neck, inserted his sword into the enormous wound, and scattered brains and blood over the pavement. "Let us go, knights," he said then. "This fellow will not rise again."

EPILOGUE

EPILOGUE

ONCE AGAIN roaring *"Réaux, réaux!"* (King's men) to clear a path through the gathering crowd, the murderers dashed from the cathedral by the way they had entered, back through the cloisters and into the palace. There they ransacked the archbishop's private rooms for incriminating documents, for they were still hoping to find proof that Thomas had plotted against the king. They seized quantities of charters, papal bulls, and private letters, which were turned over to Ranulf de Broc for transmission to the king in Normandy. Although the archbishop's property now belonged to the king until the election of a new archbishop, they acted as if they had just defeated a secular enemy in a private war; that is, they set about looting the palace, stealing gold and silver vessels, vestments, and even books. To make matters worse, they loaded these spoils on horses from the archbishop's stables. It is difficult to see how they thought they could possibly justify this spoliation either to the old king or the young; and it is not impossible that the archbishop's biographers exaggerated the casual pillaging of a few retainers whom the four barons and the de Brocs could not control. Possibly also some facts have been omitted; the four, or the de Brocs, may have decided they ought to collect valuables to cover the archbishop's debts. It is difficult to believe that the four behaved like common thieves.

That night they rode back to Saltwood Castle, leaving Robert de Broc in charge at the archiepiscopal palace. Next day they

made for de Moreville's castle of Knaresborough, in the West
Riding, safely within Archbishop Roger's province of York.
Their temporary disappearance from sight soon gave rise to leg-
ends about their fate. They were supposed to have died in the
Holy Land, where they had gone to expiate their crime, after
suffering dreadful torments. In fact they lay low for a considerable time, under sentence of excommunication but quite safe from
secular penalties because only the Church could punish the slay-
ing of an ecclesiastic. (This *reductio ad absurdum* of the principle
for which Thomas had fought was amended in 1178, when a
final settlement of the Church–State issues was reached between
Henry and Pope Alexander's legates. It was then agreed that the
murderers of clerics would be subject to the same punishments as
the murderers of laymen.) Eventually the four knights were
taken back into Henry's good graces. There is no evidence that
they profited conspicuously by the murder; but they certainly did
not suffer greatly for it, so far as can be determined on the basis of
highly inconclusive evidence.

There is no record of the fate of Hugh Mauclerc, the "evil
clerk" who contemptuously desecrated Thomas Becket's corpse.
But he proved a false prophet. On the very night of the martyrdom the monk Benedict[1] saw Thomas in a vision. The body had
earlier been placed on a bier and carried up the steps to the choir
to the high altar, where it was laid for the night.[2] In his vision
Benedict saw Thomas arise, "dazzling white and red, comely of
face, beautiful to look upon." Dressed in his full vestments, he
approached the altar as if intending to celebrate Mass. After
much hesitation, Benedict in his dream asked Thomas: "Are you
not dead, Lord?" And Thomas replied: "I was dead, but I have
risen again."

Not everyone was willing to believe this. Even as the shak-
ing monks crept back to the transept where Thomas had fallen,
the wounded Edward Grim heard some say that the archbishop

[1] Benedict subsequently became Prior of Christ Church and, seven
years later, Abbot of Peterborough; he is generally known as
Benedict of Peterborough.
[2] This fact probably gave rise to the persistent but incorrect notion
that Thomas was killed at the foot of the altar.

had deserved his fate, had brought it on himself by his obstinacy. But division of opinion about his motives and character did not last for long. Other monks, and some of the townsfolk, reverently collected the blood and brains spattered on the pavement, along with the splinters of Mauclerc's sword. And their faith that the murdered archbishop was a true martyr became certainty when Robert of Merton lifted the outer garments from the body and showed the monks that underneath his splendid robe the arch-bishop had worn a hair shirt, as well as the monastic habit. The impact of that disclosure upon a community of monks, who thus suddenly learned that the ecclesiastical superior who had come to them from "the world" had really been one of themselves in spirit, can scarcely be imagined in our less emotional age. "Then the monks, wholly transported with spiritual joy, lifted their hearts and hands to heaven, glorifying God; they gave over sorrow for rejoicing, turned their laments to cries of gladness. . . . They fell to the floor, kissing his hands and feet, calling him Saint Thomas, declaring him a holy martyr of God. All ran up to see him in haircloth whom they had seen as chancellor in purple and byssus."

The example of the monks was followed by the townsfolk. In spite of the intense darkness of a phenomenal winter thunder-storm that burst over Canterbury after the murderers had left, the townspeople thronged into the cathedral to gaze upon the new-found saint. They fell to their knees; they cut pieces from their clothing and dipped these into the blood. Adoration of the corpse might have gone on for days if Robert de Broc had not acted to check the rising popular excitement. Robert sent word to the monks that if they did not bury the body promptly he would drag it out and hang it on a gibbet or tear it to pieces with horses or throw it into a cesspool. Alarmed, aware that they now had a precious relic, the monks hastily buried their martyr in the crypt, between the altars of St. Augustine and St. John the Baptist. The interment was unceremonious; no Mass could be said because the cathedral had been desecrated by violence.

Thomas Becket died on Tuesday December 29, 1170. On Thursday, the wife of a Sussex knight, who made a vow to "Saint Thomas, martyr precious to Christ," was promptly cured of blindness. Miracles then followed by the score, by the hundreds. Tiny droplets of blood scraped from the stone floor healed the deaf, the lame, and the blind, cured dropsy, epilepsy, and leprosy, exorcised demons in possession of hapless souls. A churl's dead cow was restored to life by the martyr, who in life had always shown his special sympathy for the poor. A horse fell to its flanks into a hole in a bridge; when all efforts to help it failed, invocation of the name of Thomas of Canterbury miraculously extricated the animal. Odo of Falaise, who had lost the sight of his right eye, regained it after he had wept for the death of Thomas. Robert of Cricklade, the learned Prior of St. Frideswide, suffered for nine years from an exceedingly painful disease of the leg contracted in Sicily: prayer at the grave of St. Thomas cured the limb so thoroughly that thereafter it was stronger than his sound leg.[3]

✠ ✠ ✠

But even before the tidings of the miracles spread, the whole of the Latin West shuddered with revulsion as word of the murder sped from court to court and city to city. The peculiar circumstances of the crime, its combination of sacrilege and breach of a king's plighted word, aroused singular horror. The archbishop's death was straightway compared with the Passion of Jesus. In fact, said William FitzStephen, the murderers were worse than those who had crucified Christ, since they were fellow Christians of the archbishop and "his own sons and vassals."

Young Henry might have been expected to mourn the death of his foster father. But he only lifted hands and eyes to heaven, and said: "What a pity! But I thank Thee, God, that it was kept secret from me and that none of my men was there." It is difficult not to read a certain hypocrisy in these words.

The elder Henry was at Argentan when the news was brought to him on January 1, 1171. At the messenger's first

---

[3] Out of gratitude, the prior wrote a biography (now lost) which became the basis for the Icelandic saga of Thomas.

words, he burst into tears. He alternately wailed and fell into a stupor, so that for a time his attendants feared for his sanity or his life. For three days he stayed in his room, refusing food or consolation, while he mourned the man who for sixteen years, in friendship and enmity, had never been far from his thoughts. He mourned his friend and he mourned also the loss of his own honor, for he fully realized that everyone would believe he had contrived the murder. When he had recovered sufficiently to face his court again, he loudly called on God to witness that he had not wanted the crime, nor known of it, and that if he were guilty of it in any way, then only because he had not made sufficiently clear that his reconciliation with the archbishop was full and complete. Possibly it crossed his mind briefly that the murderers may have acted more in their own interests than his, for he considered punishing them. But he quickly realized that to do so would compromise his reputation still more; it would be said that he was sacrificing his tools to cover his own crime.

His immediate necessity was to stave off excommunication of himself and interdict on all his lands. Louis of France, Theobald of Blois, Archbishop William of Sens, and other friends of Thomas Becket were urging Pope Alexander to impose the severest censures of the Church upon Henry himself and the English bishops who had incited his anger against their archbishop. Henry enlisted his bishops to dispatch letter after letter to the Curia, testifying to his innocence. Simultaneously, he sent embassies to plead with Alexander, who was so outraged that for a time he gave orders to his attendants to admit no Englishmen to his presence. Meanwhile, the Archbishop of Sens, at the instance of King Louis and out of his own desire to avenge his friend, imposed interdict on all Henry's Continental lands. Despite appeals, the pope confirmed this sentence, although heavy bribes at the Curia, together with an abject promise to accept whatever penance the pope saw fit to order, saved Henry from excommunication and England from interdict.

Henry realized that some dramatic act on behalf of the faith was essential to restore the remnants of his reputation. Abruptly, he launched that invasion of Ireland which was to link the fates of the English and the Irish, more for ill than for good, for the

373

next seven hundred fifty years. Publicly it was proclaimed that he had taken the cross in order to bring the Irish back into the fold of the Roman Church. Privately he had the satisfaction of knowing that St. George's Channel lay between himself and papal legates, while his bishops bore the burden of attempting to exculpate him. The bishops had much to do just trying to plead their own cases; Roger of York remained in suspension for a full year, and Gilbert Foliot even longer. A year and a half passed before negotiations with the papal legates were completed. Only then did Henry return from Ireland. At Avranches, on May 21, 1172, in the presence of his son, the young king, Henry "in public audience placed his hand upon the sacred Gospels and swore that he had neither commanded nor desired the murder of the Archbishop of Canterbury, and that on hearing of Thomas's death he had sorrowed, not rejoiced. He added—although this had not been suggested as part of the oath—that "he had not grieved so much over the death of his father or mother."

At this ceremony Henry further vowed to perform any penance the cardinal-legates wished to impose. He admitted that he had been the unwitting cause of the archbishop's death in that his retainers, seeing his troubled face and eyes and hearing his complaints against Thomas Becket, avenged his wrongs without his knowledge. Cardinals Theodwin and Albert, the legates, then absolved him on conditions that represented an almost total victory for the Church. Henry was to furnish two hundred knights to fight in the Holy Land for an entire year under the command of the Templars.[4] Providing the full expense of these knights would cost him some nine thousand pounds a year. In addition, he was to restore all the possessions of Canterbury as they had been held a year before Thomas incurred his anger. But the financial burden of these penances was insignificant compared to the humiliation of the provision that obligated Henry "to renounce wholly the wicked Statutes of Clarendon and all evil customs which in his time had been introduced into the churches of God." In assenting to this clause, Henry was granting posthu-

---

[4] It is worth noting how the Templars thus profited by their old intimacy and cooperation with Thomas Becket.

mous triumph to Thomas Becket. He could no longer argue that he had introduced no new customs, only revived the usages of his grandfather's time; for now he had admitted that evil customs had been introduced and that they were indeed novelties. Abandonment of the Constitutions of Clarendon was one unequivocal feature of the so-called Concordat of Avranches. In death the archbishop was stronger than he had been while living. It has been argued that Henry conceded a little in theory, but in practice later regained all that he had yielded. But it would be fairer to say that he accepted *de jure,* if not always *de facto,* that internationalization of the Church for which Thomas Becket had shed his blood. Once Henry had made his peace with Alexander, the isolation of the English Church, which he had for so long tried to enforce, was altogether abandoned. Appeals flowed freely to Rome, and the unquestioned supremacy of the pope was fully acknowledged. It is true that compromises were subsequently reached on the respective jurisdictions of royal and ecclesiastical courts, and that the king succeeded in imposing his own choices of bishops and abbots upon the clergy. Nevertheless, the stage was already set for that dominance over England that Pope Innocent III was to assert in the reign of Henry's son John.

The news of Thomas Becket's death apparently grieved Pope Alexander as a personal loss. He too is said to have withdrawn to his chambers and shut himself off from all his associates for a full week. Alexander might indeed feel conscience-stricken; for had he been firmer in his support of Thomas over the years, the outcome might well have been different. He had told himself all along that his weakness was concession to the evil of the times, imposed by circumstances beyond his control; now, too late, he gave the lie to his own argument by unprecedented severity toward King Henry. With astonishment, gratitude, and remorse, he listened to the tales of miracles that came pouring in from Canterbury and elsewhere; and early in March of 1173 he sent the following letter to the chapter of Canterbury cathedral:

> May the whole community of the faithful rejoice in the miracles of that revered and holy man, Thomas, your archbishop. Your own hearts ought to leap with an even greater joy;

375

for you more often than others have beheld his miracles with the
eyes of faith. What is more, his most sacred body lends luster to
your church. In life, the glory of his merits and the greatness of
his soul shone forth. In death, his miracles are matter of public
record. We have, moreover, received confirmation of them by
the testimony of our beloved sons, the apostolic legates Albert,
cardinal-priest of St. Laurence in Lucina, and Theodwin, cardinal-priest of St. Vitalis. We have also deliberated with our
brother bishops. At the beginning of Lent [February 21], therefore, in the presence of a great multitude of clerics and laymen,
we have solemnly canonized the aforesaid archbishop and de-
creed that he shall be numbered among the society of martyr
saints. We command you and the whole community of the
faithful of England, by our apostolic authority, to celebrate his
feast yearly with due veneration on the day on which he ended
his life with a glorious Passion. . . .

This formal act was but the acknowledgment of an enthusiasm for the martyr so overwhelming and so widespread that it
seemed in itself something not of man but of God. Bishops and
even popes had been killed before; but such a torrent of miracles
was unique. More than five hundred of them were recorded
within the first few years after Thomas's death. But more amazing than the miracles themselves was the unceasing procession of
believers who came to touch the spot where he had fallen, to pray
not for his soul but for his intercession, and to buy the tiny lead
ampullas of his blood infinitely diluted with water. The "water of
St. Thomas" became the great panacea of the age. Pilgrims came
by the thousands and tens of thousands; and for three hundred
years they would continue to come. From parched Acre in the
Holy Land to Iceland in the northern waste of waters, Thomas
Becket soon became the saint to whom men appealed in the
crises of their lives. The word "canter" entered the English language as an abbreviation of "Canterbury gallop," the pleasant,
leisurely pace favored by Canterbury pilgrims.

Among the earliest and most notable of these pilgrims was
Henry II himself, who came in desperation hoping to make a
more lasting peace with Thomas than the reconciliation at Fréteval had been. Early in 1173, the long-smoldering sedition in

Henry's empire had erupted. Urged on by Louis of France, Queen Eleanor, and Eleanor's uncle Ralph de Faye, who had been one of Thomas Becket's bitterest enemies at court, young Henry rose in rebellion against his father. His brothers, Richard and Geoffrey, soon joined him, bringing with them much support from the discontented barons of England and the Continental domains.

Henry's misfortunes were widely attributed to divine punishment for the death of Thomas Becket. The rebels sedulously nourished this popular notion. Henry managed to control the uprising in his Continental domains, but at the cost of neglecting England. By midsummer of 1174 Richard of Ilchester, now bishop-elect of Winchester (old Henry of Blois had died in August 1171, just before the king departed for Ireland) came to Henry in Normandy. He convinced the king that all of England was in danger of being lost to the rebels. Henry embarked without delay, in spite of high winds and threatening skies. When a terrible gale sprang up, he publicly prayed that he might be granted safe passage only if his arrival would mean peace to his kingdom. The voyage from Barfleur to Southampton was completed safely; but Henry did not at once lead an army against his enemies. Instead he proceeded to emulate the humility of his German namesake of nearly a century earlier. Subsisting on a diet of bread and water, he rode straight to Canterbury. For the last part of the journey he donned a hair shirt and the woolen shift of the pilgrim, and walked barefoot in the rain from St. Dunstan's church to the cathedral. He kissed the "stone of the martyrdom," knelt at Thomas's tomb, wept and then prayed there. Gilbert Foliot, for his own penance, had to speak for the king, declaring Henry's regret that he had unwittingly prompted the murder, and announcing various grants to the monastery so that lamps might burn forever at the tomb. The Prior of Christ Church gave the king the kiss of peace. Then Henry submitted to flagellation from the bishops, the abbot, and each one of the eighty monks. All night long he stayed in the crypt, fasting and praying.

Within twenty-four hours, the new saint rewarded Henry with a miracle. The penance had taken place on Saturday, July

12. On Sunday night, back in London and trying to sleep off the effects of his exhausting vigil, Henry was awakened by a loud knocking at his door. A messenger brought word that William the Lion, King of Scots, had been taken prisoner on Saturday, just after Henry had completed his penance. The capture of King William broke the back of the rebellion in the north. "God be thanked for it," Henry exclaimed, "and Saint Thomas the Martyr and all the saints of God." Only three and a half years after Thomas's death, it had become natural even for Henry, who had known him so well in life, to address the dead man as "Saint Thomas the Martyr." *O quanta rerum mutatio!*

St. Thomas the Martyr he remained for all. Soon his other associates and former enemies came round. Richard de Lucy founded the Abbey of Lesnes in his honor, Gilbert Foliot the hospital of St. Thomas at Southwark. Even the murderer who had struck the first blow, William Tracy, gave a manor to the monastery of Christ Church in penance. All his life Thomas Becket had been much concerned with money and property, both for the material power they represented and for their symbolic value in the struggle between Church and State. After his death, he became an enormous source of revenue for the monastery of Christ Church and the city of Canterbury. Kings showered wealth upon his shrine. Soon it was covered with plates of pure gold; but the gold itself was almost hidden by an encrustation of sapphires, diamonds, rubies, and emeralds. Desiderius Erasmus, one of a host of famous pilgrims to Canterbury, saw in 1513 "inestimable treasures. . . . Every part glistened and shone and sparkled with rare and very large jewels, some of them bigger than a goose's egg." Yet this luxury was trifling compared to the wealth enjoyed by the monastic foundation of Christ Church, which remained in charge of cathedral and shrine. The cellarer of the monastery alone had thirty-eight servants under him, including such worthies as a *potagiarius*—a special cook for herbs, vegetables, and delicacies.

Fame and wealth came to an abrupt end in 1538, when Henry VIII ordered the destruction of the shrine of Thomas Becket. A complex of legend has been elaborated around this event, as around so much in the saint's birth and career. The tale is told that King Henry summoned Thomas Becket to appear for trial as a traitor to his king, and appointed a public defender (who lost his case) when the saint failed to answer the summons. The story was a fabrication; but the posthumous "punishment" of Thomas Becket by Henry VIII was real enough. The shrine was broken to pieces, Becket's bones carelessly buried in an unmarked spot, and all the gold and jewelry carted off to the royal treasury in a long procession of wagons. Henry himself later wore the "Regale of France," the great gem presented by Louis VII of France, in a ring on his thumb. In the proclamation that Henry VIII issued on November 16, 1538, to justify these proceedings, Thomas Becket was charged with having stubbornly withstood the "wholesome laws established against the enormities of the clergy by the king's highness' most noble progenitor, King Henry the Second." Henry VIII, conducting his own fight against clergy and papacy, quite correctly identified the former Archbishop of Canterbury, dead for 368 years, with the principle of clerical supremacy.

> Therfore his grace strayghtly chargeth and commandeth, that from hense forth the sayde Thomas Becket shall not be estemed, named, reputed, nor called a sayncte, but bysshop Becket, and that his ymages and pictures, through the hole realme, shall be putte downe and auoyded out of all churches, chapelles, and other places, and that from hense forthe, the dayes vsed to be festiuall in his name, shall not be obserued, nor the seruice, office, antiphones, collettes, and prayers in his name redde, but rased and put out of all the bokes.

Thus the worship of the saint ended in the Church of England; but throughout the Catholic world his feast continued to be kept, and the following words sung in the Introit in honor of "the Holy Bishop and Martyr Thomas":

Gaudeamus omnes in Domino, diem festum celebrantes sub honore Thomae Martyris; de cuius passione gaudent angeli, et collaudant Filium Dei.[5]

---

[5] Let us rejoice in the Lord, celebrating the festal day in honor of the Martyr Thomas; the angels rejoice in his martyrdom, while they praise the Son of God.

But perhaps more significant are the words of the concluding Alleluia:

Ego sum pastor bonus et cognosco oves meas et cognoscunt me meae.[6]

For in the end the quality that stands out in Thomas was his devotion to duty, to the "flock" that had been committed to his charge. Throughout his struggle with the king, he alluded to this responsibility: to his immediate dependents, to the unfortunates exiled for his sake, to the people of his province and his fellow Englishmen. Among his last words was an injunction to the murderers not to harm any of his followers. The charge of "traitor" stung him most of all because his loyalties were austere: loyalties to the king, to the Church, to the people, to his God. Unfortunately for him, they could not all be reconciled—although if he had had his will he might possibly have demonstrated that they were not incompatible. Perhaps this striving for an impossible ideal was the "saintly" quality in him that most of his critics have missed.

Certainly Thomas Becket does not seem to have been saintly, if we apply to his personality the saccharine or cliché notion of sainthood. Proud, forceful, stubborn, fond of good food and wine, more given to luxury and display than asceticism, he had been a thoroughgoing man of the world until his consecration as archbishop—except for the consistency with which he kept a vow of chastity. We have seen him leading armies, engaging in single combat, maneuvering in adroit diplomacy, losing his temper, cursing his enemies. He showed little of the sweetness, forbearance, and lovingkindness, and none of the theological originality, that had given his predecessor Anselm the nimbus of sanctity. Yet Anselm waited four hundred years for canonization; Thomas was formally enrolled in the calendar of saints in less than three years.

The miracles made the difference, of course. Some miracles were ascribed to Anselm, too; but these were paltry compared to

---

[6] I am a good shepherd and know my own sheep, and my own know me.

the hundreds, the thousands, and in the course of time the tens of thousands, connected with the name of Thomas Becket. It is difficult, in our rationalistic age, to discuss miracles at all. But in truth the nature of miracles has never changed. Even when they were frequent, they still required an act of faith. In his letter to the Canterbury monks announcing the canonization, Pope Alexander used the phrase *oculata fide,* "with the eyes of faith," or as it might perhaps be more forcibly translated, "with seeing faith." Miracles do not engender faith, they spring from it; they are evidence that sanctity is already acknowledged. The fears and hopes of an emotional populace, a sensational death, a charismatic personality—a thousand rational explanations can be offered for the psychological fact. All miracles are ultimately a theological mystery and a philosophical problem. But when we remember the crowds of "Christ's poor" who followed Thomas Becket's train wherever he went, who wept for joy on his return to Canterbury, and who lined the roads of France and England to hail him on his journeys; when we remember the substantial citizens who sought him out in spite of official warnings; and when we remember the hundreds who suffered exile for him, when only a word of submission was needed for them to obtain the king's favor and restoration of their confiscated worldly goods—when we remember all this, then perhaps we may say that the miracles came after Thomas Becket's death because all his life he had attracted love as the tallest tree in the woods attracts lightning.

Appendix

THE CONSTITUTIONS OF CLARENDON [1]

I. If a dispute shall arise between laymen, or between clerks and laymen, or between clerks, concerning advowson and presentation to churches, let it be treated and concluded in the court of the lord king.

II. Churches within the fief of the lord king cannot be granted in perpetuity without his consent and concession.

III. Clerks cited and accused of any matter shall, when summoned by the king's justice, come before the king's court to answer there concerning matters which shall seem to the king's court to be answerable there, and before the ecclesiastical court for what shall seem to be answerable there, but in such a way that the justice of the king shall send to the court of holy Church to see how the case is there tried. And if the clerk be convicted, or shall confess, the Church ought no longer to protect him.

IV. It is not lawful for archbishops, bishops and beneficed clergy of the realm to depart from the kingdom without the lord king's leave. And if they do so depart, they shall, if the king so please, give security that neither in going, nor in tarrying, nor in returning, will they contrive evil or injury against the king or the kingdom.

V. Excommunicates ought not to give pledges of security for future good behavior, nor take oaths, but only ought to give

---

[1] Reprinted by permission from *English Historical Documents*, Vol. II, 1042–1189, ed. David C. Douglas and George W. Greenaway. London: Eyre & Spottiswoode; New York: Oxford University Press; 1953.

383

sufficient pledge of security to abide by the judgment of the Church in order to obtain absolution.

VI. Laymen ought not to be accused save by accredited and lawful accusers and witnesses in the presence of the bishop, in such wise, however, that the archdeacon may not lose his right nor anything due to him thereby. And if the accused persons be such that no one either wishes or dares to prefer a charge against them, the sheriff, when requested by the bishop, shall cause twelve lawful men of the neighborhood or township to swear before the bishop that they will manifest the truth of the matter to the best of their knowledge.

VII. No one who holds of the king in chief nor any of the officers of his demesne shall be excommunicated, nor the lands of any one of them placed under interdict, unless application shall first be made to the lord king, if he be in the realm, or to his chief justice, if he be abroad, that right may be done him; in such wise that matters pertaining to the royal court shall be concluded there, and matters pertaining to the ecclesiastical court shall be sent thither to be dealt with.

VIII. With regard to appeals, if they should arise, they should proceed from the archdeacon to the bishop, and from the bishop to the archbishop. And if the archbishop should fail to do justice, the case must finally be brought to the lord king, in order that by his command the dispute may be determined in the archbishop's court, in such wise that it may proceed no further without the assent of the lord king.

IX. If a dispute shall arise between a clerk and a layman, or between a layman and a clerk, in respect of any holding which the clerk desires to treat as free alms,[2] but the layman as a lay fee, it shall be determined by the recognition of twelve lawful men through the deliberation, and in the presence of the king's chief justice, whether the holding pertains to free alms or to lay fee. And if it be judged to pertain to free alms, the plea shall be heard in the ecclesiastical court; but if to lay fee, it shall be heard in the king's court, unless both of them shall claim from the same

---

[2] Frankalmoign, purely religious tenure, which involved no temporal duties and theoretically could not be alienated.

bishop or baron. But if each of them appeal concerning this fief to the same bishop or baron, the plea shall be heard in the latter's court, in such wise that he who was originally in possession shall not lose possession by reason of the recognition that has been made, until the matter has been settled by the plea.

X. If anyone of a city or castle or borough or demesne manor of the lord king be cited by archdeacon or bishop for any offence for which he is obliged to make answer to them, and he refuse to give satisfaction at their citations, it is highly proper to place him under interdict; but he ought not to be excommunicated until application has been made to the chief officer of the lord king in that town, in order that it may be adjudged meet for him to make satisfaction. But if the king's officer fail to act in this, he himself shall be at the mercy of the lord king, and thereafter the bishop shall be allowed to coerce the accused by ecclesiastical justice.

XI. Archbishops, bishops and all beneficed clergy of the realm, who hold of the king in chief, have their possessions from the lord king by barony and are answerable for them to the king's justices and officers; they observe and perform all royal rights and customs and, like other barons, ought to be present at the judgments of the king's court together with the barons, until a case shall arise of judgment concerning mutilation or death.

XII. When an archbishopric or bishopric is vacant, or any abbey or priory of the king's demesne, it ought to be in his own hand, and he shall receive from it all revenues and profits as part of his demesne. And when the time has come to provide for the church, the lord king ought to summon the more important of the beneficed clergy of the church, and the election ought to take place in the lord king's chapel with the assent of the lord king and the advice of the clergy of the realm whom he shall summmon for this purpose. And the clerk elected shall there do homage and fealty to the lord king as his liege lord for his life and limbs and his earthly honor, saving his order, before he is consecrated.

XIII. If any of the magnates of the realm should forcibly prevent an archbishop or bishop or archdeacon from doing justice to himself or to his people, the lord king ought to bring him to justice. And if perchance anyone should forcibly dispossess the lord king of his right, the archbishop, bishops and archdeacons ought to bring him to justice, so that he may make satisfaction to the lord king.

XIV. The chattels of those who are under forfeiture to the king may not be retained by any church or cemetery against the king's justice, because they belong to the king, whether they be found within the churches or without.

XV. Pleas of debt due under pledge of faith, or even without pledge of faith, are to lie in the justice of the king.

XVI. Sons of villeins ought not to be ordained without the consent of the lord on whose land they are known to have been born.

This record of the aforesaid customs and privileges of the crown was drawn up by the archbishops, bishops, earls, barons, nobles and elders of the realm at Clarendon on the fourth day previous to the Purification of the Blessed Virgin Mary in the presence of the lord Henry and of his father, the lord king. There are, moreover, many other great customs and privileges pertaining to holy Mother Church and to the lord king and his barons of the realm which are not contained in this document. Let them be safe for holy Church and for our lord the king and his heirs and the barons of the realm. And let them be inviolably observed for ever and ever.

NOTES

The reader can easily locate the passage for which a reference is supplied by looking for the catchwords in the text on the indicated page and line. For direct quotations, the last words of the quoted passage, printed within quotation marks, serve as catchwords. For indirect quotations or statements of fact, key phrases or names from the given page, printed without quotation marks, have been used for catchwords. I am indebted to Thurman Wilkins for suggesting to me this system of keying references, which he has used in his biography, *Clarence King*.

For explanation of the abbreviated forms of the titles cited, see the left-hand column of the Bibliography.

Notes to A PREFATORY NOTE ON SOURCES

| viii:37 | Magnûsson | *Saga* II, xc |

Notes to CHAPTER I: LONDON

3:10	paragon	Norgate I, 424 f.
3:12	violent	Froude, J. A., 99
4:20	Lincolner's bid	Stenton, 173
5:10	Thierceville	*Materials* III, 15
5:21	Saracen maiden	Brown, 31; Robertson, 10
5:31	in her womb	*Materials* III, 13
6:9	"to cover"	*EHD*, 703
6:13	"friend of God"	*Saga* I, 17
6:30	Roesa	*Materials* IV, 81
7:5	"after Christ"	*Materials* II, 302 f.
7:16	"transacted"	*Materials* V, 26
7:33	foot soldiers	*Materials* III, 4
7:36	forty thousand	Lloyd, 190
8:2	"they keep"	*EHD*, 957
8:10	"godwit"	*EHD*, 958
8:24	"woolly sheep"	*EHD*, 959
9:2	"of martyrs"	*EHD*, 960

9:7	"arguments"	*EHD*, 958
9:13	"the shield"	*EHD*, 960 f.
9:18	"of animals"	*Materials* III, 11
9:23	"all things"	*Saga* I, 21
9:24	"merry"	*Materials* II, 302
9:30	schoolmasters	*Governance*, 270
10:18	complex ideas	Holmes, 23
10:21	"modern times"	*Meta.*, 67; Lloyd, 91
10:36–7	"ostentatious"	*Meta.*, 70
11:24–5	"in him"	*Saga* I, 19
12:19	"tabernacles"	*Saga* I, 35
12:22–3	in his hood	Guernes, 7 f.
12:38	"half dead"	*Materials* IV, 6

Notes to CHAPTER II: NORMAN ENGLAND

14:16	"man's land"	*EHD*, 147
14:22–3	changed hands	*EHD*, 28
15:7	"not escape"	*EHD*, 149 f.
15:18	"single battle"	*EHD*, 291
15:27	"frugality"	*EHD*, 291
17:24	"the hundred"	Stubbs, *S.C.*, 85
19:4	single day	Stenton, 15 f.
19:9	small towers	Holmes, 183 f.
19:16	"hand shackles"	Holmes, 185
21 *n.*:7	accepts	Cantor, 32
21:18	"my order"	*EHD*, 610
22:16	"judge you"	*EHD*, 617 ff.
24:7	reduce taxes	Cantor, 55
24:20	there twice	Cantor, 58
25:10	"come of it"	*EHD*, 656
25:29	"crown"	*EHD*, 659
26:4	urge submission	*EHD*, 661
26:14	"his will"	Cantor, 83; *EHD*, 664
27:22	royal treasury	Barlow, 172
27:34	"is installed"	*EHD*, 400
27:36	financial needs	Barlow, 180
28:19	condemned	*EHD*, 669 f.
28:19	morally bound	Barlow, 174
28:21	the marriage	Cantor, 128
28:37	compromise	Barlow, 180
29:9	"your fief"	See page 22.
29:15	favored	Barlow, 185 f.
29:29	silver pennies	Barlow, 187
29:38	"base coin"	Chron., A.D. 1125

Notes to CHAPTER III: YOUTH

31:2	"all things"	*Saga* I, 21
31:18	"northern lands"	*Saga* I, 21
31:22–3	"most civilized"	Simson, 106
32:6	"woman-friend"	*Saga* I, 21
32:18	"this world"	*Saga* I, 23
33:5	"miserable life"	*Saga* I, 25
33:19	population	Holmes, 64
33:22	paving	Okey, 65
33:28	Notre Dame	Holmes, 67
33:36	"at the feet"	*Meta*, 95
34:4	"ostentatious"	*Meta*, 97
34:6	"questions"	*Meta*, 96
34:12	Lombard	Gilson, 669
34:25	"from his lips"	*Meta*, 95
35:6	"to truth"	Storrs, 465
35:30	"to me"	Pieper, 89
35:34	Walter Map	Map, 48
36:6	"old problems"	*Meta*, chap. 10
36:16	"they touch"	Gilson, 160
36:18	"to lower"	Gilson, 163
36:36	*"mot a mot"*	Guernes, line 2356
37:21–2	"in the city"	*Materials* II, 361
37:32	*"curteis"*	Guernes, line 245
38:21	over a bastard	Barlow, 198
38:27	"his last"	*Gesta*, 3
39:12	"the bishops"	*EHD*, 403
39:16	"just dignity"	*EHD*, 404
40:11	"be robbers"	*EHD*, 200
41:23	"of flight"	*Gesta*, 74
41:34	"lamentation"	*Gesta*, 75
42:8	"the mighty"	*EHD*, 301
42:13	"and support"	*EHD*, 202
43:5	"questions plain"	*Saga* I, 29
43:10	"household"	*Materials* III, 15
43:21	"humpbacked"	*Materials* II, 346
44:30–1	"worldly goods"	*Materials* V, 515
44:36	government	Saltman, 165
44:37	lesser luminary	Saltman, 10
45:3	*"literatissimus"*	*Materials* III, 16
45:33	learning	Foreville, 20
45:34	Vacarius	*Poli.* VIII, 22
46:1	bloodsuckers	Lloyd, 242
46:22	Theobald	*Saga* I, 36 f.

46:36–7	"archbishop"	Radford, 40
47:29	ports watched	Saltman, 26 f.
47:36	*"navigando"*	*Materials* VI, 58
48:3	ineffectual	Milman, 244 f.
48:6	"but me"	*Hist. Pont.,* XVII
49:3–4	his commentary	Gilson, 141
49:17	"itself God"	Lloyd, 168 f.
49:24	"nominative"	Lloyd, 169
49:37	the sentence	*Hist. Pont.,* 7 f.
50:22	"foresightedness"	Radford, 45
50:31	of money	Saltman, 33
51:12	invaded England	*Gesta,* 152
51:21	sent home	*Gesta,* 153
51:30–1	"to Wallingford"	*Gesta,* 156–9
51:37	untimely death	*EHD,* 211
52:5	of his life	*EHD,* 404 ff.; Barlow 233
52:10	interregnum	Norgate I, 405

Notes to CHAPTER IV: THE KING AND HIS CHANCELLOR

53:2	a demon	Norgate I, 143
53:19	"the living"	*EHD,* 386
54:13	"his horses"	*EHD,* 422 ff.
55:4	"little hovel"	Norgate I, 412 f.
55:18	dilatoriness	Map, 303
55:27	"and French"	Map, 298
56:1	frugal meals	Stubbs, *H.I.,* 106
56:7	"and powerful"	*EHD,* 386
57:6	in attendance	Eyton, 2 f.
57:31	de Vere	*Governance,* 263
58:10–11	coronation	*Materials* III, 19
58:21	"advice"	*Materials* III, 18
58:27–8	"and advice"	Stubbs, *S.C.,* 179; *EHD,* 501
58:38	"chancellor"	*Materials* III, 173
60:4	"same age"	*Materials* III, 22 ff.
60:26	"to God"	Hutton, 16
61:7	how to behave	*Materials* V, 2
61:21	exile	Eyton, 14
61:28	complained	*Saga* I, 59
62:9	compensation	*Governance,* 262
62:11	disregarded	*Governance,* 260
62:17	Flemings	*EHD,* 323
63:14	Exchequer	*EHD,* 323
63:27	assistance	Norgate I, 144
64:8	severely ill	Saltman, 74
64:9	a daughter	Eyton, 18

64:13	were rendered	Stubbs, *S.C.*, 189
64:23	"many years"	Stubbs, *S.C.*, 199
65:3	"to ordain"	*Saga I*, 49
65:10	activities	Stubbs, *C.H.* I, 459
66:5	Lambeth	Radford, 174 ff.
67:3	charters	*Materials* IV, 246
67:12	forgery	Foreville, 91; Davis, 431
67:24	second session	Radford, 107
68:1	"lord bishop"	Radford, 185
68:3	"men know"	Radford, 172
68:26	"by you"	*Materials* IV, 255
68:34	voluntarily	*Materials* IV, 256
69:9	"any matters"	*Materials* VII, 242 f.
69:10	as evidence	Giles I, 93; Radford, 179
69:19	*"hereditario"*	*Materials* VII, 242
69:26	"his coffin"	Saltman, 158
71:28	and train	*Materials* III, 29
73:2	Paris	Holmes, 60
74:13	"and joy"	Map, 281; translation amended
74:18	all he asked	*Materials* III, 33
74:31	Knights Templar	Norgate I, 470
75:4	Geoffrey	Eyton, 40 f.
75:21	crusade	Norgate I, 453

Notes to CHAPTER V: THOMAS THE SOLDIER

76:20	"and leader"	*Poli.* VIII, 25; Radford, 88; Norgate I, 458 ff.
77:4	Midsummer Day	Norgate I, 459
78:6	three more	*Materials* III, 22
78:26	"of yeomen"	Stubbs, *S.C.*, 129; Norgate I, 459
78:32	for a year	Holmes, 289
79:2	"against Toulouse"	*Materials* V, 525
79:4	lay barons	Radford, 159
79:16	"of wickedness"	*Materials* V, 379
79:30	"life for it"	*Materials* V, 379
79:34	"military tenure"	Norgate I, 459
79:38	"and historians"	Stubbs, *C.H.* I, 456
79:38	has diminished	Barlow, 312; *Governance,* 62–91
80:13	Assize of Arms	Stubbs, *S.C.*, 154 f.
80:20	the loan	*Materials* III, 53 ff.
81:20	ill will	*Saga,* 58
81:22	"superstition"	*Materials* III, 33 f.
81:29–30	"whole province"	*Materials* III, 34
82:9	"king's enemies"	*Materials* II, 365
82:13	immediate sequel	Norgate I, 466 f.

82:23	own expense	*Materials* III, 35
83:1	"accident of battle"	Barlow, 257
83:5	"exhorted them"	*Materials* III, 35
83:10	*"chevalchier"*	Guernes, line 359
83:27	after Christmas	Eyton, 49
84:12	had died	*Materials* III, 328
84:22	political grounds	*Materials* IV, 87
84:28	"enormity"	*Materials* III, 328
85:1	Matthew	Boussard, 431
85:2	invasion	Barlow, 312
85:11	"apostolic glory"	*EHD,* 326
85:23	"and Norway"	*EHD,* 327
86:16	"Croesus"	*EHD,* 789 ff.
87:3	"his cup"	*EHD,* 795 f.

Notes to CHAPTER VI: SCHISM

89:10	him lecture	Foreville 21, *n.*2
90:5	drew his sword	Milman, 276
90:6–7	conclave	Dunker, 53
90:18	"divine judgment"	Milman, 288
90:35	"brother priests"	*Meta.,* 275
91:11	Arnulf	Norgate I, 500
91:27	"of Alexander"	*Letters of J. S.,* 202
91:29	urged Henry	Saltman, 47, 49
92 *n.*:8–9	"ought to do"	*Letters of J. S.,* 32
92 *n.*:13–14	"ascribed to me"	*Letters of J. S.,* 45;
		Materials V, 82
92:18	"of banishment"	*Letters of J. S.,* 205
92:18	testimonial	*Letters of J. S.,* 218
93:7	anxious letters	Saltman, 48
93:13	"our prince"	*Letters of J. S.,* 216 f.
93:20	"be increased"	*Letters of J. S.,* 220
93:28	their case	Saltman, 47
93:32	Henry had led	Kelly, 397; Milman, 452
94:12	"or fighting"	*Materials* III, 175
95:30	summons	*Letters of J. S.,* 224
96:21	"at once"	*Letters of J. S.,* 221 f.
97:25	"my lodging"	*Materials* III, 27 f.
98:13	at Le Mans	Eyton, 52
98:35	born in Salisbury	Webb, 1
98:38	crystal-gazing	*Poli.,* 28
99:7–8	papal court	Webb, 12
100:10	"good works"	*Poli.,* 43
100:20	"English king"	*Letters of J. S.,* 182
100:28	"of the Church"	*Poli.,* 9

100:36	"by God alone"	*Poli.*, 9 f.
101:8	"entire body"	*Poli.*, 64
101:14	"things divine"	*Poli.*, 79
101:15–16	"God himself"	*Poli.*, 80
101:33	"his virtues"	*Poli.*, 233
102:5	"gone before"	*Poli.*, 235
102:13	"bestowed on him"	*Poli.*, 233
102:15	"are groundless"	*Poli.*, 237
102:24–5	"man on earth"	*Poli.*, 258

Notes to CHAPTER VII: TOWARD CANTERBURY

105:11	"wicked men"	*Letters of J. S.*, 250 f.
105n.:3	"and the flesh"	Saltman, 55
106:17	"of the poor"	*Letters of J. S.*, 246 f.
107:9	mercenaries	Boussard, 424
106n.:23	"to his demesne"	*EHD*, 909
108:9	"to his soul"	Persius III, 30
108:10	"the Lord God"	*Materials* III, 26
109:5–6	"of the king"	*Materials* II, 305; *EHD*, 708
110:21	teach the boy	*Materials* III, 22, 176
111:1	coronation	*Materials* II, 366
111:21	"of his mind"	*Materials* III, 180; *Saga* I, 64
111:25	was staying	Eyton, 56
112:4	"between us"	*Materials* III, 180 f.
112:11	"before you"	*Saga* I, 65
112:13	*topos*	Curtius, 537
112:23	legate	*Saga* I, 67
112:25	to persuade	*Materials* IV, 87
113:11	"to the kingship"	*Materials* III, 182
113:11–12	"and limbs"	*Saga* I, 66
113:26	William Cade	Eyton, 56
114:28	"will follow"	*Materials* IV, 15
115:15	depend on that	*Materials* IV, 16
115:23	"heart and will"	*Materials* IV, 16
115:28	"royal appointment"	Poole, *FDBMC*, 181
116:1–2	"of the kingdom"	*Materials* V, 498
116:2–3	queen mother	*Materials* V, 517
116:11	disagreed	*Saga* I, 72
116:22	"to London"	*Saga* I, 73
117:12	"young king"	*Materials* IV, 16; *EHD*, 710
117:23	such a man	*Materials* V, 30
117:35	Gilbert	*Hist. Pont.*, 47
118:3	on the gospels	*Hist. Pont.*, 48
118:17–18	Church has accepted	*Hist. Pont.*, 49

118:24	respected him more	Knowles, *E.C.*, 38 ff.;
		Norgate I, 497
119:2	"the episcopate"	Webb, 61
119:14	"consequences"	Knowles, *E.C.*, 45
119:20	"and unlearned"	*Saga* I, 74–5
119:25	*"concorditer"*	*Materials* IV, 17
119:32	"Far from it"	*Saga* I, 76
119:36	"of the Church"	Guernes, 15
120:17	"to our will"	*Saga* I, 78–9
120:37	"your decision"	*Materials* IV, 17 f.; *EHD,* 711
121:16	"in great fear"	*Saga,* 80 f.
122:5	"multitude"	*Materials* IV, 18
123:27	candles	Taylor, 88 ff., 119 f.
123:31	"of people"	*Materials* IV, 19
124:20	"an archbishop"	*Materials* III, 36

Notes to CHAPTER VIII: THE NEW ARCHBISHOP

125:3	"his own heart"	*Materials* III, 185
125:7	"ten talents"	*Materials* III, 186
126:12–13	prolixity	*Materials* III, xxiv
127:10–11	"begot him"	*Materials* III, 101
127:16–17	Thury-Harcourt	Boussard, 95
127:19	*eruditi*	*Materials* III, 523–9
128:24	hidden hair shirt	*Saga* I, 94–8
128:24	tears at the Mass	*Materials* III, 210;
		Materials III, 37
128:29	"of souls"	*Materials* III, 290
129:2	poor	*Saga* I, 98–9
129:13	doubled it	*Materials* IV, 20, 90
129:17	separate table	*Saga* I, 107
129:21	sons of barons	*Materials* III, 227
129:26	cases	*Materials* III, 219 ff.
129:28	fairest of men	*Materials* III, 236
129:30	gifts	*Saga* I, 112 f.
131:11	dispensation	Guernes, 23
131:19–20	"I feel that"	Guernes, 23
131:28	larger revenues	*Saga* I, 119
132:6	documents	*Saga* I, 118
132:16	Roger's sister	*Materials* III, 43
132:32	annates	Baldwin, 73 f.
133:2	king's permission	*Materials* III, 43
133:5	Henry ignored	*Saga* I, 121
133:6	than the king	*Materials* IV, 92
133:13	see for himself	*Materials* IV, 92
133:21	conferred frequently	*Materials* III, 252 f.; *Saga* I, 121

133:23	"their complaints"	*Materials* III, 253
134:3	Gilbert	L'Huillier, 205
134:31	"your consent"	*Materials* V, 26
	"liberty"	*Materials* VI, 590
135:6–7	Henry's confessor	*Materials* V, 24, 29
135:16	sworn obedience	*Materials* V, 56
135:27	a treaty	Eyton, 80 f.
136:22	"of the realm"	*Materials* V, 33
136:29	lavish manner	*Materials* III, 254; *Saga* I, 128 ff.
136:36–7	triumphal progress	*Materials* III, 25
137:12	"after labor"	*Materials* III, 254
137:20	"finger of God"	*EHD*, 331
138:1	"provinces"	William of Newburgh, Stevenson IV–II, 462
138:12	"of churches"	William of Newburgh, Stevenson IV–II, 464
139:6	"conscience"	*EHD*, 331
139:12	"by his son"	*Materials* III, 255

Notes to CHAPTER IX: FIRST DISPUTES

140:5	"without cause"	*Materials* III, 41 f.
140:22	sheriff's aid	Cf. Hutton, 35 f.; Norgate II, 15; Robertson, 328
141:1–2	general policy	Barlow, 310 f.
141:23	"aid from them"	*Materials* II, 374
142:5–6	"of the Church"	*Materials* II, 374; Guernes, 24
142:28–9	"money and goods"	Stevenson IV–II, 748
142:37	adultery	*Materials* III, 43–5
143:17	"that sentence"	*Materials* III, 45
143:27–8	"and reputation"	Stevenson IV–II, 753
143:34	hundred murders	*EHD*, 331
144:3	Philip de Brois	*Materials* III, 45; *Materials* II, 374
144:20	"homicide"	*Materials* II, 374 f.
145:18	"of laymen"	*EHD*, 714
145:26	"is a clerk"	*Materials* II, 375 f.
146:34	to touch him	*Materials* III, 45
147:8	silver chalice	*Materials* III, 45 f.
148:19	"our strength"	*Materials* V, 48 f.
148:30	purpose was	*Materials* IV, 201
149:16	spiritual penalties	*Materials* III, 266
149:25	"punishment"	*Materials* IV, 202
150:6	"same cause"	*Materials* IV, 202
150:23	"with their kings"	*Materials* IV, 26
150:37–8	"to my customs"	*Materials* IV, 26 f.

151:6	*bona fide*	*Materials* III, 274
151:21	"already sworn"	*Materials* III, 274
151:34	general feeling	*EHD,* 330 f.
152:4–5	of the bishops	*Materials* III, 275
152:16	advised	*Saga* I, 158; *Materials* II, 377
152:32	"for him here"	*Materials* IV, 27
154:23	"to the priesthood"	*Materials* IV, 27–9

Notes to CHAPTER X: CLARENDON

156:2	"presumption"	*Materials* IV, 30
156:15	"his promises"	*Materials* IV, 31; cf. Guernes, 27 f.
156:30	Philip	*Materials* IV, 31
157:4	to the limbs	*Materials* IV, 31
157:6	the responsibility	*Saga* I, 160
157:11	been affronted	*Materials* IV, 32
157:15	"curse him"	*Materials* IV, 205
158:13	"hearing of all"	*Materials* IV, 32 f.
159:3	of l'Aumône	*Materials* IV, 33
159:7–8	"of the lion"	*Materials* IV, 33
159:35–6	"will be done"	*Materials* IV, 34 f.
160:6	"or your order"	*Materials* IV, 35
160:32	"I have done"	*Materials* IV, 36
161:30	"and constancy"	*Materials* V, 527–9
162:13	violence and fear	*Materials* VI, 521
163:17	"outrages"	*Materials* V, 398
164:6	of the king	*Cf.Foreville,* 122–61; Brooke, *E.C.,* 181–90
165:13	to writing	*Materials* V, 148 f.
165:23	"ecclesiastical law"	Stevenson V–I, 332
166:27	point by point	*Materials* III, 280 ff.
167:9	dissembling	*Saga* I, 169; *Materials* III, 288
167:19	speaking to none	*Materials* III, 288 ff.
167:32	*eruditi*	*Materials* III, 328
167:34	"before the wolf"	*Materials* II, 324
168:1	"the lord pope"	*Materials* II, 325
168:25	"arise from it"	*Materials* V, 88
169:5	the other ten	*Materials* V, 73–9
169:14	"Roman pontiff"	*Materials* V, 87
169:19	in disgust	Knowles, *E.C.,* 66; *Materials* V, 91
169:27	"of York"	*Materials* V, 112
170:34	"never despised"	*Materials* V, 101 f.
171:20	"in his absence"	*Materials* III, 49
171:27	back into port	*Materials* IV, 40

171:37	upon a phantom	*Materials* II, 325
172:10	the two of them	*Materials* III, 294
172:30–1	wilfulness	*Saga* I, 179
173:13	"deep roots"	*Materials* III, 294
173:18	"lay person"	*Saga* I, 181
173:24	reading aloud	*Saga* I, 182
174:31	at Northampton	*Materials* III, 50

Notes to CHAPTER XI: NORTHAMPTON

175:10	John the Marshal	*Materials* III, 51 ff. for entire council
175:26	perjury	Knowles, *E.C.,* 69
176:18	"to the kiss"	*Materials* III, 50
177:10	"little defense"	*Materials* III, 52
177:24	"and our lord"	*Materials* III, 52 f.
177:34	"at Clarendon"	*Materials* III, 297
178:6	Gilbert Foliot	*Materials* III, 53
178:12	lay magnates	Knowles, *E.C.,* 68
179:11	a gift	*Materials* III, 298
179:17	bail for Thomas	*Materials* III, 299
179:32	"devoured"	*Materials* III, 300
180:3–4	mind of the king	*Materials* III, 54
180:14–15	"take such advice"	*Materials* II, 327
180:27	"no longer alive"	*Materials* III, 328
181:10	"to the king"	*Materials* III, 55
181:32	kidney stone	Knowles, *E.C.,* 168
181:37	a deception	*Materials* III, 56, 300 f.; *Materials* IV, 44
183:13–14	"committed to me"	*Materials* III, 302 f.
183:18	openly emerging	*Materials* III, 303
183:28	"and the altar"	Knowles, *E.C.,* 77
184:20	"always will be"	*Materials* III, 57
184:35	"of peace"	*Materials* III, 57
185:17	"in patience"	*Materials* III, 58
187:9	"the lord pope"	*Materials* III, 63 f.
187:21	"in a bowl"	*Materials* III, 65
188:12	"could there be"	*Materials* II, 331
188:21–2	"will of God"	*Saga* I, 217 f.
188:27	"myself for it"	*Materials* II, 305
189:25	"your prohibition"	*Materials* III, 65 f.
189:28	"I hear"	*Materials* II, 332; *Saga* I, 219
190:23	"not binding"	*Materials* III, 66 f.
191:11	"was adjudged"	*Materials* III, 310
191:38	"your judgment"	*Materials* III, 66 f.
192:10	"you the lie"	*Materials* IV, 52

192:17	already killed	*Materials* II, 233
192:19	his cross	*Materials* III, 310
192:23	was to molest	*Materials* III, 69
192:27	the King's Evil	*Materials* II, 333
193:21	were to be fed	*Materials* III, 333
194:11	fall upon them	*Materials* III, 311
194:16	"and affable"	*Materials* IV, 53
	"they allege"	*Materials* III, 68
194:36	flight was born	*Materials* III, 312
195:15	pointed out	*Materials* II, 334
195:24	he replied	*Materials* III, 69
195:30	between two altars	*Materials* II, 334

Notes to CHAPTER XII: FLIGHT

199:19	as fifty	*Materials* III, 324
200:19	"the man yet"	*Materials* IV, 55
200:22	"go with him"	*Materials* IV, 55
201:2	around its neck	*Saga* I, 248 f.; *Materials* IV, 56
201:38	"as a loan"	*Materials* IV, 57
202:3	Herbert of Bosham	*Materials* III, 329
202:19	Louis of France	*Materials* III, 323
202:36	behind them	*Materials* III, 332 f.
203:26	"need arose"	*Materials* V, 134
204:5	"in my realm"	*Materials* III, 332
204:17	"against him"	*Materials* IV, 59
205:4	tradition	*Materials* III, 333
205:12	"of his enemies"	*Materials* III, 335
205:22	"to our lodging"	*Materials* III, 335
206:3–4	"to yourself"	*Materials* II, 337 f.
206:16	fell silent	*Materials* II, 338 f.
207:14	"and love"	*Materials* II, 339 f.
207:25	Alexander said	*Materials* III, 337; *Saga* I, 287
207:31	had infected	*Materials* II, 341
208:3–4	"adversaries"	*Materials* II, 340 f.
208:10	Alexander refused	*Materials* III, 74
208:29	plunder it	*Materials* III, 338
209:9	the archbishop	*Materials* III, 74
210:9	"sore afraid"	*Materials* II, 290 f.
210:21	"hands, father"	*Materials* II, 243
210:25	"possible way"	*Materials* II, 244
210:28	"pope's hands"	*Materials* III, 76
210:32	"for certain"	*Materials* II, 403
212:11	Tewkesbury's story	*Materials* III, 386 f.
212:26	"written here"	*Saga* I, 294
212:29	"pope's court"	*Saga* I, 299

213:4	*"par bel latin"*	Guernes, 73
213:22	"reason permitted"	Guernes, 73
214:2	"the peace"	*Materials* II, 345

Notes to Chapter XIII: Humility and Pride

216:10	Cistercian Rule	*Materials* II, 293
216:29	over his eyes	*Materials* II, 413
217:5–6	by gluttony	*Materials* III, 377 f.
217:20	for books	*Materials* III, 77
217:24	in the library	*Foreville*, 252 f.
218:14	"so I think"	*Materials* V, 162 f.
219:25	"concerning them"	*Materials* V, 152
219:28–9	"in England"	*Saga* I, 321
219:35	many innocents	*Materials* III, 78; *Saga* I, 349
220:6	"in the cradle"	*Saga* I, 349
220:20	kindness to them	*Materials* V, 242
221:7	*"gubernas omnia"*	*Materials* III, 78
221:14	*"non valeo"*	*Materials* III, 80
222:7–8	"vacillating minds"	*Materials* V, 162
222:25	"by others"	*Saga* I, 328–9
223:5	puppet pope	*Materials* V, 162
224:23	"of my arms"	Winston, 96 f.
224:27	"continued schism"	Bryce, 170
225:34	"him devotedly"	*Materials* V, 208
226:9	recently attached	Bryce, 199
226:19	"of my soul"	*Materials* VI, 162
226:28	upon the emperor	Reuter II, 198 ff.
226:36–7	Rainald proposed	*Materials* V, 352
227:2	"and reverence"	*Materials* V, 182
227:8	"as we do"	*Materials* V, 183
227:17	in France	Reuter II, 209
227:25–6	"of Canterbury"	*Materials* V, 428
227:34	"of England"	Winston, 413
227:38	sworn no oaths	*Materials* V, 206; *Materials* VI, 78 ff.
229:22	"your authority"	*Materials* V, 178 f.
230:2	"in this matter"	*Materials* V, 192 f.
230:16	"with patience"	*Materials* V, 175–8
230:25	"justify his cause"	*Materials* V, 203–9
230:37	in rebuke	Knowles, *E.C.*, 104–6
231:10	"of the Church"	*Materials* V, 452
231:11–12	"of your office"	*Materials* V, 453
231:25–6	"lord the king"	*Materials* V, 453
232:30	"in the earth"	Chron. Melrose, Stevenson IV–I, 130

233:24	"royal presents"	Gerald of Wales, Stevenson V–I, 218
234:13	"too much truth"	Gerald of Wales, Stevenson V–I, 219 f.
234:17	"dismissed him"	*Materials* VII, 165
235:2	"deserve credence"	*Materials* V, 197

Notes to CHAPTER XIV: VÉZELAY

236:7	making peace	*Materials* V, 198
236:23	"of a pastor"	*Materials* V, 360
236:26	"also in speech"	*Materials* III, 385
237:19	"always, my lord"	*Materials* V, 266–8
238:1–2	"of the Lord"	*Materials* V, 329
238:4–5	in all matters	*Materials* V, 331
238:21	to one another	Robertson, 182 *n.*
239:2	"and his health"	*Materials* V, 361
239:7–8	"labyrinth"	*Materials* V, 380 f.
239:13	"and soul alike"	*Materials* V, 381
239:17	by one man	*Materials* V, 381
239n.:3	Froude's translation	Froude, R. H., 150
240:28	"and vengeance"	*Materials* V, 278–82; *EHD*, 743 f.; Hutton, 120–3
241:7	of the appeal	*Materials* V, 381
241:19	Becket gone	*Materials* III, 383
241:23	satisfaction	*Materials* III, 394
241:38	told Herbert	*Materials* III, 394
242:3	Thomas concealed	*Materials* III, 391
242:9	"in his memory"	*Materials* V, 382
242:21	bits of clothing	Robertson, 165
242:27	"O king"	Daniel 3:17
243:8	fiery furnace	Calmette, 197
243:16	chains of prisoners	Calmette, 59
243:31	"many nations"	*Materials* III, 391
243:37	"to the people"	*Materials* III, 391
244:18	of anathema	*Materials* V, 383
244:35	The letter	*Materials* V, 269–78

Notes to CHAPTER XV: THE PAPER WAR

247:1	a spate of	*Materials* V, 385–401
250:3	"to our care"	*Materials* V, 403–8
250:20	"and advice"	*Materials* V, 410
250:30	calls it	*Materials* V, 459
251:7	by Thomas himself	*Materials* V, 490–512; Hutton, 136–49
252:15	another long letter	*Materials* V, 512–20

254:16	*Multiplicem nobis*	*Materials* V, 521–44; Hutton, 149–67
255:22	purchasable	Stubbs, *H.I.*, 140
258:18	of catechumens	Knowles, *E.C.*, 154
259:10	"swallow that"	Knowles, *E.C.*, 121
259:22	"to religion"	*Materials* VI, 20

Notes to CHAPTER XVI: LEGATES

261:2	Oxford	Stenton, 261
261:12	had warned	*Materials* V, 365 ff.
261:15	*Carta Caritas*	*EHD*, 689
261:21	"former chancellor"	*Materials* V, 365
261:37	lay his head	*Materials* III, 400
262:6	"other refuge"	*Materials* III, 400
262:22	"to abandon"	*Materials* III, 400
262:33	"ready for him"	*Materials* III, 401
263:17	and sociable	*Materials* III, 403 f.
263:26	John of Oxford	*Materials* V, 55–9
264:1	sent to Rome	*Materials* VI, 147
264:6	Thomas's hands	*Materials* VI, 126
264:34	"strictly secret"	*Materials* VI, 85
265:4	"absolve them"	*Materials* VI, 86
265:33	"of the Church"	*Materials* VI, 123–5
266:1	"cardinal"	*Materials* VI, 132
266:5	"of the Church"	*Materials* VI, 132
266:24	justice	*Materials* VI, 155 f.
266:26–7	"my archbishop"	*Materials* VI, 152
266:34	"time and place"	*Materials* VI, 209
267:11	"own writing"	*Materials* VI, 218
267:16	"biting sarcasms"	*Materials* VI, 220
267:21	"of the Church"	*Materials* VI, 221 f.
267:28	William	*Materials* VI, 215
268:9	"shall we do"	*Materials* VI, 162 f.
269:22–3	ceremony	Milman, 429
269:34	terrible downpour	Reuter II, 266
270:1	"before evening"	Robert de Monte, Stevenson IV–II, 766
270:8–9	from the bones	Chron. Melrose, Stevenson IV–I, 131
270:22	one-sidedly	*Materials* VI, 232 f.
270:24–5	"humiliated"	*Materials* VI, 228
270:28–9	"more justly"	*Materials* VI, 228
270:33	"of God"	*Materials* VI, 237
270:38	impression on him	*Materials* III, 411
271:13	in his stables	*Materials* VI, 247

271:31	"many others"	*Materials* VI, 262
271:38	"it fell out"	*Materials* III, 209 f.
272:9	the king's anger	*Materials* VI, 256
272:31	forefathers	*Materials* VI, 250
273:14	"to the Church"	*Materials* VI, 250 f.
274:3	on that score	*Materials* VI, 253
274:24	"hidden consent"	*Materials* III, 412
274:33	"to the king"	*Materials* III, 412
275:15	"others like him"	*Materials* VI, 225
275:26–7	to their lodgings	*Materials* VI, 269
276:3	"cardinal again"	*Materials* VI, 270
276:16	"hardly elegant"	*Materials* VI, 270
276:33–4	"joins in it"	*Materials* VI, 270 f.
277:8	"cancels debts"	*Materials* VI, 271 f.
277:36–7	his laughter	*Materials* VI, 273

Notes to CHAPTER XVII: MONTMIRAIL AND MONTMARTRE

279:7	"my blood"	*Materials* VI, 296; *EHD,* 749
279:15	"Last Judgment"	*Materials* VI, 294 f.
279:20	with the Germans	Haller III, 157
280:8	Lent of 1169	*Materials* VI, 421
280:14	"to him"	*Materials* VI, 439
280:17–18	two letters	*Materials* VI, 440
281:33	"God's honor"	*Materials* III, 419
282:21	"was renewed"	*Materials* III, 422
284:11	"than a saint"	*Materials* III, 423
284:19	"ordeal by fire"	*Materials* II, 348
284:31	"destroyed by me"	*Materials* III, 428
284:37	"my own order"	*Materials* III, 437
285:33	in chains	*Materials* III, 438
286:31	made his escape	*Materials* VI, 603
288:7	"be excommunicated"	*Materials* VI, 595; Hutton, 199 f.
288:23	"for your journey"	*Materials* VI, 599; Hutton, 199 f.
289:18	wrote to Thomas	*Materials* VII, 1
289:30	some other church	*Materials* VII, 25 f.
289:33	at his discretion	*Materials* VII, 31
289:37	from his dominions	*Materials* VII, 27
290:3	their own station	*Materials* III, 441
290:15	"another way"	*Materials* VII, 71
290:22	"and kings"	*Materials* VII, 74
290:30	"one egg"	*Materials* VII, 73
292:24	to make haste	*Materials* III, 446
293:5	"were ours"	*Materials* VII, 168
293:9	"the words"	*Materials* VII, 168
293:28	"a peace"	*Materials* III, 448

295:3	"poison"	*Materials* III, 350; III, 450; *EHD,* 752
295:29	"my blood"	*Materials* III, 451

Notes to CHAPTER XVIII: THE RECONCILIATION

296:16	"of St. Peter"	*Materials* VII, 206
297:25	"of the Church"	*Materials* VII, 279
298:1–2	"to posterity"	*Materials* VII, 279–81
298:19	"aware"	*Materials* VII, 182
298:29	"of Canterbury"	*Materials* VII, 256
298:31	strict injunction	*Materials* VII, 257
299:18–19	"such wickedness"	*Materials* VII, 217
302:21	"with you"	*Materials* VII, 307–9
302:24	a letter	*Materials* VII, 259 f.
304:31	royal robes	Salzmann, 91
305:16	at Fréteval	meeting at Fréteval: *Materials* VII, 326 ff.; III, 465 ff.; Hutton 210–13
307:14	"king assented"	*Materials* III, 466
307:29	"from a distance"	*Materials* VII, 332
308:6–7	"said of me"	*Materials* VII, 333
309:18	"subtle"	*Materials* VII, 335
309:30–1	"not abandoned"	*Materials* VII, 334
311:31	"Apostolic See"	*Materials* VII, 334
312:6–7	"demolished barns"	*Materials* VII, 402
312:34	"in the past"	*Materials* VII, 468
313:14	"to die"	*Materials* III, 113
313:20	"he was now"	*Saga* I, 469
314:9	"another time"	*Materials* III, 115
314:22	arbitrate	*Saga* I, 471
314:34	"worship me"	*Materials* III, 470
315:12	*"te, domine"*	*Materials* III, 115 f.
315:26	"royal authority"	*Materials* VII, 343; III, 112
316:10	"at Chinon"	*Materials* III, 112; *EHD,* 756
316:13	at Westminster	*Materials* VII, 389
316:21	the settlement	*Materials* VII, 383
317:8	the customs	*Materials* VII, 401 f.
317:21	"and in peace"	*Materials* VII, 400
317:27–8	"provide for him"	*Materials* III, 116
317:34	"keeping his word"	*Materials* III, 116
318:24	named Milo	*Saga* I, 485–7
318:30	"to your deaths"	*Materials* III, 472
318:37	"fulfil it"	*Materials* III, 476
319:15	"violence to us"	*Materials* VII, 403
320:10	"and truth"	*Materials* III, 119

320:29	"very countenance"	*Materials* III, 479
320:32	"one to come"	*Materials* III, 129
320:38	"Christ rules"	*Materials* III, 479 f.
321:4	"solemn day"	*Materials* III, 480

Notes to CHAPTER XIX: ENGLAND IN 1170

326:7	"little missed"	Poole, *FDTMC*, 209
326:31	"all England"	*EHD*, 408 f.; Stubbs, *S.C.*, 143 f.
330:4	"or his justices"	*EHD*, 440; Stubbs, *S.C.*, 149 f.
330:13	"than before"	*EHD*, 438
330:24	"for organization"	Salzmann, 217
330:36	"on the outside"	*EHD*, 906
332:3–4	"to your orders"	*EHD*, 907
332:17	"its legal rights"	*EHD*, 908
333:3	Arnulf	Norgate II, 132; *Materials* V, 309 f.
334:38	"and your children"	*Materials* VII, 393–5

Notes to CHAPTER XX: TWENTY-NINE DAYS

335:9	*honore regni*	*Materials* VII, 405
335:25	"false prophets"	*Materials* VII, 401
337:1	swear solemnly	*Materials* VII, 502
337:5–6	king's consent	*Materials* VII, 406
337:8	"of the Church"	*Materials* VII, 406
337:26	"put down"	*Saga* I, 498–501
338:21	"rich colors"	*Materials* III, 122
339:19	"the knife"	*Materials* III, 123
339:31	"commanded you"	*Materials* III, 123
340:3	"secret from us"	*Materials* III, 123 f.
340:10	signatory witness	*EHD*, 947
340:32	"Thank God"	*Materials* VII, 330
342:34	before High Mass	*Materials* III, 130
343:19	"leave us desolate"	*Materials* III, 484
343:21	"all darkness"	*Saga* I, 511
343:23–4	"wont to ponder"	*EHD*, 759
343:34–5	"of Canterbury"	*Materials* III, 130
343:36–7	"perpetual anathema"	*Materials* III, 485
344:2	"lord the king"	*Materials* II, 42
344:20	"an excommunicate"	*Materials* III, 130
344:34	"but turbulence"	*Materials* III, 485
344:39	"is concerned"	*Materials* III, 486
345:21	"paternal blessing"	*Materials* III, 485 f.
345:32	"the archbishop"	*Saga* I, 500
346:24	"tranquil kingdom"	*Materials* III, 128
347:18	"to please him"	*Materials* III, 128

| 349:15 | the king himself | *Materials* III, 128 |
| 349:29 | "insolence" | *Materials* III, 129 |

Notes to CHAPTER XXI: O MORS INAUDITA

| 351:title | *"O Mors Inaudita"* | *Materials* III, 144. |

For the remainder of this chapter I omit all source references. The dialogue and course of the action are reconstructed from so many sources —a phrase from Grim, a phrase from Bosham or FitzStephen or William of Canterbury, etc., that a hundred or more reference notes would be necessary to allocate every fragment of speech or information. It has seemed simpler, therefore, to give no references at all for this last chapter. I have leaned most heavily on the accounts of FitzStephen, *Materials* III, 129–49; Herbert of Bosham, *Materials* III, 491–522; Grim, *Materials* II, 429–40; but have also made use of the *Thómas Saga*, Guernes, and letters describing the murder by John of Salisbury and others (*Materials* VII, 462 ff.). Dean Stanley's *Historical Memorials of Canterbury* remains a valuable guide, although more than a hundred years have passed since its first publication.

Notes to EPILOGUE

370:30	"risen again"	*Materials* II, 27
371:20	"and byssus"	*Materials* III, 147
371:38	"to Christ"	*Materials* II, 38
372:24	"and vassals"	*Materials* III, 145
372:28	"men was there"	*Materials* III, 149
374:17	"or mother"	*Materials* VII, 514
374:34–5	"churches of God"	*Materials* VII, 515
376:15	"glorious Passion"	*Materials* VII, 545 f.
378:8	"saints of God"	*EHD,* 375
378:11	*rerum mutatio*	. . . the words of Thomas Becket to John of Oxford, *Materials* III, 116
378:29	"goose's egg"	Hutton, 268
379:14	"the Second"	Brown, 239
379:26	"all the bokes"	Borenius, 110

Note to APPENDIX

| 386:23 | "ever and ever" | *EHD,* 719–22 |

Bibliography

Adams, W. H. D.: *Great English Churchmen*. London: Society for Promoting Christian Knowledge; 1879.

Appleby, John T.: *John, King of England*. New York: Alfred A. Knopf; 1959.

————: *Henry II. The Vanquished King*. London: George Bell & Sons; 1962.

Artz, Frederick B.: *The Mind of the Middle Ages*. New York: Alfred A. Knopf; 1953.

Baldwin   Baldwin, Summerfield: *The Organization of Medieval Christianity*. New York: Henry Holt and Company; 1929.

Barlow   Barlow, Frank: *The Feudal Kingdom of England 1042–1216*. London: Longmans, Green & Co.; 1955.

————, ed.: *The Letters of Arnulf of Lisieux*. Camden Third Series. Vol. LXI. London: Royal Historical Society; 1939.

Borenius   Borenius, Tancred: *St. Thomas Becket in Art*. London: Methuen & Co.; 1932.

Boussard   Boussard, Jacques: *Le Gouvernement d'Henri II Plantagenêt*. Paris: Librairie d'Argences; 1956.

Brooke, *E.C.*   Brooke, Z. N.: *The English Church and the Papacy*. Cambridge: Cambridge University Press; 1952.

————: "The Register of Master David of London, and the Part he Played in the Becket Crisis." *Essays in History Presented to Reginald Lane Poole*. Oxford: Clarendon Press; 1927.

Brown   Brown, Paul Alonzo: *The Development of the Legend of Thomas Becket*. Philadelphia: The Pennsylvania State University Press; 1930.

Buss, Franz Joseph: *Der Heilige Thomas, Erzbischof von Canterbury und Primas von ganz England, und*

407

sein Kampf für die Freiheit der Kirche. Mainz: Kupferberg; 1856.

Butler, H. E., ed. and trans.: *The Autobiography of Giraldus Cambrensis.* London: Jonathan Cape; 1937.

Calmette   Calmette, Joseph, and David, Henri: *Les Grandes Heures de Vézelay.* Paris: Editions Sfelt; 1951.

Campbell, Lord: *Lives of the Lord Chancellors of England.* 7th edn. Vol. I. New York: Cockcroft & Company; 1878.

Cantor   Cantor, Norman F.: *Church, Kingship and Lay Investiture in England, 1089–1135.* Princeton: Princeton University Press; 1958.

Cheney, C. R.: "Magna Carta Beati Thome: Another Canterbury Forgery." *Bulletin of the Institute of Historical Research,* Vol. XXXVI (1963), pp. 1–26.

Compton, Piers: *The Turbulent Priest. A Life of St. Thomas of Canterbury.* London: Staples Press; 1957.

Coulton, C. G.: *A Medieval Garner.* London: Constable & Company; 1910.

———: *Medieval Panorama.* Cambridge: Cambridge University Press; 1958. New York: Meridian Books; 1955.

Cunnington, Susan: *The Story of Thomas Becket.* London: Harrap; 1914.

Curtius   Curtius, Ernst Robert: *European Literature and the Latin Middle Ages.* Bollingen Series XXXVI. New York: Pantheon Books; 1953.

Dark, Sidney: *Seven Archbishops.* London: Eyre & Spottiswoode; 1944.

Davis, H. W. C.: "The Chronicle of Battle Abbey." *English Historical Review,* Vol. XXIX (1914), pp. 426–34.

EHD   Douglas, David C., and Greenaway, George W., eds.: *English Historical Documents,* Vol. II, 1042–1189. London: Eyre & Spottiswoode; 1953. New York: Oxford University Press; 1953.

Duckett, Eleanor Shipley: *Carolingian Portraits.* Ann Arbor, Mich.: The University of Michigan Press; 1962.

Duggan, Alfred: *My Life for my Sheep.* New York: Coward-McCann; 1955.

Duggan, Charles: "The Becket Dispute and the Criminous Clerks." *Bulletin of the Institute of Historical Research,* Vol. XXXV (1962), pp. 1–28.

Dunken	Dunken, Gerhard: *Die politische Wirksamkeit der päpstlichen Legaten in der Zeit des Kampfes zwischen Kaisertum und Papsttum in Oberitalien unter Friedrich I.* Historische Studien, Heft 209. Berlin: Verlag Dr. Emil Ebering; 1931.
Eyton	Eyton, R. W.: *Court, Household, and Itinerary of King Henry II.* London: Taylor and Co.; 1878.
	Foreville, Raymonde: *Le Jubilé de Saint Thomas Becket. Du XIIe au XVe siècle (1220–1470).* Paris: S.E.V.P.E.N.; 1958.
Foreville	———: *L'Eglise et la Royauté en Angleterre sous Henri II Plantagenet (1154–1189).* N.p.: Bloud & Gay; 1942.
Freeman, *H.E.*	Freeman, Edward A.: "Saint Thomas of Canterbury and his Biographers." *Historical Essays.* First series. 3rd edn. London: Macmillan & Co.; 1875.
Freeman, *N.C.*	———: *The History of the Norman Conquest of England.* Vol. V. Oxford: Clarendon Press; 1876.
	———: "Mr. Froude's Life and Times of Thomas Becket." *The Contemporary Review,* Vol. XXXI (March 1878), pp. 821–42; Vol. XXXII (April 1878), pp. 116–39; Vol. XXXIII (May 1878), pp. 213–41; Vol. XXXIV (June 1878), pp. 474–500.
Froude, J. A.	Froude, James Anthony: *Life and Times of Thomas Becket.* New York: Scribner, Armstrong and Company; 1878.
Froude, R. H.	Froude, Richard Hurrell: "History of the Contest between Thomas à Becket, Archbishop of Canterbury, and Henry II, King of England." *Remains of the late reverend Richard Hurrell Froude.* Pt II, Vol. II. Derby, 1839.
Giles	Giles, J. Allen: *The Life and Letters of Thomas à Becket, now first gathered from the contemporary historians.* 2 vols. London: Whitaker & Co.; 1846.
Gilson	Gilson, Etienne: *History of Christian Philosophy in the Middle Ages.* New York: Random House; 1955.
Guernes	Guernes de Pont Sainte-Maxence: *La Vie de Saint Thomas Becket.* Ed. Emmanuel Walberg. Paris: Librairie Ancienne Honoré Champion; 1936.
Haller	Haller, Johannes: *Das Papsttum. Idee und Wirklichkeit.* Vol. III. Hamburg: Rowohlt; 1965.
	Halphen, Louis: "L'Essor de l'Europe (XIe–XIIe Siècles)." *Peuples et Civilisations. Histoire Génerale.* Paris: Librairie Felix Alcan; 1932.
Holmes	Holmes, Urban Tigner, Jr.: *Daily Living in the*

Twelfth Century. Based on the Observations of Alexander Neckham in London and Paris. Madison, Wis.: The University of Wisconsin Press; 1962.

Hook, Walter F.: *Lives of the Archbishops of Canterbury.* Vol. II. London; R. Bentley; 1860–76.

Hope, Mrs.: *The Life of S. Thomas Becket of Canterbury.* 3rd edn. London: Burns and Oates; 1891.

Hutton   Hutton, William Holden: *St. Thomas of Canterbury.* London: David Nutt; 1899.

————: *Thomas Becket.* Cambridge: Cambridge University Press; 1926.

Hist.Pont.   John of Salisbury: *The Historia Pontificalis.* Ed. Marjorie Churchill. London: Thomas Nelson and Sons; 1956.

Letters of J. S.   ————: *The Early Letters.* Ed. W. J. Milton and H. E. Butler; revised C. N. L. Brooke. London: Thomas Nelson and Sons; 1955.

Meta.   ————: *The Metalogicon.* Trans. Daniel D. McGarry. Berkeley; University of California Press; 1962.

Poli.   ————: *The Statesman's Book of John of Salisbury (Policraticus).* Trans. J. Dickinson. New York: Alfred A. Knopf; 1927.

Jolliffe, J. E. A.: *Angevin Kingship.* London: A. & C. Black; 1955.

Kelly   Kelly, Amy: *Eleanor of Aquitaine and the Four Kings.* New York: Vintage Books; 1959.

Knowles, David: "Archbishop Thomas Becket. A Character Study." *Proceedings of the British Academy.* Vol. XXXV (1949), pp. 177–205.

Knowles, E.C.   ————: *The Episcopal Colleagues of Archbishop Thomas Becket.* Cambridge: Cambridge University Press; 1951.

Lea, Henry C.: *An Historical Sketch of Sacerdotal Celibacy in the Christian Church.* Philadelphia: J. B. Lippincott & Co.; 1867.

L'Huillier   L'Huillier, A.: *Saint Thomas de Cantorbéry.* Paris: Société Générale de Librairie Catholique, Vol. I, 1891; Vol. II, 1892.

Lingard, John: *The History of England from the First Invasion by the Romans to the Accession of William and Mary in 1688.* Vol. II. London: J. C. Nimmo & Bain; 1883.

Lloyd   Lloyd, Roger: *The Golden Middle Age.* London: Longmans, Green & Co.; 1939.

Map   Map, Walter: *De nugis curialium.* Trans. Frederick

Tupper and Marbury Bladen Ogle. London: Chatto & Windus; 1924.

Marcham, Frederick George: *A History of England.* New York: The Macmillan Company; 1937.

Milman   Milman, Henry Hart: *History of Latin Christianity.* Vol. IV. New York: A. C. Armstrong and Son; 1903.

Morris, John: *The Life and Martyrdom of St. Thomas Becket.* 2nd edn. London and New York: Burns & Oates; 1885.

Murray, Margaret: *The God of the Witches.* New York: Oxford University Press; 1952.

Norgate   Norgate, Kate: *England under the Angevin Kings.* 2 vols. London: Macmillan and Co.; 1887.

Okey, Thomas: *The Story of Paris.* London: J. M. Dent; 1906.

Pain, Nesta: *The King and Becket.* London: Eyre and Spottiswoode; 1964.

Pieper   Pieper, Josef: *Scholasticism: Personalities and Problems of Medieval Philosophy.* New York: Pantheon Books; 1960.

Poole, *FDBMC*   Poole, Austin Lane: *From Domesday Book to Magna Carta, 1087–1216.* London: Oxford University Press; 1951.

———, ed.: *Medieval England.* Rewritten and rev. edn. London: Oxford University Press; 1958.

Gesta   Potter, K. R., ed.: *Gesta Stephani. The Deeds of Stephen.* Latin text and trans. with intro. and notes. London: Thomas Nelson and Sons; 1955.

Püschel, Brita: *Thomas a Becket in der Literatur.* Beiträge zur englischen Philologie, 45. Heft. Bochum-Langendreer: Verlag Heinrich Pöppinghaus; 1963.

Radford   Radford, Lewis B.: *Thomas of London Before his Consecration.* Cambridge Historical Essays No. VII. Cambridge: Cambridge University Press; 1894.

Reuter   Reuter, Hermann: *Geschichte Alexander des Dritten und der Kirche seiner Zeit.* 3 Vols. Berlin: G. W. F. Müller; 1845, 1860, 1864.

Governance   Richardson, H. G., and Sayles, G. O.: *The Governance of Mediaeval England from the Conquest to Magna Carta.* Edinburgh: The University Press; 1963.

Robertson   Robertson, James Craigie: *Becket, Archbishop of Canterbury.* London: John Murray; 1859.

Materials   ———, ed.: *Materials for the History of Thomas*

411

Becket, Archbishop of Canterbury (published under the direction of the Master of the Rolls). London; 1875 ff.

Saltman   Saltman, Avrom: *Theobald, Archbishop of Canterbury*. London: The Athlone Press; 1956.

Salzmann   Salzmann, L. F.: *Henry II*. Boston: Houghton Mifflin Company; 1914.

Simson   Simson, Otto von: *The Gothic Cathedral*. Bollingen Series XLVIII. New York: Pantheon Books; 1956.

Southern, R. W.: *The Making of the Middle Ages*. New Haven: Yale University Press; 1961.

Speaight, Robert: *Thomas Becket*. London: Longmans, Green & Co.; 1938.

Stanley   Stanley, Arthur Penrhyn: *Historical Memorials of Canterbury*. New York: Anson D. F. Randolph & Co.; 1888.

Stenton   Stenton, Doris Mary: *English Society in the Early Middle Ages*. London: Penguin Books; 1951.

Stevenson   Stevenson, Joseph: *The Church Historians of England*. Vol. IV, Pt I; Vol. IV, Pt II; Vol. V, Pt I. London: Seeleys; 1856.

Storrs   Storrs, Richard S.: *Bernard of Clairvaux*. New York: Charles Scribner's Sons; 1892.

Stubbs, *C.H.*   Stubbs, William: *The Constitutional History of England*. Vol. I. 2nd edn. Oxford: Clarendon Press; 1885.

Stubbs, *H.I.*   ———: *Historical Introductions to the Rolls Series*. Coll. and ed. Arthur Hassall. London: Longmans, Green & Co.; 1902.

Stubbs, *S.C.*   ———: *Select Charters*. 7th edn. Oxford: Clarendon Press; 1890.

Taylor   Taylor, G. R. Stirling: *The Story of Canterbury*. New York: E. P. Dutton; 1912.

Tellenbach, Gerd: *Church, State and Christian Society at the Time of the Investiture Contest*. Trans. R. F. Bennett. Oxford: Basil Blackwell; 1959.

Saga   *Thómas Saga Erkibyskups,* ed. Eiríkr Magnússon (published under the direction of the Master of the Rolls). *The Chronicles and Memorials of Great Britain and Ireland During the Middle Ages*. Vols. I and II. London: 1875–83.

Thompson, Robert Anchor: *Thomas Becket Martyr Patriot*. London: Kegan Paul, Trench; 1889.

Urry, William: *Canterbury under the Angevin Kings*. London: The Athlone Press; 1967.

Voss, Dr. Lena: *Heinrich von Blois Bischof von Winchester (1129–71)*. Historische Studien, Heft 210. Berlin: Verlag Dr. Emil Ebering; 1932.

Walberg, Emmanuel: *La Tradition hagiographique de Saint Thomas Becket avant la fin du XIIᵉ Siècle.* Paris: E. Droz; 1929.

Watt, Francis: *Canterbury Pilgrims and their Ways.* New York: Dodd, Mead and Co.; 1917.

Webb   Webb, Clement C.: *John of Salisbury.* London: Methuen & Co.; 1932.

Williamson, Hugh Ross: *The Arrow and the Sword. An Essay in Detection, being an enquiry into the nature of the deaths of William Rufus and Thomas Becket, with some reflections on the nature of medieval heresy.* London: Faber & Faber; 1947.

Winston   Winston, Richard: *Charlemagne: From the Hammer to the Cross.* New York: Vintage Books; 1960.

Index

Abelard, Peter, 34–6, 48, 138
absolution, 16, 265, 297–8, 335–6, 356–7
Adam du Petit Pont, 33
Adela (daughter of Louis VII), 280
Adela of Blois, 94
Adrian IV, 46, 66–8, 75, 85–90, 94, 102, 269, 310
Aigle, Richer de l', 12, 295
Alan of Tewkesbury, 192, 210–12, 213
Alberic, 34
Albert of St. Laurence, 374, 376
Alexander III: dealings with Becket, 26, 43, 134, 147–8, 156–7, 168–71, 176, 204–15, 216, 217, 218–23, 235–40, 248, 254, 309–10, 375–6, 381; struggle for papacy, 89–94; 136–9, 174, 224–31, 248; and Henry II, 249, 373; as mediator, 263–81, 288–96; 298–9, 306, 310–12, 345
Alfonso of Spain, 225 n.
Alfred the Great, 20, 24
Angevins, the, 40–1, 42, 50–1, 53, 56, 61, 62, 213
Anglo-Saxon Chronicle, 14–15, 19–20, 40
Anselm, Archbishop, 24–6, 28–9, 37, 115, 127, 167, 202, 217, 306, 380
antipopes, 16, 225; see also names of specific antipopes
appeals, 50, 162, 166, 170, 202; against Becket, 241, 248–51; 288, 375

archbishops: of Cologne, 4; of York, 16, 47, 67, 143; of Rouen, 41, 97, 315; see also names of specific archbishops and Canterbury, Archbishop of
archdeacons, 45–6, 97, 162, 166, 301
Arnold of Brescia, 48, 87–9, 311
Arnulf of Lisieux, 61, 91, 93, 137, 152, 155–6, 240–1, 287, 309, 333
Arundel, Earl of, 202, 206–7
Aschetinus of Leicester, 107–8
Assizes: of Arms, 80; of Clarendon, 326–30, 326 n.; of Northampton, 326 n.

Balliol, Jocelin de, 163, 244
barons: role of medieval, 4, 18–20, 164, 329–33; 27, 30; under Stephen, 38–9, 51, 62; 45; and Becket, 61, 172, 348 and n.; under Henry II, 63, 77–8, 160; at Northampton, 177–92; 229, 340
Bartholomew of Exeter, 79, 113–17, 161, 180, 188, 206
Battle Abbey, 65–70, 170
battles: see names of specific battles
Beatrice (wife of Frederick Barbarossa), 269
Becket, Agnes, 12, 220
Becket, Gilbert, 4–6, 4 n., 12, 30, 37, 42–3
Becket, Mary, 12, 220
Becket, Matilda, 5–7, 37
Becket, Rose (Rohesia), 12, 220
Bede, 217
Benedict of Peterborough, 370 and n.
Berengar, 286

i

A Note About the Author

Richard Winston was born in New York City in 1917. Over the last thirty years he has translated more than a hundred full-length books from five European languages—including the works of some of the foremost German writers —and has written two biographies, both relating to his special interest, the Middle Ages: *Charlemagne: From the Hammer to the Cross* (1954) and *Thomas Becket* (1967). Mr. Winston is married to the novelist Clara Winston, who has frequently collaborated with him on his translations. The Winstons live with their two daughters in Halifax, Vermont.

A Note on the Type

The text of this book was set on the Linotype in a face called Times Roman, designed by Stanley Morison for *The Times* (London) and first introduced by that newspaper in 1932.

Among typographers and designers of the twentieth century, Stanley Morison has been a strong forming influence, as typographical adviser to the English Monotype Corporation, as a director of two distinguished English publishing houses, and as a writer of sensibility, erudition, and keen practical sense.

Composed, printed, and bound by Kingsport Press, Inc., Kingsport, Tenn. Typography and binding design by

Warren Chappel